SLAVOPHILE EMPIRE

SLAVOPHILE EMPIRE

Imperial Russia's Illiberal Path

LAURA ENGELSTEIN

CORNELL UNIVERSITY PRESS   *Ithaca & London*

First published 2009 by Cornell University Press
First printing, Cornell Paperbacks, 2009

Printed in the United States of America

Library of Congress Cataloging-in-Publication Data

Engelstein, Laura.
 Slavophile empire : Imperial Russia's Illiberal path / Laura Engelstein.
   p. cm.
 Includes index.
 ISBN 978-0-8014-4740-2 (cloth : alk. paper) —
 ISBN 978-0-8014-7592-4 (pbk. : alk. paper)
  1. Russia—Politics and government—1801–1917. 2. Political culture—Russia—History—19th century. 3. Slavophilism—Russia—History—19th century. 4. Liberalism—Russia—History—19th century. 5. Russians—Ethnic identity—History—19th century. 6. Nationalism—Russia—History—19th century. 7. Religion and state—Russia—History—19th century. 8. Russia—Intellectual life—1801–1917. I. Title.
  DK189.E54 2009
  947.08—dc22   2009023344

Cornell University Press strives to use environmentally responsible suppliers and materials to the fullest extent possible in the publishing of its books. Such materials include vegetable-based, low-VOC inks and acid-free papers that are recycled, totally chlorine-free, or partly composed of nonwood fibers. For further information, visit our website at www.cornellpress.cornell.edu.

Cloth printing   10 9 8 7 6 5 4 3 2 1
Paperback printing   10 9 8 7 6 5 4 3 2 1

In memory of Reggie Zelnik

Contents

Preface   ix

Acknowledgments   xi

Introduction: The Discordant Choir   1

1   Combined Underdevelopment   13
Discipline and the Law in Imperial and Soviet Russia

2   Revolution and the Theater of Public Life   33
The Triumph of Extremes

3   The Dream of Civil Society   78
The Law, the State, and Religious Toleration

4   Holy Russia in Modern Times   99
The Slavophile Quest for the Lost Faith

5   Orthodox Self-Reflection in a Modernizing Age   125
The Case of Ivan and Natal'ia Kireevskii

6   Between Art and Icon   151
Aleksandr Ivanov's Russian Christ

7   The Old Slavophile Steed   192
Failed Nationalism and the Philosophers' Jewish Problem

Index   233

Preface

Twentieth-century Russia—imperial, Soviet, or post-Soviet—lacked the basic features of the Western liberal model: rule of law, civil society, and an uncensored public sphere. The autocracy and the Soviet regime rejected the model outright. It was adopted, briefly and ineffectually, between February and October 1917. After 1991 the Russian Federation again broke step, embracing a market economy, an unregulated press, and government by election. Under Putin, Russia has turned back, limiting freedom of expression, manipulating the laws, creating a form of state-centered capitalism, under a neo-nationalist flag. Even in negation, however, the Western model has exerted an obvious pull: nineteenth-century Russian intellectuals measured their case against it; the 1936 Stalin Constitution claimed to grant the most absolute freedoms of all. Critics of the West held it to its own professed standards. In the last decades of the autocracy, however, voices endorsing the Western liberal perspective were outnumbered, to the right and to the left, by those who favored illiberal options. How Russia's identity as a cultural nation at the core of an imperial state came to be defined, following the nineteenth-century Slavophile model, in terms of an antiliberal consensus is the story at the heart of this book. Focusing on the center of the political spectrum, it examines debates on religion and secularism, on the role of culture and the law under a traditional regime presiding over a modernizing society, on the status of the empire's ethnic peripheries, and on the spirit needed to mobilize a multinational empire in time of war. Such debates did not predetermine what emerged after 1917, but they foreshadowed elements of a political culture that are still in evidence today.

Acknowledgments

Several chapters of this book originally appeared in other publications. Chapter 1 was first published in the *American Historical Review* 98:2 (1993); rpt. rev., in *Foucault and the Writing of History*, ed. Jan Goldstein (Cambridge: Blackwell, 1994), 220–36; translated as "Kombinirovannaia nerazvitost': Distsiplina i pravo v tsarskoi i sovetskoi Rossii," *Novoe literaturnoe obozrenie*, no. 49 (2001). The chapter was presented at the conference, "Foucault and the Writing of History," University of Chicago, October 1991, convened by Jan Goldstein. It is reprinted here with the permission of John Wiley & Sons publishers.

Chapter 2 first appeared in *Revolution and the Meanings of Freedom in the Nineteenth Century*, ed. Isser Wolloch (Stanford: Stanford University Press, 1996), 315–57; (c) 1996 by the Board of Trustees of the Leland Stanford Jr. University, all rights reserved, by permission of the publisher, www.sup.org. The chapter was originally presented at the Center for the History of Freedom, Washington University, 1993–1994.

The first printing of chapter 3 was in *Civil Society before Democracy: Lessons from Nineteenth-Century Europe*, ed. Nancy Bermeo and Philip Nord (Lanham, Md.: Rowman and Littlefield, 2000), 23–41. It was originally presented at the conference, "Civil Society before Democracy: Lessons from Nineteenth-Century Europe," Princeton University, October 1995, convened by Nancy Bermeo and Philip Nord. It is reprinted here with permission of the publisher.

Chapters 4 and 5 were first published, respectively, in *Past and Present*, no. 173 (November 2001): 129–56, published by Oxford University Press; and *Autobiographical Practices in Russia—Autobiographische Praktiken in Russland*, ed. Jochen Hellbeck and Klaus Heller (Göttingen: Vandenhoeck & Ruprecht, 2004), 77–102. Chapter 5 was written in connection with the conference, "Autobiographical Practices in Russia and the Soviet

Union (19th–20th Centuries)," Rauischholzhausen, Germany, January 2001, convened by Jochen Hellbeck. It is reprinted with the permission of the publisher. Thanks to Jochen Hellbeck, Mark Mazower, and Irina Paperno for their helpful comments on this chapter.

Much of my research on Aleksandr Ivanov for chapter 6 was accomplished during a fellowship at the Dorothy and Lewis B. Cullman Center for Scholars and Writers at the New York Public Library in 2001–2002. I thank Peter Gay, Pamela Leo, and Edward Kasinec for making that experience a fruitful one. Thanks also to Yuri Tsivian for his encouragement and ideas.

For chapter 7, I collected much of the material on the philosophers' wartime debates in the Helsinki University Slavonic Library, with the generous and expert help of Irina Lukka. I first presented these ideas as one of the Merle Curti lectures at the University of Wisconsin, Madison, in March 2008.

All translations from foreign language texts are my own, unless otherwise noted. For Russian, I have used the Library of Congress system of transliteration. Dates in Russia before 1918 followed the Julian calendar. Archival citations use the following abbreviations: f. (*fond:* collection), op. (*opis':* inventory), d. (*delo:* file), l. or ll. (*list, listy:* sheet, sheets), ob. (*oborot:* reverse). Archives cited are: GARF (Gosudarstvennyi arkhiv Rossiiskoi Federatsii: State Archive of the Russian Federation); IRLI (Institut russkoi literatury Rossiiskoi akademii nauk: Institute of Russian Literature of the Russian Academy of Sciences).

I am grateful for the financial support of various institutions: Princeton University and Yale University for research, travel, and leave; in 1997–1998, the National Humanities Center and the John Simon Guggenheim Foundation. Thanks—personal, intellectual, and professional—to my friends and colleagues John Ackerman, Peter Brown, Francine Hirsch, Irina Paperno, and the late, much-beloved Reggie Zelnik.

SLAVOPHILE EMPIRE

Introduction

The Discordant Choir

The model of the nation that emerged in Europe after the French Revolution and the Napoleonic Wars was founded on the principles of citizenship and civil rights. To be sure, the governments that replaced the old regime did not always realize their own professed ideals. They nevertheless redefined the nature of sovereignty, recognized the value of the individual person, and delegated some degree of power to society. Nor was this model universal. Not all European states were nations. Not all nations managed to forge a sense of cultural coherence to replace the traditions they left behind.[1] The terms in which liberal society was governed continued, moreover, to evolve over the decades, as suffrage expanded and issues of social justice moved to the fore.

In this, as in other regards, the Russian Empire shared the Western experience but with a difference. The illusion of unity so useful to the consolidation of national states ill-suited the rulers of a terrain extending from the Prussian to the Chinese borders. The rhetoric of cultural identity was an instrument wielded instead against the state by the spokesmen of the empire's subject peoples, Finns, Poles, and self-declared Ukrainians, in particular.[2] The autocracy needed a unifying myth, not to build the consciousness of a nation but to counter the national urge.

---

[1] The classic statements: Eric Hobsbawm and Terence Ranger, eds., *The Invention of Tradition* (Cambridge: Cambridge University Press, 1983); Benedict Anderson, *Imagined Communities: Reflections on the Origin and Spread of Nationalism* (London: Verso, 1983). On the difficulties Germany faced in shaping this identity, see Shulamit Volkov, *Germans, Jews, and Antisemites: Trials in Emancipation* (Cambridge: Cambridge University Press, 2006), 92–93.

[2] Contemporaries understood these distinctions; see the strikingly familiar vocabulary employed by M. A. Slavinskii, "Russkaia intelligentsiia i natsional'nyi vopros," in *Intelligentsiia v Rossii: Sbornik statei* (St. Petersburg: Zemlia, 1910), 220–34, rpt. in *Vekhi: Pro et Contra,*

On matters of internal governance, the nineteenth-century autocrats drew selectively from the Western pattern-book. They codified the laws, introduced trial by jury, and expanded the opportunities for cultural and economic development. Yet they never relinquished the features of absolutism discredited in 1789: censorship, administrative repression, and arbitrary rule. Shaken by revolution in 1905 the regime grudgingly extended the promise of civil liberties and political participation, but it did not endorse the principle of individual or civic rights independent of social station; the legal system continued to recognize the sovereign's ultimate authority to supersede the power of the law.[3]

To its dying day, the autocracy operated on premises that were distinctly—and proudly—not liberal.[4] Its antiliberalism was at once economic (suspicious of the free market and nervous about the social consequences of industrial development); political (wary of delegating power and civic responsibility); and cultural (hierarchical, traditionalist, and antisecular). The imperial state was also, however, the engine of economic and institutional modernization. At the start of the eighteenth century, Peter the Great (r. 1682–1725) welcomed Western science and technology; at its end, Catherine the Great (r. 1762–1796) promoted the rational principles of the Enlightenment. The ambivalence of these monarchs toward this forward-moving enterprise is illustrated, however, in their policies toward religion. Both undermined the institutional autonomy of the Eastern Orthodox Church, which they viewed as an obstacle to social and economic progress. Yet neither abandoned the Church's role in legitimizing autocratic rule. Myths of divine sanction continued to surround the

---

ed. V. V. Sapov (St. Petersburg: Russkii Khristianskii gumanitarnyi institut, 1998), 736–48; esp. 737–39; 740–41 (comparing the Western "mononational state" [*odnonatsional'noe gosudarstvo*] to Russia, a "multinational state" [*gosudarstvo mnogonatsional'noe*]).

[3] Olga Crisp and Linda Edmondson, eds., *Civil Rights in Imperial Russia* (Oxford: Clarendon, 1989); Dov Yaroshevski, "Empire and Citizenship," in *Russia's Orient: Imperial Borderlands and Peoples, 1700–1917*, ed. Daniel R. Brower and Edward J. Lazzerini (Bloomington: Indiana University Press, 1997), 58–79; Yanni Kotsonis, "Introduction: A Modern Paradox—Subject and Citizen in Nineteenth- and Twentieth-Century Russia," in *Russian Modernity: Politics, Knowledge, Practices*, ed. David L. Hoffmann and Yanni Kotsonis (New York: St. Martin's, 2000), 1–16; Eric Lohr, "The Ideal Citizen and Real Subject in Late Imperial Russia," *Kritika* 7, no. 2 (2006): 173–94; Jane Burbank, "An Imperial Rights Regime: Law and Citizenship in the Russian Empire," *Kritika* 7, no. 3 (2006): 399–400; in response, Timothy Snyder, "The Elusive Civic Subject in Russian History," ibid., 609–17. On the debate over modernity and the liberal model, as exemplified in the difference between Zygmunt Bauman (the liberal model of equality as repressive) and Hannah Arendt (valuing the liberal promise), see the lucid exposition in Volkov, *Germans, Jews, and Antisemites*, 166–67.

[4] Retaining the term "citizenship" but specifying its distinction from the liberal model: Yaroshevski, "Empire and Citizenship," 60–61 (the Russian version as "republican citizenship"); Burbank, "Imperial Rights Regime," 400 (a "politics of rights based on difference").

imperial person; the tsar was always the Orthodox sovereign.[5] For the empire's inhabitants, religious affiliation remained an essential marker of civil status and cultural identity. Ready to employ the practical fruits of modern knowledge, the autocracy strenuously resisted the "disenchantment" of public life that Max Weber (1864–1920) counted among the symptoms of the new age.

The question of Russia's relation to the West was a subject that occupied intellectuals as well as statesmen. The narrow educated elite, steeped in Western culture and trained in Western science, articulated two conflicting visions of the empire's heritage and destiny. On the one side were those who believed that the Russian Empire, though not a nation, must aspire to the goals articulated in the West: laws, rights, individualism, and a secular public sphere able to accommodate the diversity of its religious and cultural landscape. On the other side were those who argued for a distinctively native path rooted in the dominant Eastern Orthodox tradition, alien to Roman concepts of law, communal rather than individualistic, and resolutely antisecular.

Both these camps derived their basic postulates from contemporary European thinking. In Europe, too, revolution generated a conservative, as well as a liberal, response. Exponents of Romantic nationalism rejected the Enlightenment project of social and cultural engineering. Following their lead, Russian conservatives denounced the model of the activist state promoted by Peter the Great and celebrated the attributes of religion and community that escaped its reach. At the other extreme, radicals endorsed the Enlightenment ideal of a secular public sphere within a state governed by principles of reason, not tradition. Yet they, too, found fault with the liberal model. Inspired by the socialist critique of bourgeois society (not yet implanted on Russian soil), they rejected capitalist individualism and the hierarchy of social class in favor of an egalitarian collectivist ideal. In between, moderates defended liberal rights as the basic building blocks of civil society and of an empire-wide political structure hospitable to the diversity of both cultures and persons.

The chapters in this book explore the tensions, as manifest in the Russian case, between the liberal paradigm (a secular civil society in a rule-of-law state) and the conservative antiliberal alternative (society, culture, and political institutions rooted in Eastern Orthodox traditions of authority). Those who voiced these conflicting views sometimes engaged in conversation, at other times talked past one another; they did not constitute a well-tempered choir. They did, however, shape the terms in which society at large—or at least that part of educated society concentrated in the

---

[5] On the autocracy's strategies of self-presentation: Richard S. Wortman, *Scenarios of Power: Myth and Ceremony in Russian Monarchy,* 2 vols. (Princeton: Princeton University Press, 1995, 2000).

Russian-speaking, Eastern Orthodox center, in close proximity both to Europe and to the domestic seat of power—came to think about itself and the issues that dominated late imperial political life.

The Intelligentsia

By mid-century these shapers of public discourse had come to be known as the intelligentsia. This is a fluid term, coined in the 1860s, though not widely applied for another twenty years. It conjured up stereotypes cultivated by its members on their own behalf and perpetuated by historians in retrospect.[6] As shorthand, it designated the loose fraternity of nineteenth- and early-twentieth-century thinkers, writers, journalists, pamphleteers, artists, and activists hostile to the autocracy and the social order it sustained. The label implied a particular moral tone rather than a social position; it was identified with the production of critical ideas and often with involvement in subversive political action. There was little agreement, however, on how far the term extended.[7] It was sometimes applied, well beyond the range of troublemakers or critically minded intellectuals, to embrace the array of trained professionals that emerged after the Great Reforms of the 1860s and provided the backbone of respectable public life. Insofar as they did not speak in an official role, conservative ideologues also qualified. By the end of the century the category embraced the literary and artistic lights of the modernist avant-garde, many of whom avoided any political commitment.

In all its uses, however, the label designated a source of opinion, particularly political opinion, originating outside the structures of the state or asserting its independence from official doctrines. Its roots go back to the eighteenth century, when Catherine encouraged a limited degree of civic

[6] Original myth-making but already in retrospect: P. V. Annenkov (1813–1887), "Zamechatel'noe desiatiletie (1838–1848)," in *Vospominaniia i kriticheskie ocherki: Sobranie statei i zametok, 1849–1868 gg.*, 3 vols. (St. Petersburg: Stasiulevich, 1877–1881), 3:1–224; imperfect in English: P. V. Annenkov, *The Extraordinary Decade: Literary Memoirs*, ed. Arthur P. Mendel, trans. Irwin R. Titunik (Ann Arbor: University of Michigan Press, 1968). By contrast, Herzen's memoirs, *Byloe i dumy* (1852–1868) do not use the term "intelligentsia." Perpetuating the myth: Isaiah Berlin (1909–1997), *Russian Thinkers*, ed. Henry Hardy and Aileen Kelly, 2nd ed. (London: Penguin Books, 2008); following Berlin, Tom Stoppard, *Coast of Utopia*, 3 pts. (London: Faber and Faber, 2002). For bibliographic overview: Nathaniel Knight, "Was the Intelligentsia Part of the Nation? Visions of Society in Post-Emancipation Russia," *Kritika* 7, no. 4 (2006): 733–58.

[7] Boris Kolonitskii, "Identifikatsiia rossiiskoi intelligentsii i intelligentofobiia (konets XIX–nachalo XX veka)," in *Intelligentsiia v istorii: Obrazovannyi chelovek v predstavleniiakh i sotsial'noi deistvitel'nosti*, ed. D. A. Sdvizhkov (Moscow: Institut vseobshchei istorii RAN, 2001), 150–70; in French: Boris I. Kolonickij, "Les identités de l'intelligentsia russe et l'anti-intellectualisme, fin du XIXe-début du XXe siècle," *Cahiers du monde russe* 43, no. 4 (2002): 601–16.

dialogue. The posture of active opposition was first assumed by the next generation. Home from the Napoleonic Wars, where they absorbed the lessons of the French Revolution and observed the movements of national liberation in Italy and the German lands, a group of elite guards officers staged an abortive coup in the name of a new political order. Even in defeat, the events of December 1825, which inaugurated the reign of Nicholas I (r. 1825–1855), underscored, from the perspective of the regime, the dangers of a Western orientation but at the same time the necessity of coming to terms with what that danger meant.

The so-called Decembrist Uprising was followed by the Polish revolt of 1830–1831, also spearheaded by men of rank and education, inspired in this case by the recent wave of European revolutions. In the wake of these events, Nicholas determined not only to limit independent thought and civic action. He promoted a native alternative to ideas coming from abroad that threatened the legitimacy of absolute rule. Hence the official ideology, formulated in 1833—a concession to the need for one. "Orthodoxy, Autocracy, Nationality" (*Pravoslavie, Samoderzhavie, Narodnost'*)—religious authority, political authority, and the native spirit, a cultural substitute for political nationalism, was Russia's answer to *Liberté, égalité, fraternité* and *La nation.*[8] Their opposite—obedience, hierarchy, patriarchy, and empire, as Nicholas made unmistakably clear—constituted the defining features of his rule.

The regime's response to the shock of rebellion generated a response in turn. As later dramatized in the classic memoirs of Alexander Herzen (1812–1870), *Byloe i dumy* (*My Past and Thoughts*) (1852–1868), the following generation of privileged men reacted to the fate of the Decembrists by addressing the question of where Russia should be headed. They were not yet "the intelligentsia," as it was later defined, but they had taken the first steps. Resentful of their exclusion from an active part in public life, they gathered in their drawing rooms. It was there, in the 1840s, that the enduring paradigms of Russian social thought and political action were established. Here the so-called Slavophiles argued with the so-called Westernizers about how to reconcile Russia's historical legacy with the Western values that shaped their own privileged lives and their own ways of thinking. Equally antagonistic to the autocracy in the person of Nicholas I, the

---

[8] Andrei Zorin, "Ideologiia 'Pravoslaviia-Samoderzhaviia-Narodnosti': Opyt rekonstruktsii," *Novoe literaturnoe obozrenie*, no. 26 (1997): 71–104. As Zorin explains, Count Sergei Uvarov (1786–1855) chose the Slavic "narodnost'" over the Latinate "*natsional'nost'*" in explicit rejection of the terms of nationalist ideology. This important difference is ignored, when the slogan is sometimes misquoted: e.g., Anderson, *Imagined Communities*, 83. On "narodnost'": Nathaniel Knight, "Ethnicity, Nationality, and the Masses: *Narodnost'* and Modernity in Imperial Russia," in Hoffmann and Kotsonis, *Russian Modernity*, 41–64.

two camps articulated divergent visions of the past and the future that set the terms for the liberal-antiliberal conversation.

On the one side, the Slavophiles regretted the disruption initiated by Peter the Great in what they imagined to have been the unself-conscious authenticity of traditional life. They located the vestiges of this lost ideal in the Great Russian peasant commune, remote from their own sophisticated lives. Obedient still to the direction of the village priest and the rhythms of the sacred calendar, governed by the patriarchal authority of the household head and the ritualized consensus of the village assembly, the commune presented an alternative to the self-centered existence of the Westernized upper crust. Yearning to connect with a realm seemingly untouched by time and untroubled by doubt, they saw in Orthodoxy the key to their own salvation.

On the other side, those who defended the legacy of the Enlightenment condemned the Slavophile ideal as a retrospective illusion: the Romantic vision of a harmonious, spiritually saturated culture, embracing the ill-assorted layers of imperial Russian society, was a fantasy that ignored the harsh realities of peasant life and sacrificed the individual personality to the mass.[9] The Slavophiles indeed rejected the values of personal autonomy and achievement celebrated by the European Renaissance. Imagining a resolution to their own frustrated desire for belonging, Konstantin Aksakov (1817–1860) described the village commune as a "moral choir," which allowed each voice to resonate more fully than it could on its own, achieving in consort a "triumph of the human spirit."[10]

This was the age of Herzen and his friends, the "fathers" of *Ottsy i deti* (*Fathers and Sons*) (1862), the novel by Ivan Turgenev (1818–1883) that provided a convenient gallery of current social types. Two decades later, the "sons" emerged as the acolytes of revolution, also divided into nativist (Populist) and Westernizing (Marxist) camps. Herzen himself bridged both the psychology of the generations and the values dividing them: an aristocratic, anti-autocratic free-thinker and political exile, he imagined a socialism that incorporated the best features of the Russian agrarian community (the Slavophile legacy) with the progressive attributes of the

[9] Classics: Nicholas V. Riasanovsky, *Russia and the West in the Teaching of the Slavophiles: A Study of Romantic Ideology* (Cambridge, Mass.: Harvard University Press, 1952); idem, *A Parting of Ways: Government and the Educated Public in Russia, 1801–1855* (Oxford: Clarendon, 1976); Andrzej Walicki, *The Slavophile Controversy: History of a Conservative Utopia in Nineteenth-Century Russian Thought*, trans. Hilda Andrews-Rusiecka (Oxford: Clarendon, 1975).

[10] Quoted in Nicholas V. Riasanovsky, *Russian Identities: A Historical Survey* (Oxford: Oxford University Press, 2005), 152–53. As a catchphrase for neo-Slavophile thinkers, see Abram Terts [Andrei Siniavskii], *Golos iz khora* (London: Izd-vo Stenballi, 1973); in English: *A Voice from the Chorus*, trans. Kyril FitzLyon and Max Hayward (New Haven, Conn.: Yale University Press, 1995).

West (individual rights and political liberty). He managed, therefore, to survive the twentieth century in both the official Soviet and intelligentsia pantheons.[11]

The Populists evolved from an anti-elitist Romantic faith in the virtues of the common folk in the 1860s to a Romantic reliance on heroic personal deeds and the drama of revolutionary terror a decade later. Their purest type despised mere talk (abstract thinking) and social privilege (including the advantages of high culture). They were anti-Western in their hostility to emerging capitalism but Western in their affinity for the radical socialism, and even more visceral anarchism, in contemporary Europe. When Marxism supplanted Populism in the 1890s, it inherited the taste for violence (though not in the form of heroic deeds) and hostility to social privilege, but not the opposition to Western-style progress. Embracing the legacy of Enlightenment rationalism, Marxists did not, however, accept the principles of what they derided as "bourgeois" liberalism—private property, individual rights, personal inviolability, and class-blind justice.

Precisely these values defined the outlook of the professional intelligentsia that otherwise shared the Marxist commitment to progress, reason, and secular enlightenment. These were the physicians, pedagogues, economists, and lawyers, trained in the universities that expanded after the Great Reforms, who devoted themselves to education, health, and social welfare.[12] Together with the progressive-minded gentry seeking a middle ground between repression and revolt, they endorsed the basic liberal project: respect for the law, the individual, and private property, and for freedom of speech, the press, public assembly, and religious belief. Most accepted the framework of the historic imperial state, until in 1905 they were propelled by events beyond their control into the turbulence of revolution.

Russian Contradictions

Liberalism, therefore, was not entirely lacking adherents in imperial Russia; the space between extremes was not a political void.[13] Yet liberals

[11] Martin E. Malia, *Alexander Herzen and the Birth of Russian Socialism, 1812–1855* (Cambridge, Mass.: Harvard University Press, 1961); Irina Paperno, "Introduction: Intimacy and History: The Gercen Family Drama Reconsidered," *Russian Literature* 61, nos. 1–2 (2007): 1–65.

[12] On the social program of such liberals, see Daniel Beer, *Renovating Russia: The Human Sciences and the Fate of Liberal Modernity, 1880–1930* (Ithaca: Cornell University Press, 2008).

[13] On conservatism: Edward C. Thaden, *Conservative Nationalism in Nineteenth-Century Russia* (Seattle: University of Washington Press, 1964); V. Ia. Grosul et al., eds., *Russkii konservatizm XIX stoletiia: Ideologiia i praktika* (Moscow: Progress-Traditsiia, 2000); Richard

were forced always to contend with the pressure of an antiliberal consensus. Take the case of the law. Respect for the principles of legality emerged as a hallmark of statehood in the aftermath of the French Revolution, when monarchs were overthrown and the nation declared its sovereign right to rule. Resistance to legality in the Russian case emanated from diverse sources. The autocrats themselves, although recognizing the utility of legal institutions in the new age, resented the limits to their own absolute authority. The Slavophiles, for their part, denounced both autocracy and the rule of law as alien imports destructive of the workings of the social organism. The radical Left viewed the law not as a limit on state power but as its enhancement, and hence something to disdain or subvert.

Was the law a hindrance or an opportunity? The architects of the Judicial Reform of 1864, trained in Western jurisprudence and working from within the imperial bureaucracy, created institutions at odds with the fundamentals of autocratic rule, most notably trial by jury and the irremovability of judges. They considered these institutions necessary, along with the newly created organs of local self-administration (the *zemstvos*), for maintaining orderly government after serfdom was abolished in 1861, taking with it the disciplinary power and managerial functions of the landlords.[14] The new courts were not merely updated instruments of repression, however; they provided a rare forum for the open presentation of ideas. Aware of the importance of public opinion (the rudiments of "civil society," a term in play at the time) in circumstances in which it was severely constrained, the defendants in the Populist trials of the 1870s used the courtroom to advertise their beliefs. Ably represented by lawyers who valued the importance of due process and the law, the firebrands made a mockery of their defenders' interests.

Chapter 1, "Combined Underdevelopment: Discipline and the Law in Imperial and Soviet Russia," explores the long-term consequences of a weak commitment to the rule of law. In restricting the limits of self-expression and impeding the emergence of an independent social sphere, the autocracy hindered the evolution of Western-style public life. It fostered a political environment that encouraged extremes. Hostility to the institutions of the law and to the rights they guarantee carried over into the Soviet period, which, like the autocracy, shared other features of social and economic development with the bourgeois West.

Pipes, *Russian Conservatism and Its Critics: A Study in Political Culture* (New Haven, Conn.: Yale University Press, 2005); Mikhail Luk'ianov, *Rossiiskii konservatizm i reforma, 1907–1914*, intro. Mark D. Steinberg (Stuttgart: Ibidem-Verlag, 2006).

[14] Richard S. Wortman, *The Development of a Russian Legal Consciousness* (Chicago: University of Chicago Press, 1976); Jörg Baberowski, *Autokratie und Justiz: Zum Verhältnis von Rechtsstaatlichkeit und Rückständigkeit im ausgehenden Zarenreich 1864–1914* (Frankfurt am Main: Vittorio Klostermann, 1996). On liberalism: F. A. Gaida, *Liberal'naia oppozitsiia na putiakh k vlasti: 1914—vesna 1917 g.* (Moscow: ROSSPEN, 2003).

Neither regime dispensed with the law altogether, but each attempted to constrain its possible effects. Chapter 2, "Revolution and the Theater of Public Life," demonstrates the paradoxical impact of institutions introduced by the autocracy to bolster the authority of the state, which, in fact, contributed to its erosion. The chapter focuses on the development of the nineteenth-century revolutionary movement. It puts the radicals in perspective, as a marginal group yet able to pressure those in the middle, narrowing the options available to moderates caught between the unscrupulousness of the regime and that of its most determined opponents. Beginning with the trials that both vindicated and frustrated liberal ambitions (proving how powerful the legal process could be but also how easily its advocates could be outmaneuvered on the public stage), the chapter pursues the well-known story of the continuous radicalization of society as a whole. The move to the left was prompted by the disappointed promise of the Great Reforms (the limited scope of zemstvo responsibilities, the enduring restrictions on public expression and the press, the continued use of administrative repression, and the retraction of earlier concessions), accelerated by the increasing turmoil in the laboring classes and the impatience of a younger generation trained in the universities and steeped in radical ideas. At the same time as moderates were swept along—or pushed—into the radical current by the intransigence of the regime, they persisted in seeking an alternative outcome. Mobilizing as a political force on the eve of 1905, liberals welcomed the promise of the Western-style parliamentary order that followed the revolution.

Chapter 3, "The Dream of Civil Society," outlines the moderates' efforts to construct a public sphere that, even within the framework of the monarchy, would bring this alternative to life. It demonstrates how powerfully the concept of civil society moved them but also the ineffectuality of their efforts to achieve it. The chapter concentrates on the issue of religious toleration, which reveals the workings of empire as a structure of domination. As a marker of social position, religious affiliation shaped the relationship between imperial subjects and the state. The liberals' attempt to remove this barrier and reconfigure the basis for confessional difference, from an attribute of communal belonging to a matter of personal choice, did not meet with success. As its aura faded, the autocracy clung all the more desperately to the myth of spiritual authority already eroding in the West and now also at home.[15]

The first three chapters on law and legality thus explore critical dimensions of the moderates' Westernizing urge. The two chapters on religion

---

[15] Gregory L. Freeze, "Subversive Piety: Religion and the Political Crisis in Late Imperial Russia," *Journal of Modern History* 68 (1996): 308–50; Richard S. Wortman, "Publicizing the Imperial Image in 1913," in *Self and Story in Russian History,* ed. Laura Engelstein and Stephanie Sandler (Ithaca: Cornell University Press, 2000).

that follow explore parallel efforts to resist it. Given the strength of the antiliberal consensus, it is surprising how arduous these efforts proved to be. Exploring this paradox, chapter 4, "Holy Russia in Modern Times," returns to the generation of the 1840s. It focuses on the Slavophile philosopher Aleksei Khomiakov (1804–1860), a cosmopolitan dedicated to the cause of cultural introversion. Framing his nostalgic religious enthusiasm in the context of similar European trends, the chapter illustrates the non-Russian origins of his Romantic nativism. Religious revivalism was a modern form of religious expression. The Slavophiles, in their willful archaism, were in tune with their times. Yet they understood (as did Nicholas) that tradition had to be redefined and mobilized in order to save it.

This was no easy task, even on a personal scale. Chapter 5, "Orthodox Self-Reflection in a Modernizing Age," is devoted to Khomiakov's Slavophile contemporary, Ivan Kireevskii (1806–1856), and illustrates the difficulties Europeanized intellectuals faced in their efforts to adopt the Russian path and learn to be Russian. Kireevskii would have liked to address a secular readership by publishing in the thick journals that governed public opinion, but the authorities barred him from print. Forced into domesticity and seclusion, he substituted introspection for the public role he was denied. He understood his personal quest, however, not as a search for private satisfaction but as an attempt to enter an alternate community, the unworldly world of the pious, sheltered from the ambivalences and frustrated desires of his earlier life. Yet the monks themselves had a worldly mission: to reinfuse the spiritual landscape of an increasingly secular culture with the lost allure of authentic piety, reconnecting the Westernized elite to the traditions of the Christian East.

However contemporary the overall logic of their enterprise may have been, the Slavophiles contributed to a definition of the Russian cultural nation that resisted the rationalist pressures of the disenchanted modern public sphere. They resisted the notion of civic neutrality, just as they insisted the empire be identified in terms specific to the Russian, defined as Orthodox, core. Though they criticized the particular incarnation of the autocracy embodied in the repressive regime of Nicholas I, they were imperial patriots and philosophical conservatives. It was not a simple posture to maintain. Chapter 6, "Between Art and Icon," on the much-discussed painter Aleksandr Ivanov (1806–1858), pursues the dilemma confronted by nineteenth-century Russian thinkers and artists of how to imagine a Russia that was both universal and particular, both imperial and national. Tracing the debate on Ivanov from the 1840s to the post-Soviet present, the chapter shows how the link between religion and nationalism refuses to go away, but also how difficult it was to create that link in the first place.

The question of national identity is central to many of the tensions these chapters explore, although the concept of "the national" is awkward in the Russian case. Aware of the inadequacy of the political nation as a model for the imperial Russian state, thinkers and statesmen could not avoid the terms it established. The questions they confronted reflect these tensions. On the one hand, they groped for principles of distinction that separated them from a standard they could neither fully embrace nor simply ignore. How to be Russian by borrowing state institutions and legal principles from the West? How to be Russian in relation to a universal religious mission? How to produce Russian art when living in Rome and copying the European masters? On the other hand, the dilemma related not to foreign influences but to the position of a Russian-educated elite operating in a composite imperial terrain. How to construct a sense of national pride in relation to a state that included a mix of cultures, languages, and traditions? What to do about the aspirations to autonomy or civic rights coming from groups such as the Poles and the Jews that asserted their moral and cultural self-sufficiency?

As Nicholas I had realized, the ideology of nationalism and national identity was inescapable but also inapplicable. He tried to preempt its appeal by devising alternatives of his own and exercising his powers of repression. But even conservatives caused trouble in this domain: How did Russian cultural exclusivity fit with the imperial project? How did Slavic brotherhood jive with the practical demands of power politics? World War I brought these issues to a head. The Russian imperial state, confronted by the militant nationalism of the German foe, suffered from the lack of a national ideology. Intellectuals and political figures in Russia confronted the deficit in different ways. Debates over national identity and the relationship of the Russian core to its troublesome peripheries—the Poles, the Jews, and the Baltic Germans—intensified after 1905 and climaxed under the pressure of armed conflict.

The final chapter, "The Old Slavophile Steed," explores some of the issues engaged by philosophers and ideologues during the war. These often centered on the question of the Jews and anti-Semitism. The enduring power of the Slavophile paradigm prevented even some self-designated liberals from embracing a secular, and therefore inclusive, definition of the imperial community. These politically liberal philosophical conservatives repudiated the aggressive anti-Semitism of the ideological right. Yet they were trapped in a style of thinking whose consequences were inimical to their own liberal perspective.

Less culturally disparate populations, stronger civil societies, more deeply rooted traditions of law, less encumbered freedom of expression: these were, of course, no guarantees against illiberal outcomes in the twentieth century. Anti-Semitism was a plague that respected no institutions. The Nazis equipped antiliberalism with highly modern devices—technology, bureaucracy, mass communication, and industrial mass murder.[16] Stalinism, too, was a proudly antiliberal modernizing project. But Russia's story

[16] Zygmunt Bauman, *Modernity and the Holocaust* (Ithaca: Cornell University Press, 1989).

is not one of decline from bourgeois imperfection to post-bourgeois disaster. The empire, as a political structure and as the framework for the unfolding of a rich and tragic cultural life, resisted liberalism all along. Among its most creative forces, some yearned for spiritual renewal, a return to lost cultural wholeness; others yearned for earthly perfection, a release from the irresistible progress of time; and a few pursued the utopia of reason but were left stranded on the other shore.

CHAPTER ONE

Combined Underdevelopment

Discipline and the Law in Imperial and Soviet Russia

As a political activist, Michel Foucault (1926–1984) spoke out against oppressive political regimes and allied himself, as in the case of Poland, with people who fought for political liberty and freedom of expression. Having insisted, in essays and interviews, that he appreciated the importance of the institutional context that distinguished so-called totalitarian systems from liberal states, he did not make that distinction the focus of his scholarly work but concentrated instead on the mechanisms of control characteristic of all governments in the modern era.[1] As Sheldon Wolin has written, invoking a contrast the philosopher himself would not have employed, Foucault "was not directly concerned with great tyranny but with smaller ones."[2] In fact, Foucault's theoretical interest was captured not by the problem of postliberal politics but by the origins of liberalism itself, and his condemnation of certain kinds of state systems (Communist regimes, in particular) did not fit comfortably with his insistence that constitutional forms and legal structures do not determine the workings of power in the modern world.

---

[1] Michel Foucault, *Remarks on Marx: Conversations with Duccio Trombadori,* trans. R. James Goldstein and James Cascaito (New York: Semiotext(e), 1991), 167–72. On the nature of modern government, see Michel Foucault, "Governmentality," in *The Foucault Effect: Studies in Governmentality,* ed. Graham Burchell, Colin Gordon, and Peter Miller (Chicago: University of Chicago Press, 1991), 87–104. On Foucault's life and political involvements, see Didier Eribon, *Michel Foucault,* trans. Betsy Wing (Cambridge, Mass.: Harvard University Press, 1991).

[2] Sheldon S. Wolin, "On the Theory and Practice of Power," in *After Foucault: Humanistic Knowledge, Postmodern Challenges,* ed. Jonathan Arac (New Brunswick, N.J.: Rutgers University Press, 1988), 190–91. For a similar complaint, see Michael Walzer, "The Politics of Michel Foucault," in *Foucault: A Critical Reader,* ed. David Couzens Hoy (Oxford: Blackwell, 1986), 63.

Indeed, the thrust of Foucault's critical energy was directed at identifying the "minor" tyrannies brought about by the bourgeois order that replaced the "major" tyranny of Old Regime states with the promise of civic freedom. He argued that the fundamental social category central to the bourgeois polity—that of the autonomous individual—has not, in fact, operated as the precondition for liberty and happiness but as a mechanism of domination, the agent and object of discipline exercised by society upon itself. Where monarchies once imposed order by brute force, through the coercive instruments of the state, Foucault observed, liberal capitalist societies exercise control through the gathering and production of information, the surveillance associated with these scientific projects, the imposition of categories derived from such investigation, and by inculcating mechanisms of self-censorship and self-restraint that compel people to police themselves. By exposing the disciplinary function of subjectivity (the vaunted condition of individual freedom), rationality (prized as an instrument of subjective autonomy), and sexuality (in more recent times hailed as the domain of personal liberation), Foucault unmasked the ideological nature of bourgeois claims to have improved on the overt compulsions and unabashed hierarchies of the absolutist state.[3]

The "great tyranny" that did interest Foucault was not the modern "police state" of Nazi Germany or Soviet Russia but the monarchical system of early modern Europe, which finally gave way to the deceptive liberties of the modern era. During this transition, the state ceased to display its might in exemplary theatrical spectacles of publicly inflicted bodily pain when punishing crime. Instead, it created institutions for the concealment and regimentation of offenders, who were kept alive and physically intact but out of public sight and under expert supervision. In regulating sex, the state likewise abandoned public rituals of shame or retribution, delegating the exercise of control to the more insidious offices of the trained professions.[4] The "new mechanism of power" that characterized the modern era took the form of "highly specific procedural techniques, completely novel instruments, quite different apparatuses" from those of the Old Regime and "absolutely incompatible with the relations of sovereignty" associated with absolute rule.[5]

[3] For helpful characterizations of this transition, see Walzer, "Politics of Michel Foucault," 54, 59; Hubert L. Dreyfus and Paul Rabinow, *Michel Foucault: Beyond Structuralism and Hermeneutics*, 2nd ed. (Chicago: University of Chicago Press, 1983), chap. 6; Nancy Fraser, *Unruly Practices: Power, Discourse, and Gender in Contemporary Social Theory* (Minneapolis: University of Minnesota Press, 1989), chap. 1.

[4] Leading ideas of Michel Foucault are found in *Discipline and Punish: The Birth of the Prison*, trans. Alan Sheridan (New York: Pantheon, 1977); and idem, *The History of Sexuality*, Vol. 1, *An Introduction*, trans. Robert Hurley (New York: Random House, 1978).

[5] "Two Lectures," in Michel Foucault, *Power/Knowledge: Selected Interviews and Other Writings, 1972–1977*, ed. Colin Gordon (New York: Pantheon, 1980), 104.

The transition from compulsion to discipline, in Foucault's scheme, coincided with the turn from precapitalist to capitalist social organization, from the absolutist to the constitutional state. The contrast, however, is more than a chronological blueprint. It also represents two different (though not mutually exclusive) principles of social order. The Old Regime state, which Foucault sometimes termed "the juridical monarchy," came into being as a unified center of authority, having established its domination over the competing claims of powerful and multiple rivals. The national monarchs thus identified themselves with the reign of lawfulness, the triumph over anarchy. "Western monarchies," Foucault wrote, "were constructed as systems of law, they expressed themselves through theories of law, and they made their mechanisms of power work in the form of law." But they also arrogated to themselves the right to supersede any law, and their critics came increasingly to identify them in their own right with the arbitrary disregard of formal constraints. In Foucault's view, "A tradition dating back to the eighteenth or nineteenth century has accustomed us to place absolute monarchic power on the side of the unlawful: arbitrariness, abuse, caprice, willfulness, privileges and exceptions, the traditional continuance of accomplished facts."[6]

Insofar as this critique applied the standard of the law against which to measure the practices of the Old Regime, it used the monarchy's own ideology against it and failed to represent a new and different concept of justice. Like the monarchies they replaced, bourgeois liberal regimes also used the law to legitimate their claims to political authority, but antiliberal critics went further than their eighteenth-century predecessors in arguing not merely that bourgeois states violated the legality they claimed to uphold but that legality itself was deceptive. The law, they said, was not the antidote to coercion but a covert system of domination in its own right. Such critics claimed "not only that real power escaped the rules of jurisprudence, but that the legal system itself was merely a way of exerting violence, of appropriating that violence for the benefit of the few, and of exploiting the dissymmetries and injustices of domination under cover of general law." But this critique, Foucault argued, "is still carried out on the assumption that, ideally and by nature, power must be exercised in accordance with a fundamental lawfulness."[7]

What is inadequate about this critique, in Foucault's view, is that law no longer operates as the organizing principle for the exercise and constitution of power in modern societies, despite its continuing pretensions to the contrary. The judicial system, he wrote,

is utterly incongruous with the new methods of power whose operation is not ensured by right but by technique, not by law but by normalization, not by

---

[6] Foucault, *The History of Sexuality,* 1:87; see also Foucault, "Two Lectures," 94.
[7] Foucault, *The History of Sexuality,* 1:88.

punishment but by control, methods that are employed on all levels and in forms that go beyond the state and its apparatus. We have been engaged for centuries in a type of society in which the juridical is increasingly incapable of coding power, of serving as its system of representation. Our historical gradient carries us further and further away from a reign of law that had already begun to recede into the past at a time when the French Revolution and the accompanying age of constitutions and codes seemed to destine it for a future that was at hand.

Operating through the power/knowledge nexus, dispersed (in Foucault's elusive metaphor) throughout the social fabric, the "new mechanisms of power" do not emanate from the institutions of the state or formally constituted authorities and are "probably irreducible to the representation of law."[8]

This paradigm may or may not adequately describe a transition that occurred in European nations. Even Foucault qualified his claims in ways that cloud the opposition between the two ideal types of power. In the first place, he explained, the regulatory mechanisms characteristic of the modern era find their origin in the custodial functions of the monarchical regime, deriving "at least in part, [from] those [mechanisms] that, beginning in the eighteenth century, took charge of men's existence, men as living bodies."[9] Indeed, the absolutist *Polizeistaat* did not merely punish or coerce but also intruded, examined, fostered, and shaped the economic, social, and demographic body politic. One might illustrate this awkward combination with the example of Russia's Catherine the Great, who sanctioned the slitting of criminals' nostrils and the branding of their flesh, while at the same time sponsoring foundling homes and public hospitals. The bourgeois disciplinary regime, as Foucault recognized, did not represent the complete negation of the absolutist state but rather, perpetuated certain principles of premodern "enlightened" stewardship.[10]

In the second place, while Foucault maintained that the new techniques were "absolutely incompatible with the relations of sovereignty" central to old regimes,[11] or at the very least "probably irreducible to the representation of law" that legitimated state power, he also admitted that many of the juridical forms associated with the absolutist regime "have persisted to the present."[12] Having at times argued that discipline virtually

---

[8] Ibid., 1:89.

[9] Ibid.

[10] For more on the continuity between absolutist "police" and modern discipline, see Foucault, "Governmentality," 96, 101, 104. For a historical analysis of the Polizeistaat, see Marc Raeff, *The Well-Ordered Police State: Social and Institutional Change through Law in the Germanies and Russia, 1600–1800* (New Haven, Conn.: Yale University Press, 1983).

[11] Foucault, "Two Lectures," 104.

[12] Foucault, *The History of Sexuality,* 1:89.

replaces law as the effective mechanism of power in the modern period, at other times he depicted the liberal regime as an alliance between the two distinctive—and in principle irreconcilable—forms of power. "The system of right, the domain of the law," he wrote at one point, "are permanent agents of these relations of domination, these polymorphous techniques of subjugation" associated with the disciplinary regime. The theory of sovereignty and the formal structures of the law have, he suggested, bolstered the disciplinary mechanisms in two ways (both pejorative): first, they provide ideological cover for the kinds of coercion and subjugation inherent in the dispersed techniques of power that have superseded the strong arm of the absolutist state; and, second, they are the enabling condition for discipline itself, allowing for a "democratization of sovereignty," which has shifted the hub of power in modern times from the centralized state to a public sphere whose operations are "fundamentally determined by and grounded in mechanisms of disciplinary coercion."[13]

Indeed, it would seem, the modern period is characterized not so much by its contrast with the preceding one but by its deployment of old principles to new ends. "The powers of modern society," Foucault wrote, "are exercised through, on the basis of, and by virtue of, this very heterogeneity between a public right of sovereignty and a polymorphous disciplinary mechanism." Yet the alliance is not without conflict. Rather than a clean break with the past, the bourgeois regime constitutes a parasitic encroachment on it: "as these techniques and these discourses, to which the disciplines give rise[,] invade the area of right so that the procedures of normalisation come to be ever more constantly engaged in the colonization of those of law... [and] come into ever greater conflict with the juridical systems of sovereignty."[14]

There is some question as to how Foucault himself stood in relation to the power systems he anatomized.[15] On the one hand, he straddled the two critical traditions he himself identified: the one that takes the law to task for violating its own principles (here providing ideological cover for the operation of normalizing regimes), and the one that denounces law in its own terms as a mask for domination (insofar as law without discipline—the absolutist regime—provided no better alternative). In the end, Foucault could not find an uncontaminated standpoint:

Against these usurpations by the disciplinary mechanisms,...we find that there is no solid recourse available to us today,...except that which lies

---

[13] Foucault, "Two Lectures," 96, 105. For more along these lines, see Foucault, "Governmentality."

[14] Foucault, "Two Lectures," 107.

[15] On Foucault's contradictory critique of liberal politics and the question of his own value system, see Fraser, *Unruly Practices*, chaps. 1–3.

precisely in the return to a theory of right organized around sovereignty and articulated upon its ancient principle....But I believe that we find ourselves here in a kind of blind alley: it is not through recourse to sovereignty against discipline that the effects of disciplinary power can be limited, because sovereignty and disciplinary mechanisms are two absolutely integral constituents of the general mechanism of power in our society.

This situation left him with the wistful reflection that what was needed was "a new form of right, one which must indeed be anti-disciplinarian, but at the same time liberated from the principle of sovereignty."[16] That is to say, not only do principles of legality not provide a way out of the modern dilemma but the law actually abets the modern polity's violation of the promise of freedom. It is therefore not true, in Foucault's scheme, whatever its internal contradictions, that law is the standard from which to judge the derelictions of the bourgeois disciplinary regime, because, however opposite in principle, the law is compromised as well.[17]

But no matter how complicated Foucault ultimately made the picture of modernity, he retained the distinction between Old Regimes, in which power emanated from the state, and liberal, bourgeois societies, in which power operates through "normalizing" mechanisms based on "scientific knowledge" and is implemented through disciplinary practices widely dispersed in the social body. Moreover, the chronological vector is never entirely lost: whatever the overlaps and collusions, Western nations have allegedly proceeded from absolutist monarchies, through Polizeistaat enlightened despotisms, to liberal states that delegate power through social self-regulation and control their citizens through the operational fiction of individual autonomy.

To cast an oblique light on Foucault's historical scheme as well as on his implicit (and not so implicit) political judgments, let us take the case of a nation that both contemporaries and historians have considered an example of cultural and political backwardness or, at best, of "combined development."[18] In the Russian Empire, the Old Regime survived almost

---

[16] Foucault, "Two Lectures," 107–8.

[17] Complicating matters further, Foucault occasionally spoke as though power could be "limited" and liberty protected (though, of course, not guaranteed) only within the framework of the law; see passages from "Inutile de se soulever?" *Le monde* (11 May 1979), quoted in Colin Gordon, "Governmental Rationality: An Introduction," *The Foucault Effect*, 47–48.

[18] Trotskii (1879–1940) used this term to describe how "backward" countries might skip over stages traversed by advanced nations in order to arrive at the socialist goal without enduring the requisite intervening development. It implies the coexistence of elements associated with separate time periods in the Western sequence. See Leon Trotsky, *The Russian Revolution, the Overthrow of Tsarism, and the Triumph of the Soviets*, ed. F. W. Dupee, trans. Max Eastman (New York: Doubleday, 1959), 4 ("the law of *combined development*—by

unmodified into the era in which the modern mechanisms of social control and social self-discipline derived from Western practices had already emerged. Here, the "reign of law" had not "already begun to recede," as Foucault said of the European nineteenth century, but had not yet arrived. Rather, the tsar appropriated the institutional appurtenances of a rule-of-law state (legal codes, independent judiciary, trial by jury), while continuing to exercise absolute sovereignty through the mechanisms of a virtually unimpeded administrative state. Indeed, the Russian example represents the superimposition of the three models of power chronologically separated (however imperfectly) in Foucault's scheme: the so-called juridical monarchy, the Polizeistaat, and the modern disciplinary regime. Furthermore, both the defense and the critique of the law, which Foucault identified roughly with the eighteenth and nineteenth centuries—the one holding the monarchy to the standard of its own stated claims and the other attacking the law as intrinsically obfuscatory—also coincided in time in the utterances of tsarism's liberal and radical critics. And both positions coexisted with the articulated interests of trained professionals, representing the social authority of science.

The example of Russia is also instructive as a test case for Foucault's discursive hypothesis, which locates the authority and coercive power of the disciplinary mechanisms in the production of knowledge and the implementation of scientifically legitimated norms. Although Western culture penetrated the empire's official and civic elites, and the model of Western institutions largely shaped the contours of state and social organization, the regime of "power/knowledge" never came into its own in the Russian context. Thus the modern discursive mechanisms did not produce the same effects they purportedly did in the West. Nor, for that matter, did the ideology of the law. To quote the legal scholar Bogdan Kistiakovskii (1868–1920), writing in 1909: "No one, single idea of individual freedom, of the rule of law, of the constitutional state, is the same for all nations and all times, just as no social and economic organization, capitalist or otherwise, is identical in all countries. All legal ideas acquire their own peculiar coloration and inflection in the consciousness of each separate people."[19] To examine the Russian case is to remind ourselves not to mistake Foucault's paradigm for a universal model, for some "discursively" disguised

---

which we mean a drawing together of the different stages of the journey, a combining of the separate steps, an amalgam of archaic with more contemporary forms").

[19] B. Kistiakovskii, "V zashchitu prava (Intelligentsiia i pravosoznanie)," in *Vekhi: Sbornik statei o russkoi intelligentsii,* 2nd ed. (Moscow: I. N. Kushnerev, 1909), 130. In English, as: "In Defense of Law: The Intelligentsia and Legal Consciousness," in *Vekhi/Landmarks: A Collection of Articles about the Russian Intelligentsia,* trans. and ed. Marshall S. Shatz and Judith E. Zimmerman (Armonk, N.Y.: M. E. Sharpe, 1994).

reworking of modernization theory. More to the point, it is to question whether Foucault's understanding, even of the European case, adequately addresses the political issues at stake.

Using the Russian example, I argue that law and discipline are indeed interdependent principles, but not in the pejorative sense Foucault had in mind, and that Foucault's hostility toward order (whether juridical or disciplinary) has dangerous political implications, some of which were played out on the Russian stage. It is the voice of Russian liberalism that most eloquently expresses the difficulty of negotiating the mutual relation between state and society, between law and discipline, and the urgency of that attempt. The case of the Russian Empire and its Soviet successor illustrates the civic costs of failing to achieve the invidious bourgeois solution.

In exploring this counterexample of Foucault's historical hypothesis, this chapter proceeds along two lines. First, it situates Foucault's analysis and critique of law and social order within the nineteenth-century intellectual tradition reflected in Russian discussions of the same theme. Second, it locates the discontinuity effected by modernity not in the transition from law to discipline (if evident only, in some of Foucault's renditions, in the residual incompatibility of their continued coexistence) but from administration to law as the context for disciplinary technology. In short, I argue that the contribution of liberalism is not to displace an intrinsically ideological legality with the normative power of an equally inequitable and unfree disciplinary regime[20] but to replace the alliance between discipline and the administrative state with a configuration that frames the operation of discipline within the confines of the law. In the Russian-Soviet case, by contrast, the absolutist regime was succeeded by an administrative order that rejected legality and harnessed the professional disciplines to its own repressive ends, rather than a disciplinary society limited and controlled by the authority of the law.

* * *

As commentators have often remarked, Russian intellectuals produced a critique of capitalism and bourgeois culture before either had a chance to develop on Russian soil. Alexander Herzen's disillusionment with European politics and his hope that Russia might somehow negotiate the transition from traditional exploitation to future utopia without the painful middle passage provide the classic example of this precocious dissatisfaction. The revolutions of 1905 and even 1917 occurred before the theoretically appointed hour, as Marxists were uneasily aware. In relation to the

---

[20] Fraser, in *Unruly Practices,* argues that Foucault's judgment against both law and discipline ultimately relies on the humanistic (indeed, liberal) values of autonomy, dignity, and rights that he professed to reject as elements of the power regime he criticized.

law, Russians likewise generated an anticipatory critique of institutions not yet imbued with the authority of an established order. While independent liberals and government reformers struggled to build and validate a rule-of-law state, radicals and conservatives joined in denigrating a legality that had yet to take root in social psychology or institutional practice.

For all its resemblance to Old Regimes elsewhere, tsarism did not produce a similar legal tradition. Unlike the monarchs of Western Europe, Russian rulers had not come to predominance by resolving the clash of competing particular powers but had from the beginning constituted themselves as the source of all power in the land. They had never assumed an adjudicative but always an administrative function, creating the social hierarchy from on high, as a dependency of the state. The tsarist regime's persistent antipathy to the constraints of law was obvious to contemporaries and is a commonplace of historians. Eager for the attributes of modernity but unwilling to pay the political price, the nineteenth-century tsars played with judicial reform while consistently violating the meaning of lawful rule. The reforms created institutions that in theory, and to a degree in practice, circumscribed the emperor's absolute freedom to act or, at the very least, created new tensions in the system; these reforms reflected the emergence of legal-minded modernizers both within the bureaucracy and in educated society who pressed to transform the monarchy from within.[21]

Even its flirtation with reform displayed the autocracy's quintessential character, the very features that most angered its critics: arbitrariness and self-contradiction. Thus Alexander I (r. 1801–1825) employed European experts to reorganize the existing laws into a systematic compendium yet would not accept general principles, conceptual distinctions, or any winnowing of the chaotic body of historic edicts that could challenge the autocrat's untrammeled might.[22] Russian legal commentators complained that the resulting codes were "medieval" in their deliberately fragmentary conception, a jumble of specific cases designed to inhibit the discretion

---

[21] On the judicial reforms of 1864, see Richard S. Wortman, *The Development of a Russian Legal Consciousness* (Chicago: University of Chicago Press, 1976); on the impact of the new institutions and the strength of the post-Reform legal ethos, see Jörg Baberowski, "Das Justizwesen im späten Zarenreich 1864–1914: Zum Problem von Rechtsstaatlichkeit, politischer Justiz und Rückständigkeit in Russland," *Zeitschrift für neuere Rechtsgeschichte* 3–4 (1991): 156–72; on the liberalism of legal reformers, see William G. Wagner, "The Trojan Mare: Women's Rights and Civil Rights in Late Imperial Russia," in *Civil Rights in Imperial Russia*, ed. Olga Crisp and Linda Edmondson (Oxford: Oxford University Press, 1989). On the pro-law intellectual tradition among Russian liberals, see Andrzej Walicki, *Legal Philosophies of Russian Liberalism* (Oxford: Oxford University Press, 1987).

[22] See complaints in the introduction to Ludwig Heinrich von Jakob, *Entwurf eines Criminal-Gesetzbuches für das russische Reich: Mit Anmerkungen über die bestehenden russischen Criminalgesetze; Nebst einem Anhange, welcher enthält: Kritische Bemerkungen über die von der Gesetzgebungs-Commission zu St. Petersburg herausgegebenen Criminal-Codex* (Halle: Hemmerde und Schwetschke, 1818).

of the courts.[23] During the reign of Nicholas I, who, despite his conservatism, continued to sponsor the project of codification, the bureaucrats taxed with revising the codes necessarily relied on Western precedent but carefully denied the influence of alien models, pretending their work was merely to assemble the national tradition, not inject principled modifications into the existing corpus.[24] Moreover, the tension between tradition and change worked both ways. On the one hand, allegedly progressive tsars such as Alexander II (r. 1855–1881), who instituted the judicial reforms of 1864, later inhibited the formulation and application of the law. On the other, the vigorously reactionary Alexander III (r. 1881–1894), who showed utter contempt for proper procedure and presided over a reign of "extraordinary legislation," at the same time failed to curtail the ongoing project of legal reform initiated by liberal bureaucrats in his father's time.

The radical intelligentsia was resolutely anti-legal, the mirror image of this relentlessly inconsistent autocratic state. The radicals' hostility to legal principles distinguished them from those contemporaries who saw Russia's future in the strengthening of legality, the creation of a rule-of-law state (the *Rechtsstaat*), and the inculcation of respect for the law as a cultural value. It was this conflict within the educated elite that surfaced in the trenchant essay by Bogdan Kistiakovskii, included in the 1909 volume *Vekhi* (*Landmarks*). That provocative collection of articles represented a reaction against the 1905 Revolution on the part of thinkers we might now call neoconservatives: former radicals and socially cautious liberals, in some cases repudiating their own activist past and distancing themselves from the ideological assumptions of their cultural milieu. Kistiakovskii, for his part, deplored the intelligentsia's failure to recognize the importance of formal legal guarantees securing personal rights and inviolability as necessary to the maintenance of social discipline (*sotsial'naia distsiplina*). Rather, he insisted, the protection of individual liberty and integrity was central to a civic order based on the guarantees of the law, indeed, that individual freedom was the defining feature of the rule of law.[25]

---

[23] V. D. Spasovich, quoted in N. S. Tagantsev, *Russkoe ugolovnoe pravo: Lektsii*, 2nd rev. ed. (St. Petersburg: Gosudarstvennaia tipografiia, 1902), 222.

[24] See D. N. Bludov, "Obshchaia ob"iasnitel'naia zapiska," in *Proekt ulozheniia o nakazaniiakh ugolovnykh i ispravitel'nykh, vnesennyi v 1844 godu v Gosudarstvennyi Sovet, s podrobnym oznacheniem osnovanii kazhdogo iz vnesennykh v sei proekt postanovlenii* (St. Petersburg, 1871), viii, xxx–xxxiv. All eighteenth- and nineteenth-century lawmakers in Russia and the West borrowed from each other's laws. The vector of influence usually pointed from West to East, but the Russian draft criminal code of 1903 was cited by European authorities as a model of contemporary jurisprudence. See N. S. Timasheff, "The Impact of the Penal Law of Imperial Russia on Soviet Penal Law," *American Slavic and East European Review* 10 (1953): 443.

[25] Kistiakovskii, "V zashchitu prava," 125, 132, 135, 137. On Kistiakovskii and *Vekhi*, see Walicki, *Legal Philosophies*, 374–403; also Susan Heuman, *Kistiakovsky: The Struggle*

Although the absolutist monarchy did not assure such protection, few of the regime's most outspoken enemies included it in their demands. Radicals as well as critical conservatives were skeptical of both the principle of individualism and the value of formal judicial institutions. In the 1840s the Slavophiles denigrated the Roman law tradition of the West and the individualism of bourgeois societies as related defects of modern social organization that allegedly had disrupted the communal integrity of former times. They saw in the Russian peasant commune the opposite principle of spiritual and collective solidarity, a retroactive utopia (which they sometimes imagined as contemporary) associated with a premodern wholeness, in which individual persons did not conflict with or separate from the group. The later Populists persisted in this distrust of the West, identifying the great social evil with the capitalist form of production and exalting the folk principles of the peasant commune as the basis for a future socialist transcendence. The Marxists, by contrast, celebrated the historic mission of capitalism, disdained agrarian utopianism, and expressed theoretical, though qualified, respect for the contributions of bourgeois political culture. But they, too, Kistiakovskii complained, reviled the law as an instrument of coercion, a tool of class domination. The historic failure of law to realize its promise of universality was no reason, he argued, to dispense with the promise altogether. As a constitutional liberal sympathetic to the moral claims of socialism, he granted that law might not guarantee social justice but insisted that social justice could not be achieved without a basis in law.[26]

Kistiakovskii's analysis of the legal consciousness and principle of social order manifested by the radicals in their own political practice is particularly relevant to my concerns. Instead of respecting the law as a system of externally guaranteed but widely internalized norms, Kistiakovskii observed, the Marxists instituted a system of order based on the imposition of rules and regulations. Their rigidly enforced party strictures, in his view, demonstrated the same style of bureaucratic management exemplified in the tsarist administrative state. "We [Russians]," Kistiakovskii wrote, "need external discipline precisely because we lack internal discipline. In this regard, once again, we understand the law not as a matter of legal conviction [*pravovoe ubezhdenie*] but as a form of coercive regulation [*prinuditel'noe pravilo*]. And this conception once again testifies to the low level of our legal consciousness."[27]

The regime of the individual subject, enshrined and protected in the law, exalted by the liberal Kistiakovskii, was precisely what Russian radicals

---

for National and Constitutional Rights in the Last Years of Tsarism (Cambridge, Mass.: Harvard Ukrainian Research Institute, Harvard University Press, 1998).

[26] Kistiakovskii, "V zashchitu prava," 137, 144. On Marxist attitudes toward legality, see Walicki, *Legal Philosophies*, 82–104.

[27] Kistiakovskii, "V zashchitu prava," 144, 148 (quote).

disdained. The subsumption of the individual within the class, and of class in a future classlessness, made this concept of law seem irrelevant to the revolutionary project. As Vladimir Lenin (1870–1924) was later to declare in *Gosudarstvo i revoliutsiia* (*State and Revolution*) (1917), the ideal of socialist government was one that merely administered. In a society without class conflict, only the distribution of goods and services and the assignment of tasks would be left to the public authorities, no longer impelled to keep order by coercive means. The law, as Lenin realized (and Foucault often seems to have forgotten), is not only or primarily about repression but also about the resolution or adjudication of conflict. Lenin consistently postulated that a conflict-free society might safely dispense with the law. In the end, the law disappeared and conflict remained. Repression of an administrative character resulted.

Like Russia's nineteenth-century intellectuals, Foucault was all too aware of the defects of the bourgeois regime, its false promises, its covert constraints, and so could not celebrate the advance it represented over the burdens of absolutism. Yet, unlike them, he focused his ire not on the law, a principle of limitation (repression, he called it) that had presumably ceded preeminence on the historical stage, but on the insidious mechanisms of control, functioning as cultural proliferation or incitement, that had displaced it. Foucault was exercised by the very mechanisms that instill the "internal discipline" Kistiakovskii thought essential to the maintenance of order, indeed, to the operation of the law itself. Where Foucault emphasized the coming to predominance of "discourse" (power/knowledge) over prohibition as the regulatory principle of modern life, Kistiakovskii emphasized their mutual dependence. Insofar as Foucault, too, recognized a complicity between the two principles of order, it was a negative one, in which the facade of legality concealed the inequities of discipline, rather than discipline enabling the realization of the law.

In the Russian situation, the two groups to defend the principle of legality were, on the one side, certain bureaucrats and official servitors (the authors of judicial reform within the Ministry of Justice or the men who served as justices of the peace after 1864) and, on the other, professionals outside government like Kistiakovskii himself. The professionals outside government were in the position of having to defend both law and discipline at the same time, to insist on the interdependence, rather than the opposition, between institutional and dispersed authority. Insofar as they engaged in the business of social discipline, these professionals were the natural heirs to the autocratic Polizeistaat tradition, yet they actively opposed the official incarnation of Polizeistaat administrative rule in the interests of a civic autonomy protected by the rule of law (the Rechtsstaat principle).

Whereas in Europe the preconditions for and continuing context of disciplinary authority were established by the law-abiding state (in however imperfect a guise), in Russia both the reign of law and the ascendance of bourgeois discipline remained largely hypothetical. Jealous of its monopoly on tutelage, the autocracy obstructed attempts by the cultural elite to exercise its own kind of influence on the social body. The efforts of pedagogues, engineers, and other members of the professional intelligentsia to educate workers and provide social services were impeded by bureaucratic interference no less than the endeavors of physicians to raise the level of public hygiene.[28] Far from understanding that the delegation of disciplinary authority would have strengthened its own regulatory hand while winning the loyalty of the modern professional class, the tsarist regime was reluctant to evolve in the direction taken by Old Regimes in the West. It was as unwilling to allow alternative sources of custodial influence as it was jealous of the intrinsic power of the law.

The regime's reluctance to disperse the mechanisms of social discipline weakened, however, in the last years of imperial rule, as the growing complexity of the modern sector and the spread of education and technology strengthened the professional cohort and multiplied the kinds of social problems with which such mechanisms contend. Thus, at the turn of the century, the police entertained an experiment in state-sponsored labor unions, which enlisted the help of liberal professionals, while the 1905 Revolution netted the long-desired opening of a (restricted) parliamentary arena and the guarantee of minimal civil rights. The elite, for their part, also lost some of their defiance. Before 1905 the possibility of popular mobilization, whether desired or feared in educated circles depending on the particular ideological cast, was in all cases less of a certainty than the burden of repression from above. With the revolution, however, this potential became a reality. In response, many moderates (including the *Vekhi* group) who had sympathized with the Left lost their enthusiasm for political extremes or articulated long-held but previously muted doubts.

At the same time trained practitioners began to lose some of their hostility to state intercession and discovered a new enthusiasm for technologies of public intervention. While some populist-minded physicians, for example, continued to oppose bureaucratic strategies for health delivery and public hygiene in the name of independent, localized deployment of professional expertise, many of their colleagues joined hands with the central bureaucracy in the name of efficiency and modern technique. Those who decided that professional authority could be strengthened in league with, rather than opposition to, the state included more than a few Bolsheviks

---

[28] See Reginald E. Zelnik, "The Russian Working Class in Comparative Perspective, 1870–1914," paper presented at the Conference on Germany and Russia in the Twentieth Century, Philadelphia, 19–22 September 1991; and Nancy Mandelker Frieden, *Russian Physicians in an Era of Reform and Revolution, 1856–1905* (Princeton: Princeton University Press, 1981).

by political conviction.[29] The old Polizeistaat principle, which never trafficked in the pretensions of legality but functioned in a crudely regulatory mode often in conflict with the operation of the law, was acquiring a new plausibility in professional circles on the eve of World War I.

This principle seems to have beguiled the Bolshevik professionals who also helped found the postrevolutionary disciplinary regime. For what evolved after October 1917 was an alliance between the old tutelary state and the new disciplinary mechanisms but without the legal protections that Russian liberals had earlier considered essential to the disciplinary project and that Rechtsstaat reformers had tried to insinuate into the autocratic context.[30] The alliance was reinforced during the Stalin years, when a reconstituted technological elite was recruited as the system's social and ideological mainstay.[31] Ultimately, however, the experts were thoroughly subordinated to the interests of the state, and the scientific standards once evoked to legitimate Marxist claims to truth now depended on Marxism for their own legitimation. The absence of a legal context evidently proved fatal to the disciplinary authority inherent in professional expertise.

The radical intelligentsia's pervasive disdain for the law came into its own as public policy after 1917. At first elevated to an official philosophy, the critique of the law as an instrument of class domination justified courts operating in the absence of written rules and applying principles of "class justice" that violated the basic liberal postulates of lawful rule.[32] As in the tsarist regime, in which juridical status had determined one's relation to the law and one's vulnerability to punishment, so attributes of social position (in this case, socioeconomic or ideologically constructed)

---

[29] See the argument in John F. Hutchinson, *Politics and Public Health in Revolutionary Russia, 1890–1918* (Baltimore, Md.: Johns Hopkins University Press, 1990); and idem, "'Who Killed Cock Robin?': An Inquiry into the Death of Zemstvo Medicine," in *Health and Society in Revolutionary Russia,* ed. Susan Gross Solomon and John F. Hutchinson (Bloomington: Indiana University Press, 1990).

[30] I take my distance here from two opposing interpretations of the relationship between the tsarist and Soviet regimes. Richard Pipes has argued that the Bolshevik state perpetuated the repressive characteristics of the late autocracy: see, for example, his *Legalised Lawlessness: Soviet Revolutionary Justice* (London: Institute for European Defence and Strategic Studies, 1986). Jörg Baberowski counters by arguing that tsarism was "well on the way" to a Rechtsstaat when the revolution interrupted this development and eliminated the progressive legal personnel responsible for the change: "Das Justizwesen," 158, 162, 170. While I agree with Pipes that the Soviet system reflected certain institutional and cultural continuities with the tsarist regime and that Soviet pretensions to legality were hollow, I see the autocracy as less monolithic than he does, though not as deeply transformed as Baberowski maintains.

[31] This point emerges in Hutchinson, *Politics and Public Health*. On the Stalinist period, see Kendall E. Bailes, *Technology and Society under Lenin and Stalin: Origins of the Soviet Technical Intelligentsia, 1917–1941* (Princeton: Princeton University Press, 1978).

[32] On the articulated hostility to the law in the 1920s and the preference for technical administration, see Robert Sharlet, "Pashukanis and the Withering Away of the Law in the USSR," in *Cultural Revolution in Russia, 1928–1931,* ed. Sheila Fitzpatrick (Bloomington: Indiana University Press, 1978), 176–80.

affected one's susceptibility to repression. When the legal apparatus of the new regime achieved a greater degree of institutionalization, after the first Soviet criminal code was published in 1922, certain liberal principles of jurisprudence were still ignored. For example, crimes were punishable retroactively and by analogy: a person might be penalized for an act that had not been illegal at the time it occurred, and acts not defined as criminal in the statutes might be prosecuted because they resembled others that were. Despite the outward forms of legality (the famous Constitution of 1936, the codes and court system), law did not survive into the Stalinist period in any meaningful sense but operated as an instrument of administrative rule.[33] As in the tsarist regime, the business of repression was conducted both judicially in the courts and extra-judicially by the ordinary and political police.[34] Precisely because of the law's subordination to the ideological purposes of the party-state, discipline also lost the relative autonomy (its separation from sovereignty) it manifests in bourgeois regimes.

A nice example of the perils of discipline operating in the absence of law, taken from the early postrevolutionary years, is a trial of male homosexuals staged in Petrograd in 1922.[35] The men in question had met periodically in an apartment that was raided by the political police (the Cheka) on suspicion that the gatherings concealed a political purpose. The intruders found no counterrevolutionary conspirators but instead a group of men dressed as heterosexual pairs, some in male and others in female attire.

The lot was arrested and tried for public indecency. No other charge could be brought, because the participants had not been apprehended in the course of sexual activity and also because no criminal law forbade the act of anal intercourse between consenting adult men (the old definition of

---

[33] On the appropriation of law in the service of the new regime, see Eugene Huskey, *Russian Lawyers and the Soviet State: The Origins and Development of the Soviet Bar, 1917–1939* (Princeton: Princeton University Press, 1986).

[34] See Peter H. Solomon Jr., "Soviet Penal Policy, 1917–1934: A Reinterpretation," *Slavic Review* 39 (1980): 200–203. Elsewhere Solomon argued that the Soviet legal system at first encompassed a range of infractions formerly processed by administrative procedure under tsarist rule, and only in 1925, as a response to overloading in the courts, diverted many petty cases to nonjudicial institutions: "Criminalization and Decriminalization in Soviet Criminal Policy, 1917–1941," *Law and Society Review* 16 (1981–1982): 10, 13. The operation of the administrative alternative was so arbitrary and ineffective, however, that the relevant (petty) crimes were reassigned to the regular courts in the late 1930s: ibid., 26–27, 35–37. But even before 1925, when all crime was supposed to be handled by the regular courts, the political police ran its own (administrative) penal system for serious transgressions: Solomon, "Soviet Penal Policy," 197, 200–201. In 1936 the regime reasserted the importance of the law as an instrument of governance, rejecting the prevalent hostility to the formal aspects of the law (see Sharlet, "Pashukanis," 187), but this shift did not mean that "bourgeois" notions of legality (due process, equality before the law, fair and consistent punishment) were adopted or that recourse to administrative repression was abandoned.

[35] G. R., "Protsessy gomoseksualistov," *Ezhenedel'nik sovetskoi iustitsii*, no. 33 (1922): 16–17.

sodomy in the abrogated tsarist criminal code),[36] in which they presumably might have engaged.

The charge of public indecency was thus an improvised way of bringing the men to criminal account, although it did not suit the circumstances (the men were not comporting themselves in public) and did not conform to any legal offense. The significance of this charge was different, as the justification reported in the legal press makes clear: the prosecution of these men, it was said, formed part of a campaign to clean up public morals conducted in the interests of the nation's biological welfare. The effort at moral surveillance, which acquired special urgency in the confused early years of the New Economic Policy,[37] smacked of the old Polizeistaat rationale for the state's intervention in sexual affairs. It recalled the language and purpose of the tsarist criminal code, framed during the reign of Nicholas I and lasting in substance until 1917, which included the sexual offenses, among them sodomy, under violations of "public morality" (obshchestvennaia nravstvennost') and more generally of "public orderliness and decorum" (obshchestvennoe blagoustroistvo i blagochinie). In so doing, the code underscored the analogy between the role of the statutory law in enforcing sexual norms (classed as a matter of public decorum rather than interpersonal conflict) and the function of the police, which maintained standards of propriety through administrative rather than judicial means.

Objecting to the use of judicial institutions to impose the kind of discipline properly left to the police, liberal reformers had fashioned a new criminal code (completed in 1903 but never enacted), which recast sexual offenses as violations of a person's right to physical and psychic integrity. In decriminalizing sodomy, early Soviet lawmakers had taken the reformers' principles further than they themselves had been willing to go. (The 1903 code continued to penalize sodomy, despite objections from within the progressive legal community.) Yet the new regime's hostility to legality opened the door to mechanisms of control rooted in the same administrative tradition that Old Regime reformers had opposed. These mechanisms were buttressed, however, by the authority of "bourgeois" science. In the absence not only of particular statutes but of any guarantee of due process, Soviet courts used professional experts to justify repressive measures not specified in laws or decrees. Thus the prosecution in the 1922 trial summoned the eminent psychiatrist Vladimir Bekhterev (1857–1927), a

[36] See Laura Engelstein, The Keys to Happiness: Sex and the Search for Modernity in Fin-de-Siècle Russia (Ithaca: Cornell University Press, 1992), chap. 2; also idem, "Soviet Policy toward Male Homosexuality: Its Origins and Historical Roots," Journal of Homosexuality 29, nos. 2–3 (1995): 155–78.

[37] See Eric Naiman, "The Case of Chubarov Alley: Collective Rape, Utopian Desire, and the Mentality of NEP," Russian History 17 (1990): 7.

prominent member of the prerevolutionary professional elite, who willingly pronounced on the social harm attendant on the free practice of homosexual sex and recommended the application of penal sanctions. By dubbing the defendants an organically defective breed, he translated the issue of political control (the policing of public gatherings) into a scientific, medical prophylaxis (the policing of contagious pathologies).[38] Bekhterev provided the expert testimony, quintessentially in the "disciplinary" mode, that helped condemn the men for behavior not included in the criminal code, which is to say, not against the law.

Both the role of the political police and Bekhterev's public hygiene argument underscore the extent to which sexual regulation continued to fall within the province of the administrative state. It was precisely this third term in the social control equation, the old-style administrative state, that in Russia never evolved into the bourgeois disciplinary order. Rather, it survived the failure of liberalism to serve as the basis of the Soviet regime, updated and fortified by modern technology and a more aggressive ideology of public intrusion. In the early days of the New Economic Policy, the weight of scientific opinion, heir to the disciplinary authority of the bourgeois professions, reinforced the official project of social control and social engineering. Later, as Stalin consolidated his hold on power, science itself fell under the domination of political orthodoxy; then homosexuality became the disease of fascism and counterrevolution, rather than the medical pathology some experts had earlier seen it to be.[39]

The case of abortion again shows how prerevolutionary professional discourse set the terms of early Soviet practice and, like the case of homosexuality, also demonstrates the social consequences of discipline forming an alliance with the administrative state in the absence of legal protection. In the few years before the outbreak of World War I, jurists and physicians hotly debated the question of abortion law, which under the tsarist code penalized the medical practitioners as well as the pregnant women. The arguments articulated in the debate defined three possible positions on the question. Although all agreed that the existing statute needed reform, many insisted that abortion must remain a crime. The majority, however, favored decriminalization. Abortion, they contended, could not be effectively controlled through legal repression (penal sanctions) but should be regulated by professional discretion. Far from being punished for providing abortions, they asserted, physicians should be empowered by the state to

[38] Indeed, as reliance on legality weakened, psychiatry assumed a more central role in Soviet legal proceedings: Sharlet, "Pashukanis," 179.

[39] See Engelstein, "Soviet Policy toward Male Homosexuality." Also Dan Healey, *Homosexual Desire in Revolutionary Russia: The Regulation of Sexual and Gender Dissent* (Chicago: University of Chicago Press, 2001).

allocate and administer them. The third position, held by only a handful of participants, rejected both these policies in favor of the pregnant woman's absolute right of personal self-determination.[40]

In political terms, those taking the first position (for the continued relevance of the criminal law) tended to be stringent liberals, whereas those assuming the second sat further to the left, even though few identified themselves in openly partisan terms. Self-declared feminists could be found in all three camps, while women (the few who entered the debate) clustered around the third pole. The October Revolution institutionalized the second, "disciplinary" model. Abortion was decriminalized in 1920, but absolute prohibition was not replaced with the positive right to abortion. Instead, women were obliged to apply to clinics, where physicians were authorized to decide who would have access to professional care. The test case in the prerevolutionary debate had been the educated, privileged woman who wished to limit family size, supposedly for reasons of comfort or vanity. Champions of women's sexual self-determination defended the right to abort even for women such as these, while enemies of that principle used this group as a negative symbol of selfish individualism. As it turned out, no woman in the 1920s could argue successfully that she was entitled to the procedure on purely idiosyncratic grounds. Only material need or serious medical deficiency qualified an applicant for help.[41] In 1936 Stalin re-criminalized abortion, thus returning to the tsarist *status quo ante*. Referring to this change, Commissar of Justice Nikolai Krylenko (1885–1938) remarked, "A basic mistake is made in every case by those women who consider 'freedom of abortion' as one of their civil rights."[42]

* * *

What conclusions can be drawn from the Russian-Soviet case that are relevant to evaluating the paradigms supplied by Foucault in deciphering the modalities of power in the modern world? In what sense can he help us

---

[40] For the issues in the debate, see *Otchet desiatogo obshchego sobraniia russkoi gruppy mezhdunarodnogo soiuza kriminalistov, 13–16 fevralia 1914 g. v Petrograde* (Petrograd: Tip. Dvigatel', 1916); for further documentation and discussion, see Laura Engelstein, "Abortion and the Civic Order: The Legal and Medical Debates, 1911–1914," in *Russia's Women: Accommodation, Resistance, Transformation,* ed. Barbara Alpern Engel, Barbara Evans Clements, and Christine D. Worobec (Berkeley: University of California Press, 1991).

[41] On abortion in the 1920s, see Wendy Goldman, "Women, Abortion, and the State, 1917–36," in Engel, Clements, and Worobec, *Russia's Women;* also Susan Gross Solomon, "The Demographic Argument in Soviet Debates over the Legalization of Abortion in the 1920s," *Cahiers du monde russe et soviétique* 33 (1992): 59–82. As in the case of Bekhterev, continuity was provided on a personal as well as ideological level. Mikhail Gernet (1874–1953), who articulated the middle, "disciplinary" position in the prewar debates, survived into the Soviet period as a distinguished legal sociologist.

[42] Quoted in Goldman, "Women, Abortion, and the State," 265.

understand the "great tyrannies" of our age? I suggest that it was his own cultural context that caused him to neglect what was most radical about the very regime whose seductive comforts he deplored. For all his iconoclasm, Foucault, we must remember, lived not in Russia but in France, where he had the luxury to denounce the insidious intrusions of the disciplinary professions and the entangling effects of bourgeois liberation. France is a country in which the juridical monarchy indeed gave rise to the rule of law as well as to its critique, in which Old Regime legalism produced the bourgeois legal regime, which buttresses the vaunted subject that the disciplinary project also invokes and deploys.

The liberal state is not perfect. Beginning in the nineteenth century, critics already complained that the operation of the vaunted public sphere, with its attendant freedoms and connection to political authority, depended on a monopoly of access. Marxists and feminists (in their respective varieties) have explained both the principle and the function of these exclusions on different grounds. The existence (indeed origins) of regulated prostitution in Western Europe demonstrates, for example, that administrative incursions on legal rights were not unique to absolutism. And it is certainly not the case that the existence of a legal apparatus and a rule-of-law tradition guarantees the realization of civil and political justice. But one cannot conclude from the negative example that their presence is irrelevant to the chances of success. What distinguishes post-liberal repressive regimes from the inequitable but more porous "bourgeois" variety is not the presence or absence of social "self-regulation" (whose mechanisms, moreover, are not everywhere the same) but the nature of the political apparatus, including its legal ethos, and its relation to other forms of control. The importance of these imperfect, but indispensable, institutional guarantees is what Russian professionals, chafing under the constraints of the shamelessly antilegal imperial regime, repeatedly invoked.[43]

Not surprisingly Russian liberals, no less than their Western counterparts, sometimes hesitated before the full implications of their own ideas: displaying wariness in regard to women's suffrage and a residual paternalism (though it was the Provisional Government that granted women the vote in 1917, along with civil rights for ethnic minorities), moral revulsion at sexual variation, condescension toward non-Russian local cultures, and at times unseemly nationalist zeal. They also demonstrated ambivalences of their own: chronic doubts about the liberal sacred canon and often a sentimental affection for the political Left, which had little use for their niceties. Even to the best Russian liberal, individualism was both an ardently desired prize and a threat to cultural values that distinguished their world from "out there," a place that often seemed better but also spiritu-

---

[43] See Laura Engelstein, "Reply," *American Historical Review* 97, no. 2 (1993): 380.

ally impoverished; private property and the marketplace (whether in goods or culture) seemed deeply troublesome attainments; and the rigors of bourgeois morality struck them as narrow and vain. They felt themselves blessed or cursed with a social conscience. As the psychiatrist Nikolai Bazhenov (1856–1923) remarked in 1906, Russia was both too early and too late for liberalism. "The time for purely political revolutions has long passed," he wrote. "Russia will witness the struggle for land as well as for legality [*pravo*], and not for land alone but for the establishment of social and economic justice [*spravedlivost'*]."[44] In the end, it was not only legality that got short shrift but also social justice.

In Russia liberalism ultimately failed, and the custodial state survived by enlisting and absorbing the agencies of social self-formation it inherited in embryonic form. In contrast to the imperfect world of capitalist liberalism, which both extends and violates the promise of rights, the Soviet regime long offered discipline without rights. This was not merely the old Polizeistaat under new ideological auspices—the return of Catherine the Terrible—but its refurbishment with new tactics, by which society was enlisted to do its own policing but in which the discursive authority of the professional disciplines, speaking in the name of "science," functioned only as a dependency of the state. The very meaning of "discipline," as invoked by Foucault in the bourgeois context to signify social self-regulation through the dissemination of scientifically validated norms and professional practices, resulting in the politically useful subterfuge of individual sovereignty, loses its sense in the Soviet context, although it is certainly true that control in Soviet society was not merely exercised by state institutions "from the top down." Without the guarantees promised by the law, even if not always successfully provided, authority, it would seem, cannot reside in society. Without a measure of autonomy, without even the appearance of autonomy, as in the Soviet case, there has historically been no tension between subjectivity and submission. The Soviet regime, often used to symbolize the essence of modern tyranny, has, more accurately, provided an example of illusory modernity, an administrative state that mobilizes disciplines not free in either fact or pretense. In the Soviet aftermath, the "deceptive" visions of civic modernity still remain an alluring dream. Russia is a society that has yet to generate the luxury of a Michel Foucault to push it to consider the enticements of paradox.

[44] N. N. Bazhenov, *Psikhologiia i politika* (Moscow: I. D. Sytin, 1905), 6.

CHAPTER TWO

Revolution and the Theater of Public Life

The Triumph of Extremes

Russian intellectuals and statesmen of the second half of the nineteenth century associated Europe, for good or for ill, with the emerging future and Russia with a past that resisted forward movement. They were burdened still with that relic of pre-1789 Europe, an absolute monarchy, which limited their ability to shape the world in which they lived. They were surrounded with a vast peasantry mired in misery, bound by tradition, and largely unaffected by the advances of scientific knowledge.

The Europe to which these Russians compared themselves had, of course, more than one face. The legacy of the French Revolution endowed it with concepts of rights and citizenship and with a new idea of nationhood. It rearranged state boundaries and created new empires and new nations. It produced new kinds of wealth and new kinds of poverty, new hierarchies and new models of the good society, new techniques for governing new kinds of populations. In Foucault's terms, it created new modalities of power and new ideologies with which to implement and conceal them. It also set in motion a chain of revolutionary upheavals and inspired a century of social thought devoted to understanding and often promulgating revolution. It was both orderly and agitated—replete with the contradictions Karl Marx delighted in revealing.

The Russian Empire had a different set of tensions. The 1905 Revolution compelled the tsar to grant the rudiments of modern political life: a parliament and the promise of limited civil rights. But the regime retained its administrative prerogatives, and the exercise of imperial rule, though sometimes challenged, was never seriously impaired.[1] Indeed, the use of

---

[1] For a precise definition of the sovereign's absolute power, see "Miatezh," in *Ugolovnoe ulozhenie: Proekt redaktsionnoi komissii i ob"iasneniia k nemu*, 8 vols. (St. Petersburg: Tip. Pravitel'stvuiushego senata, 1897), 2:34.

extrajudicial, administrative repression reached its apex in the years after 1905.[2] Yet if imperial Russia failed to be modern, in its own as well as Western eyes, it was nevertheless of its age. Although lacking the ideals of citizenship and the French sense of the empowered nation, it was affected by the thinking that accompanied the new European order. It experienced the early stages of social and economic transformation linked to industrial production and technological change sweeping across Europe—the railroads, factories, automobiles, telephones, warships, street lights, streetcars, art museums, advertising, mass-circulation newspapers, illustrated magazines, psychiatrists, self-help manuals, feminism, socialism, and anti-Semitism.

If Russia was the last exemplar of unmitigated absolute rule among the European powers, it was also notorious as a breeding ground of revolutionary ideology and eventually a revolutionary movement. One mirrored the other—a confrontation of extremes. Yet here, too, Russia echoed the experience of contemporary Europe, where revolutions were a chronic occurrence. Radical ideas streamed across the borders, from West to East, where they confronted both the archaic framework of the autocratic regime and the elements of a new social formation emerging under the ambivalent sponsorship of the state, aware of the dangers not only of modernity but of backwardness as well.

Organized challenges to tsarist authority punctuated the long nineteenth century. Between the massive popular uprising of 1773–1774, inspired by the Cossack leader Emelian Pugachev (1740–1775), and the convulsive upheaval of 1905, Russia experienced three localized cases of rebellion: the failed coup of 1825 led by imperial guards officers returned from the Napoleonic campaigns; the failed revolt of 1830–1831 led by Polish officers emulating the European example; and the Polish Uprising of 1863, following Russia's defeat in the Crimean War. The 1905 Revolution, involving all segments of imperial society, gave rise to a brief decade of quasi-parliamentary political life (the last three years consumed by the trauma of World War I), after which the empire succumbed to the most dramatic upheaval of all.

The Bolshevik victory ensured that enormous effort would be devoted in retrospect to studying the origins and character of the revolutionary movement that prepared the triumphal outcome. For most of the preceding fifty years, in fact, the radicals were few in number. Their impact was magnified, however, through the prism of a disgruntled educated public that continued to expand, in the absence of features that constituted civil

---

[2] Volker Rabe, *Der Widerspruch von Rechtsstaatlichkeit und strafen der Verwaltung in Russland 1881–1917: Motive, Handhabung und Auswirkungen der administrativen Verbannung von Revolutionären.* Wissenschaftliche Beiträge Karlsruhe, no. 14 (Karlsruhe: M. Wahl, 1985), 143–56.

society in the West—freedom of expression, freedom of choice, and public responsibility. This stunted context helps explain how the myth of revolution came to exert such enormous power, even among those who saw clearly where the dangers lay.

* * *

The story of revolution and potential revolution in nineteenth-century Russia can best be told in three registers. First, it involves an activist state that exemplified arbitrary power by ignoring or changing the rules it established. Second, it concerns the efforts of educated people outside the state apparatus to challenge its claims to legitimacy and either modify its operations or bring it crashing to the ground. Some tried to mobilize the force of popular discontent for political ends, but many spent at least as much effort communicating with officialdom and with leaders of the cultural establishment. Intellectual resistance to absolutism was not restricted to the ideological fringe. It was vastly more widespread and diverse. Without the receptive audience of an alienated professional and privileged class, the radicals would not have loomed as large on the political landscape. Third, the story entails a long tradition of popular resistance and revolt, which sometimes erupted in violence but more often simmered below an ominous surface compliance.

Until the end of the nineteenth century, the major challenge to the regime's political complacency was enacted not in the village or the factory but on the stage of public opinion, as a conversation among the privileged few. Despite the efforts of intelligentsia activists to build a popular movement beginning in the 1870s, their systematic contacts with the common folk were limited. By the 1890s they had indeed developed a small following of politically educated workers, but these did not represent the broad laboring mass. When in the course of that decade textile workers launched a wave of giant strikes, this was not the result of direct political intervention. Likewise, in 1905, radicals helped shape working-class protests once these had begun, but their influence was always tenuous. In terms of bringing the crisis of 1905 to a head, they were more important as ideological gadflies among the disaffected elite, pushing frustrated moderates toward ever more daring gestures of political defiance. The radicals did not stand outside the bounds of the emerging public sphere in which educated Russians struggled against their political disenfranchisement. Whatever one may think of the ultimate consequences of October 1917, the revolutionary challenge that preceded it was not the work of social riff-raff, intellectual fanatics, or criminal misfits, but of respected men with connections in the halls of power and rich cultural capital. Their allies were less respected, often younger and more impatient, but not isolated from the whole. Nor was 1905 a playground on which the influence of educated leaders—moderate or extreme—held absolute sway; traditions of popular mobilization shaped the contours of collective behavior more decisively than any brand of ideological exhortation.

Cossacks and Gentlemen

The story of revolutionary agitation and upheaval in tsarist Russia begins in the eighteenth century. All the essential elements are in place by the time Alexander I comes to the throne in 1801: a politics of radical rupture and cultural innovation implemented by the state; the institutional basis of public opinion, which turns the official ideology of enlightenment against the principles embodied in serfdom and autocratic rule; and the violence of popular rebellion. The policies of Peter the Great exemplified the primary contradiction of Russian absolutism: the inculcation of Western principles, including the institution of the law, using the unlimited powers of a coercive state. Catherine the Great raised this contradiction to an acute degree by assuming the mantle of enlightened despot. Having colluded in the murder of her husband, Peter III (r. 1762), the empress advertised her devotion to the rule of law while never abandoning her belief in absolute power.[3] She fostered public discussion by authorizing the first private printing presses, encouraging the publication of satirical journals, and inviting her subjects to communicate their suggestions for legal reform.[4] She did not, however, allow any challenge to imperial authority, refusing to institutionalize the legal principles proclaimed in her famous Instruction of 1767, revoking the right to private publishing when it suited her whim, confiscating manuscripts that displeased her, and sending intellectually obstreperous subjects to prison for appropriating the values she herself proclaimed.

The greatest challenge to Catherine's rule came, however, not from the cultural elite but from her lowliest subjects, inhabitants of the imperial frontier inspired by a crafty veteran of military service, the Cossack Emelian Pugachev. A clever propagandist as well as charismatic chief, Pugachev led his followers in a bloody assault on the persons and property of the landed class, which lasted from 1773 to 1774 and culminated in a prolonged struggle with the imperial armed forces. The rebellion united the discontents of a motley following, angered by the regime's violation of traditional norms and incursions on particular freedoms: Cossacks, defending their autonomy; serfs and factory workers, fleeing bondage and

---

[3] See contradictions in the text of her Instruction: Paul Dukes, ed., *Russia under Catherine the Great*, Vol. 2, *Catherine the Great's Instruction (Nakaz) to the Legislative Commission, 1767* (Newtonville, Mass.: Oriental Research Partners, 1977).

[4] Gary Marker, *Publishing, Printing, and the Origins of Intellectual Life in Russia, 1700–1800* (Princeton: Princeton University Press, 1985).

exploitation; religious sectarians and dissenting priests, guarding out-lawed practices; miners and foundry workers; misfits and vagrants (army deserters, fugitive convicts, bandits); and members of non-Russian tribal communities.

Styling himself the true tsar Peter III, Pugachev issued numerous decrees and missives couched in the language and form of imperial authority. Surrounded by a mimetic court, complete with rituals and courtiers named after Catherine's favorites, the rebel captain disciplined his followers with the same sort of penalties inflicted by the state, including hanging and threats of torture. Pugachev and his men exhibited extreme ferocity in attacking their enemies and their property: factories were destroyed; towns, monasteries, and churches stripped and smashed; estates set to the torch, contents as well as structures obliterated. Members of the nobility met gruesome deaths at the rebels' hands, usually in summary fashion. Sometimes, in his capacity as "monarch," Pugachev held court and imposed sentences upon them.[5]

Pugachev had confronted Catherine not only with the use of armed force (learned in the imperial army) but also with purloined signs of authority: the name of a dead tsar, the symbols of imperial office, and the rituals of formal justice. Catherine replied in kind, with military might, judicial authority, and the ritualized language of retribution. In the end Pugachev's followers renounced their allegiance. Betrayed by fellow Cossacks, Pugachev was captured and interrogated, placed in an iron cage, and taken to Moscow, where the public could marvel at his shame.[6]

Catherine now had to please two audiences with vastly different expectations: an imagined European public of modern views and a Russian one that anticipated the pleasure of revenge. With an eye on Western opinion, the empress insisted on a proper trial. Though Pugachev's followers met truly grisly deaths, and nobles wished to spare the leader no possible torment, Catherine instructed the judges to exercise moderation, so as not to offend her own "love of humanity" or earn the country a reputation for "barbarity."[7] On 10 January 1775, on a square below the Kremlin, Pugachev was therefore decapitated before being cut apart. The corpse must be left on display, wrote the official in charge of the proceedings, "in order to impress the restless mob," enraged by "the well-known ferocity and inhumanity of the miscreant and his henchmen."[8] The crowd must

---

[5] Paul Avrich, *Russian Rebels, 1600–1800* (New York: Schocken Books, 1972), 195–96, 203–5, 217–21, 233, 235. My interpretation of Pugachev follows Avrich.

[6] Ibid., 242.

[7] Quoted in R. V. Ovchinnikov, "Sledstvie i sud nad E. I. Pugachevym," *Voprosy istorii,* no. 3 (1966): 126–28 (quotes, 128); also idem, "Sledstvie," *Voprosy istorii,* no. 9 (1966): 141, 145; and Avrich, *Russian Rebels,* 243.

[8] Document in Ovchinnikov, "Sledstvie," *Voprosy istorii,* no. 9, 146.

also watch the culprit die. Those who gathered to witness the execution saw the rebel cross himself and bow. Before the axe severed the head from his body, he spoke his final words: "Farewell, Christian folk; forgive me for all my offenses before you; farewell, Christian folk."[9]

The execution was the third since the death penalty had purportedly been abolished in 1753. Despite her scruples, Catherine thus seemed to have acted in contradiction not only to her self-proclaimed enlightened principles but also to the law of the land.[10] Yet the decision was consistent with the views expressed in the Bible of enlightened jurisprudence, *Dei delitti e dele pene (Essay on Crimes and Punishments)* (1764), by Cesare Beccaria (1738–1794), which had influenced the empress's own Instruction. Though Beccaria denounced the use of torture and the death sentence, he believed that corporal punishment was appropriate for certain crimes and considered death the proper response to rebellion.[11] Subsequently, in 1824, the State Council decided that the decrees of 1753 and 1754 had not intended to eliminate the death penalty altogether, and certainly not in cases involving attacks on the sovereign or the state.[12] The death penalty was valued not only for its practical effects (eliminating the culprit) but for its psychological and symbolic power.[13] It remained in the tsarist criminal code until 1917, although it was restricted to crimes against the state and quarantine violations. At the same time, and increasingly after 1881, the death penalty was inflicted on civilians convicted of a wider range of crimes by the military courts, which were governed by separate statutes.[14]

[9] Dmitriev's memoirs, quoted in Alexander Pushkin, *The History of Pugachev,* trans. Earl Sampson (Ann Arbor, Mich.: Ardis, 1983), 108.

[10] Decree no. 10101 (1753), *Polnoe sobranie zakonov Rossiiskoi imperii,* 45 vols. (St. Petersburg: Tip. II Otdeleniia Sobstvennoi Ego Imperatorskogo Velichestva Kantseliarii, 1830), 13:838–39. Also embodied in the law of 30 September 1754 (no. 10306); see N. S. Tagantsev, *Russkoe ugolovnoe pravo: Lektsii,* 2 vols. (St. Petersburg: Gosudarstvennaia tipografiia, 1902), 2:973–74. Also Peter Liessem, "Die Todesstrafe im späten Zarenreich: Rechtslage, Realität und öffentliche Diskussion," *Jahrbücher für Geschichte Osteuropas* 37, no. 4 (1989): 493.

[11] Cesare Beccaria, *An Essay on Crimes and Punishments,* trans. from the Italian of Beccaria with commentary by Voltaire, trans. from the French, 5th ed. (London: E. Hodson for J. Bone, 1801), 95, 76, 100. See T. Cizova, "Beccaria in Russia," *Slavonic and East European Review* 40 (1961/1962): 392, 396.

[12] On interpretation, see D. N. Bludov, "Obshchaia ob"iasnitel'naia zapiska," in *Proekt ulozheniia o nakazaniiakh ugolovnykh i ispravitel'nykh, vnesennyi v 1844 godu v Gosudarstvennyi Sovet, s podrobnym oznachenie osnovanii kazhdogo iz vnesennyki v sei proekt postanovlenii* (St. Petersburg, 1871), li; also Tagantsev, *Russkoe ugolovnoe pravo,* 2:975.

[13] Count Dmitrii Bludov (1785–1869), author of the revised criminal code of 1845, noted that the death penalty was necessary to produce a "salutary psychological effect" (*spasitel'no deistvovat' na umy*): Bludov, "Obshchaia ob"iasnitel'naia zapiska," lii.

[14] Before the use of corporal punishment was severely restricted in 1863 and 1871, culprits often died from its physical effects. See Donald Rawson, "The Death Penalty in Late Tsarist Russia: An Investigation of Judicial Procedures," *Russian History* 11 (spring 1984): 29–52; and Tagantsev, *Russkoe ugolovnoe pravo,* 2:977–79.

The confrontations between sovereign and rebel reveal a persistent confusion, on both sides, between the literal and the symbolic registers. In the case of errant intellectuals, Catherine punished cultural expression as though it were physical insubordination. Aleksandr Radishchev (1749–1802) became a criminal for having published a book critical of the monarch. Catherine is said to have called him "a rebel, worse than Pugachev."[15] Though the seditious author was condemned to death, the empress was hampered by the niceties of the law in imposing the sentence. She had to contend not only with the decrees of 1753 and 1754, but also with the 1785 Charter of the Nobility, which granted exemption from corporal punishment. In view of these limitations, Catherine commuted Radishchev's sentence to ten years' exile in eastern Siberia and stripped him of his rank, honors, rights, and privileges. Treated harshly while in prison and interrogated at great length, Radishchev did not undergo a public trial; his fate was decided behind closed doors by high judicial officials.[16] On the way to Siberia, he was kept in fetters, a mark of humiliation, but no crowd assembled to register his shame.

Radishchev's subsequent fate mirrored the changing politics of succeeding reigns and showed the extent to which the intellectual preoccupations of rulers were intertwined with those of their critics. The early years of the nineteenth century were marked by high-minded rhetoric and projects of institutional reform. During his brief reign from 1796 to 1801, Paul repudiated the principles once espoused by his mother, but under Alexander I the Enlightenment once again became the language of legitimacy as well as opposition. Four days after coming to the throne, Alexander restored Radishchev to his rank and honors. The former exile was soon appointed to an imperial commission charged with revising the laws. He dreamed of establishing a legal system in Russia comparable to the English system he so admired, but his hope proved vain. In 1802 Radishchev took his own life, in a calculated gesture of protest against the tsar who had set him free but who disappointed his faith in the promise of enlightenment from above.[17]

[15] Remarks of a contemporary, quoted in Roderick Page Thaler, "Introduction," in Aleksandr Nikolaevich Radishchev, *A Journey from St. Petersburg to Moscow*, trans. Leo Wiener, ed. Roderick Page Thaler (Cambridge, Mass.: Harvard University Press, 1958), 11.

[16] See Thaler, "Introduction," 11–12; also D. S. Babkin, *Protsess A. N. Radishcheva* (Moscow-Leningrad: Izd-vo Akademii nauk SSSR, 1952), 56–59, 268, 271–72, 276–77. Babkin does not mention a public ceremony of dishonor in his heavily ideological account of Radishchev's heroic suffering.

[17] Thaler, "Introduction," 14, 16–19. On Radishchev's suicide and the Roman model, see Iurii M. Lotman, "The Poetics of Everyday Behavior in Eighteenth-Century Russian Culture," in Iurii M. Lotman, Lidiia Ia. Ginsburg, and Boris A. Uspenskii, *The Semiotics of Russian Cultural History*, ed. Alexander D. and Alice Stone Nakhimovsky (Ithaca: Cornell University Press, 1985), 90–92. Political suicide was a theatrical gesture that had gained currency in France during the revolution, where the practice drew on the same classical and

Like Radishchev, many of the guards officers who staged the Decembrist Uprising of 1825 were aristocrats close to the throne who embraced the principles of the Enlightenment. In the aftermath of Alexander I's death, when the order of succession was still unclear (the heir had secretly renounced his claim, and the next in line, the future Nicholas I, did not immediately assume the throne), the officers attempted to block the transfer of power by means of an armed insurrection on St. Petersburg's Senate Square and armed resistance in the south. Aspiring to replace the absolutist monarchy with a different kind of political regime, their venture represented a transition between old and new styles of political action. On the one hand, they followed the tradition of the palace coup, in which highly placed courtiers meddled in the process of succession, either by physically dispatching the legitimate heir or promoting one contender over another. Like the tsaricides who did away with Peter III and later Paul, the Decembrists were privileged men who took it upon themselves to determine who should hold supreme power. On the other hand, in challenging the legitimacy of autocratic rule, the conspirators also represented something new. While Alexander flirted with the idea of a constitution and the rule of law, authorizing projects of reform (though strictly behind closed doors), the Decembrists also worked on plans for change. They joined Masonic lodges and formed their own secret committees, in which they dreamed of transforming the principles of enlightened governance into the outline of a renovated state.[18]

They did not work entirely in private, however. Their goal was not only to achieve practical victory but also to make a moral impression on the society in which they moved. Even before they took to the streets with their ill-fated final performance, they enacted their disaffection in the ballrooms and salons of the capital. As Iurii Lotman has so brilliantly observed, they used the cultural idiom of their own aristocratic world to fashion a language of rebellion and even a new social type, in opposition to, but also in dialogue with, the representatives of power. Exploiting the ritualized structure of their social milieu, they inverted its meanings, attending balls in order ostentatiously not to dance, staging feasts in order not to drink to

---

Enlightenment sources that inspired Radishchev. See Dorinda Outram, *The Body and the French Revolution: Sex, Class, and Political Culture* (New Haven, Conn.: Yale University Press, 1989), 90–105; also Andrzej Walicki, *A History of Russian Thought: From the Enlightenment to Marxism* (Stanford: Stanford University Press, 1979), 39.

[18] For documents, see Marc Raeff, *The Decembrist Movement* (Englewood Cliffs, N.J.: Prentice Hall, 1966); for a standard account, see Anatole G. Mazour, *The First Russian Revolution, 1825* (Stanford: Stanford University Press, 1937). On official projects for reform, see S. V. Mironenko, *Samoderzhavie i reformy: Politicheskaia bor'ba v Rossii v nachale XIX v.* (Moscow: Nauka, 1989). The Russian-language literature on 1825 is vast; see S. V. Mironenko, ed., *Dvizhenie dekabristov: Ukazatel' literatury, 1977–1992* (Moscow: GPIB, 1994); Pavel Il'in, ed., *14 dekabria 1825 g.: Istochniki, issledovaniia, istoriografiia, bibliografiia*, directed by Sergei Erlikh, 7 vols. (St. Petersburg: Nestor, 1997–2005).

excess. They imbued every word and gesture with moral significance and were highly sensitive to the impression they produced.[19]

If the rebels' behavior reflected their sensitivity to the importance of public opinion, the opening act of their final drama had disappointing results. The popular audience, composed of the troops who might have rallied to their cause, did not respond as hoped, and Nicholas seized the heroic lead, establishing the legitimacy of his rule by using force against the traitors.[20] The second act of the Decembrist drama had no audience at all but occurred as a private performance, enacted and witnessed by the principals alone; there was no public trial. Brought from their gloomy cells one by one, the culprits were questioned by Nicholas personally. A commission was appointed to ferret out the particulars of the plot.[21] The evidence and charges were heard by a specially appointed court, which met only to endorse the commission's findings. The defendants first learned of the proceedings when the results were announced. Half the original 579 brought to trial were acquitted; of the 121 identified as ringleaders, five were sentenced to be quartered, thirty-one to beheading, and the rest to exile and hard labor. Nicholas commuted the sentences to hanging for the five defendants (including the poet Kondratii Ryleev [1795–1826]) and hard labor for the thirty-one. The pretense of a trial was apparently designed to impress the world with Russia's respect for lawful procedure.[22]

The third act of the Decembrist drama involved execution, exile, and posthumous myth. The hangings were carried out at three in the morning before a small audience. The five men were first stripped of their military honors in a ceremony of symbolic degradation, including the breaking of swords. The bodies were neither mutilated nor displayed but buried in secret. Alexander Herzen recalls in his memoirs that the public was nevertheless shocked by the death sentences.[23] These were not, after all,

---

[19] Lotman, "The Decembrist in Daily Life," in Lotman, Ginsburg, and Uspenskii, *Semiotics.*

[20] Richard Wortman has argued that Peter the Great set a pattern by which acts of founding violence became central to the symbolics of imperial legitimation; see his *Scenarios of Power: Myth and Ceremony in Russian Monarchy,* Vol. 1, *From Peter the Great to the Death of Nicholas I* (Princeton: Princeton University Press, 1995). Thanks to the Decembrists, this pattern was replicated even for Nicholas, the ideological conservative who reigned in the name of dynastic continuity, not rupture.

[21] Mazour, *First Russian Revolution,* 205–9. Friends and associates of the accused were among the investigators, making it difficult for the prisoners to view their questioners as enemies or political abstractions. Lotman, "Decembrist," 143.

[22] Mazour, *First Russian Revolution,* 210–14. The information the prosecution accumulated constitutes the basis of what we know about the event and much of what we know of the conspirators' ideas, but it was not available to contemporaries. For Nicholas's belief that the Decembrist trial had convinced the world of Russia's respect for legality, see A. A. Kizevetter, "Imperator Nikolai I, kak konstitutsionnyi monarkh," in *Istoricheskie ocherki* (Moscow: A. A. Levenson, 1912; rpt. The Hague: Mouton, 1967), 405.

[23] Mazour, *First Russian Revolution,* 220; Herzen cited, ibid., 214.

bloodthirsty brigands from the imperial frontier but one's own equals and friends.

Unlike Radishchev, the executed Decembrists did not control the circumstances of their demise. They did not turn their final moments into one last chance to speak through calculated gestures. Rather, the survivors spoke to their fellow countrymen through the pathos of the journey into exile. Their dignity, their continued loyalty to the cause (advertised through the circulation of letters and news), the self-sacrifice of their wives in following them into captivity—this mythic afterlife in the wake of "civil death" completed the narrative of heroic self-dramatization.[24]

All three acts of resistance—Pugachev, Radishchev, and the Decembrists—deployed official rhetoric and ceremony for subversive ends. Whether Pugachev's "true" tsar and his mimetic court, Radishchev's invocation of the dialogue of enlightened monarch and loyal interlocutor, or the guards officers' secret societies, constitutional dreams, and military heroics—all used the idiom of political legitimacy to challenge the claims of the absolutist state. For most of the intellectual and cultural elite, the Decembrist revolt severed the connection between court ideology and public values. The contrast, however, was not absolute. Nicholas continued to tinker with the problem of eliminating serfdom (in secret, just as Alexander had done); and some of the institutional reforms such as codification of the laws, begun but abandoned in the preceding reign, were accomplished in the reign that despised Western influences and the rule of law.[25] But Nicholas broke with the posture of enlightenment and Westernization, which had dominated the court at the start of the century and remained the idiom of much of educated society (though in educated circles, as well as at court, conservatism found a newly influential voice). Intolerant of any unauthorized form of expression, Nicholas made free thinking a crime—the natural extension of Catherine's response to Radishchev, though in his case ideologically more consistent.

The legal context shaped not only the consequences of revolt but its very definition. The Criminal Code of 1845 (in effect until 1917) defined "crimes against the state" in broad terms, to cover three kinds of actions: physical assault on the person of the tsar (or members of the imperial household); mass uprising; and propaganda hostile to the sovereign or government or inciting to rebellion. Any role in planning or executing attacks on the imperial person or household, successful or unsuccessful, was

[24] Radishchev's exile and his sister-in-law's decision to follow him to Siberia had made no such impression on his contemporaries and exercised no enduring fascination. In the space of thirty years, as Lotman notes ("Decembrist," 121–22), formerly neutral gestures had acquired new meaning.

[25] On codification under Nicholas I, see A. A. Kizevetter, "Vnutrenniaia politika v tsarstvovanie imperatora Nikolaia I," in *Istoricheskie Ocherki,* 494–97.

punishable by death, as was any role in promoting insurrection. Failure to report knowledge of these plans or actions to the authorities was also a crime. Prohibited forms of expression included "bold speech" critical of the government, the production or dissemination of insulting or disrespectful texts and images, as well as damage to likenesses of the sovereign.[26]

These laws drew on precedents dating back to the seventeenth century, which treated with equal severity the mere intent to rebel, preparation for revolt, and attempts to execute the plans. The early decrees also outlawed associations promoting such goals, communicating these purposes to others, or failing to report them to the authorities. The 1845 code perpetuated this legacy by defining subversive intention in the broadest possible terms and uniformly applying the death penalty to the full range of subversive acts. Russia was not, of course, the only nation to punish attempts at insurrection with death, but European codes exempted cases where plans were never carried out or conspirators were foiled in the early stages. Late-nineteenth-century Russian legal reformers believed that the death penalty was appropriate in cases of attempted insurrection, but criticized the existing code for failing to distinguish between more or less direct threats to the established order and between degrees of criminal responsibility. The abuse of ultimate sanctions, they argued, encouraged extremism among critics of the regime, who were bound to suffer in the greatest measure for the least involvement in the most tenuously subversive acts.[27]

It was therefore easy to fall afoul of the law. The law, moreover, was not always the favored instrument of repression; administrative reprisals were more common still. Petr Chaadaev (1794–1856) was declared insane and placed under police and medical supervision for having published the first of his "Philosophical Letters," in 1836. Alexander Herzen was sent into administrative exile on several occasions. As these examples show, however, Nicholas's reign was a period largely of intellectual, not practical, opposition. Only one "conspiracy" against the established order—the socialist discussion group led by Mikhail Petrashevskii (1821–1866)—was uncovered by the vigilant police, and even that never translated talk into action.

The one active challenge Nicholas confronted after 1825 had nothing to do with the psychological and philosophical turmoil of the Russian elites or with the anger of the Russian masses. The Polish Uprising of 1830–1831

---

[26] See articles 241–52 in *Ulozhenie o nakazaniiakh ugolovnykh i ispravitel'nykh 1885 goda*, ed. N. S. Tagantsev (St. Petersburg, 1901), 253–59.

[27] "Miatezh," in *Ugolovnoe ulozhenie*, 2:10, 16–20, 24–25, 40–41, 45–46. For the origins of this legal tradition, see N. N. Evreinov, *Istoriia telesnykh nakazanii v Rossii* (St. Petersburg: Izd. V. Ilinchika, 1913), 23, 25; and James Cracraft, "Opposition to Peter the Great," in *Imperial Russia, 1700–1917: State, Society, Opposition*, ed. Ezra Mendelsohn and Marshall S. Shatz (DeKalb: Northern Illinois University Press, 1988), 23, 25–26.

originated in the political discontents and Romantic longings of army officers, who, like their Russian counterparts, and in the same years, formed secret societies and dreamed of national liberation. They demanded full implementation of the Polish Constitution recognized by Russia in 1815 and return of the formerly Polish provinces that had been incorporated directly into the Russian part of the empire.[28] The Polish rebels did not share the Decembrists' vision of social and constitutional change and were not involved in their plans, but contact with the Decembrists led to the arrest and trial of a few Polish officers, who thereby achieved the status of national martyrs. The symbolic link between the two movements was underscored in January 1831, when the rebellious Diet commemorated the Decembrists' execution six years earlier and declared Nicholas no longer king of Poland.[29]

The events of November 1830 were sparked by a group of younger officers galvanized to action by the example of revolution in Belgium and France, by the news that Nicholas was preparing to send Lithuanian and Polish troops to help suppress it, and by the rumor that Grand Duke Constantine (1779–1831), the tsar's brother in charge of Poland, was preparing to arrest the conspirators before they had a chance to proceed with their plans. No less inept than the Decembrists when it came to practical steps, the rebels bungled the beginning of the coup. Having attacked the grand duke's residence, they failed to seize him, and they found no senior officers who would agree to assume command. The awkward start escalated into a serious challenge, however, when the lower classes of Warsaw rallied to the rebels' cause and when moderate leaders, and eventually the Diet itself, lent their support to the struggle against Russia. Constantine's refusal to apply armed force at the very beginning permitted the movement to build up steam. Apparently troubled by legal considerations, the grand duke believed that Poland's status as a separate political unit limited Russia's right to impose itself on Polish affairs.[30]

---

[28] On political divisions within the Polish elite before incorporation into the Russian Empire and on Polish attitudes toward the Constitution of 1815 at the time it was introduced, see Andrzej Walicki, *Russia, Poland, and Universal Regeneration: Studies in Russian and Polish Thought of the Romantic Epoch* (Notre Dame, Ind.: University of Notre Dame Press, 1991), 5–6.

[29] Norman Davies, *God's Playground: A History of Poland,* 2 vols. (Oxford: Clarendon, 1981), 2:321.

[30] W. Bruce Lincoln, *Nicholas I: Emperor and Autocrat of All the Russias* (Bloomington: Indiana University Press, 1978), 138–39. For Constantine's scruples, see Kizevetter, "Imperator Nikolai I." For narrative accounts of 1830, see R. F. Leslie, *Polish Politics and the Revolution of November 1830* (London: Athlone, 1956), 117–23; Piotr S. Wandycz, *The Lands of Partitioned Poland, 1795–1918* (Seattle: University of Washington Press, 1974), 105–17; and W. F. Reddaway et al., eds., *The Cambridge History of Poland, from Augustus II to Pilsudski (1697–1935)* (Cambridge: Cambridge University Press, 1941; rpt. New York, 1971), 295–310.

Though Nicholas, too, allowed himself to be governed in some respects by the provisions of the Polish Constitution, he took immediate steps to crush the insurrection. Refusing to consider the appeals of Polish moderates, the tsar sent troops to restore order. Despite considerable ineptitude on the part of Polish commanders, it nevertheless took the Russians nine months to bring the Poles to their knees.[31] Without the backing of the Western powers, which refused to intervene on Poland's behalf, the rebels ultimately were unable to withstand military repression. The fight for national independence could not be won on the battlefield. In ideological terms the Polish elite was divided between the conservative to moderate majority, which rejected any program of social reform, and a small number of radicals. These were the only ones to gain a popular following, and that only in the towns. The peasantry as a whole viewed the war with Russia as a conflict between landlords and tsar, and resented being called upon to fight. In the amputated eastern provinces, many Lithuanian peasants supported the Polish cause but most Ukrainian peasants were anti-Polish.[32] In the aftermath many prominent figures emigrated; the officers and implicated civilians who remained behind were tried and sentenced to severe penalties, though none was put to death. Poland lost the limited autonomy it had enjoyed since 1815: the rights granted in the constitution were suspended, the independent army, Diet, and universities abolished.[33] Polish nationalist feeling and resentment of Russian domination were reinforced by defeat.

If one thinks of the Polish events as an echo of the Decembrist debacle, Nicholas can be said to have gotten satisfaction once again by asserting military preeminence and using the courts to teach a political lesson. Combating the revolutions of 1848 and their domestic consequences proved a more complex undertaking. Nature and politics seemed to conspire in that year: a bad harvest led to famine, followed by a cholera epidemic, and drought encouraged widespread fires; the threat of revolution, meanwhile, swept ever eastward across the European continent. After seditious leaflets of foreign origin appeared in Poland and the Baltic and western provinces in March 1848, Nicholas announced his readiness to defend Holy Russia against the revolutionary peril and sent troops into the region. A year later he sent forces into Hungary to support Hapsburg rule. From the start, the regime had feared that unrest would erupt in Russia itself. Officials warned against the spread of "communist" ideas. Censorship was

[31] Lincoln, *Nicholas*, 140–43.

[32] See Davies, *God's Playground*, 2:324–25; Leslie, *Polish Politics*, 257; Wandycz, *Lands of Partitioned Poland*, 105–17; and Michael T. Florinsky, *Russia: A History and an Interpretation*, 2 vols. (New York: Macmillan, 1953), 2:757–64.

[33] Davies, *God's Playground*, 2:331–32. For the 250 condemned to death though never executed, see M. N. Gernet, O. B. Gol'dovskii, and I. N. Sakharov, eds., *Protiv smertnoi kazni: Sbornik statei* (Moscow: Tip. I.D. Sufina, 1907), 386–94.

extended to a ludicrous degree, leading a contemporary to complain that the tsar was waging a "Holy War against scholarship and knowledge." It was in this context that the members of Petrashevskii's socialist discussion group (including Fedor Dostoevskii) were arrested and condemned to death in 1849. So oppressive was the campaign against free expression that even moderates exulted in 1855, when the "thirty-year tyranny" of Nicholas's reign finally ended.[34]

Reform and Rebellion

With the death of Nicholas I and the Crimean defeat, an important shift occurred in the relationship between Russia's three dynamic elements— activist state, educated society, and restive populace. In some obvious ways Nicholas had repudiated the principles of his predecessor's reign: where Alexander I, until his last years, had kept alive the prospect of enlightened governance, Nicholas made conservatism his official creed and military discipline his civic model. Alexander had raised hopes of reform; Nicholas had dashed them. Yet there were striking similarities. Both contemplated, behind the closed doors of secret committees, the modification of serfdom. Before 1812 Alexander had fostered rumors of constitutional change, but in the end neither monarch did anything to weaken the autocracy's power.

By contrast, Alexander II initiated a process of reform that not only resulted in real social and institutional change but for the first time opened the door to public participation in political affairs. The making of peasant emancipation and the "Great Reforms" involved the joint activity of progressive bureaucrats, who had nurtured hopes for change in the inhospitable climate of the preceding reign, and representatives of the nobility. To facilitate their task the state allowed a limited circulation of opinion and the airing of conflicting ideas (the famous "artificial *glasnost'*"). The regime was thus more energetic (unsettling rather than merely intrusive) and more tolerant than it had been for more than thirty years.

The educated elite flourished under the new dispensation. From highly placed personages, prominent landowners, and staid university professors to disgruntled former students, professional journalists, and radical aristocratic émigrés, all engaged in what might be considered a national conversation. Debate and civic activity were facilitated by a number of institutional changes. The relaxation of censorship permitted the formation of professional journals and associations that widened the range of discourse on public affairs. The organs of local self-government known as zemstvos, introduced in 1864, became the focus of hitherto unthinkable

---

[34] Lincoln, *Nicholas*, 271–77, 287–89, 313–15, 318–22, 320 (Holy War), 323 (Kavelin on tyranny).

civic activity, providing a context in which respected public figures could press for a broader mandate, for the introduction of constitutional change, and for a legitimate role in national life. The elected delegates progressed, with ever increasing disaffection, from respectful petitions to the tsar in the 1860s to gatherings of angry notables in the 1890s to the awkward alliance of socially modest but morally intense paid professionals and their well-born but increasingly frustrated gentry employers on the eve of 1905.

If zemstvo activism had a long fuse, which eventually helped spark the outbreak of revolution, the immediate impact of the judicial reforms, also implemented in 1864, was more dramatic. With new rules of procedure, an independent bar, legally protected judges, trial by jury, public access, and published proceedings, the new courtrooms offered a rare opportunity for tolerated free speech. For defendants, their lawyers, sometimes even the judges, and certainly for the public at large, they served as a substitute for political life. While establishment liberals welcomed the changes in their own terms, as a step toward constitutional government and the rule of law, hot-headed members of the younger generation used the platform provided by the regime as a stage on which to dramatize their opposition to moderation and compromise of any sort.

The terms of emancipation, announced on 19 February 1861, ended peasant bondage but left the former serfs with meager allotments of land, heavy financial burdens, and continuing civic liabilities. In the wake of the disappointing decree, the young radicals had set their hopes on provoking a popular revolution, but they had less success delivering their message of liberation in the village than before the courts. The third element in the revolutionary equation—the nation at large—was fitfully restive throughout those years but generally unresponsive to the issues that moved the privileged few. Peasant disturbances in the reign of Nicholas I increased with rumors of impending liberation. During the Crimean War, peasants enlisted in the hope of gaining freedom in return; afterward thousands moved to the Crimea, expecting to settle there as free men. The authorities had been frightened by a peasant rebellion in Austrian Galicia in 1846 and anticipated the worst in 1861.[35] Once the decision had been made, authorities feared that the good news would itself generate unrest.

Indeed a spate of disorders followed the announcement of the terms of emancipation, which gravely disappointed peasant hopes, but violence was rare. In the most famous incident, villagers in the hamlet of Bezdna

---

[35] Historians have debated the extent to which Alexander II was motivated by the specter of peasant violence in finally embarking on emancipation as a way to ward off disorder from below. For the standard Soviet view, see M. V. Nechkina, "The Reform as a By-Product of the Revolutionary Struggle," in *Emancipation of the Russian Serfs*, ed. Terence Emmons (New York: Holt, Rinehart and Winston, 1970), 66–71. Compare Alfred J. Rieber, "The Politics of Emancipation," in *The Politics of Autocracy: Letters of Alexander II to Prince A. I. Bariatin-skii, 1857–1864*, ed. Alfred J. Rieber (Paris: Mouton, 1966), 15–58.

insisted they had found "true freedom" in the emancipation decree and had divined the tsar's real motives behind the misguided claims of his agents in the field. Anton Petrov, a semi-literate peasant, "discovered" the word "freedom" in the official text. Neighbors who heard his message and refused to believe he was wrong were dispersed by gunshot and a number were killed. Petrov was seized and shot. The survivors professed the loyalty of their intentions.[36] But the Bezdna incident, strikingly symbolic though it was, was notable for its isolation.

The most serious challenge to the regime in the 1860s did not stem from tensions within Russian society but from the frustrated aspirations of Polish nationalists. Russia's defeat in the Crimean War and the death of Nicholas I had raised Polish hopes of a new dispensation. But Alexander II, although conciliatory, was firm. Ready to tolerate a wider range of cultural activity than Nicholas had been, the tsar appointed officials sympathetic to Polish interests but he refused to relax control over Polish life. As early as June 1860, Polish students and returned émigrés, inspired by the Italian Risorgimento, mounted public demonstrations in the streets of Warsaw; further demonstrations, in February and April 1861, were violently dispersed by imperial troops. As in 1830, Polish moderates tried to elicit concessions from the imperial authorities; their efforts this time met with a certain success. But the radicals once again pursued a more aggressive course. By the fall of 1861, the tsar had declared military rule. Churches and synagogues closed in protest.

In the end Russian policy helped consolidate a united national front of radicals and moderates. In August 1862, when Constantine arrived in Warsaw to assume the post of viceroy, an attempt was made on his life. In response, Constantine and Alexander Wielopolski (1803–1877), then head of the Polish government, ordered the perpetrators publicly hanged. In the wake of this ill-considered attempt at symbolic intimidation, Polish leaders buried their differences in obdurate resistance to Russian domination. Despite these divisions and the movement's lack of support from peasants in significant parts of the kingdom and eastern provinces, the insult to national pride and the desire for autonomy kept the cause alive.

In September 1862 the leadership constituted itself Poland's national government, and on 22 January 1863 announced a state of insurrection. It declared equal rights for all Polish citizens regardless of religion or ethnic descent, and offered the peasants land and freedom. In April the tsar made a conciliatory offer, including amnesty for those who surrendered arms. Meanwhile, England and France supported Polish demands for restoration

[36] See Terence Emmons, "The Peasant and the Emancipation," in *The Peasant in Nineteenth-Century Russia*, ed. Wayne S. Vucinich (Stanford: Stanford University Press, 1968), 41–71, esp. 48–50, 54–55; and Daniel Field, *Rebels in the Name of the Tsar* (Boston: Houghton Mifflin, 1976; rpt. Boston, 1989), 31–111.

of the 1815 constitution, and the return of Lithuania and Ruthenia to the Polish kingdom. But the Poles refused the tsar's offer, and the Western powers failed to intervene. Popular backing for the Polish cause remained uneven; Russia ultimately secured peasant support by instituting agrarian reforms favorable to peasant interests. The Poles continued to differ among themselves over the purposes of the insurrection, and they failed to gain the sympathy of Russian liberals, most of whom saw the struggle not as a matter of political principle but of power politics, a conflict between states. Ultimately the Poles were defeated by force of arms, and the last of their commanders were hanged on a square in Warsaw. In the aftermath Russia confiscated gentry estates, eliminated the qualified autonomy granted by the constitution of 1815 (already partly eroded after 1831), and introduced a policy of cultural and administrative Russification.[37]

The Polish rebellion challenged the integrity of the empire and resulted in a prolonged military confrontation, and yet, by definition, it was a limited threat. More disturbing, because it was more pervasive and harder to defeat, was the development of cultural and political disaffection among the Russian elite. University students were quick to respond to the freedoms promised by the new era. Their activism represents a classic example of the energy generated between the contradictory poles of tsarist policy. Admission had been expanded after 1855 to include young men of humble background; diversity and relative freedom of speech on university grounds promoted fervent intellectual debate, which in turn led the authorities to restrict the students' liberties and their scholarships. Restrictions on what had so recently been conferred provoked more meetings and discussion. In 1861 the indignant young men poured into the streets in St. Petersburg's first public demonstration. The authorities at first tolerated the protests, but they soon lost patience and closed down the universities.

The young people who caused this trouble constituted a new generation in cultural as well as biological terms. Its members were generally less exalted in family origin than the highly cultivated, socially prestigious men of the 1830s and 1840s who had nourished critical ideas in the shelter of private salons. The newcomers were often ill-mannered, aggrieved, and prone to ideological grandiosity. They repudiated established ideas and social forms, and the absolutes of religion and beauty, in the name of a worldly social good; devoted to Reason, Science, and Materialism, they subordinated art to practical purposes, yet set their hearts on the utopian dream of universal happiness. The generation of the 1860s was the first to be dubbed "the intelligentsia," to denote a particular cast of mind and intensity of moral commitment.

---

[37] On 1863, see Davies, *God's Playground*, 2:348–63; Florinsky, *Russia*, 2:909–18; Wandycz, *Lands of Partitioned Poland*, 155–79; *Cambridge History of Poland*, 365–86.

Sociology certainly separated the figures of the 1830s and 1840s from their successors. Well-bred, sure of his personal importance, the wealthy Alexander Herzen chafed under the petty humiliations supplied by the administrative regime. A proud individualist, he also disdained the vulgar laissez-faire individualism of the bourgeois Europe he encountered after 1847. Nikolai Chernyshevskii (1828–1889) and his peers, by contrast, were obliged to improvise a sense of social worth. Their intellectual assurance obscured agonies of personal unease. Yet a sociological ground shift cannot account for the persistence of the project of self-fashioning that spans the generations—from the Eugene Onegins and Decembrists of the 1820s, to Herzen and Nikolai Ogarev (1813–1877) adopting the model of Romantic friendship and later the sentimental free thinking of George Sand, to the mock Bazarovs of the 1860s.[38]

The self-styled new men and women of the 1860s chose as their guide Chernyshevskii's novel *Chto delat'? (What Is to Be Done?)* (1863). Vissarion Belinskii (1811–1848) had told them that literature was a social enterprise; texts were to describe the world, reveal its defects, and propose remedies. In fact, its effects were not only social but personal. Chernyshevskii's novel provided the younger generation with the model for a distinctive cultural style, affecting the shape of haircuts, the terms of romance, as well as political ideas. So convinced were contemporaries (not the radicals alone) of the power of literature that the establishment liberal Boris Chicherin (1828–1904) blamed Chernyshevskii for "inject[ing] the revolutionary poison into our life." The authorities were just as literal-minded. In 1862 Chernyshevskii was arrested and charged with having written a radical proclamation and instigating public disturbances. Despite the complete absence of proof, he was convicted.[39] The novel was published, by an oversight of the censor, while Chernyshevskii was in prison.

---

[38] Bazarov was the hero of Ivan Turgenev's novel, *Fathers and Sons* (1862). On the concept of the intelligentsia, see Martin Malia, "What Is the Intelligentsia?" *Daedalus* (summer 1960): 441–58; and Michel Confino, "On Intellectuals and Intellectual Traditions in Eighteenth- and Nineteenth-Century Russia," *Daedalus* (spring 1972): 117–49. The men of the 1840s are conventionally described as the first generation of the intelligentsia, and the men and women of the 1860s as the second. Michael Confino ("On Intellectuals") argues, however, that only the generation of the 1860s fits the strict definition of the intelligentsia, characterized by a sense of social estrangement and intense moral commitment to civic or political action. For a recent discussion of the concept, see Nathaniel Knight, "Was the Intelligentsia Part of the Nation? Visions of Society in Post-Emancipation Russia," *Kritika* 7, no. 4 (2006): 733–58.

[39] See Irina Paperno, *Chernyshevsky and the Age of Realism* (Stanford: Stanford University Press, 1988), 21 (Chicherin quoted), 22 (arrest). For specific charges, see *Vedomosti S.-Peterburgskoi gorodskoi politsii,* 17 maia 1864, no. 108, quoted in *Gosudarstvennye prestupleniia v Rossii v XIX veke: Sbornik izvlechennykh iz offitsial'nykh izdanii pravitel'stvennykh soobshchenii,* ed. B. Bazilevskii [B. Bogucharskii], 3 vols. (St. Petersburg: Russkaia skoropechatnia, 1906), 1:123.

What Is to Be Done? presented a cast of characters on which to model one's behavior—the selfless, though self-assertive woman; the gentle, self-abnegating man; and the ruthless, self-disciplined revolutionary. The author also became a hero in his own right. Chernyshevskii's conduct at his civil execution and his subsequent dignity in exile produced a saintly aura around his person.[40] The execution also afforded an opportunity for public participation in the drama of political martyrdom. The deprivation of juridical rights and social status, known as "civil death" (*grazhdanskaia smert'*), was marked by a public ceremony. The purpose of the performance was to induce contrition in the condemned and leave an "edifying" impression on the crowd.[41] Symptoms of this edification were demonstrated by the response in May 1862, when one of Chernyshevskii's followers was sentenced to exile for distributing a subversive pamphlet. In the words of a witness, spectators at the ceremony "expressed the bestial desire that [the culprit's] head be cut off, that he be flogged with the knout or at least tied to the column with his head down, as he had dared to go against the tsar."[42]

Things were different in Chernyshevskii's case. Early in the morning on 19 May 1864, a well-dressed group assembled in the heavy rain on St. Petersburg's Mytninskaia Square.[43] As the sentence was read, Chernyshevskii stood hatless, in prisoner's garb. As was the custom, his crime was inscribed on a board hung around his neck. He paid little attention to the proceedings and showed no remorse—for a "crime" he had in any case not committed. The executioner lowered him to his knees and broke a sword over his head, then chained him to the pillory for the required ten minutes of silence. The crowd then thronged the carriage bearing the prisoner away. Admirers threw flowers in his direction and followed in his tracks. One started the cry, "Farewell [*proshchai*], Chernyshevskii!!" Others yelled the more poignant, "Till the next time [*do svidaniia*]!" Even after the police tried to hurry the convoy along, people continued in pursuit, crying out and waving kerchiefs and caps.[44]

---

[40] Nicholas Ishutin (1840–1879), sentenced to hard labor for his part in the attempted assassination of the tsar in 1866, considered Chernyshevskii as one of the world's three great men, along with Jesus and St. Paul. Franco Venturi, *Roots of Revolution: A History of the Populist and Socialist Movements in Nineteenth Century Russia,* intro. Isaiah Berlin, trans. Francis Haskell (New York: Grosset and Dunlap, 1966), 331.

[41] The term "edifying" (*pouchitel'noe*) was used by the 1864 judicial reform commission, complaining that this effect was no longer produced: quoted in N. V. Murav'ev, "Obriad publichnoi kazni" (*Iuridicheskii vestnik,* nos. 7 and 8 [1874]), rpt. in idem, *Iz proshloi deiatel'nosti,* 2 vols. (St. Petersburg: M. M. Stasiulevich, 1900), 1:19.

[42] Quoted in Venturi, *Roots,* 240 (trans. modified).

[43] Eyewitness account in N. A. Alekseev, ed., *Protsess N. G. Chernyshevskogo: Arkhivnye dokumenty* (Saratov: Saratovskoe oblastnoe gosudarstvennoe izdatel'stvo, 1939), 354–55.

[44] A note on the ambiguities of status and the discord between juridical and cultural meanings in late tsarist Russia: although Chernyshevskii, in his modest personal demeanor and clerical family background, represented the archetypal intellectual commoner, he was

Thus did heroes become criminals and criminals become heroes. The public no longer consisted of local inhabitants drawn by curiosity to the site of easy moral drama, ready to throw the unfortunate miscreant a few spare kopecks for Christ's sake.[45] The public in May 1864 was a select group determined to frustrate official intentions. And unlike Pugachev, who in traditional fashion begged forgiveness of the crowd, or those among the Decembrists and the Petrashevtsy who repented of their ways,[46] Chernyshevskii rejected the terms of his condemnation. His demonstrative indifference to the process of public humiliation, as well as his followers' celebratory response, defeated the edifying purpose of the occasion.

The history of these rituals shows that the symbolic repertory of absolutism, on which they so heavily relied, had begun to lose its hold. In 1864 the judicial reform commission complained that public executions had ceased to function as serious political theater, becoming instead "a frivolous spectacle."[47] One could bind Pugachev in chains and expect the ladies to faint and the crowd to howl, but spectator and perpetrator were no longer what they once had been. Even after 1864 crowds were sometimes indifferent or even hostile to the fate of condemned revolutionaries, but the results were no longer predictable.[48] What had been, in Pugachev's time, "terrifying and meaningful," was now often "a sad and vulgar comedy"[49]—or worse, an occasion for ritualized inversions. The reversal of signification that occurred between 1864 and 1881 under the pressure of the radical assault led to the abolition of public executions and the removal of political cases from the (semi-open) civilian to the closed military

---

legally a member of the nobility. Having earned the civil service rank of *tituliarnyi sovetnik,* which conferred the status of "personal" nobility, he was entitled to have a sword broken over his head as a token of civic degradation. Nikolai Gogol's famous downtrodden hero, the clerk Akakii Akak'evich in *"Shinel'"* (The Overcoat) (1842), an object of universal derision, belonged to the same rank. See Seymour Becker, *Nobility and Privilege in Late Imperial Russia* (DeKalb: University of Northern Illinois Press, 1985), 91, 95, 97.

[45] Murav'ev, "Obriad," 42.

[46] Avrahm Yarmolinsky, *Road to Revolution: A Century of Russian Radicalism* (New York: Macmillan, 1959), 82.

[47] Quoted in Murav'ev, "Obriad," 19 (*prazdnoe zrelishche*).

[48] On reaction to Pugachev, see Pushkin, *History,* 106–7. Local citizens watched impassively the civil execution of three of Nechaev's followers: Venturi, *Roots,* 77. The crowd at Nechaev's own ceremony was hostile: ibid., 387; and N. A. Troitskii, *Tsarskie sudy protiv revoliutsionnoi Rossii: Politicheskie protsessy 1871–1880 gg.* (Saratov: Izd-vo Saratovskogo universiteta, 1976), 150. No one gathered to consecrate Karakozov's death, but the civil execution of the followers of Aleksandr Dolgushin (1848–1885) on 6 May 1875 provided an occasion for public theater similar to the performance at Chernyshevskii's "execution" ten years before: see N. A. Troitskii, *Tsarizm pod sudom progressivnoi obshchestvennosti, 1866–1895 gg.* (Moscow: Mysl', 1979), 132; also Venturi, *Roots,* 500–501. On the Dolgushin case, see Bazilevskii, *Gosudarstvennye prestupleniia,* 1:254–318.

[49] Murav'ev, "Obriad," 48.

courts.[50] Legal procedure and publicity both suffered a defeat, but so, too, did the regime. Not only had the modern features of the reformed judicial system veered out of control, but the archaic elements of traditional discipline had also gone off course.

Populists on Trial

What began in the aftermath of 1861 as a scattershot series of disturbances and demonstrations soon gave rise to an organized movement of opposition among the disenchanted "children" of the 1860s. The Populists (Narodniki), as they were called, tried to undermine the autocratic regime and instigate revolution in a number of ways: by encouraging the peasantry to rise up against the old order; by promoting the moral value of popular liberation among educated society; and by using violence to attack and kill members of the regime, most importantly the tsar himself. Uniting the movement's disparate groups and varied strategies was a belief in the moral superiority of the peasantry and its collective way of life, hostility to modern forms of social organization, and an exalted spirit of self-sacrifice. The story of the Populist epoch is one of diversity and disagreement, and also, as in the case of the Decembrists, of public posturing and myth making.

The earliest formal organization to emerge after 1861 called itself Land and Liberty (Zemlia i volia)—Nikolai Ogarev's answer to the rhetorical question, "What do the people want?" The activities and outlook of this organization were modest. Having opened a bookshop and library to educate Russian society, its members were arrested for corresponding with Herzen in London and the group soon dissolved. At the same time others rejected the painstaking work of cultural uplift. In 1862 the first "Russian Jacobins," as Franco Venturi calls them, launched the manifesto "Young Russia," which called for violent revolution, to be followed by a dictatorship of the revolutionary party during the transition to a democratic, federative, collectivist popular regime. Members of Land and Liberty objected to such impatience, insisting that their job was not to make a revolution for the people but to assist them once they rebelled on their own and, moreover, to moderate the violence the rebels were sure to inflict on the privileged classes.[51] This disagreement embodied a tension that was to divide Populism throughout its existence: whether to act in the name of the people, if necessary without their participation, or limit oneself to

---

[50] For comments on the changed moral impact of public executions as one of the reasons for their removal from public sight after 1881, see "Nakazaniia," in *Ugolovnoe ulozhenie* (1897), 1:124.

[51] Venturi, *Roots*, 260–64, 275, 285–99.

helping them actualize their own presumably rebellious desires; whether to destroy the architecture of privilege and scorn its occupants or find allies among the progressive elite; whether to encourage violence or avoid it.

Until 1866 exhortations to violence had been merely rhetorical. In that year Dmitrii Karakozov (1840–1866) attempted to assassinate the tsar. With no clear vision of what was supposed to ensue, Karakozov failed to win the support of his friends in the group led by Nikolai Ishutin (1840–1879) and proceeded on his own. Having shot and missed, he was arrested along with the others. Karakozov was tried and hanged; Ishutin, who denounced the act, was reprieved on the scaffold and died in prison. The deed served only to alienate liberal sympathies and push the government toward greater intolerance of radical ideas. The crowd at Karakozov's execution—several thousand strong—did not greet him as a hero.[52]

Even among radical youth, his gesture was unpopular. The various groups that formed in the last years of the 1860s preferred to work among the people rather than take potshots at the regime. Karakozov's act did, however, spark the imagination of a man even more obsessed, and certainly more ruthless, than himself: the infamous Sergei Nechaev (1847–1882). Nechaev was a charismatic "man of the people," who wanted nothing so much as to escape his common roots. Having impressed the leading lights of Populist ideology, Nechaev collaborated with Peter Tkachev (1844–1886) and Mikhail Bakunin (1814–1876) in defining the figure of the dedicated revolutionary. This type was an outlaw operating beyond the pale of civil society, one who had "broken every tie with…the civil order, with the educated world and all laws, conventions and generally accepted conditions, and with the ethics of this world." Bakunin believed that this voluntary outlaw, dedicated to total destruction, would make common cause with the Romantic criminals of popular legend, revolutionary brigands in the style of the by now mythic Pugachev.[53]

Despite their collaboration, Bakunin and Nechaev were separated by an important difference: the anarchist Bakunin dreamed of spontaneous destruction, whereas Nechaev envisioned the overthrow of the existing order as the work of a conspiratorial core. It was not this distinction, however, that finally drove them apart, but the uninhibited ruthlessness of Nechaev's methods. After a spell in Europe hobnobbing with radical émigrés of the older generation, Nechaev slipped back into Russia where he created an organization with alleged ties to the international revolutionary movement. Suspecting an associate of disloyalty, Nechaev had persuaded other members of his small dedicated band to collaborate in the young man's murder. The deed was swiftly uncovered; Nechaev's followers were arrested and

---

[52] Ibid., chap. 14; Bazilevskii, *Gosudarstvennye prestupleniia*, 1:135–51. Also, Claudia Verhoeven, *The Odd Man Karakozov: Imperial Russia, Modernity, and the Birth of Terrorism* (Ithaca: Cornell University Press, 2009).

[53] "Revolutionary Catechism" (1869), quoted in Venturi, *Roots*, 365; see also 369.

tried; Nechaev himself was extradited from Switzerland, whence he had fled, tried in 1873, and sent to prison, where he died of scurvy in 1882.[54] His civil execution was held at dawn on 25 January 1873. The few people gathered at the scaffold heard him shout: "Down with the tsar! Long live freedom! Long live the free Russian people [narod]!"[55] The crowd showed no sympathy but, according to the police report, responded to this outburst with the cry: "For this he should be shot!"[56] Even Bakunin repudiated the man he had earlier hailed as a "young fanatic."[57]

In the aftermath of Karakozov's failure and Nechaev's ignominious end, both violence and personal heroism fell into disrepute. The young people who dreamed of social justice now stressed the ethical basis of their endeavor, dedicating themselves to the "people's cause" in a spirit of almost religious fervor. Although there was no single Populist ideology, the attitudes reflected in the movement of the early 1870s converged around generally shared assumptions. These spokesmen of agrarian socialism represented themselves as agents of the people's good. The young men and women who abandoned comfortable family lives to toil in the villages in the summer of 1874 urgently tried to speak to the people but generally insisted they wanted the people to speak for themselves. Feeling morally obliged to repay the luxury of social privilege, the radicals launched their pilgrimages to the rural heartland in the spirit of collective self-sacrifice. They denounced political institutions as instruments of oppression, scorned constitutional distinctions as an indulgence of interest only to the elite, and believed their movement would swell from below to institute a paradise of social equality. Some favored peaceful "propaganda" (the followers of Petr Lavrov [1823–1900]), others provocation (the Bakuninite "rebels") as a means to start the peasants off, but, in either case, the movement would be massive and democratic.

Because the Populists took as their ideal the collective organization of peasant life and denounced the individualism, social hierarchy, and economic exploitation of Western capitalism, they hoped to forestall the further erosion of traditional peasant ways. In the spirit of Alexander Herzen, they counted Russia's "backwardness" a moral blessing.[58] Thus speed was of the essence. It was not only the rigidity and intolerance of the regime that threatened their enterprise but the regime's readiness (however limited) for change. Insofar as the autocracy promoted economic modernization, it

---

[54] See ibid., chap. 15.

[55] Quoted in Troitskii, Tsarskie sudy, 150.

[56] "Obriad publichnoi kazni nad S. G. Nechaevym," Krasnyi arkhiv 1 (1922): 280–81; also Murav'ev, "Obriad," 40–41.

[57] Quoted in Venturi, Roots, 364. On Nechaev and his relation to Bakunin, see Michael Confino, "Introduction," Violence dans la violence: Le débat Bakounine-Nečaev (Paris: F. Maspero, 1973), 13–93.

[58] See Andrzej Walicki, The Controversy over Capitalism (Oxford: Clarendon, 1969); Walicki, History of Russian Thought, chap. 10; also Martin Malia, Alexander Herzen and the Birth of Russian Socialism (Cambridge, Mass.: Harvard University Press, 1961).

contributed to the demise of old social forms; insofar as it modified its own structure to allow limited public participation in administrative and legal affairs, it opened the door to the further development of the principles of individual rights and freedom of expression. Whereas the regime feared the destabilizing potential of such change, the radicals worried that increased national wealth and extended political liberties would produce a stable social order based on civic inequality and economic exploitation much harder to challenge than the oppressive, slow-moving system currently in place.

Initially, therefore, the Populists rejected the value of political change and focused instead on mobilizing broad social forces against the regime, not in order to achieve liberty in a formal sense but to promote social justice by direct action. The second Land and Liberty organization, established in 1876, concentrated on propagandizing the peasants, while also making contacts among St. Petersburg workers. But, as in the first encounters of 1874, the activists were disappointed with the people's response. By the end of the 1870s the Populists had recognized the need to address the broader political context. Adopting contradictory tactics, on the one hand, they used existing institutions to promote their ideas and gain a following in educated society. On the other, they tried to destroy the institutions they made use of. For example, the terrorists brought to trial for acts of violence against the state exploited the courtroom as an opportunity to address the public and the scaffold as a stage on which to enact the heroism of ultimate self-sacrifice and dramatize the villainy of the established order.

The striking contradictions of the post-reform monarchy were underscored by these political trials. For the generation that came of age after the judicial reforms, the legal system presented both a threat and an opportunity. The new courtrooms constituted a protected zone of free speech, in which subversive ideas not only found utterance but reached the widest possible audience. The 1864 statutes had introduced trial by jury for serious criminal cases but made an exception for crimes against the state, which were to be heard in special chambers. Correct procedure was nevertheless to be observed, and except in cases of seditious speech, trials were open to the public.[59] Despite its general suspicion of both law and public life, the regime was at first convinced that this system could work in its favor. Officials apparently believed that exposure to the radicals' ideas would educate respectable society to their dangers and deprive the revolutionaries of their mysterious allure.[60]

---

[59] Articles 1030–32, 1050, 1055–56, "Ustav ugolovnogo sudoproizvodstva, Razdel vtoroi: O sudoproizvodstve po gosudarstvennym prestupleniiam," in *Rossiiskoe zakonodatel'stvo X–XX vekov*, Vol. 8, *Sudebnaia reforma*, ed. B. V. Vilenskii (Moscow: Iuridicheskaia literatura, 1991), 220–21, 223. Also Troitskii, *Tsarskie sudy*, 107 (on closed doors).

[60] Committee of Ministers, opinion of March 1875, quoted in Venturi, *Roots*, 585. This opinion was expressed after some of the rules had already been changed to limit the impact of

The first trials immediately made clear, however, that the impact on public opinion was just the opposite. The confrontations with authority were at least as significant in making the Populists into a public force as their contacts with the people they hoped to arouse. From the government's point of view, the first problem was the relative autonomy of the reformed judiciary. In the trial of Nechaev's followers (1871) the judges, and even the prosecutors, strictly observed the rules of proper procedure. The accused were treated with respect, and the verdict was restrained; half the group was acquitted. The second problem was the unpredictability of the effect. The trial drew an eager and varied audience, ranging from officials to ordinary people, but composed mostly of students. Far from discrediting the defendants, their speeches made a vivid impression on the public. The right-wing press condemned the outcome, but others hailed the accused for their moral fortitude or praised the result as a triumph of legal principle.[61]

The authorities were dismayed at the outcome but could not argue that the rules had been ignored. The tsar considered the verdict scandalous and asked the minister of justice to protest, but there was no legal basis for doing so. Legal principle, however, could not prevail in an autocratic state. Two elements of the original procedure were soon altered: preliminary investigations were removed from the purview of the judicial authorities and transferred to that of the police; and political cases were shifted from the regular courts and assigned to a special arm of the Senate, which had the option of sitting behind closed doors. From now on, published accounts of trial proceedings were truncated and the right of appeal was curtailed. The pitfalls of the political trial, which seemed to have vindicated rather than discredited the accused, were avoided in the case of Nechaev himself. In 1873 he was tried for premeditated murder as a common criminal, not a political offender. The jury returned a verdict of hard labor, which the tsar increased to life in prison.[62]

Even with these adjustments, the radicals still succeeded in using the courtroom to propagate their ideas and appeal to public sympathies. Their moral impact was greatest in the two cases in which the defendants were charged not with violence but with conducting propaganda or participating in an illegal association—the Trial of the 50 (March 1877) and the

---

trials but before the two major trials of 1877 and 1878, which did the greatest damage from the government's point of view.

[61] Troitskii, *Tsarskie sudy*, 127–28, 133, 135, 137–38; also Bazilevskii, *Gosudarstvennye prestupleniia*, 1:159–227.

[62] Laws of 19 May 1871 (transfer inquiry) and 7 June 1872 (Osoboe prisutstvie Pravitel'stvuiushchego senata): Troitskii, *Tsarskie sudy*, 99, 101. The law of 4 February 1875 imposed further limitations on published accounts: ibid., 107–8; 147–50 (1873 trial). It was the first time a tsar had intervened to increase the severity of a sentence (even Nicholas I had exercised his imperial prerogative to mitigate the sentences imposed on the Decembrists).

Trial of the 193 (October 1877 to January 1878). Eager to perform well, the prisoners rehearsed their speeches under the indifferent eye of the prison guards. In court they appeared as paragons of moral rectitude and champions of free thought, confronting the absolutist state with a posture of absolute virtue.[63]

The defendants in the "monster trial" of the 193 made the most of the courtroom setting. Protesting the tight controls on public access, the accused demanded their right to an open hearing.[64] The audience of officials and policemen hardly constituted "the public," complained Ippolit Myshkin: "To call this public access [*publichnost'*] is to make a mockery of one of the basic principles of the new judicial process." He insisted on the right to explain his beliefs "to all members of society not just a few bureaucrats."[65] When Myshkin was allowed to address the court, he complained that he was not permitted to speak freely (*net publichnosti, net glasnosti*). "Here one can not speak the truth," he railed. "Every honest word is stifled.... This is no court but a hollow comedy."[66] This was indeed ironic language for people who scoffed at the law and seized every occasion to stage political theater of their own.

Most amazing about this trial was not in fact the limited public access but rather the respect for due process that prevailed, despite the theatrics of the accused and the literal disorder in the courtroom. When the senators sitting in judgment proposed that the case be transferred to a military court, the eminent legal scholar, Nikolai Tagantsev (1843–1923), persuaded them to continue. Although ultimately the court affirmed the existence of a "criminal association," the verdict was mild. The senators emphasized the mitigating circumstances of the crimes and asked the tsar for leniency. But the minister of justice urged him to reject the plea, which Alexander did, increasing the severity of the sentences.[67] Even so, the tsar's caprice missed the mark: those released included Sofiia Perovskaia (1854–1881) and Aleksandr Zheliabov (1851–1881), both later involved in Alexander's assassination. Of the 193 accused, only 64 were convicted. More than 100 innocent people had languished in prison, subject to harsh conditions and physical mistreatment, for three years awaiting trial. The defendants emerged from the ordeal with a new sense of collective identity, as victims of official malfeasance and the object of public sympathy.[68]

---

[63] See Venturi, *Roots*, 586.

[64] Troitskii, *Tsarskie sudy*, 187–90.

[65] Bazilevskii, *Gosudarstvennye prestupleniia*, 3:3–4. The Judicial Statutes of 1864, in fact, provided for closed trials in just such cases.

[66] Troitskii, *Tsarskie sudy*, 194–95. Venturi, *Roots*, 590 (trans. modified).

[67] Troitskii, *Tsarskie sudy*, 196–98.

[68] A. F. Koni, "Vospominaniia o dele Very Zasulich," in *Sobranie sochinenii*, 8 vols. (Moscow: Iuridicheskaia literatura, 1966), 2:63–64. The acquitted remained in St. Petersburg and spoke of their experiences, increasing public indignation: ibid., 2:78.

Under these circumstances, the sense of "justice" (both fairness and fair play) manifested by the principals in the trials (court personnel, lawyers, and jurymen) did not necessarily lead them to observe the content or formalities of the law. The trial in March 1878 of Vera Zasulich (1851–1919) was the most famous instance in which the verdict constituted a moral but not a strictly legal decision. The day after the Trial of the 193 ended, Zasulich shot and wounded, but failed to kill, the municipal governor of St. Petersburg, Fedor Trepov (1809–1889), who had ordered the flogging of a political prisoner for refusing to remove his cap in the official's presence. The flogging had been approved by the minister of justice; the victim later died. Zasulich did not deny her deed, which occurred in front of witnesses, and she was apprehended on the spot. Like Nechaev, Zasulich was tried not for a crime against the state but as a common criminal, for attempted murder. In her case, however, the strategy misfired.[69]

Still eager for the prestige associated with formal justice and intent on depriving the terrorists of the aura of heroic devotion to a cause, the Ministry of Justice decided to risk an open trial by jury.[70] The St. Petersburg circuit court, presided over by Anatolii Koni (1844–1927), displayed remarkable independence, observed due process, and opened its doors to the public and the press. The argument centered on who had acted with greater contempt for the law, Trepov by beating the student in his custody (unlawfully inflicting corporal punishment on a gentleman) or Zasulich by shooting Trepov ("taking the law into her own hands," the prosecutor said).[71] The jury, composed of educated city dwellers and lowly functionaries, was so impressed with the morality of her cause, that it minimized the obvious fact of the shooting.[72] The acquittal provoked a public demonstration of rejoicing, as Zasulich was whisked away by the crowd. Too late, the tsar tried to have Zasulich rearrested (she escaped) and would have liked to dismiss the court in its entirety. In an interesting example of the limits of law and lawlessness in the honeymoon years of legal reform, the tsar was apparently hampered from doing so by the elaborate procedure demanded (by law) for the dismissal of judges. The Senate nevertheless annulled the court's ruling.[73]

---

[69] On Zasulich, see Jay Bergman, *Vera Zasulich: A Biography* (Stanford: Stanford University Press, 1975); Ana Siljak, *Angel of Vengeance: The "Girl Assassin," the Governor of St. Petersburg, and Russia's Revolutionary World* (New York: St. Martin's, 2008).

[70] For the circumstances and official justification of the trial, including suppression of its political motives, see Koni, "Vospominaniia," 66–67, 73, 75.

[71] Troitskii, *Tsarskie sudy,* 216 (*samoupravstvo*).

[72] Venturi, *Roots,* 60. Koni remarks that, according to law, Zasulich should have been convicted and then given a mild sentence in recognition of the nature of her motives. Since Trepov remained unpunished for his misdeed, the jury violated the letter of the law to compensate for the government's disregard of justice: Koni, "Vospominaniia," 74–75.

[73] Koni, who had rejected the request by the minister of justice to manipulate the outcome of the trial, now refused to be pressured into resigning. See Koni, "Predislovie," *Sobranie sochinenii,* 2:15–16; Koni, "Vospominaniia," 202–12; Troitskii, *Tsarskie sudy,* 217–18.

As the authorities continued to interfere with proper procedure, their tenuous claim to lawfulness was further eroded. The revolutionaries were cast in the role of defending justice, not in the sense of fairness (social justice or morality) but in the sense of rights and protections. When Ivan Koval'skii (1850–1878) was sentenced to death by a military court in July 1878 for armed resistance to arrest, an army officer complained: "In Russia there is no law. Koval'skii was tried in public [*glasno*], but his fate was sealed behind the scenes [*bezglasno*]."[74] When General Nikolai Mezentsov (1827–1878), head of the Third Section of His Imperial Majesty's Own Chancellery, comprising the gendarmes and the political police, was shot by Koval'skii's friends two days after his execution, the moral balance did not shift in the regime's favor.[75] A crucial attribute of "justice," in the minds both of the accused and of the public, was access—"glasnost'." What occurred behind closed doors was morally and politically reprehensible. The political trials had become tribunals, in which the defendants played dramatic roles in a spellbinding theater of ideas. Despite their contradictory views of the institution that brought them together, judges and lawyers became the radicals' allies in a struggle with the administration and the Crown. Soviet historians used to say that "bourgeois justice" (primarily in the person of high-minded defense attorneys) was morally enhanced by its association with the revolutionary cause, but one can more reasonably argue that the revolutionary enterprise was ennobled by the dignity of justice, which championed the rule of law even on behalf of the lawless.

The attorneys, to a man, were defenders of legality, not partisans of revolution. They were often distinguished members of the profession. In the words of Vladimir Spasovich (1829–1906), they were "the knights of the living, free ... word." They spoke not only in defense of their clients' rights but in defense of their own freedom to speak. The authorities acknowledged their power by limiting their ability to use it. In 1872 the Ministry of Justice advised the senators to prevent attorneys from "develop[ing] arguments contrary to the law," and in 1882 the minister of war instructed the military courts to prohibit defense attorneys from using "inappropriate criticism, metaphors, allegories, and other oratorical devices."[76]

The defendants praised their defenders: one of the accused at the Trial of the 193 said the lawyers not only helped the group's legal cause but "to a significant degree enhanced the trial's political meaning and its influence

---

[74] Quoted in Troitskii, *Tsarskie sudy,* 226.

[75] Venturi, *Roots,* 610.

[76] Quotes in Troitskii, *Tsarizm,* 185, 212 and 206. Although the transfer to military courts violated the 1864 statutes and the rules governing military justice according to the 1881 decrees were harder on civilian defendants than were the statutes governing regular courts, military lawyers nevertheless adhered to standards of professional conduct and respected the procedural framework in which they worked: see William C. Fuller Jr., *Civil-Military Conflict in Imperial Russia, 1881–1914* (Princeton: Princeton University Press, 1985), 124–27.

on public opinion."[77] Attorneys typically stressed their clients' moral purity (women stood as icons in this regard: Sofiia Bardina [1852–1883], Zasulich, Perovskaia).[78] Even in the case of the tsaricides, lawyers blamed the government for driving the conspirators to extremes. They challenged the very definition of criminality: Petr Aleksandrov (1836–1893), who had prosecuted Nechaev's followers in 1871, argued in defense of Zasulich in 1878: "What was yesterday considered a political crime, today or tomorrow will become a highly regarded feat of civic prowess. Political crimes often represent values that have not sufficiently matured, for which the time is not yet ripe." One radical said of Aleksandrov: "He did not so much defend Zasulich as indict the entire [political] system."[79]

The authorities apparently shared this view: a police officer complained that the speeches for the defense, "besides the influence they exert on the unfortunate outcome of the trials, engender intellectual ferment and dissatisfaction and by undermining the foundation of government authority, more than anything else breed support for agitation." Until 1881 trial proceedings were published in the newspapers, which provided detailed (if incomplete) reports with the appeal of serial thrillers. A few journals ran into trouble with the censor for openly supporting the defendants and their cause. Sympathizers hectographed accounts of the trials which circulated among the public. The radicals also made deliberate appeals to moderate opinion, emphasizing the issue of political freedom, guaranteed, of course, by proper legal procedure, as central to the interests of Russian society at large. After 1881, however, trial proceedings were no longer reported.[80]

"Who was serving whom?" Lenin might have asked. The Populists believed that the professionals were promoting the cause of revolution by depicting them as self-sacrificing idealists, victims rather than perpetrators of violence and lawlessness. The lawyers saw the situation in reverse. During the Trial of the 50, Spasovich remarked to one of the accused: "Do you know that nevertheless you are working not for social revolution, which is still far away. You are doing no more than clear the path for us

---

[77] Quoted in Troitskii, *Tsarizm*, 219.

[78] The question of women, as actors and icons, in the Populist movement is an important one. For self-portraits of female activists, see Barbara Alpern Engel and Clifford N. Rosenthal, eds., *Five Sisters: Women against the Tsar* (New York: Knopf, 1975). For attitudes toward women radicals and on the question of whether female culprits should be subjected to corporal punishment, see Koni, "Vospominaniia," 47–48. On images of sexual purity and pollution, see Troitskii, *Tsarizm*, 214, 218; and idem, *Tsarskie sudy*, 191.

[79] Troitskii, *Tsarizm*, 228, 221–22 (quoting Aleksandrov), 223 (quoting D. M. Gertsenshtein). Just as Aleksandrov had once left the prosecutor's bench for the bar, two of the prosecutors in the Zasulich trial resigned to work for the defense. On the role of attorneys, see N. A. Troitskii, *Advokatura v Rossii i politicheskie protsessy 1866–1904 gg.* (Tula: Avtograf, 2000).

[80] Troitskii, *Tsarizm*, 230 (breed support); 52, 107, 109–10, 123–28; also idem, *Tsarskie sudy*, 267–68.

'bourgeois-liberals,' as you call us. We will make use of your efforts and your sacrifices."[81] Indeed, the experience of the trials provoked a strong mood of support for the principles of legality. Translations of Beccaria's treatise appeared in 1878 and 1879. Establishment liberals issued appeals for constitutional protections and the rule of law, which were published abroad and smuggled back into Russia.

The courtrooms thus provided an arena for the exercise of public opinion, for a form of participation in civic affairs that was at the same time a protest against the limits of that possibility. This was as true for the audience as for the principals. People slipped into the courtrooms (two thousand at Zasulich's trial). Crowds gathered at executions: eighty thousand for Aleksandr Solov'ev (1846–1879) in 1879, and one hundred thousand for the tsaricides in April 1881. The regime had banked on the malleability of the audience: the "simple folk," whose emotions could be plied by well-staged spectacles of suffering. It had not counted on a "public," whose reactions to edifying displays could not be controlled.[82]

The government's disdain for correct procedure only encouraged the mimetic tendencies among the Populists. The sequence of arrests, resistance, trials, and executions, coming upon the radicals' failure to inspire rebellion among the folk, enhanced their preference for terror. Land and Liberty vowed to "disorganize the state," to exploit the appeal to well-meaning liberals for revolutionary purposes. In March 1879 an attempt was made to assassinate Aleksandr Drentel'n (1820–1888), who had replaced the late Mezentsov as head of the Third Section. In April, with the organization's tacit approval, Aleksandr Solov'ev took a shot at the tsar; he was hanged a month later. In August, Land and Liberty made Alexander's assassination its top priority.[83] At this point the tension between partisans of social revolution and of terror finally broke the organization apart. Those who stuck with the "orthodox" approach of revolution from below left to form a group called Black Repartition, which was soon decimated by arrests. Those committed to terror dubbed themselves the People's Will, or the People's Freedom (Narodnaia volia). It was they who plotted and carried out the assassination of Alexander II on 1 March 1881. Their case was the last of the period's big political trials and their execution the last to be staged before a crowd.

Workers and Social Democrats

The triumph of terror was also its undoing. The people did not respond with favor to the assassination of the tsar. The regime moved political trials to the military courts, curtailed publicity, and conducted subsequent executions within prison walls. In August 1881 exceptional legislation, known as the "Regulations on Measures for the Protection of State Security and Public Tranquility," imposed an emergency regime, in some cases amounting to martial law, which allowed the administrative apparatus to ignore the procedural restraints enacted in 1864. Introduced as a temporary measure, these laws were not consistently invoked, but they remained in force until 1917.[84]

Thanks to this legislation and to other changes in legal procedure, the courtroom ceased to function as a forum for the expression of political ideas and the occasion for moralistic self-dramatization. As the regime curtailed the institutional gains of the 1860s, terror diminished and opposition took new forms: Marxist Social Democrats offered an ideological and organizational alternative to Populism, and polite society began to mobilize in support of the liberal cause. Factory workers embarked on massive strikes to improve economic conditions.[85] As the high drama of early Populism faded, deep processes of social and cultural transformation were at work altering the disposition of political forces. The long-desired climax that came in 1905 was not the movement early radicals had dreamed of. Modernity, not tradition, proved the key to political transformation, just as tsarist officials had feared.

Yet it was tsarist policy that set the stage for the process of change. The stimulation of economic development emerged from the same calculation that lay behind emancipation and the Great Reforms: Russia must modernize to retain its stature in the international arena. The social consequences of this policy initiative could not, however, be controlled by the old legal instruments and administrative techniques. Cities grew and the industrial workforce expanded. More peasants than ever before sold their labor in rural hiring markets, engaged in crafts and cottage production, and left home for seasonal factory employment. Meanwhile, the lives of villagers left behind were altered by contact with printed material, manufactured goods, new styles of clothing, and the tall tales of boastful friends. Factories appeared in the countryside as well as in urban centers; a large proportion of manufacture occurred in rural settings. Yet, even

---

[84] Moving political cases to military courts had begun in 1878; see Rawson, "Death Penalty," 38. The exceptional laws of 1881 allowed administrative authorities to transfer civilian cases to military courts operating under the laws of wartime, which greatly extended the number of cases in which the death penalty could be imposed. See Fuller, *Civil-Military Conflict*, chap. 4; also Tagantsev, *Russkoe ugolovnoe pravo*, 2:978–79; also Jonathan W. Daly, "On the Significance of Emergency Legislation in Late Imperial Russia," *Slavic Review* 54 (fall 1995): 602–29; idem, *Autocracy under Siege: Security Police and Opposition in Russia, 1866–1905* (DeKalb: Northern Illinois University Press, 1998).

[85] On this period, see Norman M. Naimark, *Terrorists and Social Democrats: The Russian Revolutionary Movement under Alexander III* (Cambridge, Mass.: Harvard University Press, 1983), 5–7, 14, 35–38.

surrounded by fields and muddy roads, work in a nearby textile mill was different.[86]

The process of social transformation and extended cultural opportunity initiated in 1861 affected the privileged as well as the common folk. With the expansion of higher education, the professions grew in size and developed an organizational context. Despite tight controls over public association, the trained elite formed its own groups, societies, and journals. Science, progress, and enlightenment were the dominant values of the 1860s and 1870s. Economists and physicians studied Russia's changing social landscape and devised ways in which scientific knowledge might promote the national and popular welfare.[87] The young "nihilists" and rationalist utilitarian critics of the 1860s merely reflected the spirit of the times in their scientific fervor and enthusiasm for spreading the light. Although they warned of the dangers of modernity, the Populists, too, participated in the enterprise of enlightenment. In addition to bringing knowledge to the village, early Populists also founded study circles for workers. They sometimes claimed they sought only to profit from the workers' village ties and persisted in believing that factory hands retained their country values, but, in fact, it was easier to communicate with people who had left the rural context behind (if not necessarily forever).[88]

In the wake of the Great Reforms, establishment professionals turned to the study of social problems: economists, labor specialists, ethnographers, and physicians produced information useful to the formation of social policy and participated in programs of social improvement. The radical devotee and the state servitor, however, were far from confronting each other

---

[86] On the formation of a working class and urban-rural interaction, see Robert Eugene Johnson, *Peasant and Proletarian: The Working Class of Moscow in the Late Nineteenth Century* (New Brunswick, N.J.: Rutgers University Press, 1979). On changes in rural culture, see Ben Eklof, *Russian Peasant Schools: Officialdom, Village Culture, and Popular Pedagogy, 1861–1914* (Berkeley: University of California Press, 1986); and Jeffrey Brooks, *When Russia Learned to Read: Literacy and Popular Literature, 1861–1917* (Princeton: Princeton University Press, 1985).

[87] On growth of a professional class, see V. R. Leikina-Svirskaia, *Intelligentsia v Rossii vo vtoroi polovine XIX veka* (Moscow: Mysl', 1971); Richard S. Wortman, *Development of a Russian Legal Consciousness* (Chicago: University of Chicago Press, 1976); Nancy Mandelker Frieden, *Russian Physicians in an Era of Reform and Revolution, 1856–1905* (Princeton: Princeton University Press, 1981); Harley D. Balzer, ed., *Russia's Missing Middle Class: The Professions in Russian History* (Armonk, N.Y.: M. E. Sharpe, 1996); Elise Kimerling Wirtschafter, *Social Identity in Imperial Russia* (DeKalb: Northern Illinois University Press, 1997), chap. 3. On the natural sciences, see Kendall E. Bailes, *Science and Russian Culture in an Age of Revolutions: V. I. Vernadsky and His Scientific School, 1863–1945* (Bloomington: Indiana University Press, 1990); and Michael D. Gordin, *A Well-Ordered Thing: Dmitrii Mendeleev and the Shadow of the Periodic Table* (New York: Basic Books, 2004).

[88] See Venturi, *Roots*, chap. 19.

across an abyss; instead, they occupied points on a continuum.[89] At the same time, the Populist ethos was considerably wider and more pervasive than the number of its heroic protagonists in the 1870s would suggest. A set of attitudes associated with Populism permeated the thinking of wide strata of educated society. Many socially engaged professionals shared the Populists' idealized vision of the common folk.

The diffuse Populism of the 1880s also differed from the hard core in its attachment to the liberal ideals of civil rights, individualism, and the rule of law. Many marked by its spirit managed to combine this outlook with the kind of paternalism that motivated tsarist social policy. The case of factory legislation, for example, shows how official and oppositional values converged: these laws were designed by bureaucrats as much to fulfill the traditional obligations of the custodial state as to ward off the "proletarianization" of the industrial labor force. In protecting workers from the exploitation of the profit-seeking boss, the regulations expressed the distaste for capitalist mores that persisted within the government, despite the promotion of industry and enterprise by forward-looking officials.[90] This distaste was shared by Populists, both hard and soft.

Despite these congruences, professionals resented the administrative state, and their antagonism grew as the century progressed. They themselves did not want to be subject to state control; if social discipline were to be exercised, they wanted to administer it themselves. They wanted the right to form associations, hold meetings, raise questions, print articles, and determine policy. They wanted a civil society in which to exercise the authority generated by knowledge, cultural standing, and scientific expertise. So resistant, however, was the regime to sharing its mandate with the social and cultural elite that the beneficiaries of the state's half-hearted measures of reform found the ambivalence more than they could bear.

The roots of liberal constitutionalism go back to the 1860s, when some provincial gentry pressured the tsar to widen the opportunities for public involvement in government.[91] The terror campaign of the 1870s and the administrative reprisals it provoked elicited a renewed burst of activism in respectable circles. Believing terror and repression were two sides of the same coin, some zemstvo delegates called on the revolutionaries to abandon violence and join in the movement for reform (the offer was refused)

[89] On society's involvement in the labor question, see Reginald E. Zelnik, *Labor and Society in Tsarist Russia: The Factory Workers of St. Petersburg* (Stanford: Stanford University Press, 1971); on links between radicals and bureaucrats, see the case described in E. Willis Brooks, "The Improbable Connection: D. A. Miljutin and N. G. Černyševskij, 1848–1862," *Jahrbücher für Geschichte Osteuropas* 37, no. 1 (1989): 21–44.

[90] See Naimark, *Terrorists,* 34–35.

[91] See Terence Emmons, *The Russian Landed Gentry and the Peasant Emancipation of 1861* (Cambridge: Cambridge University Press, 1968).

and on the regime to create the preconditions for normal civic life.[92] The tsar took a step toward accommodating these initiatives in 1880, when he appointed the conciliatory Count Mikhail Loris-Melikov (1826–1888) as minister of internal affairs, but the potential for reform was once again extinguished on 1 March 1881.

The break was not, however, absolute. Alexander III may have wanted to undo major features of the judicial reforms, but even his powers were not unconstrained. The process of industrial development could not be reversed. Russia's performance in the war against Turkey (1877–1878) suffered from some of the same technological deficiencies apparent in the Crimean War. Economic traditionalism was not a policy option. Moreover, the progressive spirit that animated the bureaucracy in Alexander II's day persisted into the 1880s. Members of the State Council did not always hide their disagreement with the new monarch's ideas.[93] In some cases ministries undertook projects of reform, such as plans to redraft the civil and criminal codes, that hardly matched the spirit of the new era.[94]

Not surprisingly the balance weighed in the monarch's favor: the restrictions on due process already introduced in the 1870s in response to the Populist trials remained on the books. The dominance of police over judicial authority was consolidated: in August 1881, as we have seen, political trials were shifted from the regular to the military courts and local officials acquired extraordinary repressive powers; in 1889 the elected justices of the peace were replaced by the so-called land captains appointed by the central administration; in 1890 the powers of the zemstvos were curtailed. Official tolerance for criticism reached an all-time low, and conservatives denounced the institutional legacy of the Great Reforms as politically subversive. Arrests and trials of radical activists continued at a vigorous pace, though not in open court, until their organizations were decimated.[95]

But dissatisfaction was mutual. Educated society blamed the devastating famine of 1891–1892 on the government's economic policies. The impression arose that officials were incapable of dealing with the catastrophe they had unleashed. Local gentry, distinguished intellectuals (Lev Tolstoi

[92] The tsar had helped endow the Bulgarian people with a political constitution after liberating them from Turkish rule. A group of zemstvo men from Tver asked why he denied Russians the same "opportunity to progress along the path of gradual and lawful development." Shmuel Galai, *The Liberation Movement in Russia, 1900–1905* (Cambridge: Cambridge University Press, 1973), 10–13, 16 (quote).

[93] See Heidi Whelan, *Alexander III and the State Council: Bureaucracy and Counter-Reform in Late Imperial Russia* (New Brunswick, N.J.: Rutgers University Press, 1982).

[94] For the work of these commissions, see Laura Engelstein, *The Keys to Happiness: Sex and the Search for Modernity in Fin-de-Siècle Russia* (Ithaca: Cornell University Press, 1992), 22–23; and William G. Wagner, *Marriage, Property, and Law in Late Imperial Russia* (Oxford: Clarendon, 1994).

[95] Naimark, *Terrorists*, 21–22, 42 (almost six thousand members of Narodnaia volia were sentenced from 1881 to 1894).

most notably), rural physicians, and concerned city dwellers volunteered their help. It was in a similar spirit of civic patriotism that the Tver gentry addressed the new ruler upon his accession to the throne in 1894. They called for him to respect the rule of law, including individual and civil rights, and in particular freedom of expression. Nicholas, in his famous reply, denounced the petition as an expression of dangerous and "senseless" dreams.[96]

At the start of the last Romanov reign respectable society thus found itself caught between two opposing forces: an administratively active but politically rigid regime that stubbornly denied it access to power; and an ideologically impatient intelligentsia eager to destroy the basis for political stability and social cohesion. This intelligentsia did not set the revolutionary crisis in motion and never exercised anything resembling control over the popular forces that joined in the fray. It nevertheless produced a language of politics and offered a map of the social terrain that governed the way participants understood their own actions and how commentators later described the events. It is therefore important to take note of the ideological watershed that occurred in the 1890s among the heirs to Populist radicalism.

Populism as a movement was shattered by political repression. Terror had neither brought down the autocracy nor slowed the capitalist tide. The "people" had not risen in revolt but were assuming a new social profile. Marxism appealed to Russian intellectuals in the 1890s because it accepted and explained the facts of economic and social change. Rather than deplore the advent of capitalism as the doom of popular liberation, Marxists hailed its arrival as a necessary step in the transition to a socialist future. But Marxism in its Western European version did not fit the Russian case. Russia was undeniably acquiring the elements of a capitalist system of production. Yet the country was still predominantly agrarian. Absolutism had not given way to the bourgeois constitutionalism expected to accompany the capitalist order and understood by Marx as the precondition for the emergence of truly democratic public institutions. Some Marxists argued, therefore, that in Russia the proletariat would play an even more essential role than in the West, providing the cutting edge not only for the ultimate socialist revolution but also for the more immediate, so-called democratic one. Marxist theory thus assimilated the Russian case to a universal paradigm while making allowance for its peculiarities. Instead of insisting that revolutionaries fight the tide of progress, as the Populists had done, Marxists offered the hope that history might be on their side.[97]

---

[96] An echo of Alexander II's admonition to the Poles in 1856—"*Pas de rêveries, messieurs.*" Quoted in Davies, *God's Playground*, 2:348. Both warnings had the effect of provoking opposition.

[97] On the debate on capitalism among Populists and Marxists, see Walicki, *Controversy*.

Marxism also provided the framework for a radical culture that drew on Populist precedent while marking a distinctive turn. Competing for influence, Marxists took pains to distance themselves from their forerunners, stressing their acceptance of capitalist development and the workers' key role in the revolutionary cause. In turning toward the proletariat and renouncing terror, they were in fact continuing the recent shift in the Populists' own orientation. Although more strictly defined, Marxism also resembled Populism in providing intellectual (and tactical) options for political activists hostile to the tsarist regime. Some Marxists, on the model of Lavrov, emphasized grass-roots work and propaganda; others, echoing Bakunin, proclaimed their faith in the masses' elemental urge to revolt; still others, in the spirit of Tkachev, stressed party leadership and the role of violence.

Although no single version of Marxism at first prevailed, the idea of orthodoxy itself exercised a powerful authority, replacing the aura of moral prowess with which the Populist heroes had invested themselves. Deliberately exacerbating theoretical differences, Lenin imposed ideological standards that served disciplinary ends. The Bolshevik-Menshevik split that crystallized in 1903 exemplifies the manufactured incompatibility that helped Lenin seize the organizational upper hand. The split also reflected the tension between the revolutionary voluntarism of Marx's political thinking and the evolutionary implications of his historical analysis. Mensheviks emphasized the need to build a mass following and stressed democratic process within the party. They were ready to ally with opposition liberals in overturning absolutism and establishing a bourgeois-democratic regime. The Bolsheviks, no less convinced that the winds of history were blowing their way, nevertheless stressed the need to manage one's sails and move in advance of the current. Revolution would never emerge from below; it must be launched by a disciplined conspiratorial party.[98] But not even Lenin abandoned the ideal of the revolutionary mass movement. He envisaged a party that would not replace but lead the proletariat in its designated historical role, even if the workers were not entirely clear where they were headed.

What indeed had the people been doing since emancipation that kept the intelligentsia's revolutionary hopes alive? What, in particular, had the proletarian newcomers contributed to the potential for a popular movement?

Peasant unrest fluctuated with the hardships of the agrarian economy. It also responded to policy changes and public events: the Crimean War, emancipation, the assassination of Alexander II. The forms of rebellion and the values to which they were attached were largely traditional,

---

[98] On the split, see Leopold H. Haimson, *The Russian Marxists and the Origins of Bolshevism* (Cambridge, Mass.: Harvard University Press, 1955).

however. As we have seen, the peasants of Bezdna resisted the terms of liberation by appealing to the authority of the tsar. The same tactic (or belief) characterized other examples of peasant defiance in the 1870s, leading the Populists to admit that their best hope was not to challenge the people's resilient monarchism but to "put the revolutionary party in the place that the mythical Tsar now holds in the eyes of our citizens."[99]

Far from embracing the Populists as substitutes for the monarch's divine will, the people expressed their indignation at Alexander's death in a form more compatible with the values of autocracy than the ideals of its intellectual critics. The anti-Jewish pogrom, a common form of popular violence in the post-emancipation years, emerged with renewed vigor after 1881. At once a vestige of archaic attitudes and a reflection of social change, pogroms originated not in the villages but in the towns. They were set in motion by workers of various sorts—those somewhat detached from their communities (migrants and the unemployed) but also those perfectly well integrated (artisans, craftsmen, factory hands, and railway men).[100] For all their ugliness, moreover, pogroms had their own "moral economy," if one can extend E. P. Thompson's limited sense of the term to cover demonic forms of community.[101] They revealed an inner logic, a recognizable choreography, a sense of grievance, and a coherent vision of the world as a place of traditional values violated by invidious outsiders connected with commercial gain (the Jews). Tolerated or sometimes encouraged by local authorities, the pogroms were not instigated from outside. If tsars and ministers shared the mythology behind the disorders, they condemned the riots themselves, fearing the target would shift from the Jews to the upper classes and the regime itself as the ultimate sources of popular misery. The Populists, for their part, deplored the mythology but celebrated the events as harbingers of larger, more systematic unrest.

If sometimes folk attitudes were clearly unacceptable, at other times rebellion presented radical leaders with a confusing mix of conduct and views. Populists were often mortified, and more often frustrated, by the actual belief systems they encountered in the villages. They were considerably more successful in their interchanges with workers, who had access to urban life and its cultural opportunities; but if departure from the countryside made laborers more receptive to new ideas, the experience of change did not necessarily bring enlightenment. The pogroms, after all, were not

---

[99] Quoted in Venturi, *Roots*, 640. On examples from the 1870s, see Field, *Rebels*, chap. 3.
[100] See John D. Klier and Shlomo Lambroza, eds., *Pogroms: Anti-Jewish Violence in Modern Russian History* (Cambridge: Cambridge University Press, 1992), esp. the chapters by Michael Aronson, Erich Haberer, Lambroza, and Hans Rogger.
[101] E. P. Thompson, *Customs in Common: Studies in Traditional Popular Culture* (New York: New Press, 1993), 188–91, 260, 336, 340, 344.

initiated by the most remote, traditional peasants but by workers or part-time peasants with a wider exposure to the world.

Shifting from peasants to workers as the target of political mobilization did not resolve the ambiguities of social definition or cultural outlook. In trying to establish an ideological link with their putative constituency, Marxists focused much of their debates on the question of whether Russian workers constituted a class (the proletariat) in the classic sense of the term, and the kind of consciousness these workers (proletariat or not) could be said to have developed. Recognizing that Russian workers were not uniformly or deeply urbanized (their families remained in the villages; they retained ties to the land and went home for the holidays) and many were virtual peasants still (textile operatives being the prime example), Social Democrats struggled with the same problem of "backwardness" the Populists had confronted in reverse. This proletariat (in the loose sense of the term) had not only to perform both the democratic and the socialist revolutions but to do so with a fractured sociological and cultural profile. How could a social formation lacking a proper class constitution (varied relations to the means of production, uncertain connection to city life, deep ties to patriarchal custom) produce "class consciousness," let alone "revolutionary class consciousness"?[102] Insofar as such half-baked proletarians did in the end generate widespread disorders, was their activism a product of their modern half or of their incomplete modernity?[103]

In fact, most activists neglected these theoretical niceties and behaved as though workers could learn the basic lessons of socialism from the experience of factory labor, economic exploitation, and political oppression, regardless of the anomalies of their lives. It was clear, after all, that common people, from peasants to workers, no matter how raw, were capable of concerted mass action. Early protests by serfs attached to factories, wage bargaining in the rural labor markets, and, most dramatically, the spontaneous textile strikes of the 1870s and 1890s proved the point.[104] Radicals therefore concentrated on producing a stratum of educated workers, exposed to culture in general and to socialist ideas in particular, that would

[102] See Reginald E. Zelnik, "Russian Workers and the Revolutionary Movement," *Journal of Social History* 6, no. 2 (1972–73): 214–36.

[103] Adam Ulam argued, for example, that the Russian Revolution was not a product of class formation and class conflict, as Marxists liked to believe, but a product of retarded social development, a symptom of the incompleteness of Russia's economic development in the early twentieth century: see Adam B. Ulam, *The Unfinished Revolution: An Essay on the Sources of Influence of Marxism and Communism* (New York: Random House, 1960).

[104] See Reginald Zelnik, "The Peasant and the Factory," in Vucinich, *The Peasant in Nineteenth-Century Russia;* Zelnik, *Labor and Society,* chap. 9; Johnson, *Peasant and Proletarian,* chap. 7; Timothy Mixter, "The Hiring Market as Workers' Turf: Migrant Agricultural Laborers and the Mobilization of Collective Action in the Steppe Grainbelt of European Russia, 1853–1913," in *Peasant Economy, Culture, and Politics,* ed. Esther Kingston-Mann and Timothy Mixter (Princeton: Princeton University Press, 1991).

bring ideological direction to the rebellious but unstable mass. Candidates for this politicized labor elite emerged in the last decades of the century as a result of the expansion of industrial production, the increased demand for literate, skilled workers, and the workers' own thirst for self-improvement. But although ambitious working men and radical activists came into frequent contact, these "advanced" men were not necessarily more amenable to intelligentsia interests than their "backward" brethren were, though for different reasons.[105] Some wanted culture, not revolution, and others wanted revolution but on their own terms. In either case, they were not passive objects of political manipulation.

From the intelligentsia point of view, workers remained unreliable both practically and ideologically. In terms of action, some were more likely to mobilize than others; some were resistant, others receptive, to formal organization. Many joined collective protests only under the threat or impact of violence coming from their mates. In terms of values and aspirations, workers responded to various appeals. In the attempt to undercut the attraction of socialist ideas and forestall labor protest, the regime had done its best to promote the workers' economic interests and thus present itself, in paternalistic guise, as champion of the popular good against the exploitation of greedy bosses. Officially sponsored factory legislation limited hours and conditions of employment and defined certain rights and standards of conduct in the workplace. At the turn of the century the police undertook the even bolder step of forming authorized labor associations, hoping in like fashion to defuse the radical appeal by satisfying so-called economic grievances.[106]

This tactic mirrored Lenin's fear that the urge for self-betterment that lay behind popular unrest could be satisfied within the bounds of the status quo, or some modified version of it, without challenging the existing social hierarchy or the political framework of autocracy. Yet both factory laws and police unions demonstrated the complexity of the popular response. Often workers welcomed the opportunity to improve their

---

[105] See Reginald E. Zelnik, ed., *A Radical Worker in Tsarist Russia: The Autobiography of Semen Ivanovich Kanatchikov,* trans. idem (Stanford: Stanford University Press, 1986); idem, "Russian Bebels: An Introduction to the Memoirs of Semen Kanatchikov and Matvei Fisher," *Russian Review* 35, no. 3 (July 1976): 249–89; and 35, no. 4 (October 1976): 417–47; idem, "'To the Unaccustomed Eye': Religion and Irreligion in the Experience of St. Petersburg Workers in the 1870s," *Russian History* 16, nos. 2–4 (1989): 297–326; and Allan K. Wildman, *The Making of a Workers' Revolution: Russian Social Democracy, 1891–1903* (Chicago: University of Chicago Press, 1967).

[106] See Jeremiah Schneiderman, *Sergei Zubatov and Revolutionary Marxism: The Struggle for the Working Class in Tsarist Russia* (Ithaca: Cornell University Press, 1976); Gerald D. Surh, "Petersburg's First Mass Labor Organization: The Assembly of Russian Workers and Father Gapon," *Russian Review* 40, no. 3 (1981): 241–62; and 40, no. 4 (1981): 412–41; and Laura Engelstein, *Moscow, 1905: Working-Class Organization and Political Conflict* (Stanford: Stanford University Press, 1982), 59–62, 79–81.

lot and willingly joined the unions. As Mark Steinberg has argued in the case of the printers, the most highly educated of skilled workers, and in 1905 at the forefront of labor militancy, their outlook on the world was fully compatible with the conventional paternalism of their employers.[107] Conservative expectations were nevertheless foiled. By introducing the notion of "the worker" as a unifying rubric, marked by the possession of a special booklet and qualifying for special rules and specified treatment, the factory laws encouraged a sense of social coherence that transcended the differences between actual workers. The experiment in police unionism proved even more dangerous. To demonstrate their authenticity, these unions organized and financed strikes that sometimes got out of hand. Factory owners protested that political loyalty was being purchased at their economic expense. Officials themselves finally realized they had helped promote exactly the kind of collective action they deplored. Once the crisis of 1905 exploded, workers who had previously been involved in police unions proved unusually susceptible to radical appeals and exceptionally likely to join or form new organizations.

Russian workers were a diverse lot (not even including their geographic and ethnic variations). Buffeted by changing social and economic circumstances and by competing value systems, some made deliberate choices and others vacillated between extremes. Still others acquired the cultural attributes of the working-class elite, which might incline them either to accommodation or to a career of professional revolt. If they were ideologically fickle, workers also learned from experience, and experience seemed to dispose them to revolutionary ideals—but not always and not exclusively. If we saddle ourselves with the notion of class consciousness, we are bound to seek a consistent outlook tied to economic and social circumstances. But some of the very same workers who went on strike and rallied to socialist slogans were capable on occasion of attacking Jews and bristling at offense to the tsar.[108] Lynching a plant manager may seem less objectionable than killing a Jew, because the manager exercises direct power over his subordinates, whereas the Jews, particularly the impoverished victims of violence, were as vulnerable as their assailants, if not more so. But who is to say that the Jewish threat was any less "real" to the peasant or railway man steeped in anti-Semitic fears and prompted by right-wing agitation than the manager's abuse of authority to the worker on his shift? If we discount the power of symbols, then no ideology makes sense. And, after all, the

---

[107] Mark Steinberg, *Moral Communities: The Culture of Class Relations in the Russian Printing Industry, 1867–1907* (Berkeley: University of California Press, 1992), following E. P. Thompson's argument for the paternalism of the eighteenth-century moral economy.

[108] See Charters Wynn, *Workers, Strikes, and Pogroms: The Donbass-Dnepr Bend in Late Imperial Russia, 1870–1905* (Princeton: Princeton University Press, 1992), chap. 7.

absurdities of anti-Semitism were rife in educated circles; why should the common folk be immune?[109]

Peasants, too, were capable of a range of collective behavior. In addition to the pogroms involving both workers and peasants, which reemerged in waves of increasing virulence in 1903 and again in 1905, and the widespread violence in the countryside during the revolutionary years, a capacity for self-discipline also emerged. In the general social mobilization of 1905, some peasants organized meetings on the model of the traditional village assemblies, where they debated the ideas of schoolteachers, zemstvo employees, and activists from the cities, and elected delegates to congresses and a national "peasant union."[110] In their capacity as soldiers and sailors, peasants mutinied in massive numbers, sometimes to the accompaniment of political slogans, sometimes not. John Bushnell has argued that peasant-soldiers disobeyed only when they felt discipline weaken; as soon as superiors recovered their nerve, order returned. In short, like the perpetrators of pogroms who struck after the murder of Alexander II, the mutineers did not so much defy authority as take advantage of its breach.[111]

Society against the State

However uncertain the political awareness of workers and peasants, the 1905 Revolution, when it finally came, presented a massive challenge to the principles embodied in the autocratic regime. Not only did it unite the disparate constituents of Russian society in a movement for fundamental change in relations of power and deference, whether enacted on the factory floor or on the governing boards of city councils. It also linked the articulate political goals of the educated elite to the visceral unhappiness of the popular masses, combining classic elements of peasant revolt with patterns

[109] Lenin solved the problem of the masses' unreliability by substituting party domination for the spontaneous impulses of the crowd. But this was a radical solution, not fulfilled in practice before 1917, even by the Bolsheviks themselves, and rejected by most Social Democrats as contrary to the movement's values as well as its ideas. See Zelnik, "Russian Workers."

[110] See Scott J. Seregny, "Peasants and Politics: Peasant Unions during the 1905 Revolution" in Kington-Mann and Mixter, *Peasant Economy, Culture, and Politics*, 341–77; also Seregny, *Russian Teachers and Peasant Revolution: The Politics of Education in 1905* (Bloomington: Indiana University Press, 1989), chaps. 7, 8. For more on peasant political activity, see Maureen Perrie, "The Russian Peasant Movement of 1905–7: Its Social Composition and Revolutionary Significance," in *The World of the Russian Peasant: Post-Emancipation Culture and Society*, ed. Ben Eklof and Stephen P. Frank (Boston: Unwin Hyman, 1990); and Robert Edelman, *Proletarian Peasants: The Revolution of 1905 in Russia's Southwest* (Ithaca: Cornell University Press, 1987).

[111] John Bushnell, *Mutiny and Repression: Russian Soldiers in the Revolution of 1905–1906* (Bloomington: Indiana University Press, 1985).

of behavior, organizational forms, and political ideology generated by the modern sector of Russian life. Set off in January 1905, when troops opened fire on a procession of respectful workers petitioning the tsar, the revolution reached a bloody climax in December of that year, when politicized workers, now militant and armed, confronted government troops over the rooftops of a Moscow factory district. Persisting into 1906, in a profusion of violence on both sides, the revolution finally gave way to the routine of newly instituted electoral politics, a concession wrested from the reluctant regime only under the pressure of violent confrontation.

If the revolution was "popular" in the sense of all-encompassing, it was not popular in its origins. Initiative in bringing opposition to a head came from the privileged, not the downtrodden. While intelligentsia radicals had been laboring to build a popular base, critics of autocracy among the gentry and professional classes built a political movement centered on their own civic claims. Just as the regime's contempt for its own legal institutions prompted law-abiding attorneys to defend the honor of their radical clientele, so restrictions on the legitimate activities of trained professionals and notables (limits on the professional autonomy of physicians, interference in the activities of zemstvo delegates) generated widespread discontent among groups with no sympathy for revolutionary methods or goals.[112] Educated men and women who found their ordinary affairs imbued with political meaning soon progressed to the formation of associations with overtly political goals.

In the same period radical activity also took more solid, though still illegal, organizational form. In 1898 the Social Democrats established themselves as a formal party. In 1901 Populism reemerged in the shape of the Socialist Revolutionary Party, which championed the rights of the "laboring masses," peasant and worker alike, and revived the tradition of political terror. Assassins removed the minister of education in 1901 and successive ministers of internal affairs in 1902 and 1904.[113] Disobedience among university students reflected the rising level of public impatience. Acting without their elders' inhibitions, students staged massive demonstrations which led to massive arrests, defied academic authorities and the police, and boycotted classes. When the Ministry of Education threatened the miscreants with military conscription, the educated public took the students' side;[114] after all, these were their own children. Also helping to maintain a sense of common cause among the disparate strands of disaffected opinion was the government's unwillingness to tell them apart: in

---

[112] See Galai, *Liberation*, 144–55.

[113] On the second wave of terror, see Anna Geifman, *Thou Shalt Kill: Revolutionary Terrorism in Russia, 1894–1917* (Princeton: Princeton University Press, 1993).

[114] On student unrest, see Galai, *Liberation*, 90–91; see also Samuel D. Kassow, *Students, Professors, and the State in Tsarist Russia* (Berkeley: University of California Press, 1989).

the eyes of the officials, radicals and reformers were equally suspect. It was no less illegal to meet in a private apartment to discuss civic affairs than to establish a revolutionary party. Laws banning strikes and labor unions similarly made it hard for workers to ignore the political consequences of economic self-defense.

In the end the regime so narrowed the compass of legitimate public action that confrontation was almost inevitable. The revolution, when it finally erupted, began as an outgrowth of strikes in St. Petersburg metal factories that had been organized by a government-sponsored labor association. On 9 January, soon dubbed Bloody Sunday, a procession of workers led by the Orthodox priest Father Georgii Gapon (1870–1906) made its way toward the Winter Palace with a petition for the tsar. Originally recruited by the police, Gapon had built a mass organization, without abandoning the classic rhetoric of traditional popular protest. Imploring justice from the throne, as peasants for generations had done, Gapon's followers were stopped by gunfire before they reached their goal. The shooting at Bezdna had not affected the ancient compact between faithful folk and benevolent ruler. Now the magic no longer worked. The massacre was the signal for a general explosion of popular indignation: thousands of workers through-out the empire walked off the job.[115]

The January strikes were not the work of agitators. Instead, the readi-ness of laborers to take to the streets, and, of course, the public response to the shooting, reflected the degree to which society as a whole believed the tsar's mandate had failed. After arousing initial enthusiasm, the war against Japan, begun in 1904, soon resulted in humiliating Russian losses that alienated public opinion. Peasants suffering from land hunger and heavy taxation had rioted in 1902–1903, the same year that strikes peaked in the south and massive pogroms swept the southwest. However isolated the common villager may have been from national affairs, the peasantry was not in fact insulated. News reached far beyond the cities, through rumor and, more recently, the press. As soldiers, peasants were called upon to contain civil disorders (to restrain pogroms, stop strikes, and ultimately suppress the revolution); in 1904 they were mobilized to fight in Japan.

---

[115] On the social dynamics of the revolution, see Henry Reichman, *Railwaymen and Revolution: Russia, 1905* (Berkeley: University of California Press, 1987); Gerald D. Surh, *1905 in St. Petersburg: Labor, Society, and Revolution* (Stanford: Stanford University Press, 1989); Steinberg, *Moral Communities;* Wynn, *Workers, Strikes, and Pogroms;* Robert Wein-berg, *The Revolution of 1905 in Odessa: Blood on the Steps* (Bloomington: Indiana Univer-sity Press, 1993). For a reliable overall narrative, see Abraham Ascher, *The Revolution of 1905,* 2 vols. (Stanford: Stanford University Press, 1988–1992). The Russian-language litera-ture is vast; see E. D. Chermenskii, ed., *Pervaia rossiiskaia revoliutsiia 1905–1907 gg.: Ob-zor sovetskoi i zarubezhnoi literatury: Sbornik obzorov* (Moscow: INION AN SSSR, 1991); A. P. Korelin and S. V. Tiutiukin, eds., *Pervaia revoliutsiia v Rossii: Vzgliad cherez stoletie* (Moscow: Pamiatniki istoricheskoi mysli, 2005); Jan Kusber and Andreas Frings, eds., *Das Zarenreich, das Jahr 1905 und seine Wirkungen: Bestandsaufnahmen* (Berlin: Lit, 2007).

Conscription itself provoked dismay and disorder. Not one corner of the social landscape was sheltered from the impact of structural change, free from doubt as to the legitimacy of the old social contract, or unaffected by the willful and inconsistent policies of a fearful and repressive regime.

The comprehensive sweep of this disaffection generated the political volatility, but also the creativity, of the revolutionary events. In urban communities the breakdown of order brought disparate social groups into contact for the first time. Workers met students in university lecture halls. Printers met municipal employees on city squares. Neighborhoods formed councils (the "*sovet*" [soviet], a term that had not yet acquired its future political meaning), in which delegates from different factories joined to oversee local affairs. Each time the government summoned a committee to quiet the unrest, elections were held, representatives constituted; when the committee was dispersed, the constituency had learned a lesson in electoral process and acquired another layer of distrust for the regime.

Most notable about 1905 was not the continued existence of archaic patterns of popular revolt, its least surprising feature, but the extent to which the common folk engaged in novel forms of collective action and responded to the rhythms and aspirations of a cross-class social movement. Indeed, if one looks for the points at which political meaning and social participation crystallized, they are to be found at the intersection of class and cultural categories: where professional staff met gentry notables in zemstvo administration; where blue- and white-collar employees crossed paths in the transport, communications, or public service sector; where educated noncommissioned officers commanded urban garrisons; where skilled metalworkers plied their trade amid the common labor force of giant mills; where recruits returned to the village or peasants returned from factory jobs.[116]

In this context, radical ideology provided symbolic cohesion where social reality was fragmented and diverse. It served as the lingua franca of the revolution. Russia had no true proletariat (if one existed anywhere) but rather a congeries of artisanal trades, skilled shop workers, manual laborers, machine operatives, service workers, and shop clerks. Among these the trained and literate provided the political lead; the destitute and oppressed followed in their wake. The place of a true bourgeoisie was occupied by a range of respectable types: entrepreneurs and industrialists, defensive about their social standing in a culture hostile to commercial life; professionals (doctors and lawyers); establishment intellectuals (professors and journalists); artists, writers, and performers; and the "petty bourgeois" fringe (office workers, teachers, librarians, and bank clerks). Among these the capitalists did not stand out as a unified group determined to translate

---

[116] This argument is made by Engelstein in *Moscow, 1905.*

economic power into political rights.[117] And, conversely, the "bourgeois" role was often filled by players from the premodern sector: notably gentry liberals immersed in provincial affairs.

Despite the imperfect profile and precocious "proletarian" thrust of 1905, it was nevertheless understood by participants as the "bourgeois" revolution. While social claims energized the "masses," whose mobilization gave the political element the force it needed to prevail, constitutional demands provided the common denominator around which educated society could adhere. Yet the pathos of the revolution, like the moral drama of the Populist trials, stemmed not from the aspirations of the moderates but from the heroic gestures of those on the social or ideological edge. The idea of socialism exerted a charismatic appeal that transcended sociological frontiers: liberals acknowledged the importance of the social question, as they struggled for basic political rights;[118] rallying to the proletarian flag, pharmacy clerks left their conciliatory employers alone in the shops, bemoaning the shattered bonds of patriarchal fellowship, struck with the incongruity of their assistants' claims.[119] Finally, the apocalyptic showdown in December 1905 between armed workers and tsarist forces intensified the "proletariat's" symbolic allure.

Yet the revolution did not topple the regime. Rather, the combined assault of society across the board—from city halls to peasant villages, battleships, railroad lines, post offices, armaments plants, and restaurants—forced the tsar to resume his role as political demiurge. The Manifesto of 17 October 1905 established a parliament and promised limited civil rights. Would the civil society that managed a fragile coherence in the course of that year survive the transition to institutional routine? Would the radicals who rallied their troops to the constitutional cause respect this solidarity or be driven by the lure of ideological extremes? Would the absolutist state encourage them in this direction, or would it permit the evolution of public life to proceed? Would it re-evoke the massive disaffection that preceded 1905 by violating its own rules and maintaining the administrative ideal? Would the popular forces that fueled the mass movement in 1905 continue to expand and accumulate resentment, while keeping alive the memory of that astonishing moment when their power finally struck home? These questions were still unsettled when the 1905 revolution came to an end.

---

[117] On the political fragmentation of the industrial bourgeoisie, see Alfred J. Rieber, *Merchants and Entrepreneurs in Imperial Russia* (Chapel Hill: University of North Carolina Press, 1982); also Ruth Amende Roosa, "Russian Industrialists, Politics, and Labor Reform in 1905," *Russian History* 2, no. 2 (1975): 124–48.

[118] Galai, *Liberation*, 181 (citing Sergei Bulgakov).

[119] See Engelstein, *Moscow, 1905*, 121.

CHAPTER THREE

The Dream of Civil Society

The Law, the State, and Religious Toleration

The history of nineteenth-century Russia's political movements demonstrates the paradoxical character of the autocratic regime. While the authorities lavishly exercised their power to prohibit, punish, and repress, their policies at the same time created new sources of resistance. The professions were useful, technology indispensable (hence the need for education and scientific knowledge), but the growing cultural elite demanded conditions of self-expression and self-regulation that challenged the principles of absolute rule. The official response to these demands proved self-defeating. The refusal to grant the rights that would have enabled power to operate outside the state undermined the support the state needed for its own survival.

The myth of revolution had an appeal even to liberal believers in the rule of law, the authority of science, and the rights of the individual, who were unable to exercise power on their own behalf. It expressed their desperation. Once the structures of political life were introduced in October 1905, the liberals withdrew their sympathies. These were again aroused when the scope of self-representation and the constraints on the emperor's sovereign rule were constantly retracted. In the final crisis—the outbreak of war in 1914—society rose to the occasion. It performed functions the state could not perform, enjoying a breadth of movement and engagement it had never before enjoyed. The task at hand was designed, however, not to strengthen the social organism but to buttress the state in the conduct of a war that demanded ever more state control and intervention.[1] It was not a moment for freedom of expression—not for any of the warring nations. In Russia,

---

[1] Peter Holquist, "What's so Revolutionary about the Russian Revolution? State Practices and the New-Style Politics, 1914–21," in *Russian Modernity: Politics, Knowledge, Practices,* ed. David L. Hoffmann and Yanni Kotsonis (New York: St. Martin's, 2000), 87–111.

however, it was a time for the state not only to expand its writ but also to lose control of its own operations. Here is when the imperial state ended by destroying the last vestiges of social coherence, creating an inner crisis that no authority could then resolve. The tsar's inability to delegate power, the army's assault on the population of the western borderlands, the violation of any shred of legality in the name of military rule created chaos and disorder. The poor performance of the troops in the field demoralized the public and the men at the front. Society, though mobilized, rallied on behalf of a regime that was digging its own grave.

But we are ahead of ourselves. Before the edifice had yet crumbled, Russian liberals aspired to the role of fortifiers. They wished to build and inhabit a structure composed of willing and self-defining citizens, not subjects, protected from unwarranted intrusion, free to operate in a public sphere in which their choices mattered. It was a model they took from the West and one they considered indispensable to the national (in this case, imperial) welfare and survival. It was not a subversive vision but a constructive one. They were patriots and imperialists (in the domestic sense). In addressing the issue of religion and religious tolerance, these liberals focused on one of the pillars of traditional authority. They had no wish to do without it. They wished merely to assign it a more modern, less traditional role—as a moral force, not an arm of the state. The failure of this aspiration demonstrates the limits to what could be achieved in the final years of imperial power.

*   *   *

In searching for the emergence of "civil society," historians assume there is a connection between forms of public association and expression and the political character of modern states, but the connection is not easily established. The prototype of civil society is hard to define, and its local embodiments do not always match the ideal. Political regimes, furthermore, change over time: Germany has been authoritarian, fascist, and democratic, all in one century. But in one respect agreement reigns: Western European and North American nations to some degree have generated an autonomous public life that helps sustain the democratic (or at least participatory) political impulse. On the margins of the European state system, sharing but not fully integrating the Western cultural heritage, Russia, it is said, has always lacked just these civic and political traits. Antonio Gramsci (1891–1937) provides the classic statement of this contrast: "In Russia," he wrote in the 1920s, "the state was everything, civil society was primordial and gelatinous; in the West there was a proper relation between state and civil society, and when the state trembled a sturdy structure of civil society was at once revealed." When in 1917 the Russian autocracy not only trembled but tumbled to the ground, there was no "powerful system of fortresses and earthworks," in Gramsci's phrase, to prevent the Bolsheviks from erecting another absolutist regime in its place.[2]

The end of Communism raised the issue yet again. Some commentators associate the failure of post-Soviet Russia to establish viable political institutions and an orderly public life with the state's ability to impair or extinguish civil society.[3] That the Soviet system collapsed from within has convinced others, to the contrary, that social forces must have been at work in its demise. They conclude that elements of a civil society escaped the stranglehold of the allegedly "total" state and created the pressure for change.[4] In the same optimistic vein, some historians are finding evidence of a vital pre-1917 "middle sphere" that challenges the notion of Russian exceptionalism and offers present-day democrats a cultural precedent.[5]

These old and new arguments invite us to revisit the question of what relation the concept of civil society in fact bears to the political life of imperial Russia. This chapter argues that Gramsci was both right and wrong. The state was indeed powerful and strictly patrolled the social landscape, suspicious of any force outside its control. Yet the tsars could not rule entirely as they pleased but had to contend with public opinion, if only on a limited scale. Society was not formless. Even the intolerant Nicholas I accepted the existence of philanthropic associations, a type of civic participation, though often self-generated, embodying the same values and devotion to hierarchy as the regime. Nor, try as he might, could he extinguish the discontent of intellectuals in the universities and drawing rooms of the capitals. Although most were loyal monarchists, they denounced the persistence of serfdom, chafed under the censorship of ideas, and thirsted for influence in public affairs.

When Alexander II abolished serfdom and initiated the Great Reforms of 1861–1864, he acted not only in response to Russia's defeat in the

---

[2] Antonio Gramsci, *Selections from the Prison Notebooks (1929–1935)*, quoted in Geoff Eley, "Nations, Publics, and Political Cultures: Placing Habermas in the Nineteenth Century," in *Habermas and the Public Sphere*, ed. Craig Calhoun (Cambridge, Mass.: MIT Press, 1992), 325.

[3] Martin Malia, *The Soviet Tragedy: A History of Socialism in Russia, 1917–1991* (New York: Free Press, 1994), says there was a civil society in tsarist Russia (67) but calls it "exceptionally weak" (70). Having asserted that its weakness left a "social void" that facilitated the Bolsheviks' coming to power (134–35), he then blames the Soviet regime for destroying "civil society." He dates this event variously as 1918 (120), 1920 (133), and 1930 (437), in the last case defining civil society as the "independent peasantry." He sees the return of civil society, if only in a "relatively unstructured form," as a product, not cause, of the system's eventual "implosion" but judges it too weak to sustain a post-Communist democratic structure (498). Despite the confusion in Malia's argument, his prediction was on the mark.

[4] Moshe Lewin, *The Gorbachev Phenomenon: A Historical Interpretation* (Berkeley: University of California Press, 1988), 80.

[5] See Edith W Clowes, Samuel D. Kassow, and James L. West, eds., *Between Tsar and People: Educated Society and the Quest for Public Identity in Late Imperial Russia* (Princeton: Princeton University Press, 1991), 6–7.

Crimean War but also under pressure from intellectuals, forward-looking bureaucrats, and progressive members of the imperial family. He thus acknowledged that Russia's standing as an international power depended on its encouraging some of the features that sustained civil society in the West: the production and dispersion of science, technology, and other forms of knowledge; a professional elite; a market-driven labor force; a trained and literate army; and courts of law for the regulation of disputes.

In the absence of enabling political conditions, however, these changes generated an ambivalent and tension-ridden result: both the desire to perform the functions of an "actually existing civil society" and its chronic frustration. Yet the desire itself mitigated the contradiction: it is a case of wishful thinking embodying the wish. In struggling to produce what they thought of as the civil society they lacked, Russians de facto enacted its possibility at home, while at the same time experiencing the limits imposed by their own situation. Their efforts, which, I argue, partially exemplified what they were striving for, took two forms: first, a critique of existing arrangements; and, second, projects of reform designed to overcome the restrictions under which they suffered and bring Russia into line with the imagined ideal.

It should be said, however, that not all people who acted as though they were members of a recognizable civil society subscribed in principle to the goal of bringing it about. Some of the active participants in public debate over issues such as reform of the civil and criminal codes were ideological conservatives who defended patriarchal values and paternalistic government.[6] For liberals, however, the concept of civil society exercised a strong symbolic influence independent of its practical realization, while the process of articulating the goal brought it closer to home. Yet the dream did not come to pass, either before or after 1917. And this, as all parties to the conflict—would-be citizens, no less than autocrats and commissars—understood all too well, depended not so much on the contours of the social landscape as on its relation to the power of the state.

This understanding was embedded in the vocabulary of social description that Russians themselves devised. Nineteenth-century intellectuals were, of course, familiar with the notion of civil society as articulated in Western thought, but they also used terms adapted to the local configuration. They viewed their own history as the interaction of three forces: the state (*gosudarstvo*), the people (*narod*), and something called "society" or "the public" (*obshchestvo, obshchestvennost'*). The latter was a cultural category that largely overlapped a sociological domain. Encompassing the educated residents of Russia's Westernized cities, the term "society"

---

[6] See William G. Wagner, "Ideology, Identity, and the Emergence of a Middle Class," in Clowes, Kassow, and West, *Between Tsar and People*, 162–63.

distinguished them, on the one hand, from bureaucrats (no less educated or urban but servants of the regime) and, on the other, from the common folk. Bureaucrats exercised power and established policy. They played a political role but only as instruments of the state. Members of "society" had political opinions, often, but not always, critical of the established order. Until the 1905 Revolution induced the tsar to establish a national parliament and relax the censorship laws, freedom of expression was limited and society had few opportunities to play a constructive political role.[7]

Despite the three-part scheme, there was, in fact, no clean sociological divide in nineteenth-century Russia between state servitors and members of "society." Individual careers crossed the line; professions included public and private sectors; civic associations united officials and independent activists. Yet the contrast stood for an important principle: the possibility of public activity independent of the state—the dream in which "society" became "civil society," a matter not of persons or social categories but of structures. This vision took hold in the second half of the century, once the Great Reforms had inaugurated a new relationship between the autocracy and its subjects, educated and uneducated alike.[8] These reforms ended bonded labor and reconfigured the social map. They also created institutions of local self-administration (the zemstvos) and revamped the operation of the law. They did not, however, change the law's statutory content or modify the absolutist basis of autocratic rule.

The new dispensation allowed "society" to enter more actively into public affairs. But at the same time that the educated elite welcomed this chance, it spawned an offshoot opposed to any such participation: the so-called intelligentsia, dedicated to overturning the existing order and hostile to any constitutional reform. Though not responsible for the outbreak of revolution in 1905, radicals embraced the project of total transformation. The upheaval did not, however, destroy the old regime. To quell the wave of opposition engulfing the empire, Nicholas II (r. 1894–1917) authorized elections to a State Duma and the formation of recognized political parties. The tsar promised to endow the population with the "foundations of civic freedom based on the principles of real personal inviolability, freedom of conscience, speech, assembly, and union."[9]

This concession to some extent represented a victory of social forces over the state. But it was also one of the final examples of the monarchy's

---

[7] See Clowes, Kassow, and West, *Between Tsar and People*; Louise McReynolds, *The News under Russia's Old Regime: The Development of a Mass-Circulation Press* (Princeton: Princeton University Press, 1991); and Harley D. Balzer, ed., *Russia's Missing Middle Class: The Professions in Russian History* (Armonk, N.Y.: M. E. Sharpe, 1996).

[8] See Ben Eklof, John Bushnell, and Larissa Zakharova, eds., *Russia's Great Reforms, 1855–1881* (Bloomington: Indiana University Press, 1994).

[9] Manifesto of 17 October 1905, quoted in Abraham Ascher, *The Revolution of 1905: Russia in Disarray* (Stanford: Stanford University Press, 1988), 229.

long history of managing the society it ruled, hoping to encourage the national welfare while exercising maximum control. Beginning with the reign of Peter the Great, cultural standards as well as social standing were imposed by an active, interventionist regime. Noble status was a function of state service, not a mark of autonomy. Catherine the Great aspired to create by fiat both a proto-middle class and a public opinion worthy of a European nation. Where Peter sponsored the publication of works promoting technological advance, Catherine opened the door to private publishing and encouraged the airing of opinions in the press. Nikolai Novikov (1744–1818), at once publisher, author, and sponsor of educational and charitable ventures, exemplified the possibilities of independent cultural initiative. Freemasonry offered a context for civic activity, sustained a network of social ties, and promoted public responsibility.[10]

Eighteenth-century Russia had a lively public life. Private presses, a market in print, debating societies, literary salons, private theaters, public lectures, Masonic lodges—all linked inhabitants of the capitals and provincial centers in something of an empirewide conversation. Yet this world was limited in scope, audience, and resources, and was fatally dependent on the autocrat's goodwill. Catherine, when it pleased her, cracked down on independent publishers. When Aleksandr Radishchev printed, at his own expense, an attack on serfdom and absolute rule, she sent him to Siberia. Novikov weathered the end of Catherine's reign in prison. Alexander I outlawed the Freemasons in 1822.

Perhaps more striking than the occasions when the sovereign intervened to quash the expression of ideas was the cozy relationship that prevailed between ruler and opinion makers under Catherine and Alexander I. Even Catherine's critics shared her professed Enlightenment views. Radishchev, who returned to the capital after the empress's death, served in various official roles. The court and high society of Alexander's time constituted a close-knit world, in which religious enthusiasm set the dominant tone. Reformers and conservatives may have differed in their ideas, but they were intimately connected and all close to the throne. Educated men and women of the period met in drawing rooms and private clubs, most famously the literary societies frequented by writers such as Aleksandr Pushkin (1799–1837). By contrast, the men who staged the ill-fated Decembrist Uprising in 1825 had concocted their plans and articulated their ideas in the shelter of secret societies modeled on the Masonic lodges and nationalist associations of contemporary Europe. But the leaders themselves belonged to the

---

[10] See Gary Marker, *Publishing, Printing, and the Origins of Intellectual Life in Russia: 1700–1800* (Princeton: Princeton University Press, 1985); Douglas Smith, *Working the Rough Stone: Freemasonry and Society in Eighteenth-Century Russia* (DeKalb: Northern Illinois University Press, 1999).

world they opposed. The officials who investigated and tried the rebels were often their relatives and friends.[11]

The distinction between official circles and "the public" with opinions first achieved symbolic importance only in the reign of Nicholas I. In the 1840s cultivated men gathered in one another's homes to discuss the taboo questions of the day through the respectable detour of philosophy and literature. These were still gentlemen of the aristocracy, intellectual amateurs who had honed their wits in the lecture halls of Moscow University and then survived on personal incomes. Westernizers and Slavophiles amiably agreed to disagree with their partners in conversation, and all were hostile to Nicholas's oppressive rule. Publishing critical ideas was still a risky venture. Petr Chaadaev was sent to a madhouse and his editor banished for printing the famous "Philosophical Letter" in which Chaadaev argued that Russia had been stranded on the margins of Western civilization. Alexander Herzen put his dangerous ideas to paper only when safely abroad.[12]

The turning point came with the Great Reforms, the joint product of imperial initiative, bureaucratic involvement, and public participation. Enlightened principles and the spirit of professionalism had invaded the establishment, and the aristocracy was invited to help shape its own fate, although only its terms, not its direction, were open to discussion. Any contemplation of change sponsored either by Alexander I or Nicholas I had been confined to secret committees. News circulated not by press release but by rumor only. The key term linked to the Great Reforms, in contrast, was glasnost'—public accessibility, if only within limited bounds. It was a process open to outside participation and to the movement of ideas.[13]

Hoping to reinforce the basis of traditional autocratic rule by controlled application of its opposite principles, Alexander conceded some of the basic elements of modern Western society: a free labor supply, expanded educational access, institutions of public responsibility (the zemstvos), and, most incompatible of all with the still intact framework of autocracy, an independent judiciary.[14] These changes ended by establishing the

---

[11] See Nicholas V. Riasanovsky, *A Parting of the Ways: Government and the Educated Public in Russia, 1801–1855* (Oxford: Clarendon, 1976), chap. 2; Alexander M. Martin, *Romantics, Reformers, Reactionaries: Russian Conservative Thought and Politics in the Reign of Alexander I* (DeKalb: Northern Illinois University Press, 1997); Iurii M. Lotman, "The Decembrist in Daily Life (Everyday Behavior as a Historical-Psychological Category)," in *The Semiotics of Russian Cultural History*, ed. Alexander D. Nakhimovsky and Alice Stone Nakhimovsky (Ithaca: Cornell University Press, 1985); William Mills Todd, *Fiction and Society in the Age of Pushkin: Ideology, Institutions, and Narrative* (Cambridge, Mass.: Harvard University Press, 1986).

[12] Riasanovsky, *Parting of the Ways*, pt. 2.

[13] See W. Bruce Lincoln, *In the Vanguard of Reform: Russia's Enlightened Bureaucrats, 1825–1861* (DeKalb: Northern Illinois University Press, 1982).

[14] See Richard S. Wortman, *The Development of a Russian Legal Consciousness* (Chicago: University of Chicago Press, 1976).

component parts of what in the Western context can be called civil society: an expansion of publishing, periodicals in particular; the proliferation of professional organizations with a specialized press and claims to cultural authority; the opening of new venues of civic association; and the extension of educational opportunity beyond the narrow service-oriented elite. Indeed, the tenor of public discourse shifted. Doctors, lawyers, statisticians, and economists held opinions on social issues, and because their activities were so heavily monitored and constrained, they also developed opinions on directly political questions.[15]

The reforms had immediately generated a movement in some sections of the nobility for the extension of political rights: capping the zemstvo foundation with a constitutional roof was the demand.[16] At first, the elected noble deputies to the provincial zemstvo assemblies aimed at the establishment of a constitutional monarchy. Under the pressure of official intolerance and gathering social conflict, they moved ever farther to the left, finding themselves eventually in alliance with radical forces in what became the 1905 Revolution. Their efforts at responsible political activity must be considered part of the general tendency of post-Reform, educated Russians to fashion a basis for civic life within the constraints of a relentlessly administrative regime. Yet this very regime had conceded the rudiments of an independent judicial system. If the zemstvo constitutionalists spoke as elected representatives of local elites, legal professionals spoke and acted in the name of the principles articulated by the Judicial Reforms of 1864, defending them against the same authority that had installed them. But professionalism in this period was a force that transcended the state–society divide.[17] The substance of the reform was the work of trained lawyers within the bureaucracy: here professionals worked in concert with the state to shape institutions that would considerably alter the state's relation to its subjects and enhance the lawyers' own public role. Independent legal practitioners then elaborated these principles in directions they had not been intended to go.

The Judicial Reforms created a sheltered arena, sanctioned by the state, in which information could be exchanged, opinions articulated, and conflicting interests confronted, perhaps even reconciled. According to the new rules, the courts were to deliberate in public, respect due process,

---

[15] See, for example, Nancy Mandelker Frieden, *Russian Physicians in an Era of Reform and Revolution, 1856–1905* (Princeton: Princeton University Press, 1981); and John F. Hutchinson, *Politics and Public Health in Revolutionary Russia, 1890–1918* (Baltimore, Md.: Johns Hopkins University Press, 1990).

[16] See Terence Emmons, *The Russian Landed Gentry and the Peasant Emancipation of 1861* (Cambridge: Cambridge University Press, 1968).

[17] On the professional integrity of state prosecutors, see A. F. Koni, "Vospominaniia o dele Very Zasulich," in *Sobranie sochinenii*, 8 vols. (Moscow: Iuridicheskaia literatura, 1966), 2:81–84.

and submit all cases except crimes against the state to decision by jury. Professional standards were monitored by an independent bar, and judges could not be removed, in principle even by the monarch. Although the emperors in fact retained the privilege, as well as the right, to supersede any provision of the law, they were surprisingly reluctant to violate this particular rule.[18] In the courtroom, before a public audience and in the presence of journalists free to publish their reports, defendants and their attorneys enjoyed the freedom of speech inaccessible to law-abiding subjects of the empire in their daily lives. Even during the honeymoon of reform, censorship persisted, public assemblies were monitored by the police, expressions of critical opinion were subject to criminal proceedings, and the activities of professional associations were kept within regulated bounds. The new courtrooms, by contrast, permitted the open expression of subversive ideas.

The freedom they granted led, of course, to the courts' undoing. The social and legal changes introduced by the reforms generated not only a new range of constructive civic engagement (on the part of physicians, lawyers, economists, and other professionals) but also a tendency to radical disaffection, embodied in the newly hatched intelligentsia. Young, angry, disappointed with the limited extent of reform, this cohort set itself in opposition not only to the absolutist regime but also to those still committed to institutional change. When they were arrested in the 1870s for preaching revolution in the villages, the activists used their trials as occasions to articulate their ideas. They combined a vision of social justice with a contempt for precisely those institutions that threatened them with repression but also enabled them to address a wider public than they would have reached in any other way. And it was their performances before the bench, their impassioned speeches, their posture as martyrs to autocratic tyranny that made them heroes of liberation in the eyes of an educated public that did not share their extreme views. This sympathy emerged in response not only to court theatrics but resulted also from a shared dissatisfaction with the tensions at the heart of the reforms. The refurbished envelope of due process still contained the outmoded statutes of the pre-Reform criminal code, which determined that subversive speech no less than active rebellion should put these young rebels within reach of Siberia or even the scaffold.

The simultaneous appearance of liberal and radical figures on the new public stage of post-Reform Russia was not, however, a function of its

---

[18] Jörg Baberowski, *Autokratie und Justiz: Zum Verhältnis von Rechtsstaatlichkeit und Rückständigkeit im ausgehenden Zarenreich 1864–1914* (Frankfurt am Main: Vittorio Klostermann, 1996); Eugene Huskey, *Russian Lawyers and the Soviet State: The Origins and Development of the Soviet Bar, 1917–1939* (Princeton: Princeton University Press, 1986), chap. 1; Jane Burbank, "Discipline and Punish in the Moscow Bar Association," *Russian Review* 54, no. 1 (1995): 44–64; Koni, "Vospominaniia," 203–9.

"backwardness." Even in Western Europe, as Geoff Eley notes, the liberal public sphere never monopolized civic life, either in opposition to the Old Regime or as the kernel of an evolving bourgeois polity. From the start it was accompanied by a rival force: the plebeian or radical public, which used the same opportunity for open discussion to challenge the social basis of bourgeois domination.[19] But if radicals in Europe pushed to democratize the political process, radicals in Russia denounced that very process as a tool of bourgeois oppression, no less nefarious (perhaps even more so) than the overt repressions of the police-administrative regime. This hostility to the law and to the respectable public's constitutional aspirations did not prevent the self-styled revolutionaries from invoking liberal values on their own behalf and from using the opportunities liberal institutions provided. Thus Populist defendants insisted on their right to an audience, while denouncing the legal guarantees that gave them that right. They enlisted the services of liberal attorneys, while mocking their faith in due process. They mocked the idea of formal justice itself.

Having failed to secure a popular following by strategies of political propaganda—their failed mission to the countryside, where they preached to deaf ears—the Populists directed their eloquence at their peers. If they spoke in the interests of the excluded populace, however, they certainly did not represent it. They did not constitute a plebeian, as opposed to a liberal-bourgeois, public. Indeed, the only public they could address was that same "society" that marked itself off as much from the "people" as from the "state." And this distinction was sociologically more accurate in the first instance than in the second. In fact, the Populist orators on the judicial stage were not public figures in the civic sense but rather emblems of exclusion. They did not speak for themselves but in the voice of self-denial, as ventriloquists, in the name of a social group whose interests conflicted, moreover, with those of the groups from which the spokesmen came. Seeking to minimize their personal roles, even as they claimed the stage for their own, their rhetoric was one of abnegation—welcoming harsh verdicts, courting exile, eager for the stigma of civil death.

Women, it has often been noted, were active in the Populist movement not only as terrorist accomplices but also as speakers in the famous trials. Their prominence does not mean that the movement was "feminist." The charismatic Populist women demonstrated in their very persons the self-imposed marginality of the movement for which they stood—its desire not to be part of an established public sphere, a civil society predicated on participation in community affairs, designed to enlarge and enhance the political capacity of the educated classes and, by extension, of the popular ones. They represented the renunciation of cultural as well as social privilege, a

[19] Eley, "Nations," 307.

self-sacrifice and self-denial most strikingly embodied in the female sex. Some of these women abandoned their own children and husbands or lovers for the sake of the cause. But this apparent egoism rendered them no less iconic of feminine selflessness: in leaving their domestic roles behind they did not aspire to public recognition (as "emancipated women" might) but to a place beyond social claims or public responsibilities. They aspired to sainthood, and this is how they were understood.

In using the courtroom as a stage, the Populists of the 1870s managed not only to engineer their own removal from the public world through sentencing and exile but also to contribute to the destruction of the very boards on which they stood. The dramatic impact of the spectacle they created on the public opinion they despised prompted the regime to remove political trials from the courts and pursue the anti-Populist campaign by means of administrative repression: courts-martial, summary convictions, executions behind closed doors. The new courts were not themselves dismantled, but they ceased to provide a tribunal for political speech.

Lawyers and legal experts of the same liberal persuasion as those who had defended the radicals in the name of due process and the rule of law did not abandon their campaign for the affirmation and extension of these principles. Although their efforts challenged the underlying principles of autocracy, they did not operate entirely outside the state or in opposition to it. Legal scholars praised the institutions of Western law in the pages of the journal of the Ministry of Justice. Indeed, the ministry was, for awhile, something of a snake in the bosom of the absolutist regime. Appointed to head it by Alexander II, Dmitrii Nabokov (1826–1904) retained his post long enough into the conservative 1880s to initiate reform of the pre-1864 civil and criminal codes. Commissions composed of state servitors and distinguished members of the legal profession met in closed session, but they widely canvassed the opinion of administrators and scholars in relation to range of questions raised in both codes, and they published extensive commentaries on foreign laws. Neither their research nor their proceedings reached the wider public, but debate on the issues flooded the professional press and, in the case of marriage and inheritance law, provoked an outpouring of public opinion. These discussions evoked the "dream of a civil society" that haunted the Russian educated public, which, in debating, created that very "civil society" (if only in embryo), *iavochnym poriadkom*, without official permission, by the seat of their pants.[20]

---

[20] On civil code reform, see William G. Wagner, *Marriage, Property, and Law in Late Imperial Russia* (Oxford: Clarendon, 1994); on criminal code reform, see Laura Engelstein, *The Keys to Happiness: Sex and the Search for Modernity in Fin-de-Siècle Russia* (Ithaca: Cornell University Press, 1992), chaps. 1–2. Nabokov was the father of the liberal activist Vladimir Dmitrievich Nabokov (1869–1922) and the grandfather of the novelist.

The key distinction in the debates on the definition of private and public life and the relation between state, society, and the individual (the issues raised in civil and criminal code reform) concerned the nature of the state and the kind of law necessary to fulfill that dream. The answer was obvious. Most of the Russian legal community wanted the rule of law (the Rechtsstaat), not the vestigial eighteenth-century model of administrative rule and state tutelage over public life (the Polizeistaat) that had persisted into the modern age. Only under the shelter of a legal edifice construed in this sense, constructed and empowered by the state as a matter of course, but keeping the state itself at a distance from its subjects, could public life thrive.

An issue key to the relation of state and society concerned the laws governing religion. These were of particular importance in an empire whose populations embraced many different confessions. The official state religion was the Russian Orthodox Church, which occupied a privileged position in relation to the other faiths but was administratively subordinate to secular authority. In supporting government policy and discouraging movements for change, it fulfilled its official, conservative mission. Indeed, Church authorities resisted the proposed reforms of the civil code concerning divorce and family life, as well as the revision of the laws governing religious worship. Insofar as these campaigns involved not only civil servants but also representatives of public opinion, the Church can be said in both cases to have contributed to civic debate, in the interests, however, of maintaining administrative control over public life and limiting the range of personal self-determination.

The Church thus participated in public debate only to restrict the scope of civil society. Yet the Church could not entirely escape the subversive encroachments of civic discourse. During the period of the Great Reforms, voices within the Church advocated changes in its own internal structures, and during the 1905 Revolution, a movement for the reorganization of Church governance on a conciliar model echoed political themes articulated in the secular realm. Within the Orthodox fold significant differences of opinion made themselves heard even in peaceful times. A range of periodicals associated with various branches of the Church commented on secular as well as religious themes from differing points of view. Orthodoxy also influenced public life in another way. Providing a spiritual rationale and moral context for independent philanthropic activity, it strengthened the fabric of informal associations through which society governed its own affairs, sometimes in concert with government efforts, sometimes on its own.[21]

---

[21] See I. S. Belliustin, *Description of the Clergy in Rural Russia: The Memoir of a Nineteenth-Century Parish Priest*, ed. Gregory L. Freeze (Ithaca: Cornell University Press, 1985). Also Marc Szeftel, "Church and State in Imperial Russia"; John Meyendorff, "Russian

Although associated with traditional values of deference and hierarchy, the Church did not thus function as a simple impediment to the evolution of civic life. As the established religion, institutionally and politically tied to the state, Orthodoxy could offer no independent platform for the expression of public opinion. Even its opposition to change was expressed "in house," as it were, as a function of its bureaucratic office. Yet it should be remembered, on the one hand, that conservative, as well as liberal, ideas could animate public-spirited minds and, on the other, that conservative institutions did not always stifle demands for change. Religious precepts inspired civic activism and political critiques (the case of the Slavophiles), and some clergymen managed to articulate dissenting positions without leaving the fold. In this sense, the situation of the Church mirrored the experience of society at large: forbidden from occupying neutral space, opinion makers used the structures designed to restrict their activity for precisely the purposes they were supposed to obstruct.

Those who had abandoned Orthodoxy for heretical versions of the faith were long unable to contribute anything to public discourse. The Old Believers who had confronted the monarch with pious resistance two hundred years earlier had by now made their peace with the state but continued to function outside the law. Until late in the nineteenth century when policy began to change, the regime reinforced the community's doctrinal isolation with civil disabilities and restrictions on confessional life. After 1905 the Old Believers began publishing journals of their own, but other dissenters continued to suffer more aggressive forms of exclusion, pushing them literally off the social map.[22]

The juridical status of religion not only affected the development of public life and civic culture. It became an issue hotly debated as part of the process of strengthening the rudiments of civil society in the last years of tsarist rule. The Christian Orthodox Catholic Eastern Church was defined by law as the "preeminent and predominant religion" of the empire, subject to the administrative authority of the state. In view of the empire's cultural diversity, however, the law also promised adherents of other religions the freedom to worship "in the various languages and according to

---

Bishops and Church Reform in 1905"; and Paul R. Valliere, "The Idea of a Council in Russian Orthodoxy in 1905," in *Russian Orthodoxy under the Old Regime*, ed. Robert L. Nichols and Theofanis George Stavrou (Minneapolis: University of Minnesota Press, 1978); Adele Lindenmeyr, *Poverty Is Not a Vice: Charity, Society, and the State in Imperial Russia* (Princeton: Princeton University Press, 1996).

[22] See Robert O. Crummey, *The Old Believers and the World of Anti-Christ: The Vyg Community and the Russian State, 1694–1855* (Madison: University of Wisconsin Press, 1970); Manfred Hildermeier, "Alter Glaube und neue Welt: Zur Sozialgeschichte des Raskol im 18. und 19. Jahrhundert," *Jahrbücher für Geschichte Osteuropas* 38, no. 3 (1990): 372–98; and no. 4 (1990): 504–25; and Roy R. Robson, *Old Believers in Modern Russia* (DeKalb: Northern Illinois University Press, 1995). On the Skoptsy, see Laura Engelstein, *Castration and the Heavenly Kingdom: A Russian Folktale* (Ithaca: Cornell University Press, 1999).

the laws and confessions of their ancestors," as well as the right to govern their own communities through institutions created by the state.[23] This "freedom of religion" (*svoboda very*) was, however, a peculiar grant. In the first place, the freedom to worship consisted of the right to persist in the faith of one's ancestors, that is, to continue to belong to the religious community into which one had been born. It did not endow individual believers with the right to change religious affiliation. Second, the price of recognition was subordination to administrative authority. And, third, recognition did not mean equality.

The laws on religion established a hierarchy of belief that positioned the various creeds according to their relationship to the dominant one. In addition to Orthodoxy, the state recognized four religions as legitimate faiths. The most respected were the non-Orthodox Christians (*inoslavnye*), also known as "Christians of foreign confessions" (*khristiane inostrannykh ispovedanii*): Protestants and Roman Catholics. Below them in rank were the non-Christians, or "those of other faiths" (*inovertsy*): Jews and Muslims. Pagan belief systems, though not institutionalized, were included in this second category, reflecting negatively on the status of the monotheistic traditions with which they were grouped. Deviations from Orthodoxy, such as the Old Belief and its sectarian offshoots, were not recognized as religions at all. These heretics had no right to conduct worship, enact marriages, empower a clergy, or govern their own affairs. Membership in some of these groups qualified as a criminal offense. Under the principle of "religious toleration," understood as respect for the established Church, the law prohibited attempts to convert adherents of the recognized religions to any but the Orthodox faith, which alone had the right to proselytize. Indeed, the law made it virtually impossible to abandon the Church under any circumstances.[24]

Russians who thought of themselves either as inhabiting an existing civil society or helping to bring one to life criticized the disposition of religious affairs under imperial law and offered corresponding visions of how religion ought to be governed. Three of these alternatives illustrate the range of opinion on this matter. The first, published in 1895, was formulated by the editorial commission charged with revising the criminal code.[25] The

---

[23] Articles 40, 43, 45, and 46, in *Svod zakonov rossiiskoi imperii*, ed. A. F. Volkov and Iu. D. Filipov, 4th ed., 16 vols. (St. Petersburg: Obshchestvennaia pol'za, 1904), 1:3–4.

[24] Articles 70 and 77, in *Svod*, 14:75–76. See Paul W. Werth, "The Limits of Religious Ascription: Baptized Tatars and the Revision of 'Apostasy,' 1840s–1905," *Russian Review* 59, no. 4 (2000): 493–511; idem, "Toward 'Freedom of Conscience': Catholicism, Law, and the Contours of Religious Liberty in Late Imperial Russia," *Kritika* 7, no. 4 (2006): 843–63; idem, "Freedom of Conscience in Imperial Russia: A *Begriffsgeschichte*" (unpublished paper, American Association for the Advancement of Slavic Studies, November 2007; courtesy of the author).

[25] *Ugolovnoe ulozhenie: Proekt redaktsionnoi komissii i ob"iasneniia k nemu* (henceforth *UU*), 8 vols. (St. Petersburg: Pravitel'stvuiushchii senat, 1895), 4:3–147.

second, published in 1900 by a major legal journal, is the work of a liberal professor of jurisprudence.[26] The third consists of proposals and debates in the State Duma following the 1905 Revolution. Each instance is a variation on the "dream" that is the subject of this chapter.

In relation to certain themes the editorial commission offered fundamental challenges to the principles embodied in the existing criminal code, dating from the reign of Nicholas I. Most of its members prided themselves on a progressive, secular view of the law. In the case of religion, however, their proposals were cautious. The active code positioned crimes against religion immediately after crimes against the state in order of political importance, on the grounds that "crimes against religion are in essence also rebellion against the secular authority." The commission agreed that the state must continue in the role of guardian of religious values, because "religion and the church are among the most important foundations of the political and social system." This was all the more so in Russia, "where the principles of the Christian faith and the Orthodox Church form the unifying link that holds together the numerous and varied elements of the population." The reformers viewed religion as a social good in which the state had a protective interest, rather than an aspect of personal life subject only to private determination in which the state must not interfere. Questions of faith, therefore, could not be left entirely to the individual conscience.[27]

The commission, judging that the current level of intrusion was nevertheless extreme, argued, somewhat obscurely, that precisely because "church and family are fundamental to our public community [gosudarstvennoe obshchezhitie], attacks on religion and the church should be separated from attacks on the state and its institutions."[28] The draft code thus removed the section on crimes against religion from its privileged position immediately following crimes against the state and inserted it between threats to public welfare and crimes against the person. The repositioning was also a redefinition: religion bordered the public and the private, not the public and the political, in the commission's view. But even this modification departed too radically from tradition to find favor with the Ministry of Justice and the Holy Synod, which, in reviewing the draft, returned the statutes to their accustomed location.[29]

Repositioning aside, the existing statutes remained virtually unaltered. The reformers sustained the state's obligation to endorse certain values

[26] M. A. Reisner, "Moral', pravo i religiia po deistvuiushchemu russkomu zakonu," pts. 1–4, Vestnik prava (1900): no. 3, 1–18; no. 4–5, 1–49; no. 8, 1–34; no. 10, 1–46. Rpt. in idem, Gosudarstvo i veruiushchaia lichnost': Sbornik statei (St. Petersburg: Obshchestvennaia pol'za, 1905), 141–267. Here cited from Vestnik prava.

[27] UU, 4:48, 50 (quotes), 105.

[28] Ibid., 4:51.

[29] Ardalion Popov, Sud i nakazaniia za prestupleniia protiv very i nravstvennosti po russkomu pravu (Kazan: Imperatorskii universitet, 1904), 497.

over others, defending the prohibition of socially harmful faiths (Mormons were among their examples) and retaining the state's authority over propaganda and conversion. Though mitigating the penalties imposed, the commission thus retained the hierarchy of protected and stigmatized creeds and continued to rank the harm alleged to result from conversion according to the status of the confessions involved. As their language and legal caution suggest, the reformers did not envision a civil society composed of rights-bearing individuals. They endorsed a polity composed of collective bodies (families, confessions) sustaining an otherwise fragmented imperial conglomeration. In some areas of the law the reformers valued individual rights above respect for traditional hierarchies, but not in this case.[30]

One commentator explained the commission's muddle on the grounds that existing law on religion was so far removed from modern principles of jurisprudence that any reform in the modern spirit would have amounted to a complete and politically unacceptable challenge to the entire system.[31] Unconstrained by bureaucratic obligations, Professor Mikhail Reisner (1868–1928) of Tomsk University formulated a more radical critique of the laws on religion than his colleagues on the editorial commission. He was also more explicit in his vision of the civil society he hoped would emerge from changes in the legal edifice. Reisner criticized the monarchy for continuing to adhere to the model of the eighteenth-century Polizeistaat, which supervised moral behavior by intervening in its subjects' private lives; tightly controlled the associations to which they belonged, including religious communities; penalized deviation from officially sanctioned norms; and limited the individual's ability to choose, even among acceptable options. In gaining legitimacy, however, religious institutions lost spiritual authority, and their members lost the true benefits of faith. "Our law," Reisner complained, "does not observe the division between the state and the religious communities. It acknowledges neither their freedom, nor the freedom of personal belief and conscience." By endowing certain faiths with official status, the state was pursuing a political mission, using police enforcement and bureaucratic control. This mission was intended to secure the loyalty of the component peoples of the empire, while keeping them in their proper place. "Our law is interested in religion primarily as the basis of national identity [natsional'nost']," Reisner critically observed, "as the spiritual nerve of the various tribes and peoples, not as one or another form of a person's relation to God."[32]

While professing devotion to spiritual values, the state manifested an entirely instrumental conception of religion. "Our law supposes that

---

[30] UU, 4:104–5, 116; Popov, Sud, 479–82; also Wagner, Marriage; and Engelstein, Keys.
[31] Popov, Sud, 471–72, 486–87.
[32] Reisner, "Moral'," pt. 2, 6, 47. For other Russian jurists of the period who shared many of Reisner's opinions, see Popov, Sud, 452–64.

religion is not practiced by individual persons but by national-spiritual entities—peoples, nations, tribes. But, in fact, religion will always be religion, and its true receptacle is not the nation but the individual human heart." The policy of dividing the spiritual field into official categories, prohibiting the formation of new confessions, and preventing believers from moving between them had created a discrepancy between the formal structure and the essence of belief. "With the exception of a few members of the 'harmful' sects," Reisner noted, "the entire population is listed under the recognized confessions. What it actually believes, how it worships, or if it believes anything at all—is another question." Only the abolition of religious censorship, guaranteed freedom of discussion and the press, and the universal right to promote one's faith would allow believers to make their own spiritual decisions and develop a culture of moral commitment to replace habits of obedience and deceit.[33]

The model Reisner contrasted to the repressive and punitive Polizeistaat was the "cultural rule-of-law state [*kul'turno-pravovoe gosudarstvo*]," a Rechtsstaat in which law made room for the creative operation of cultural influences. Instead of trying to impose morality by force, this type of state recognizes "that the bearer of morality can only be the free, moral individual, that this individual cannot be created by magical powers but only through the strengthening of a series of social, legal, and political conditions, of which the most important is freedom guaranteed by law [*pravovaia svoboda*]." Far from harming religion, the rule-of-law state fosters the emergence of a free church that "develops the enterprise and energy found neither in a church swallowed up by the state, nor, all the more so, a theocracy." Only a legal structure that protected, rather than intruded, would permit the growth of self-governing religious associations that fostered the moral improvement of their members, allowing society to develop a moral sensibility of its own. By breaking the identification of secular with church authority, the rule-of-law state "provides each individual with freedom—that greatest of conditions for moral development—and in this way raises the moral level of its citizens."[34]

Reisner's attack on administrative rule and his endorsement of a modern law-abiding state protective of individual rights, including freedom of conscience, reflected the liberal values associated with the opposition movement that emerged in the decades preceding 1905. In meetings assembled in private parlors without police approval (often dispersed by the police); in banquets dedicated to mobilizing educated opinion on the model of 1848; in newspapers published abroad; in associations such as the one called "Conversation" (*Beseda*), joined by men who wanted freedoms but not constitutions; in congresses on public health and in zemstvo

---

[33] Reisner, "Moral'," pt. 3, 8–10; pt. 4, 18–38.
[34] Ibid., pt. 3, 3; pt. 4, 1–3.

assemblies—the so-called Liberation Movement took form. The result of this process can be seen, in fact, as constituting a self-declared civil society determined, iavochnym poriadkom, to wrest the Rechtsstaat from the hands of *Polizei*. Although revolution was not what these gentlemen (and the rare professional woman) had in mind, it was revolution—an act of violence, not discussion, fueled by popular anger, not well-articulated dissatisfaction, and animated by the slogans and symbols of the radical left, indifferent to legal scruple of any kind—that caused the regime to concede some of the constitutional demands the spokesmen of mobilized civil society put forth.[35]

The Manifesto of 17 October 1905, designed to subdue the revolutionary crisis, promised to guarantee basic civil liberties and opened the way to electoral politics and parliamentary debates. But even before this constitutional watershed, an imperial decree of 17 April 1905, "On strengthening the principles of religious toleration [*veroterpimost'*]," guaranteed "to each of Our subjects freedom of belief and prayer according to the dictates of his conscience."[36] Its main contribution was to open the possibility of abandoning Orthodoxy, but only in the direction of other Christian faiths. It also recognized Old Belief as a legitimate confession. The decree originated as a response to political disorders in the Baltic and Volga regions, where numerous Catholics, Protestants, and Muslims had been baptized into Orthodoxy. Loyal to their native beliefs, they were unable formally to leave the Orthodox Church without forfeiting their civil rights and risking confiscation of property and even their children. The 17 April decree made it possible for such converts legally to resume their original identities. That the decree was less a matter of principle than a strategic political concession confirmed Professor Reisner's objection to the foundations of tsarist law.[37]

Once the State Duma convened in 1906, it pressed for the extension of the principles outlined but unfulfilled by the decree. At first the movement for reform had the support of Minister of the Interior Petr Stolypin (1862–1911). Faced with opposition from the Synod and right-wing forces, Stolypin eventually changed his mind, and none of the Duma proposals ever became law. The proposals remained hypothetical, but the issues and arguments embodied in the reform campaign nevertheless demonstrate the conflict between "dream" and reality when it came to building the architecture of civil society, even in post-1905 Russia. In May 1906, for example, a group of Duma deputies presented a bill on "freedom of

---

[35] See Shmuel Galai, *The Liberation Movement in Russia, 1900–1905* (Cambridge: Cambridge University Press, 1973); Ascher, *The Revolution of 1905*.

[36] "Imennoi Vysochaishii ukaz, dannyi Senatu: Ob ukreplenii nachal veroterpimosti" (no. 26125), *Polnoe sobranie zakonov rossiiskoi imperii*, ser. 3, 33 vols. (St. Petersburg: Gosudarstvennaia tipografia, 1905), 25:257–58.

[37] See M. A. Reisner, "Svoboda sovesti i zakon 17 aprelia 1905 g.," in *Gosudarstvo i veruiushchaia lichnost'*, 416–17.

conscience" (*svoboda sovesti*). The choice of terms underscored their interest in strengthening the individual's right to define his own spiritual identity. By contrast, the term "religious toleration" (veroterpimost') used in the title of the 17 April decree emphasized the state's relation to confessional authority. In substituting the phrase "according to the dictates of his conscience" for the current phrase "according to the laws and confessions of their ancestors," the text of the decree had departed from the existing framework, which was designed to prevent adherents from making choices of their own. But though it allowed people to move among the Christian faiths, the decree maintained the Orthodox monopoly on propaganda, still penalized conversion from Christian to non-Christian creeds, and failed to recognize the possibility of legally refusing any religious affiliation at all. By contrast, the Duma bill, in addition to granting citizens the freedom to choose among the recognized faiths, form new ones, or remain outside organized religious life, declared all confessions of equal legal standing, with the right to seek converts outside the fold.[38]

In responding to the bill, the Ministry of Internal Affairs outlined the consequences for the regulation of civil life. First, the state would cease to interpose itself between individual believers and the institutions governing religious practice. The state would also cease to regulate the religious dimension of marriage and would abdicate its power to influence the religious identity of children. In addition to limiting its own powers, the state would have to create new secular institutions: civil oaths, civil marriages, and nonconfessional burials. The ministry raised four main objections to the bill. First, it argued that certain communities were national as well as religious in character. Even if, as the bill demanded, no civil disabilities were attached to membership in any faith, the state would nevertheless be justified in limiting the rights of groups such as the Jews and the Poles, on political, not confessional, grounds. Second, it insisted that the Orthodox Church retain its close association with the state. Third, it was equally important that the state continue to regulate parents' rights to influence their children's religious identity. And, finally, it denied that all religions deserved equal treatment. It goes without saying that the Holy Synod objected to any diminution of the Orthodox Church's central role in public affairs, including its monopoly on propaganda and its right to influence the conditions of interconfessional marriage.[39]

---

[38] "Materialy po voprosu o svobode sovesti," Arkhiv Rossiiskoi Akademii Nauk [ARAN], f. 192, op. 3, d. 17, ll. 15–18 ("Osnovnye polozheniia zakonoproekta o svobode sovesti"). See also Peter Waldron, "Religious Toleration in Late Imperial Russia," in *Civil Rights in Imperial Russia,* ed. Olga Crisp and Linda Edmondson (Oxford: Oxford University Press, 1989), 112–13, 117.

[39] "Materialy po voprosu o svobode sovesti," ARAN, f. 192, op. 3, d. 17, ll. 19–24 (Ministerstvo vnutrennikh del, Departament dukhovnykh del inostrannykh ispovedanii, 16 June

What can we conclude from these three views of the civil constitution of religious life, in terms of their content and their fate? First, it can be said that between 1895 and 1906 acceptable opinion on the matter had moved some distance along the continuum from traditional to progressive. The editorial commission appointed in the 1880s had been unwilling or unable seriously to challenge the bureaucratic construction of religion as an affair of state and a matter of regulated institutions, not personal or even communal autonomy. Its timid move toward attenuating the political implications of religion and associating it more closely with the operation of civic life met with official disapproval. The draft itself, even in amended form, never became law. By 1905, however, the tsar himself was ready to narrow the scope of state intervention in religious life, beyond the extent the reformers had dared envision a decade before. But the decree of 17 April announced no new general principles, offering merely a series of specific provisions. Nor did its publication alter the behavior of the administrative authorities. Nor, when it came to completing the decree with legislative enactments, did the ministers endorse the Duma proposals. These proposals embodied the dream of a civil society, in which a public, composed of rights-bearing individuals, could shape its own moral and cultural universe, protected, rather than constrained, by the law. The proposals emanated, furthermore, from members of an active public, now constituted in relation to an empire-wide representative body.

Thus progress had been made, both in paradigm and in practice. Yet how much had actually changed? The old criminal statutes remained on the books. The Duma proposals went down to defeat. The Orthodox Church retained its monopoly on preaching to the unconverted; civil marriage did not exist; Jews still suffered state-sponsored discrimination—indeed state-sponsored persecution (for example, the trial of Mendel Beilis [1874–1934] in 1911–1913, when the Ministry of Justice brought charges of ritual blood slaughter against a Jewish artisan)—and the Duma itself was dissolved by imperial decree when its temper displeased the sovereign or his ministers. Ethnic and religious equality along with universal—male and female—suffrage, were achieved only after February 1917. When the Bolsheviks came to power in October they endorsed the separation of church and state for their own reasons. Michael Reisner, now an official of the Commissariat of Justice, helped draft the new laws. This legislation granted freedom of conscience to the private person along the lines Reisner and other liberals had envisioned. At the same time, however, it destroyed the institutional basis of belief by depriving religious associations of juridical rights. Eventually they were also forbidden to spread their beliefs.

1906, no. 3432, "Po proektu osnovnykh polozhenii o svobode sovesti"); ll. 27–48 (Ministerstvo vnutrennikh del, 1906, "Spravka o svobode sovesti").

Atheism replaced Orthodoxy as the state-sponsored dogma.[40] Whatever Reisner's original motives in defending the moral power, hence civic value, of freely chosen faith, the new regime did not abolish state control in order to enhance the moral autonomy of citizens occupying public space. Its goal was rather to obliterate religion altogether, first as social practice and ultimately as private conviction. Law served the Soviet regime not to limit the role of the state but to enhance its power by rhetorical means, mobilizing the illusion of legality in the service of administrative lawlessness.[41]

To return to Gramsci and the connection between public life and political institutions, one might conclude that civil society under the autocracy was indeed "primordial" in lacking a spine, an architecture sustained by the law, which would guarantee its independence. In the Soviet period, religious association succumbed to repression, along with other forms of public life. Yet both regimes collapsed in the end—not from the assault of civic forces, too weak in either case to attack from within, but from their own shortcomings. Their failure, in the name of security, to allow these forces to gather strength was perhaps as fatal to the existence of the states involved as it was to the political development they stunted.

---

[40] See Joshua Rothenberg, "The Legal Status of Religion in the Soviet Union," in *Aspects of Religion in the Soviet Union, 1917–1967*, ed. Richard H. Marshall Jr. (Chicago: University of Chicago Press, 1971), 63–64, 82; John Shelton Curtiss, *The Russian Church and the Soviet State, 1917–1950* (Boston: Little, Brown, 1953), 230. For texts, see "K istorii otdeleniia tserkvi ot gosudarstva i shkoly ot tserkvi v SSSR: Dokumenty i materialy," *Voprosy istorii religii i ateizma: Sbornik statei*, Vol. 5 (Moscow: Akademiia nauk, 1958), 19–22.

[41] See William B. Husband, *"Godless Communists": Atheism and Society in Soviet Russia, 1917–1932* (DeKalb: Northern Illinois University Press, 2000).

CHAPTER FOUR

Holy Russia in Modern Times

The Slavophile Quest for the Lost Faith

Alas, "love thy neighbor" offers no response to questions
about the composition of light, the nature of chemical
reactions or the law of the conservation of energy.
Christianity,... increasingly reduced to moral truisms... which
cannot help mankind resolve the great problems of hunger,
poverty, toil or the economic system,... occupies only a tiny
corner in contemporary civilization.

— VASILII ROZANOV, *Russkaia tserkov'* (1909)

Chernyshevskii and Pobedonostsev, the great radical and
the great reactionary, were perhaps the only two men of the
[nineteenth] century who really believed in God. Of course, an
incalculable number of peasants and old women also believed
in God; but they were not the makers of history and culture.
Culture was made by a handful of mournful skeptics who
thirsted for God simply because they had no God.

— ABRAM TERTZ [ANDREI SINIAVSKII],
The Trial Begins, and On Socialist Realism (1960)

In arguing for the privatization of religious life, the most thorough-going
of the liberals pursued a model of individual moral responsibility, and
hence also of the morally accountable actor in civic affairs—the citizen.
In that respect the argument for privatization was also a call for the re-
construction of public life. But conservatives also believed that Russian
religious life needed renovation. They, too, rejected the instrumental use

of religion as a state institution (although, as patriots, they were inconsistent on this point). They, too, believed that the substance of religious faith was endangered by the post-Petrine constellation. But instead of wishing religion to retreat from the public arena, they presented the Orthodox legacy as a model for social and political life. Seeking to return the educated classes to the native tradition, they realized that tradition itself must be renewed. Trying in this way to emphasize Russia's distinctive features, they joined a debate current in countries already experiencing the transformation they themselves wished to prevent. The problem itself was a modern one.

* * *

What defines the modern age? As science and technology develop, faith in religion declines. This assumption has been shared by those who applaud it as well as those who regret it. On the one side, for example, A. N. Wilson laments the progress of unbelief in the last two hundred years. In *God's Funeral*, the title borrowed from Thomas Hardy's dirge for "our myth's oblivion," Wilson endorses Thomas Carlyle's doleful assessment of the threshold event of the new era: "What had been poured forth at the French Revolution was something rather more destructive than the vials of the Apocalypse. It was the dawning of the Modern." As Peter Gay comments in a review, "Wilson leaves no doubt that the 'Modern' with its impudent challenge to time-honored faiths, was a disaster from start to finish."[1] On the other side, historians have tended to celebrate the European nineteenth century as "part of the grand narrative of secularization" inaugurated by the science-minded Enlightenment, to whose values they subscribe.[2]

The secularization thesis, which once dominated the social sciences, stresses the institutional and intellectual shifts that displaced religion from the center of European politics and culture. But, as Peter Gay observes, the picture is not that simple: "The age of Darwin was also the age of Newman."[3] The spread of public education did not inhibit the power

[1] Quote from A. N. Wilson, *God's Funeral* (New York: W. W. Norton, 1999), 69; cited in Peter Gay, "But Is It True? In God's Own Afterlife," *Times Literary Supplement*, 23 July 1999, 5.

[2] Margaret Lavinia Anderson, "The Limits of Secularization: On the Problem of the Catholic Revival in Nineteenth-Century Germany," *History Journal* 38, no. 3 (1995): 618; Phillip E. Hammond, "Introduction," in *The Sacred in a Secular Age: Toward Revision in the Scientific Study of Religion*, ed. Phillip E. Hammond (Berkeley: University of California Press, 1985), 1. See also Bryan Wilson, "Secularization: The Inherited Model," in ibid., 14.

[3] Gay, "But Is It True?" For a general discussion, see Roy Wallace and Steve Bruce, "Secularization: The Orthodox Model," in *Religion and Modernization: Sociologists and Historians Debate the Secularization Thesis*, ed. Steve Bruce (Oxford: Clarendon, 1992).

of evangelical Protestantism in Victorian England, and Catholic revivals encouraged popular piety in Germany, Ireland, and France.[4] Today's proponents of creationism are derided by the general public for clinging obstinately to false beliefs. But the very existence of creationism testifies to religion's enduring power to shape the way some people, even in high-tech lands, understand the world. Even A. N. Wilson is happy to announce that God is not dead after all. The twentieth century, he writes, confirms "the palpable and visible strength of the Christian thing, the Christian idea."[5] But adjustments that accept the continuing vitality of spiritual conviction even in the contemporary West still acknowledge that religion is no longer central to the organization of public life in the industrialized nations.[6]

When it comes to Russia, however, the assumptions are reversed. The nineteenth century produced the story not only of Europe as the land of reason and progress but also of Russia as a land of Christian endurance and cultural inertia. While post-Enlightenment Europeans boasted of their break with tradition, the Russian Empire acquired the reputation, partly home-made, of failing to keep pace with time.[7] This image of a stubbornly pious Russia was not dislodged by evidence that science, technology, and cultural change had begun, by the turn of the twentieth century, to destabilize familiar values and ways of life even there. It is an image that has survived the reign of Communism and its fall.[8] Looking for an icon of spiritual survival in the face of modernity's most concerted assaults, A. N. Wilson recounts an incident in the life of Alexander Solzhenitsyn (1918–2008), newly liberated from a Stalinist camp, whose heart is touched by the sight of a peasant woman making the sign of the cross.[9] Evoking Solzhenitsyn's

---

[4] Anderson, "Limits of Secularization," 648–49; Emmet Larkin, *The Historical Dimensions of Irish Catholicism* (Washington, D.C.: Catholic University of America Press, 1984), chap. 2; Thomas A. Kselman, *Miracles and Prophecies in Nineteenth-Century France* (New Brunswick, N.J.: Rutgers University Press, 1983); David Blackbourn, *Marpingen: Apparitions of the Virgin Mary in Bismarckian Germany* (Oxford: Clarendon, 1993); Ruth Harris, *Lourdes: Body and Spirit in the Secular Age* (London: Allen Lane, 1999).

[5] Wilson, *God's Funeral*, 354.

[6] See James T. Richardson, "Studies of Conversion: Secularization or Re-Enchantment?" in Hammond, *The Sacred in a Secular Age*, 113; Rodney Stark, "Church and Sect," in ibid., 134; Wilson, "Secularization," 19. Also Charles Taylor, "Foreword," in Marcel Gauchet, *The Disenchantment of the World: A Political History of Religion*, trans. Oscar Burge (Princeton: Princeton University Press, 1997), ix–x; Talal Asad, *Genealogies of Religion: Discipline and Reasons of Power in Christianity and Islam* (Baltimore, Md.: Johns Hopkins University Press, 1993), 28–29, 39.

[7] B. Grois, "Poisk russkoi natsional'noi identichnosti," *Voprosy filosofii* 1 (1992): 52–60.

[8] For example: "As modernization challenged tradition in Russia, it...encountered Orthodoxy at virtually every turn": William B. Husband, ed., *The Human Tradition in Modern Russia* (Wilmington, Del.: SR Books, 2000), 3–4.

[9] Wilson, *God's Funeral*, 337; quoting D. M. Thomas's version of Solzhenitsyn's account.

story, Wilson echoes a myth that Russian intellectuals have created about their culture's relation to and difference from the West.

In the realm of stereotypes East-West mirrors, in mutually reinforcing pairs, tradition-modernity, instinct-reason, religious-secular, and Russia-Europe. Historians inherit from each side a dominant version of itself, celebrated or deplored in different degrees, which must then be refuted or endorsed. This chapter begins instead by supposing that nineteenth-century Russia and Europe were moving on parallel tracks; that religion, as ethos and observance, was evolving in tandem with other cultural forms in Russia as well as in Europe. Reframing the question in terms of parallels rather than contrasts does not dispute the power of the grand oppositions between old and new, East and West, to shape the way Europeans and Russians have positioned themselves in space and time. But imperial Russia was, in fact, on the level both of the state and educated society, a participant in contemporary trends. Even the ancestors of Solzhenitsyn's peasant crone—the populace at the greatest remove from the nation's sophisticated upper crust and most closely identified by that elite with a resilient traditional core—felt the impact of change.

The discovery of tradition was itself a modern enterprise.[10] Russians, like their contemporaries abroad, reacted to Enlightenment iconoclasm by reconstituting the past. For example, only after the Napoleonic Wars did educated Russians, accustomed to European styles, begin to value Orthodox icons, not as objects of worship but as works of art to be treasured as a cultural legacy. Families now paid attention to the icons they already possessed; the wealthy started to collect them. Icons discarded by churches were rescued from neglect; many were restored to their original condition and for the first time hung in museums. New icons were painted to look like old ones. In the early twentieth century modernist artists cherished the "primitive" style that cultured Russians had originally denigrated as crude.[11]

If tradition was the subject of conscious reflection everywhere, the notion of "the modern" was a controversial and highly politicized one in the Russian case. Modernity came to Russia as a state-sponsored project at the beginning of the eighteenth century. Looking to Europe for technical knowledge, cultural paradigms, and instruments of rule, Peter the

---

[10] Eric Hobsbawm, "Introduction: Inventing Traditions," in *The Invention of Tradition,* ed. Eric Hobsbawm and Terence Ranger (Cambridge: Cambridge University Press, 1983), 1–14.

[11] See G. I. Vzdornov, *Istoriia otkrytiia i izucheniia russkoi srednevekovoi zhivopisi: XIX vek* (Moscow: Iskusstvo, 1986); Shirley A. Glade, "A Heritage Discovered Anew: Russia's Reevaluation of Pre-Petrine Icons in the Late Tsarist and Early Soviet Periods," *Canadian-American Slavic Studies* 26 (1992): 145–95; O. Iu. Tarasov, *Ikona i blagochestie: Ocherki ikonnogo dela v imperatorskoi Rossii* (Moscow: Progress-kul'tura: Traditsiia, 1995).

Great, as is well known, created a virtue of innovation.[12] His predecessors had already turned to European artists and craftsmen for expertise. They had adopted foreign symbols and military techniques. Elements of Latin Christianity had affected the teachings and practices of the Orthodox Church. Seventeenth-century Russian culture had begun to distinguish between secular and sacred modes of expression.[13] Peter was different, however, in proclaiming the start of a new era. He linked the onset of "modernity" to the introduction of European culture and the fight against ignorance and tradition. In contrasting the public or political realm with the domain of religion, he instituted a new civil alphabet demarcating secular from sacred texts, and he labeled the language of holiness Church Slavonic to maintain its distance from the newly codified literary tongue.[14] He also subordinated the Church to bureaucratic control, establishing the lay office of over-procurator to run the Holy Synod, which exercised final authority over the episcopal elite. Incorporating sacred elements into court life, he did so in a mocking or provocative spirit that demonstrated his power to manipulate the trappings of the faith and define the political meanings of culture.[15]

Europeans acknowledged Peter and his eighteenth-century successors as enlightened monarchs in the contemporary mode and recognized the refitted empire as part of the international state system.[16] They accepted the terms in which Peter couched his war on the recalcitrant native culture—including the traditions of the Orthodox Church. Recalling the changes the tsar had imposed in the religious domain, an English Protestant, writing a century later, praised "the value of that reformation, which Peter, so justly styled the Great, wrought upon the Russian church, which, before

[12] Richard S. Wortman, *Scenarios of Power: Myth and Ceremony in Russian Monarchy*, 2 vols. (Princeton: Princeton University Press, 1995, 2000), 1:18.

[13] See Nikolaos A. Chrissidis, "Creating the New Educated Elite: Learning and Faith in Moscow's Slavo-Greek-Latin Academy, 1685–1730" (Ph.D. diss., Yale University, 2000).

[14] See V. M. Zhivov, *Iazyk i kul'tura v Rossii XVIII veka* (Moscow: Shkola "Iazyki russkoi kul'tury," 1996). On the seventeenth century, see also idem, "Religious Reform and the Emergence of the Individual in Russian Seventeenth-Century Literature," in *Religion and Culture in Early Modern Russia and Ukraine*, ed. Samuel H. Baron and Nancy Shields Kollmann (DeKalb: Northern Illinois University Press, 1997), 184–98; Paul Bushkovitch, *Religion and Society in Russia: The Sixteenth and Seventeenth Centuries* (Oxford: Oxford University Press, 1992), introduction.

[15] See B. A. Uspenskij, "Historia sub specie semioticae" (1974), in *Soviet Semiotics: An Anthology*, ed. and trans. Daniel P. Lucid (Baltimore, Md.: Johns Hopkins University Press, 1977), 107–15; Ernest A. Zitser, *The Transfigured Kingdom: Sacred Parody and Charismatic Authority at the Court of Peter the Great* (Ithaca: Cornell University Press, 2004).

[16] See Larry Wolff, *Inventing Eastern Europe: The Map of Civilization in the Mind of the Enlightenment* (Stanford: Stanford University Press, 1994); Martin Malia, *Russia under Western Eyes: From the Bronze Horseman to the Lenin Mausoleum* (Cambridge, Mass.: Harvard University Press, 1999).

his time, lay in a state of the utmost ignorance and degradation."[17] From within the Orthodox fold, Father Georges Florovsky (1893–1979) viewed Peter's policies as a blow to religion. "What is innovative in this Petrine reform," he wrote in 1937, "is not westernization but secularization."[18] Deprived of institutional autonomy, the Church continued to serve the needs of a state that now conceived its own objectives in secular terms and demanded that the Church meet secular standards. Peter's strategy of subordinating and denigrating the faith did not, however, survive his reign. The Holy Synod continued to govern the Church at the highest levels, but later sovereigns mobilized the resources and charisma of religion to bolster imperial rule.

The Orthodox Church, for its part, was deeply influenced by secular trends and struggled to adjust to the changing political context. As an institution, Gregory Freeze has argued, it was in some ways enhanced by incorporation into the state. The Holy Synod centralized and streamlined the clerical chain of command and presided over the restructuring of ecclesiastical administration. The hierarchs were able to exercise more effective control over subordinates and over practical affairs. In contrast to their predecessors, eighteenth-century prelates were well-educated, worldly men. Under the thumb of this sophisticated elite, the ordinary priesthood, by contrast, suffered from inappropriate and inadequate training, economic hardship, and all too close an association with the reality of village life.[19] If the average parish priest did not experience a cultural transformation, the Church as a whole emerged from the state-imposed changes better able to function in an increasingly rationalized public sphere.

In the Muscovite era, the Orthodox Church had been more independent but also closely implicated in legitimating princely rule. In Peter's wake, religion continued to provide the tsars with support and justification. The new symbiosis demonstrated, however, that both church and state had changed. What Viktor Zhivov calls the "cultural synthesis of absolutism" began to crystallize in the mid-eighteenth century. It incorporated both spiritual and secular forms of expression into a unified court culture symbolizing the all-pervasive character of the autocratic regime.[20]

---

[17] Robert Pinkerton, *The Present State of the Greek Church in Russia, or, A Summary of Christian Divinity; by Platon, late Metropolitan of Moscow.* Translated from the Slavonian. With a Preliminary Memoir on the Ecclesiastical Establishment in Russia; and an Appendix, Containing an Account of the Origin and Different Sects of Russian Dissenters (New York: Collins, 1815), 26.

[18] Georges Florovsky, *Puti russkogo bogosloviia* (Paris: YMCA, 1937); translated as *Ways of Russian Theology*, ed. Richard S. Haugh, trans. Robert L. Nichols, 2 vols. (Belmont, Mass.: Nordland, 1979), 1:114.

[19] Gregory L. Freeze, *The Russian Levites: Parish Clergy in the Eighteenth Century* (Cambridge, Mass.: Harvard University Press, 1977).

[20] Zhivov, *Iazyk*, 368–69. For other approaches to the synthesis, see Stephen Lessing Baehr, *The Paradise Myth of Eighteenth-Century Russia: Utopian Patterns in Early Secular*

Under Catherine the Great, bishops educated in Western thought shaped a spiritual vocabulary compatible with Enlightenment principles of morality and rational exposition. Men of letters as well as churchmen forged a literary language that blended elements of Church Slavonic and the vernacular; the production of sermons, on the one hand, and dictionaries, on the other, testified to the existence of an "enlightened Orthodoxy," in which faith and reason found common ground. Metropolitan Gavriil (Petrov) (1730–1801), for example, preached in a Protestant vein; Archpriest Petr Alekseev (1727–1801) helped compose the Academy dictionary of the Russian literary language, which drew on sacred as well as secular texts for linguistic models.[21]

Enlisting elements of Orthodoxy in the project of state-sponsored culture (the "mirage" of official Enlightenment, in Zhivov's phrase),[22] Catherine nevertheless continued Peter's policy of undermining the institutional autonomy of the Church. The confiscation of Church lands had a particularly damaging effect on the monasteries, which she viewed, in the Petrine spirit, as parasites on the social organism.[23] She promoted the reform of religious education and resisted the Church's efforts to persecute false belief. Her tolerance for Old Believers and heretics, as well as her support for minority confessions,[24] had little to do, however, with civil rights. A pragmatic response suited her cameralist attitude toward governance. Religious conflict threatened social tranquility. Persecution confirmed "fanatics" in their zeal, and fanaticism itself was detrimental. Also with an eye to the general welfare, Catherine preferred the priesthood to the monks and hierarchs, valuing the priests' pastoral ministry as a social service.[25]

Despite their connection to the contemplative life, the monks were more powerful than the priests in both the political and ecclesiastical spheres. In resisting the monarch's demands, they had more to lose. Metropolitan Arsenii (Matseevich) (1697–1772) was detonsured and exiled for protesting

Russian Literature and Culture (Stanford: Stanford University Press, 1991); Marcus C. Levitt, "The Rapprochement between Secular and Religious Culture in Mid-to-Late Eighteenth-Century Russia" (unpublished paper, Tenth International Congress of the Enlightenment, Dublin, July 1999; courtesy of the author).

[21] Zhivov, *Iazyk*, 372–76, 403–6.

[22] Ibid., 375.

[23] On confiscation, see Isabel de Madariaga, *Russia in the Age of Catherine the Great* (New Haven, Conn.: Yale University Press, 1981), 111–22.

[24] Isabel de Madariaga, *Politics and Culture in Eighteenth-Century Russia* (London: Addison Wesley Longman, 1998), 90–91; Robert D. Crews, *For Prophet and Tsar: Islam and Empire in Russia and Central Asia* (Cambridge, Mass.: Harvard University Press, 2006).

[25] Olga A. Tsapina, "Secularization and Opposition in the Time of Catherine the Great," in *Religion and Politics in Enlightenment Europe,* ed. Dale Van Kley and James E. Bradley (Notre Dame, Ind.: University of Notre Dame Press, 2001), 334–89; idem, "The Image of the Quaker and Critique of Enthusiasm in Early Modern Russia," *Russian History* 24, no. 3 (1997): 251–77.

against the seizure of monastery lands, and his example had the desired inhibiting effect on his colleagues.[26] A knowledgeable foreigner described Catherine's dilemma in promoting a secular agenda:

> The monastic order...cannot be altogether abolished among the Russians, without an essential change in the constitution of their church; for the higher ranks of the clergy can only be chosen from amongst the monks. On this account, it is an object of great importance to the government, that such men should enter into this order, as may afterwards prove worthy the offices of spiritual fathers and rulers of the people.[27]

Indeed, Catherine improved the quality of the episcopal elite by appointing talented men of intellectual stature. Metropolitan Platon (Levshin) (1737–1812) was educated in the Slavonic-Greek-Latin Academy, along with the future luminaries of secular culture, the poet Vasilii Trediakovskii (1703–1769) and the scientist Mikhail Lomonosov (1711–1765). Favored by Catherine for his learning, Platon was proficient in Latin and French. He impressed foreigners with his intellectual breadth, spirit of tolerance (toward Old Believers, though not toward Catholics or Jews), and rhetorical skills. Emperor Joseph II (1741–1790), on a visit to Russia, remarked that Platon was "plus philosophe que prêtre." His sermons and compositions were translated into foreign languages, published abroad and admired, by Voltaire among others, for their stylistic polish. In a sermon at the tomb of Peter the Great, delivered to celebrate the Russian victory over the Turks in 1770, Platon extolled that emperor's achievements.[28]

Despite his Western training and loyalty to the throne, Platon defended the autonomy of spiritual values. He resented the extent to which the monarch dominated Church governance by manipulating the membership and policies of the Holy Synod. Together with Gavriil, another of Catherine's protégés, he championed the importance of Orthodox mystical asceticism, of which the empress did not approve. This posture also set him at odds with outspoken defenders of the priesthood such as Archpriest Petr Alekseev. Conversant with Western theology, especially the Presbyterian brand, Alekseev attacked the hierarchs, endorsed Catherine's anti-monasticism, and proposed a Protestant-style reorganization of the priesthood along professional lines.[29]

---

[26] *Polnyi pravoslavnyi bogoslovskii entsiklopedicheskii slovar'*, 2 vols. (St. Petersburg: P. P. Soikin, 1913), 1:231–32; K. A. Papmehl, *Metropolitan Platon of Moscow (Petr Levshin, 1737–1812): The Enlightened Prelate, Scholar and Educator* (Newtonville, Mass.: Oriental Research Partners, 1983), 34.

[27] Pinkerton, "Preliminary Memoir," 23.

[28] Papmehl, *Metropolitan Platon*, 24, 79, 106.

[29] Tsapina, "Secularization and Opposition."

Clearly the division between Enlightenment and spirituality did not run simply between church and state, nor did it sharply distinguish priests and bishops. It sometimes even bisected individual souls. A loyal practitioner of enlightened court rhetoric and a graduate, along with Platon, of the Slavonic-Greek-Latin Academy dominated by a Latin-based curriculum, Metropolitan Gavriil was at the same time a devotee of asceticism, who promoted the patristic legacy and sponsored the monastic revival. Nor were spiritual and rational always distinct in the lay world. The most famous of the eighteenth-century Russian civic enlighteners, Nikolai Novikov, was initially encouraged by Catherine in his socially constructive activities (charity, publishing, and education) but was later punished for his association with the mystical Martinist branch of Freemasonry. Metropolitan Platon defended him as a good Christian, but Catherine was nervous in the wake of the French Revolution about the political consequences of the Enlightenment and retracted her earlier support. Novikov's ventures represented, to some extent, the emancipation of cultural expression from state tutelage, and because Catherine considered culture a matter of state, his independence was his undoing.[30] The mysticism with which he was charged also made him politically suspect, since it was associated with the monastic elite.

By the Napoleonic period, the political balance had shifted. The religious enthusiasm that captivated Alexander I and his court signaled the collapse of the Catherinian cultural synthesis. Like their contemporaries abroad, educated Russians were disillusioned with Enlightenment ideals. They turned, however, not to standard-issue Orthodoxy but to European-style mysticism instead. Alexander's own inclinations led him to embrace a Romantic Pietism. Prince Aleksandr Golitsyn (1773–1844), appointed to head the Holy Synod, shared the tsar's spiritual tastes.[31] The days of "enlightened Orthodoxy" were over, but for all their pious rhetoric, subsequent tsars were no less instrumental in promoting the faith than the anticlerical Peter and Catherine. The aggressively conservative Nicholas I valued the Orthodox Church as an arm of the state, not as the repository of absolute truth.[32] In his reign, the procurator of the Holy Synod radically curtailed the bishops' powers; tightened the censorship of religious ideas, thus stifling the Church's own intellectual development; and reoriented the clergy toward a more pragmatic, less sacramental role.[33] Coping with defeat in the Crimean War, Alexander II liberated the serfs and instituted

[30] Zhivov, *Iazyk,* 371–72, 425–26.

[31] See Alexander M. Martin, *Romantics, Reformers, Reactionaries: Russian Conservative Thought and Politics in the Reign of Alexander I* (DeKalb: Northern Illinois University Press, 1997).

[32] Andrei Zorin, "Ideologiia 'Pravoslaviia-Samoderzhaviia-Narodnosti': Opyt rekonstruktsii," *Novoe literaturnoe obozrenie* 26 (1997): 71–104.

[33] Gregory L. Freeze, *The Parish Clergy in Nineteenth-Century Russia: Crisis, Reform, Counter-Reform* (Princeton: Princeton University Press, 1983), 16–18, 45.

the Great Reforms, endowing Russia with a modern judiciary and institutions of local self-government, and also improved the conditions of clerical life. Following his father's assassination, Alexander III reversed course, presenting himself in archaic terms as a national monarch, surrounded by religious pageantry and cloaked in traditionalist garb.[34] The deeply devout Nicholas II, whose regime was buffeted by social unrest and elite discontent, continued in the same vein, orchestrating the canonization of saints as a device for bolstering popular support.[35]

In the face of social and institutional change, the language and symbols of religion were read as continuous with the past, yet the Church itself was not unaffected by shifts in the culture at large. Nor was it insulated from foreign influences. Building on earlier contacts with Western Christianity, eighteenth-century Russian seminaries exposed their students to contemporary philosophy and spiritual trends such as Pietism. Metropolitans Platon (Levshin) and Filaret (Drozdov) (1782–1867) selectively invoked Western ideas for their own purposes.[36] Indeed, Filaret's career demonstrates the contradictory cross-currents that swept Russian politics and culture in the first half of the nineteenth century, when he was the Church's most authoritative spokesman. In sponsoring the translation of the Bible from Slavonic into the vernacular, he reflected the Protestant influence that permeated the seminaries, an influence reinforced by the foreign Bible missionaries who flocked to St. Petersburg during the reign of Alexander I.[37] The Alexandrine years were a time, as Florovsky complains, when "the [Russian] soul completely gave itself over to Europe."[38] Under Nicholas I, however, Filaret was dismissed from his position in the Holy Synod, partly for having supported the translation project, of which the energetic and conservative procurator disapproved.[39]

But although Filaret promoted scholarship and the spread of religious knowledge, he was no liberal.[40] The author of the proclamation announcing

---

[34] See Wortman, *Scenarios of Power,* Vol. 2, pt. 2.

[35] Gregory L. Freeze, "Subversive Piety: Religion and the Political Crisis in Late Imperial Russia," *Journal of Modern History* 68 (1996): 308–50.

[36] *Polnyi pravoslavnyi bogoslovskii entsiklopedicheskii slovar',* 2:1812–13, 2231–32; Robert L. Nichols, "Orthodoxy and Russia's Enlightenment, 1762–1825," in *Russian Orthodoxy under the Old Regime,* ed. Robert L. Nichols and Theofanis George Stavrou (Minneapolis: University of Minnesota Press, 1978), 67–89; Florovsky, *Ways of Russian Theology,* 141–46, 201–20, 331.

[37] Florovsky, *Ways of Russian Theology,* 213; Stephen K. Batalden, "Printing the Bible in the Reign of Alexander I: Toward a Reinterpretation of the Imperial Bible Society," in *Church, Nation, and State in Russia and Ukraine,* ed. Geoffrey A. Hosking (Houndmills, Basingstoke: Macmillan, 1991), 65–78.

[38] Florovsky, *Ways of Russian Theology,* 162.

[39] Freeze, *Parish Clergy,* 19, 23, 34–35.

[40] See M. S. Korzun, "Gosudarstvenno-pravoslavnaia sotsial'naia doktrina v svete uchenii mitropolitov Platona i Filareta," in *Spornye problemy istorii russkoi obshchestvennoi mysli*

the emancipation of the serfs (an act he personally opposed), he was a stubborn defender of corporal punishment and came increasingly to resist any attempt at Church reform, an issue that gained widespread endorsement in the 1860s.[41] But even his opposition to change connected him to current trends. As the Anglican dean Arthur Penrhyn Stanley (1815–1881) remarked in 1862, "the venerable Metropolitan of Moscow, represents, in some measure at least, the effect of that vast wave of reactionary feeling which...has passed over the whole of Europe."[42] In the Russian context, moreover, the lines between modern and traditional were not clearly drawn. Under the banner of political and cultural conservatism, Nicholas I sponsored reforms intended to professionalize the priesthood and diminish the power of bishops, who were castigated for their Westernized views.[43] Despite his conflict with the secular authorities, Filaret expressed a similar mixture of resistance and adaptation to the cultural and institutional demands of a changing world.[44]

Another attempt to strengthen the Church in modern times by drawing on tradition can be discerned in the revival of monasticism that occurred in the last decades of the eighteenth century. Peter the Great had tried to convert the monasteries into charitable organizations. Catherine's confiscation of Church lands in 1764 drastically reduced the monasteries' power and number.[45] It did not take long, however, for some of the remaining sites to become centers of spiritual renewal. Charismatic men of the cloth, such as the monk Paisii Velichkovskii (1722–1794), revitalized the Greek tradition of spiritual elders (*starchestvo*) and produced an inspirational literature drawn from hesychast sources. Hesychasm was a form of contemplative Orthodox mysticism that stressed the worshiper's inward mental focus and outward stillness. Repetition of the Jesus Prayer, an appeal for God's mercy mumbled continuously under one's breath, was designed to connect the supplicant with the Holy Spirit.[46] It is easy to forget, how-

---

(*do nachala XIX veka*) (Moscow: Rossiiskaia akademiia nauk, Institut rossiiskoi istorii, 1992), 49–52.

[41] See Freeze, *Parish Clergy*, 23–24. See also the hostile remarks in Michael T. Florinsky, *Russia: A History and an Interpretation*, 2 vols. (New York: Macmillan, 1953), 2:888, 906. For a sympathetic treatment, see Robert Lewis Nichols, "Metropolitan Filaret of Moscow and the Awakening of Orthodoxy" (Ph.D. diss., University of Washington, 1972).

[42] Arthur Penrhyn Stanley, *Lectures on the History of the Eastern Church*, 2nd ed. (New York: Scribner's, 1862), 525.

[43] Freeze, *Parish Clergy*, 17.

[44] On how Filaret's image and reputation evolved, see O. E. Maiorova, "Mitropolit moskovskii Filaret v obshchestvennom soznanii kontsa XIX veka," in *Lotmanskii sbornik*, ed. E. V. Permiakov, 2 vols. (Moscow: ITS-Garant, 1994–1997), 2:615–38.

[45] Mitr. Trifon (Turkestanov), *Drevnekhristianskie i optinskie startsy* (Moscow: Martis, 1997), 146–49.

[46] On the monk and theologian Gregory Palamas (1296–1359), with whom this tradition is connected, see John Meyendorff, "Introduction," in Gregory Palamas, *The Triads*, ed. John

ever, that the hesychast tradition needed to be resurrected before it became widely known. The compilation of texts by the Eastern Church Fathers called the *Philokalia*, from which these practices were drawn, was first published in Greek in 1782, translated into Slavonic by Velichkovskii in 1793, under the sponsorship of Metropolitan Gavriil, and into the vernacular Russian only in 1894.[47] Metropolitan Platon, praised by Joseph II as a "philosophe," rebuilt the sixteenth-century Optina Hermitage, which had since fallen into disuse, and it became the focal point of the contemplative style. The style's inspiration, however, was not purely Orthodox in origin. As Robert Nichols puts it, "The contemplative life rediscovered on Mount Athos... was not and could not be in Russia a simple recovery of an earlier Eastern Orthodox mystical and eremitical tradition. Rather, the awakening included those elements but it also owed something to Catholicism and Protestant pietism."[48] Starchestvo, as Vladimir Lossky (1903–1958) remarks, was "at once so traditional and so surprising in its novelty."[49]

The revived eldership was indeed a synthesis, not only of Western and Eastern Christian themes but also of the contemplative and energetic mission. Though the elders emerged in answer to the aggressive secularism of the eighteenth century, they did not preach withdrawal from the world. Perhaps reflecting prevalent Enlightenment views, they counseled a spiritual life that encouraged engagement as well as retreat. Catherine the Great took charity out of the hands of the Church and created new institutions to oversee relief for the poor. It was, however, as Adele Lindenmeyr points out, a religious ethos that motivated the charitable undertakings of nineteenth-century polite society.[50] Caring for the poor involved the participation of laypeople as well as monastics, and, in this sense, the traditionalist elders, in leading the worldly back to God, encouraged them to connect with the world.

The Orthodox Church thus entered the nineteenth century with an intellectual elite steeped in Western learning but determined to shape a native

Meyendorff, trans. Nicholas Gendle (New York: Paulist Press, 1983). See also Timothy Ware, *The Orthodox Church*, rev. ed. (London: Penguin, 1993), 62–70.

[47] Abbott Gleason, *European and Muscovite: Ivan Kireevsky and the Origins of Slavophilism* (Cambridge, Mass.: Harvard University Press, 1972), 321; Zhivov, *Iazyk*, 375.

[48] Robert L. Nichols, "The Orthodox Elders (*Startsy*) of Imperial Russia," *Modern Greek Studies Yearbook* 1 (1985): 8, 3–6 (quote).

[49] Vladimir Lossky, "Les Starets d'Optino," in Vladimir Lossky and Nicolas Arseniev, *La Paternité spirituelle en Russie aux XVIIIème et XIXème siècles* (Bégrolles-en-Mauge: Abbaye de Bellefontaine, 1977), 93. In *Brat'ia Karamazovy* (1880), Dostoevskii reminds his readers that the figure of Father Zosima, based on the Optina elders, represents a type of devotion only recently revived: Fyodor Dostoevsky, *The Brothers Karamazov*, trans. Richard Pevear and Larissa Volokhonsky (New York: Vintage, 1991), 27. See chapter 5 for more on this figure.

[50] Adele Lindenmeyr, *Poverty Is Not a Vice: Charity, Society, and the State in Imperial Russia* (Princeton: Princeton University Press, 1996).

cultural style. Nicholas I shared the nativism but repudiated the model of the West. In his reign, piety was attached to imperial ideology, not, as was the case under Catherine the Great, in order to enlist churchmen in the enterprise of enlightenment. Nicholas, on the contrary, borrowed the aura of stability and continuity associated with a purportedly unchanging national faith for purposes of state. Whereas Catholic conversion and mystical enthusiasm had been the fashion in the court of Alexander I, Nicholas determined to restore the prestige of Orthodoxy among the cultural elite. This same desire was also evident in some aristocratic circles, but intellectuals resented the monarch's heavy-handed intrusion into Church affairs and the restrictions he imposed on free expression.

It was in this context that the Slavophiles developed their model of opposing types, pitting the rational West against the spiritual East, the heartless engine of absolutism against the organic wholeness of the Orthodox Church. They welcomed Russia's resistance to the inroads of modernity and hailed the persistence of archetypes derived from the principles of the Eastern faith. In their eyes, the communalism of the peasant world replicated in social terms the merging of self-in-spirit of the Orthodox religious community. Aleksei Khomiakov used the term *sobornost'* to describe this type of harmonious spiritual life, which he understood to be the antithesis of both Western individualism and the authoritarian Roman Church. Indeed, the concept of sobornost' became shorthand for what was distinctive about the Russian culture that Peter the Great had not managed to legislate away. In the words of Nikolai Berdiaev (1874–1948), a prominent figure in the early twentieth-century Orthodox revival: "The Slavophiles not only defined our national consciousness as religious in spirit and purpose, but formulated the basic theme of East and West. This theme suffused the entire intellectual life of nineteenth-century Russia."[51]

Whatever they may have cherished, however, about the real or imagined past, the Slavophiles' style of thinking was neither archaic nor specifically Russian. Like their debating partners, the so-called Westernizers, they received an excellent European education and read German philosophy. Andrzej Walicki describes them as Romantic conservatives.[52] Enamored of folk simplicity, they were not in principle hostile to science, which they considered a different, if more limited, mode of apperception than religious inspiration.[53] Ivan Kireevskii's pious father, an eccentric landed gentleman,

[51] Nikolai Berdiaev, *Aleksei Stepanovich Khomiakov* (Moscow: Put', 1912), 28. See also B. F. Egorov, V. A. Kotel'nikov, and Iu. V. Stennik, eds., *Slavianofil'stvo i sovremennost': Sbornik statei* (St. Petersburg: Nauka, 1994).

[52] Andrzej Walicki, *The Slavophile Controversy: History of a Conservative Utopia in Nineteenth-Century Russian Thought*, trans. Hilda Andrews-Rusiecka (Oxford: Clarendon, 1975).

[53] Letter from I. V. Kireevskii to A. S. Khomiakov, 15 July 1840, quoted in *Polnoe sobranie sochinenii I. V. Kireevskogo v dvukh tomakh*, ed. M. Gershenzon, 2 vols. (Moscow: Tip. Moskovskogo universiteta, 1911), 1:67.

Fig. 1. Aleksei Khomiakov. *Polnoe sobranie sochinenii Alekseia Stepanovicha Khomiakova* [Complete Works of Aleksei Stepanovich Khomiakov], 3rd ed. rev., 2 vols. (Moscow: Universitetskaia tipografiia, 1900), vol. 1: frontispiece. Courtesy Sterling Memorial Library, Yale University.

had a fascination with chemistry and medicine.[54] Raised in a European-oriented household, Khomiakov was the inventor of a steam engine, patented in England, which he displayed in London at the Great Exhibition of 1851.[55] Dean Stanley remarked that Khomiakov combined "devotion to his ancestral belief with a fearless spirit of inquiry both into ecclesiastical and sacred records. He was fully versed in German theology.... He himself entered freely into the difficulties raised of late by Biblical criticism. Yet he never wavered in his faith and practice as an 'Orthodox Christian.' "[56]

Their unabashed piety may have impressed English divines, but it made the Slavophiles feel out of place at home. Khomiakov commented in 1846 that he was not too old to have "seen the day when it was publicly either scoffed at or at least treated with manifest contempt by [too many in] our [high] society; when [I] myself, who was bred in a religious family and have never been ashamed of adhering strictly to the rites of the Church, was either supposed a sycophant or considered as a disguised Romanist; for nobody supposed the possibility of civilization and Orthodoxy being united."[57]

They were not, however, ordinary churchgoers, any more than they were complacent monarchists. Despite their philosophical conservatism, they were critical of the absolutist regime and of the institution of serfdom. Wishing to separate the Orthodox legacy from its involvement in structures of rule, they sometimes espoused contradictory positions. The Aksakovs, for example, distrusted Filaret (Drozdov) because of his closeness to power, although they respected his talents and mind. They also championed Russia's role as defender of Orthodoxy during the Crimean War.[58] Ivan Kireevskii found a partial solution to this dilemma in the Optina elders, who offered a point of contact with formal religion, while allowing him to keep a safe distance from the Church in its official role. His wife was close to the monk Filaret (Novospasskii) (1758–1842), whose influence helped precipitate her husband's "conversion" from casual to intense involvement in the faith. Kireevskii later collaborated with the

[54] Gleason, *European and Muscovite*, 9.

[55] W. J. Birkbeck, ed., *Russia and the English Church during the Last Fifty Years, Containing a Correspondence between Mr. William Palmer, Fellow of Magdalen College, Oxford, and M. Khomiakoff, in the Years 1844–1854* (London: Published for the Eastern Church Association [by] Rivington, Percival, 1895), 107. On his many talents, see V. A. Koshelev, "Paradoksy Khomiakova," in A. S. Khomiakov, *Sochineniia v dvukh tomakh*, Vol. 1, *Raboty po istoriosofii* (Moscow: Moskovskii filosofskii fond, Izd-vo "Medium," Zhurnal Voprosy filosofii, 1994), 4. On his upbringing, see N. N. Mazur, "K rannei biografii A. S. Khomiakova (1810–1820)," in Permiakov, *Lotmanskii sbornik*, 2:195–223.

[56] Stanley, *Lectures*, 526.

[57] Birkbeck, *Russia and the English Church*, 71 (bracketed words in text).

[58] N. V. Golitsyn and P. E. Shchegolev, eds., *Dnevnik Very Sergeevny Aksakovoi, 1853–1855* (St. Petersburg: Ogni, 1913), 16, 20, 73.

Optina elder Father Makarii (Ivanov) (1788–1860) in translating the writings of the Church Fathers.[59]

Most interesting of all, perhaps, in trying to gauge the relationship between spiritual revival and the modern spirit is to position the Slavophiles in relation to like-minded thinkers in the West, those nineteenth-century Europeans who also took religion seriously and made it the center of their moral and intellectual lives. The case of Khomiakov is instructive. The exact contemporary of John Henry Newman (1801–1890), he corresponded with William Palmer (1811–1879), one of the Oxford Tractarians. The two exchanged opinions about Christianity in its various incarnations and about Russia in particular. Khomiakov had written a series of theological essays in French, first published abroad to avoid censorship restrictions and only later translated into Russian.[60] His letters to Palmer were written in superb Victorian English.

The members of the Oxford movement were in a situation somewhat analogous to that of the Slavophiles: as intellectuals and pious men, they resented the established Church's subordination to secular authority, from which its privileged position derived. As patriots, however, they sought a spiritual outcome that was in some sense still national but also universal. They debated only where this "catholic" principle might lie. Nor did they see the search for spiritual continuity as a flight from the present. At a moment when many of their contemporaries had abandoned religion, they expected traditional forms to satisfy a contemporary need.

The preoccupations of the Slavophiles are usually discussed in terms of Russia's internal dialogues and dilemmas or as an example of the appropriation of Western styles of thought. They can also be seen as part of an international conversation on the nature of modern Christianity. Indeed, Jaroslav Pelikan, in his history of Christian doctrine, uses the term "sobornost" as the heading for his chapter on nineteenth-century ecclesiology. "A sign of its [Eastern Orthodoxy's] increasing influence [in the nineteenth century]," he writes, "was the adoption, as almost a technical term, of the Russian word 'sobornost' by Western theologians of many linguistic and denominational traditions." In the sense of distinguishing "Eastern ecclesiology from both the 'papal monarchy' of Roman Catholicism and the 'sola Scriptura' of Protestantism," the term sobornost', he explains, "entered the vocabulary and the thought world of the West."[61] While recognizing

[59] Nicolas Arseniev, *La Sainte Moscou: Tableau de la vie religieuse et intellectuelle russe au XIXe siècle* (Paris: Éditions du Cerf, 1948), 66, 69, 75; Gleason, *European and Muscovite*, 139–41, 236–57.

[60] See commentary in A. S. Khomiakov, *Sochineniia v dvukh tomakh*, Vol. 2, *Raboty po bogosloviiu* (Moscow: Moskovskii filosofskii fond, Izd-vo "Medium," Zhurnal Voprosy filosofii, 1994), 350–53.

[61] Jaroslav Pelikan, *Christian Doctrine and Modern Culture (Since 1700)* (Chicago: University of Chicago Press, 1989), 287.

these differences, Western theologians were interested in the search for common ground. Palmer, for example, argued for the harmony between Anglican and Orthodox doctrine in a book published in 1846. He sent complimentary copies of the book not only to Khomiakov but also to Metropolitan Filaret and others in Moscow.[62]

Khomiakov, for his part, emphasized difference. Conceiving the ideal church as disconnected from the exercise of worldly power, he praised the timeless "ark of Orthodoxy," which, unlike the contentious Protestants and Catholics, "alone rides safe and unhurt through storms and billows."[63] This model of detachment allowed his ideas to survive their original context and elicit a prolonged intellectual response. As part of a continuing dialogue with the past, the priest and philosopher-theologian Pavel Florenskii (1882–1937) took Khomiakov to task for inventing the religion he wished to believe in. Nikolai Berdiaev observed that, while Khomiakov stressed the principle of love and the believer's creative inner spirit, Florenskii more accurately identified the historical Church with the principle of authority.[64]

Despite variations in their response to the Slavophile paradigm or to Khomiakov's ideas, thinkers in this neo-theological vein understand him as a creative mind, working with a cultural (and specifically religious) legacy to fashion something new. They themselves bridge the distance between modern and traditional styles of thought. A remarkable polymath, Florenskii wrote on geometry, art history, and linguistics, as well as religion; he edited the Soviet *Tekhnicheskaia entsiklopediia* (*Technical Encyclopedia*) from 1927 to 1933.[65] The difficulties in separating East from West, and modern from archaic, are vividly demonstrated, however, by the less edifying dimension of Florenskii's worldview. As revealed in recently disclosed archival material, he held violently anti-Semitic opinions that he conveyed privately to the openly anti-Semitic Vasilii Rozanov (1856–1919).[66] Crude

---

[62] *A Harmony of Anglican Doctrine with the Doctrine of the Catholic and Apostolic Church of the East* (Aberdeen, U.K.: A. Brown, 1846), cited in Birkbeck, *Russia and the English Church*, 41–42.

[63] Birkbeck, *Russia and the English Church*, 71.

[64] N. A. Berdiaev, "Khomiakov i sviashch. Florenskii," in *P. A. Florenskii: Pro et contra: Lichnost' i tvorchestvo Pavla Florenskogo v otsenke russkikh myslitelei i issledovatelei: Antologiia*, ed. K. G. Isupov (St. Petersburg: Izd-vo Russkogo khristianskogo gumanitarnogo instituta, 1996), 380–89.

[65] See Peyton Engel, "Background," in *Russian Religious Thought*, ed. Judith Deutsch Kornblatt and Richard F. Gustafson (Madison: University of Wisconsin Press, 1994), 91–94.

[66] See "Prilozhenie vtoroe" and notes to *Oboniatel'noe i osiazatel'noe otnoshenie evreev k krovi (1914)*, in V. V. Rozanov, *Sakharna*, ed. A. N. Nikoliukin (Moscow: Izd. "Respublika," 1998), 356–68, 337–38. Also, Michael Hagemeister and Torsten Metelka, eds., *Materialien zu Pavel Florenskij*, 2 vols. (Berlin: Edition Kontext, 1999, 2001), vol. 2. For a range of views on Rozanov, see V. A. Fateev, ed., *V. V. Rozanov: Pro et contra: Lichnost' i tvorchestvo Vasiliia Rozanova v otsenke russkikh myslitelei i issledovatelei: Antologiia*, 2 vols. (St. Petersburg: Russkii khristianskii gumanitarnii institut, 1995).

anti-Semitism was not exclusive to Russia, of course. Sergei Nilus (1862–1929), who published the so-called *Protokoly sionskich mudretsov* (*Protocols of the Elders of Zion*) (1905), was inspired by material from the contemporary West.[67] Nor were these views a relic of the distant past. Anti-Semitism, as a political ideology, attained a new virulence at the turn of the twentieth century. The *Protocols* has maintained its popularity well into the present.

Whatever else Florenskii may have believed, he seems to have resolved the tension that A. N. Wilson charts for the Victorian age, when science appeared to threaten religion with extinction. In Russia, too, the challenge presented by the views of Charles Darwin (1809–1882) led to crisis and debate. *On the Origin of Species* (1859) and *Descent of Man* (1871) were quickly translated into Russian.[68] Russian scientists and social thinkers met the challenge in two ways. Those who accepted the basic concept of the struggle for existence tended to modify its individualistic cast to include various forms of cooperation or group cohesion.[69] Those who rejected Darwin's ideas in turn took two alternative tacks. In religious circles some critics questioned the scientific enterprise itself; others used the authority of science to find fault with Darwin's methods. They insisted, however, on the need for Orthodoxy to address the challenge science posed.[70] In joining the debate, as Alexander Vucinich points out, theologians "involve[d] the church in the discussion of modern knowledge."[71] This discussion was part of a wide-ranging display of opinions and exchange of ideas in the pages of the many religious journals founded in the wake of the Great Reforms, paralleling the expansion of the secular press.[72]

This discussion had an obviously political side. On the one hand, the post-Reform generation of radical intellectuals espoused a credo of empiricism, materialism, utilitarianism, and anticlericalism. All that was "tradition" had to go. On the other, conservatives such as Fedor Dostoevskii (1821–1881) attacked the so-called nihilists on religious grounds. Nikolai

---

[67] See Michael Hagemeister, "Eine Apokalypse unserer Zeit: Die Prophezeiungen des heiligen Serafim von Sarov über das Kommen des Antichrist und das Ende der Welt," in *Finis mundi: Endzeiten und Weltenden im östlichen Europa,* ed. Joachim Hosler and Wolfgang Kessler (Stuttgart: F. Steiner Verlag, 1998), 41–60.

[68] Alexander Vucinich, *Darwin in Russian Thought* (Berkeley: University of California Press, 1988), 100.

[69] See Daniel P. Todes, *Darwin without Malthus: The Struggle for Existence in Russian Evolutionary Thought* (New York: Oxford University Press, 1989).

[70] See, for example, V. I. Dobrotvorskii, "O kharaktere prezhnego perioda nashei dukhovnoi zhurnalistiki i sovremennykh ee zadachakh," *Dukhovnyi vestnik* (April 1862): 446–77; idem, "Odin iz dukhovnykh nedugov v sovremennom obrazovannom obshchestve," *Dukhovnyi vestnik* (October 1862): 191–223.

[71] Vucinich, *Darwin,* 107.

[72] See Robert H. Davis, "Nineteenth-Century Russian Religious-Theological Journals: Structure and Access," *St. Vladimir's Theological Quarterly* 33, no. 3 (1989): 235–59.

Danilevskii (1822–1885) made the case that Darwin's vision of ruthless competition, no less than his relentless materialism, was peculiarly English. Indeed, Danilevskii viewed science itself as an essential component of European culture. He defined Russia, by contrast, in spiritual terms. That Danilevskii was a practicing scientist (a member of the Imperial Russian Geographical Society, he was an expert on fish) only gave his objections more weight. Philosophers and theologians who defended the Russian legacy while remaining open to modern ideas thus found common ground with more intransigent thinkers such as Konstantin Leont'ev (1831–1891), who insisted that rationalism was a Western flaw.[73] In the middle stood moderate liberals who envisioned a modern culture that respected the methods of science but also embraced the higher truths of religion. "Progressive people feel obliged to treat religion with hostility or contempt," complained Boris Chicherin (1828–1904) in 1879. "Religion, along with philosophy, is seen as the obsolete remnant of infantile prejudices. But if anything is a sign of outmoded thinking," he remarked, "it is a purely negative attitude toward religion."[74]

In negotiating between scientific rationalism, on the one hand, and conventional piety, on the other, some people chose a middle course. In France and England, no less than in Russia, spiritualism and the occult were popular alternatives to both materialism and the established faiths. The theosophical movement was founded in 1875 by the Russian-born Helena Blavatsky (1831–1891), who at the time made her home in New York. In Russia, spiritism was embraced by the eminent folklorist, lexicographer, and defender of official Orthodoxy, Vladimir Dal' (1801–1872), who converted from Lutheranism on his deathbed. Its principles were elaborated by Aleksandr Aksakov (1823–1903), a junior member of the celebrated Slavophile family, who claimed to demonstrate its precepts in modern scientific terms. He was vigorously challenged by the famed chemist Dmitrii Mendeleev (1834–1904). The Russian Spiritualist Society organized a congress in Moscow in 1906. Many of the artists and writers of the Russian Silver Age were steeped in theosophical, anthroposophical, and spiritualist lore, and the last three tsars found the occult appealing. In this inclination, the Russian elites followed international fashion.[75] Out of date in Nicholas II's

[73] Vucinich, *Darwin*, chap. 4. See the positive review of Danilevskii's treatment of Darwin in the journal of the Kharkov Ecclesiastic Academy: I. Chistovich, "Darvinizm: Kriticheskoe issledovanie N. Ia. Danilevskogo," *Vera i razum: Zhurnal bogoslovsko-filosofskii* 2, pt. 1 (1886): 131–36.

[74] B. N. Chicherin, *Nauka i religiia* (Moscow: Martynov, 1879), v–vi.

[75] See Maria Carlson, *"No Religion Higher Than Truth": A History of the Theosophical Movement in Russia, 1875–1922* (Princeton: Princeton University Press, 1993), 23–26, 29. Having demonstrated that mystical and occult traditions originated in Europe, Carlson nevertheless endorses the stereotype of Russian culture that her evidence undermines: "Beneath that veneer [of rationalism introduced by Peter the Great] still lay the analogical, nonlinear,

reign was not the existence of Rasputin but the persistence of the autocratic regime.

The spiritual quest of fin-de-siècle Russians thus extended beyond the boundaries of Orthodox belief, while at the same time theological preoccupations penetrated lay culture. The Church, meanwhile, was buffeted by the same intellectual and political winds that affected educated society at large. The era of the Great Reforms stimulated arguments for innovation that echoed some of the themes developed by Archpriest Alekseev in the eighteenth century.[76] Pointing to the existence of Orthodox confraternities in pre-Petrine Russia, some clergymen used that model to restructure parish organization and draw the laity into spiritual and charitable work.[77] The revived confraternities mobilized tradition as a foundation on which to build something new: an arena in which the Church and the public could join in addressing social ills such as ignorance and destitution. Other forms of clerical activism included the intensified efforts of missionaries to convert domestic heathens and combat heresy, an impulse they shared with Western Christians, as Westerners approvingly observed.[78]

By the early twentieth century the intelligentsia included liberals who demanded freedom of conscience and philosophers who invited clergymen to join them in debate. The well-known story of the Religious-Philosophical Society is intimately connected with the flowering of the so-called Russian religious renaissance, associated with the names of Vladimir Solov'ev (1853–1900), Vasilii Rozanov, and Nikolai Berdiaev.[79] The Church hierarchy, meanwhile, persisted in opposing reform of the laws governing marriage and divorce. It resisted any attempt to reduce the privileges accorded

---

intuitive frame of mind that characterizes Russian thought even today" (ibid., 16). Also: Michael D. Gordin, *A Well-Ordered Thing: Dmitrii Mendeleev and the Shadow of the Periodic Table* (New York: Basic Books, 2004).

[76] See Freeze, *Parish Clergy;* I. S. Belliustin, *Description of the Clergy in Rural Russia: The Memoir of a Nineteenth-Century Parish Priest,* ed. Gregory L. Freeze (Ithaca: Cornell University Press, 1985); A. A. Papkov, *Tserkovno-obshchestvennye voprosy v epokhu tsaria-osvoboditelia (1855–1870)* (St. Petersburg: A. P. Lopukhin, 1902).

[77] Lindenmeyr, *Poverty Is Not a Vice,* 132–36; Papkov, *Tserkovno-obshchestvennye voprosy,* 53, 74–76. The diocesan gazettes (*eparkhial'nye vedomosti*), which began publishing in the 1860s, provide a record of the confraternities' activity.

[78] Stanley, *Lectures,* 525. See Eugene Smirnoff, *A Short Account of the Historical Development and Present Position of Russian Orthodox Missions* (London: Rivingtons, 1903); Robert P. Geraci and Michael Khodarkovsky, eds., *Of Religion and Empire: Missions, Conversion, and Tolerance in Tsarist Russia* (Ithaca: Cornell University Press, 2001).

[79] Jutta Scherrer, *Die Petersburger Religiös-Philosophischen Vereinigungen: Die Entwicklung des religiösen Selbstverständnisses ihrer Intelligencija-Mitglieder (1901–1917).* Forschungen zur Osteuropäischen Geschichte, Bd. 19 (Wiesbaden: Otto Harrassowitz, 1973); A. V. Sobolev, "K istorii religiozno-filosofskogo obshchestva pamiati Vladimira Solov'eva," *Istoriko-filosofskii ezhegodnik '92* (Moscow: Nauka, 1994): 102–14; Kristiane Burchardi, *Die Moskauer "Religiös-Philosophische Vladimir-Solov'ev-Gesellschaft" (1905–1918)* (Wiesbaden: Harrassowitz Verlag, 1998).

the official state religion, but the 1905 Revolution elicited calls for changes in the form of Church governance from within the clergy itself.[80]

Some myths, however, survive the contradictions they encompass: theologians criticizing Darwin on scientific grounds; scientists defending the logical necessity of divine creation; Slavophiles engaged in dialogue with Oxford intellectuals who reproached them for lacking missionary zeal; tsars enforcing respect for tradition while looking outside the Church for otherworldly support. But these eddies of contention affected only the surface of national life. Or so it seemed to the contenders. These same educated elites, so sensitive to the shifting currents of contemporary thought, were also partly responsible for the impression that, beyond the range of their journals and debates, Russia was a repository of untroubled faith, lodged in the uncorrupted common folk. The Slavophile insistence on Russia's historic continuity with the spirit of Eastern Christianity, facilitated precisely by the country's marginal relation to European culture, was a persistent trope, powerfully embodied in Dostoevskii's reactionary politics (contrasting so dramatically with his precociously modern prose) and rearticulated in Solzhenitsyn's stubbornly old-style nationalist ideal.[81] We return to the pious crone.

If there are grounds for supposing that imperial Russia resisted the impact of cultural modernity, it should be found in the peasant residuum, not in the complicated thought patterns of the intellectual elite. But the question of popular Orthodoxy is difficult to untangle. Modern scholarship is scanty, and the classics on the subject merely confirm their authors' Slavophile assumptions.[82] A renewed tendency to see the folk as permeated with an all-embracing Christian ethos emerges in some post-Soviet writing, in reaction to decades of denial and distortion.[83] To what extent the peasants

[80] Peter Waldron, "Religious Toleration in Late Imperial Russia," in *Civil Rights in Russia*, ed. Olga Crisp and Linda Edmondson (Oxford: Clarenden, 1989), 103–19; William G. Wagner, *Marriage, Property, and Law in Late Imperial Russia* (Oxford: Clarenden, 1993); John Meyendorff, "Russian Bishops and Church Reform in 1905," and Paul R. Valliere, "The Idea of a Council in Russian Orthodoxy in 1905," in Nichols and Stavrou, *Russian Orthodoxy under the Old Regime*, 183–201.

[81] For post-Soviet versions, see James P. Scanlan, "Interpretations and Uses of Slavophilism in Recent Russian Thought," in idem, *Russian Thought after Communism: The Recovery of a Philosophical Heritage* (Armonk, N.Y.: M. E. Sharpe, 1994), 31–61.

[82] G. P. Fedotov, *Stikhi dukhovnye: Russkaia narodnaia vera po dukhovnym stikham*, ed. A. L. Toporkov (Paris: YMCA, 1935; rpr. Moscow: Progress-Gnozis, 1991); Pierre Pascal, *Religion of the Russian People*, trans. Rowan Williams (London: Mowbrays, 1976); Andrei Siniavskii, *Ivan-durak: Ocherk russkoi narodnoi very* (Paris: Sintaksis, 1991); in English: Andrei Sinyavsky, *Ivan the Fool: Russian Folk Belief: A Cultural History*, trans. Joanne Turnbull and Nikolai Formozov (Moscow: Glas; [Chicago]: Distributed by Northwestern University Press, 2007). Siniavskii's politics cannot adequately be described as Slavophile, but his view of folk religion in this text reflects that tradition.

[83] See M. M. Gromyko, "O narodnom blagochestii u russkikh XIX veka," in *Pravoslavie i russkaia narodnaia kul'tura*, ed. M. M. Gromyko et al., Vol. 1 (Moscow:

were ignorant of doctrine, as the clergy often complained, or resourceful in shaping local and spontaneous versions of the faith is a question further research needs to ponder.[84]

Clearly, however, the religion practiced by Russian-speaking peasants revealed an inventiveness not always pleasing to the Church. Vera Shevzov has demonstrated that villagers were deeply attached to their parish institutions but also developed local forms of expression, which were sometimes tolerated and sometimes condemned.[85] Brenda Meehan has shown how pious women who withdrew from ordinary life without Church sanction might be recognized by their neighbors as especially devout.[86] Ordinary city dwellers, including factory workers, found new outlets for religious feeling. In St. Petersburg, the Orthodox priests Father Georgi Gapon and Father John of Kronstadt (1829–1908) attracted followers with a combination of old-style pastoral care and new-style welfare populism. Gapon built a social movement that precipitated the outbreak of revolution in 1905. Father John, by contrast, demonstrated complete loyalty to the established order. He combined the skills of the miracle-worker with those of the publicity-seeker to make himself an object of veneration in his lifetime.[87]

The most significant variation on Orthodoxy dramatically at odds with the norm was the Old Belief. Originating in the seventeenth century as a reaction among the clerical elite against innovations in liturgy and ritual imposed with the support of the tsar by Patriarch Nikon (1605–1681), its leaders defied the authority of both state and church. Adherents main-

Kooperatsionno-metodicheskii tsentr prikladnoi etnografii In-ta etnografii i antropologii RAN, 1993), 144–82; A. A. Panchenko, "Introduction," in *Issledovaniia v oblasti narodnogo pravoslaviia: Derevenskie sviatyni Severo-Zapada Rossii* (St. Petersburg: Aleteiia, 1998).

[84] See Gregory L. Freeze, "The Rechristianization of Russia: The Church and Popular Religion, 1750–1850," *Studia Slavica Finlandensia* 6 (1990): 101–36; Simon Dixon, "How Holy Was Holy Russia? Rediscovering Russian Religion," in *Reinterpreting Russia,* ed. Geoffrey Hosking and Robert Service (London: Arnold, 1999), 21–39; Chris J. Chulos, *Converging Worlds: Religion and Community in Peasant Russia, 1861–1917* (DeKalb: Northern Illinois University Press, 2003).

[85] Vera Shevzov, "Miracle-Working Icons, Laity, and Authority in the Russian Orthodox Church, 1861–1917," *Russian Review* 58 (1999): 26–48; idem, "Chapels and the Ecclesial World of Prerevolutionary Russian Peasants," *Slavic Review* 55, no. 3 (1996): 585–613; idem, *Russian Orthodoxy on the Eve of Revolution* (Oxford: Oxford University Press, 2004).

[86] Brenda Meehan, *Holy Women of Russia: The Lives of Five Orthodox Women Offer Spiritual Guidance for Today* (New York: Harper, 1993).

[87] Gerald D. Surh, "Petersburg's First Mass Labor Organization: The Assembly of Russian Workers and Father Gapon," *Russian Review* 40, no. 3 (1981): 241–62; no. 4 (1981): 412–41; Nadieszda Kizenko, *A Prodigal Saint: Father John of Kronstadt and the Russian People* (University Park: Pennsylvania State University Press, 2000). Also Mark D. Steinberg, "Workers on the Cross: Religious Imagination in the Writings of Russian Workers, 1910–1924," *Russian Review* 53 (1994): 213–39; Jennifer Hedda, *His Kingdom Come: Orthodox Pastorship and Social Activism in Revolutionary Russia* (DeKalb: Northern Illinois University Press, 2008).

tained their traditionalist beliefs in the face of vigorous persecution. Rejecting the very principle of change, they insisted on the sanctity of sacred rites
and objects. Their reverence for the precise wording of holy texts and for
ancient icons made them seem archaic or literal-minded to outsiders, but
the community eventually made peace with the world, engaging successfully in agriculture and trade, in which it showed remarkable realism and
adaptability.[88] By the twentieth century its members occupied every level
of the social hierarchy, from villagers to Moscow city councilmen. Some
forms of folk piety, such as the veneration of relics and faith in wonder-
working icons, could also be viewed as archaic, but these had the approval
of the Church.[89] Among groups the Church condemned, some were better
described as rationalistic. Certain mid-nineteenth-century Ukrainian peasants, for example, influenced by neighboring German settlers, adopted a
form of evangelical Lutheranism (*Shtundizm,* from the German "*Stunde*"),
and Baptism had a large following.[90]

Peasants, in short, were capable of various forms of religious expression. The Slavophile ideal may perhaps be found at some point in the
spectrum, but, considering the Russian-speaking people as a whole, no one
type does justice to the range. The Slavophiles liked to think that the core
of folk sensibility grew from age-old cultural roots. But even if we search
the Christian register for what seems to be the most archaic version of
all, we will find that it, too, responded to changes around it. Consider the
mystical ascetic community known as the *Skoptsy,* which practiced self-
castration.[91] Throughout the 150 years of the group's existence, from the
mid-eighteenth to the early-twentieth century, the Skoptsy were decried as
a throwback to a primitive age.[92] The ritual originated, however, no earlier

[88] See V. V. Rozanov, "Psikhologiia russkogo raskola," in idem, *Religiia i kul'tura: Sbornik
statei* (St. Petersburg: Pertsov-Merkushev, 1899). Also Manfred Hildermeier, "Alter Glaube
und neue Welt: Zur Sozialgeschichte des Raskol im 18. und 19. Jahrhundert," *Jahrbücher
für Geschichte Osteuropas* 38 (1990): 372–98, 504–25; Georg B. Michels, *At War with
the Church: Religious Dissent in Seventeenth-Century Russia* (Stanford: Stanford University
Press, 1999); Roy R. Robson, *Old Believers in Modern Russia* (DeKalb: Northern Illinois
University Press, 1995).

[89] The Church, however, was caught in the conflict of cultures. By the late nineteenth
century clergymen sometimes enlisted physicians to help verify the validity of miracle cures.
See Christine D. Worobec, *Possessed: Women, Witches, and Demons in Imperial Russia*
(DeKalb: Northern Illinois University Press, 2001), 56.

[90] Sergei I. Zhuk, *Russia's Lost Reformation: Peasants, Millennialism, and Radical Sects
in Southern Russia and Ukraine, 1830–1917* (Washington, D.C.: Woodrow Wilson Center
Press, 2004). Also Heather J. Coleman, *Russian Baptists and Spiritual Revolution, 1905–
1929* (Bloomington: Indiana University Press, 2005).

[91] See Laura Engelstein, *Castration and the Heavenly Kingdom: A Russian Folktale*
(Ithaca: Cornell University Press, 1999).

[92] For interpretations of the Skoptsy as archaic, see Claudio Sergio Ingerflom, "Commu-
nistes contre castrats (1929–1930): Les Enjeux du conflit," in Nikolaï Volkov, *La Secte russe
des castrats,* ed. Claudio Sergio Ingerflom, trans. Zoé Andreyev (Paris: Les belles lettres, 1995),

than the mid-eighteenth century. In applying the techniques of animal husbandry to the purification of his human flock, the sect's founding prophet, a charismatic peasant, offered personal salvation through communion with the Holy Spirit.[93] Skoptsy worship also included repetitious prayer and fervent dancing, practices the community borrowed from an existing movement known as the Christ Faith, or *Khlysty*, which also imposed self-denial, though not castration, on its members. In a more sublimated way, hesychast teaching focused on the reception of the Holy Spirit through constant prayer and self-forgetting.

Russian intellectuals at the turn of the twentieth century believed that folk mystics embodied a distinctively native approach to the spiritual life.[94] If the Optina style itself incorporated some non-Orthodox elements, however, the same could be said for the popular version. A visiting Silesian mystic, Quirinus Kuhlman, was executed as a Quaker heretic by Princess Sofia (1657–1704) in 1689. In denouncing the Khlysty as a "Quaker heresy" fifty years later, Orthodox clergymen condemned the "enthusiastic" style as a Protestant import. In so doing they betrayed their own debt to foreign sources, borrowing a rhetorical turn from English polemics denouncing sectarian fanatics.[95] Aside from the specifics of castration, the ecstatic forms of worship and ascetic principles adopted by the Skoptsy and Khlysty did indeed share certain features with the Christian mysticism that flourished in late-eighteenth-century England and Germany. The rhythmic dancing, chants, and sexual abstinence resemble the practices elaborated by the English Shakers in the very same decades. Not just the timing of its appearance but also the persistence of the "enthusiastic" style conforms to a European pattern. The nineteenth century, as noted, did not exhibit a simple decline in what an increasingly secular public considered old styles of worship.

Manifestations of Christian piety evoking an earlier age were not confined, as these examples show, to the nation which itself seemed anachronistic. Russian sectarians were, moreover, a curious amalgam of pious primitivism and worldly savoir-faire. Old Believers clung to their beards and succeeded at commerce. Eventually they abandoned some of the habits that had set them apart, building urban communities and participating in civic affairs. Smaller, more resistant groups such as the *Dukhobortsy* (Spirit-Wrestlers), who got into trouble for refusing to bear arms or cooperate

---

ix–lxiii; Aleksandr Etkind, "Russkie skoptsy: Opyt istorii," *Zvezda* 4 (1995): 131–63; idem, *Khlyst: Sekty, literatura i revoliutsiia* (Moscow: Novoe literaturnoe obozrenie, 1998), pt 1.

[93] These objections are raised by Viktor Zhivov, "Skoptsy v russkoi kul'ture: Po povodu knigi N. Volkova," *Novoe literaturnoe obozrenie* 18 (1996): 396–400.

[94] See Aleksandr Etkind, "Khlysty, dekadenty, bol'sheviki: Nachalo veka v arkhive Mikhaila Prishvina," *Oktiabr'* 11 (1996): 155–76; idem, *Khlyst*.

[95] Tsapina, "Image of the Quaker."

with the authorities, were also capable agriculturalists.[96] No less stubborn in defense of their core beliefs, the Skoptsy were adept at coping with their material and cultural surroundings. The forms of expression they used to consolidate their membership, communicate with the outside world, and understand their relationship to the host culture changed over time. They eagerly sat to have their photographs taken and arranged to have their legends and verses published in a book. They used telephones and hired attorneys. Some acquired considerable wealth.[97]

What conclusions can we draw about the relationship of imperial Russia to cultural modernity, based on the character of its religious life? On the level of institutions, the state and Church present a mixed picture. Conservative and tradition-minded, they sustained each other in maintaining the social and ideological status quo. As an agent of social transformation, on the one hand, and the enemy of independent public life, on the other, the state also strained this alliance. In the spirit of enlightened despotism, the monarchs deprived the Orthodox Church of administrative autonomy and weakened its economic base.[98] Incorporated into the bureaucratic apparatus, the Church was, in a sense, modernized against its will. Some clergymen responded by addressing the cultural challenges of the age; others promoted institutional reform as a way to enhance the Church's influence and power. On the level of intellectual life, the profile is also confusing. The Slavophiles extolled an ideal of the past, even as they engaged contemporary religious and philosophical issues. They understood their affinity with Europeans grappling with similar spiritual concerns. Finally, on the level of popular expression, it is clear that old and new were also interconnected. Even the most rigid and literal-minded outliers on the sectarian frontier, the aggressively pious Skoptsy, were far from immune to the advantages and excitements of the modern age.

If the secularization thesis cannot withstand scrutiny, perhaps the notion of modernity also needs to be revised. We should not be surprised to learn that World War I provoked a surge of religious feeling among European combatants.[99] We cannot describe the tsarist army command as archaic, on the basis of the virulent anti-Semitism it displayed in relation to

---

[96] See Nicholas B. Breyfogle, "Building Doukhoboriia: Religious Culture, Social Identity, and Russian Colonization in Transcaucasia, 1845–1895," *Canadian Ethnic Studies* 27, no. 3 (1995): 24–51.

[97] On evolving forms of Skoptsy expression, see Laura Engelstein, "Personal Testimony and the Defense of Faith: Skoptsy Telling Tales," in *Self and Story in Russia*, ed. Laura Engelstein and Stephanie Sandler (Ithaca: Cornell University Press, 2000), 330–50. On wealth, see G. N. Ul'ianova, *Blagotvoritel'nost' moskovskikh predprinimatelei, 1860–1914* (Moscow: Mosgosarkhiv, 1999), 450–53, and passim.

[98] G. L. Freeze, "Handmaiden of the State? The Church in Imperial Russia Reconsidered," *Journal of Ecclesiastical History* 36 (1985): 82–102.

[99] Annette Becker, *La Guerre et la foi: De la mort à la mémoire, 1914–1930* (Paris: A. Colin, 1994).

the Jews of the western provinces during that war.[100] Both anti-Semitism and ethnic persecution were the wave of the future. Nor should we designate as a cultural anachronism the fact that many Russians greeted the end of Romanov rule as a literally miraculous occurrence.[101] When the Bolsheviks assumed the mantle of modernity and consigned religion to the relics of the past they were engaging in ideological warfare.

[100] Eric Lohr, "The Russian Army and the Jews: Mass Deportation, Hostages, and Violence during World War I," *Russian Review* 60, no. 3 (2001): 404–19.

[101] Boris Kolonitskii, "The 'Russian Idea' and the Ideology of the February Revolution," in *Empire and Society: New Approaches to Russian History,* ed. Teruyuki Hara and Kimitaka Matsuzato (Sapporo: Slavic Research Center, Hokkaido University, 1997), 41–71.

CHAPTER FIVE

Orthodox Self-Reflection in a Modernizing Age

The Case of Ivan and Natal'ia Kireevskii

In explaining the origins of modern individuality as it emerged in the West, Max Weber and Michel Foucault focus on the transformation of religious patterns of thought and behavior. Weber asserts that Protestant self-discipline laid the foundation for the habits of thrift and self-denial needed for commercial success. Foucault sees the practice of confession in the Catholic Church as a model adapted by the professional disciplines in monitoring personal conduct and imposing social norms. Both argue that the secular version substitutes worldly values (reason, success, personal autonomy) for spiritual values (faith, salvation, self-abnegation), while conserving the psychological structures and even the techniques (confession, self-scrutiny, asceticism) that religion pioneers.

Drawing on the same philosophical traditions that shaped the theories of Weber and Foucault, nineteenth-century Russian intellectuals also grappled with cultural definitions of subjectivity. From their Eastern perspective, they were aware not only of what they owed to their European training but also of the features distinguishing their backgrounds from the legacy of the West. The Slavophiles, in particular, focused on two related themes: the impact of different religious traditions in their respective cultural settings, and the degree to which these different traditions had resisted the challenge of secular values and thought. Though all modern cultures, they believed, showed the imprint of their religious origins, some were more vulnerable than others to eventual loss of faith.

In contrasting East and West, Russia and Europe, as two historical models, the Slavophiles compared forms of Christianity, degrees of secularization (or de-sacralization), and styles of personal self-realization. Aleksei Khomiakov described the Latin Christianity of the West, which included both Roman Catholicism and its Protestant offshoot, as contaminated at the root by the spirit of rationalism derived from classical sources. Because of this inheritance, European culture was destined to succumb to the process in which reason ultimately displaces religion as the measure of truth and the test of moral standards.[1] Separated from the classical world, Eastern Orthodoxy, by contrast, had avoided this contamination and was more resistant to secular styles of thought.

Religious traditions, the Slavophiles believed, affected the historical evolution of the cultures they marked but also generated particular types of personality or psychological organization. Cultures favoring rational analysis and intellectual abstraction emphasized the features common to humanity in general and, at the same time, the autonomy of actual persons—endorsing the equivalence of all men in their civic capacity and also the necessity of their fending for themselves. The Slavophiles identified Eastern Orthodoxy, by contrast, with the opposite principle. In stressing psychological wholeness over abstract thought, and social attachments over individual rights and differences, the Orthodox tradition, they maintained, inhibited the type of individualism that flourished in the West.

Many educated nineteenth-century Russians, like some of their European contemporaries, abandoned the faith in which they were raised and followed the progression identified by Weber and Foucault, in which patterns established in religious life are transmuted into secular structures.[2] Others, however, took the opposite route, attempting to recapture a religious dimension with which they had lost contact. This chapter explores one such case as a prism through which to investigate the Russian understanding of individuality and its links to Orthodox practice. The case is that of Ivan Kireevskii and his wife, Natal'ia née Arbeneva (1809–1900). Kireevskii's story offers a study in re-sacralization, but such a conscious reaching for immediacy (the desire to "re-enchant" the world) is itself a symptom of modern life. The Slavophiles were modern men, yearning for something they felt they lacked, who looked for cultural supports conducive to their effort. It was a style of self-fashioning also evident in the life stories of Vladimir Solov'ev and Lev Tolstoi (1828–1910), who later in the century experienced conversions from skepticism back to faith, as a defining feature of intellectual identity.[3]

Despite the grand generalizations proposed by Slavophile theory, however, the question of what exactly constituted the Orthodox experience—

---

[1] V. V. Zen'kovskii, *Istoriia russkoi filosofii*, 2 vols. (Paris: YMCA, 1948), 1:214. For the affinity between the Slavophile paradigm and the thought of Ferdinand Tönnies and Max Weber, see Andrzej Walicki, *A History of Russian Thought*, trans. Hilda Andrews-Rusiecka (Stanford: Stanford University Press, 1979), 108–9.

[2] See Laurie Manchester, "The Secularization of the Search for Salvation," *Slavic Review* 57, no. 1 (1998): 50–76; idem, *Holy Fathers, Secular Sons: Clergy, Intelligentsia, and the Modern Self in Revolutionary Russia* (DeKalb: Northern Illinois University Press, 2008).

[3] See Inessa Medzhibovskaya, *Tolstoy and the Religious Culture of His Time: A Biography of a Long Conversation, 1845–1887* (Lanham, Md.: Lexington Books, 2008).

preserved, lost, or regained—is not simple. As the Slavophiles realized, the impact of Orthodoxy in nineteenth-century Russia varied. Popular observance, which provided the core of Russian village life, often diverged from the precepts of the Church.[4] The options available to ordinary people suggest, moreover, that religious practices functioned not only to cement community bonds; they also provided personal alternatives that fit within the scope of communal norms. Some village women withdrew from family obligations but were respected as lay celibates; some eccentrics were treated as holy fools.[5] Nor did social change always weaken religious conviction. Soviet narratives of political coming-to-consciousness depict the abandonment of religion as a necessary step in the process of popular self-emancipation.[6] In moving to the cities and entering the factories, some peasants indeed neglected religion or rejected it outright, but most undoubtedly did not.

The association of faith with tradition and its loss with material progress, an assumption both Slavophiles and Marxists shared, does not adequately reflect the pattern that emerged either in Russia or in Europe.[7] On the one hand, Russian factory owners often clung to the familiar rituals, organizing prayer services and invoking the blessings of priests.[8] Among less educated groups, on the other hand, the persistence of the sacred did not always signal cultural stagnation. Some workers used the language of religion as a means to express a new sense of personal achievement and individual identity.[9] Father John of Kronstadt attracted an array of followers in the St. Petersburg population, who continued to seek comfort in the faith. Though confession is not of central importance in Orthodox life,[10] his followers often wrote letters describing their private anguish and

[4] Vera Shevzov, "Miracle-Working Icons, Laity, and Authority in the Russian Orthodox Church, 1861–1917," *Russian Review* 58 (1999): 26–48; idem, "Chapels and the Ecclesial World of Prerevolutionary Russian Peasants," *Slavic Review* 55, no. 3 (1996): 585–613; idem, *Russian Orthodoxy on the Eve of Revolution* (Oxford: Oxford University Press, 2004).

[5] For some examples, see Brenda Meehan, *Holy Women of Russia: The Lives of Five Orthodox Women Offer Spiritual Guidance for Today* (San Francisco: Harper, 1993).

[6] Reginald E. Zelnik, ed., *A Radical Worker in Tsarist Russia: The Autobiography of Semen Kanatchikov,* trans. idem (Stanford: Stanford University Press, 1986).

[7] See Werner K. Blessing, "Reform, Restauration, Rezession: Kirchenreligion und Volksreligiosität zwischen Aufklärung und Industrialisierung," in *Volksreligiosität in der modernen Sozialgeschichte,* ed. Wolfgang Schieder (Göttingen: Vandenhoeck & Ruprecht, 1986), 97–122; and Friedrich Wilhelm Graf, "'Dechristianisierung': Zur Problemgeschichte eines kulturpolitischen Topos," in *Säkularisierung, Dechristianisierung, Rechristianisierung im neuzeitlichen Europa: Bilanz und Perspektiven der Forschung,* ed. Hartmut Lehmann (Göttingen: Vandenhoeck & Ruprecht, 1997), 32–66.

[8] Mark D. Steinberg, *Moral Communities: The Culture of Class Relations in the Russian Printing Industry, 1867–1907* (Berkeley: University of California Press, 1992), 61–66.

[9] Mark D. Steinberg, "Workers on the Cross: Religious Imagination in the Writings of Russian Workers, 1910–1924," *Russian Review* 53 (1994): 213–39.

[10] See Timothy Ware, *The Orthodox Church,* rev. ed. (London: Penguin, 1993), 290; John Meyendorff, *Byzantine Theology: Historical Trends and Doctrinal Themes,* rev. ed. (New York: Fordham University Press, 1983), 195–96.

asking for a personal response. Many participated in mass public confessions, a style of ministry the Church viewed as irregular but which clearly satisfied a widespread demand.[11]

The more privileged classes likewise managed to integrate Orthodox observance with a variety of life choices. The story of Ivan Tolchenov (b. 1754), an eighteenth-century merchant who kept an extensive diary, shows how church attendance and conventional piety might coexist with worldly goals of social and material advancement.[12] In the diary he recorded the struggle to improve his social standing and commented on his own personal qualities. He showed no special interest in religion; his faith did not prompt him to greater self-awareness but was something he took for granted. Fedor Chizhov (1811–1877), a minor Slavophile intellectual, combined piety with a successful career as railroad magnate and financier.[13] At the top of the social hierarchy, Orthodoxy provided the ritual underpinnings of court culture. Although it failed in some cases to satisfy personal needs, the outcome was not to discredit the importance of religion. Under Alexander I, conversion to Catholicism became popular among the ladies of the court. In the manner of the European women writers they were fond of reading, they kept journals and wrote memoirs and novels.[14] The fashion for Catholicism was part of the era's Romantic search for personal expression and spiritual exaltation. It was a sign of the gap between the Westernized, highly self-conscious elite and the uneducated church-going masses.

It was precisely the conventional faith, which heretics, mystics, and Catholic converts spurned, that Nicholas I determined to reinforce. High society had gone astray—witness the conduct of the Decembrists. The doctrine of official nationality, introduced by Minister of Education Count Sergei Uvarov (1786–1855) in 1833, stressed the close association between church and state; it drew the equation between cultural and political

[11] Nadieszda Kizenko, *A Prodigal Saint: Father John of Kronstadt and the Russian People* (University Park: Pennsylvania State University Press, 2000).

[12] David L. Ransel, "Enlightenment and Tradition: The Aestheticized Life of an Eighteenth-Century Provincial Merchant," in *Self and Story in Russian History*, ed. Laura Engelstein and Stephanie Sandler (Ithaca: Cornell University Press, 2000), 305–29; idem, *A Russian Merchant's Tale: The Life and Adventures of Ivan Alekseevich Tolchenov, Based on his Diary* (Bloomington: Indiana University Press, 2009).

[13] Inna Simonova, *Fedor Chizhov* (Moscow: Molodaia gvardiia, 2002); Thomas C. Owen, *Dilemmas of Russian Capitalism: Fedor Chizhov and Corporate Enterprise in the Railroad Age* (Cambridge, Mass.: Harvard University Press, 2005).

[14] Elena Gretchanaja, "Marginalität als Mechanismus der Selbsterkenntnis: Autobiographische Texte russischer Katholikinnen des frühen 19. Jahrhunderts," in *Autobiographical Practices in Russia—Autobiographische Praktiken in Russland*, ed. Jochen Hellbeck and Klaus Heller (Göttingen: Vandenhoeck & Ruprecht, 2004), 49–76. Also Nadejda Gorodetzky, "Princess Zinaida Volkonsky," in *Oxford Slavonic Papers*, ed. S. Konovalov, Vol. 5 (1954): 93–106.

devotion. This policy had the support of conservative intellectuals such as Mikhail Pogodin (1800–1875) and Stepan Shevyrev (1806–1864).[15] Others, such as Ivan Kireevskii, Konstantin Aksakov, and Aleksei Khomiakov criticized the Church's public role, preferring a more inward form of piety. In seeking to elaborate modern forms of Orthodox theology, responsive to developments in Western thought and capable of meeting contemporary cultural demands, they resented the restrictions imposed by the Holy Synod and the ecclesiastical censors.[16]

Unlike the spiritual enthusiasts of Alexander I's time, the Slavophiles created a distinctive identity by embracing, rather than rejecting or questioning, the Orthodox faith. Yet this tradition could not be embraced without conscious effort. Fortunately, Kireevskii wrote, "the Russian style of life," abandoned by the sophisticated elite in favor of Western customs and learning, had survived among the common folk. But, as he complained, it "is now practiced almost automatically, as a matter of tradition, no longer shaped by the power of creative thought, no longer animated, as in the olden days, by the congenial influence of the upper classes, nor harmonizing, as once upon a time, with the main currents of the country's intellectual life."[17] Kireevskii wished neither to bring back the past, nor reject the rationality of the West in favor of an unthinking faith associated with the East. He wanted, instead, to achieve a synthetic wholeness in which abstract reason would not conflict with the truths of revelation, the common folk and cultivated elite would meet on the grounds of an enlightened faith, and the individual person would lead a harmonious life of personal, intellectual, and social coherence.

The Slavophiles determined to mend the breach between old and new, East and West, that had arisen in post-Petrine Russia. They aimed to rethink the place of Orthodoxy in relation both to the European culture in which they had been raised and to their own personal ambitions. In

[15] In their advocacy of the native faith, however, both Uvarov and Shevyrev were influenced by European culture—German philosophy, in the case of Uvarov, Catholicism in that of Shevyrev. See V. A. Koshelev, "Slavianofily i ofitsial'naia narodnost'," in *Slavianofil'stvo i sovremennost': Sbornik statei*, ed. B. F. Egorov, V. A. Kotel'nikov, and Iu. V. Stennik (St. Petersburg: RAN-Nauka, 1994), 122–35; Andrei Zorin, "Ideologiia 'Pravoslaviia-Samoderzhaviia-Narodnosti': Opyt rekonstruktsii," *Novoe literaturnoe obozrenie* 26 (1997): 71–104; Paul Bushkovitch, "Orthodoxy and Old Rus' in the Thought of S. P. Shevyrev," *Forschungen zur osteuropäischen Geschichte*, bd. 46 (Berlin, 1992): 203–20.

[16] See A. Kotovin, *Dukhovnaia tsenzura v Rossii (1799–1855 gg.)* (St. Petersburg: Rodnik, 1909), chap. 4.

[17] I. V. Kireevskii, "O kharaktere prosveshcheniia Evropy i o ego otnoshenii k prosveshcheniiu Rossii," in *Polnoe sobranie sochinenii I. V. Kireevskogo*, ed. M. Gershenzon, 2 vols. (Moscow: Tip. Imp. Moskovskogo universiteta, 1911), 1:203; in English: "On the Nature of European Culture and Its Relation to the Culture of Russia: Letter to Count E. E. Komarovskii" (1852), in *Russian Intellectual History: An Anthology*, ed. Marc Raeff (New York: Harcourt Brace, 1966), 195 (translation modified).

so doing, they pitted themselves against the standard-bearers of institutional authority and to some extent broke with the easy conventions of their social milieu, in which a comfortable piety was taken for granted. They did not, however, break with the aristocratic way of life that nurtured individual self-expression, in the context of strong family ties. They might anguish over their distance from what they imagined as harmonious peasant ways, but their own households reflected the intermingling of private and social claims that constituted the Slavophile ideal. It was a world in which intimacy usually enjoyed company. Intellectual activity flourished in private salons; verses circulated in personal albums. Kireevskii, Aksakov, and Khomiakov frequented the same drawing rooms and were to some degree related to one another. They were also highly self-conscious, idiosyncratic intellectuals determined to adhere to the inherited faith against the challenge of secular thinking and also against the backdrop of domesticated observance and unexamined belief to which they were accustomed.

As is well known, Ivan Kireevskii articulated an ideal of personal wholeness, which he connected with the spiritual practices of the Orthodox Church and, in particular, with its monastic culture.[18] Yet his own biography illustrates the difficulty in reconciling the elements of a European upbringing with the model of psychological harmony he admired. His case exemplifies the conflict between secular styles of personality and the values associated with the religious life. It also demonstrates one of the guiding principles of Kireevskii's mature thought: the capacity of ideas to exist as living forces, not impersonal abstractions. Indeed, the influences that shaped his intellectual development were all embodied in personal relationships. His mother, Avdot'ia Elagina (1789–1877), Kireevskaia by her first marriage, hosted the most important Moscow literary salon of the 1830s. Her second husband, Aleksei Elagin (d. 1846), the stepfather to whom Kireevskii was deeply attached, was an admirer of Friedrich Schelling (1775–1884). The poet Vasilii Zhukovskii (1783–1852), Avdot'ia's uncle, was a close friend of the household. When Kireevskii, as a young man, set out for Berlin, Zhukovskii presented him with letters of introduction, which allowed him to make the acquaintance of Georg Friedrich Wilhelm Hegel (1770–1831). In Munich, he met Schelling. An essential element in Schelling's thought, as in German idealism in general, was the effort to resolve the tension between reason and revelation. At home, the question of Orthodoxy's place in the Russian cultural heritage was at the center of discussion in those years, but religion played only a conventional role in

---

[18] On the centrality of the concept of the integrated personality, see M. [O.] Gershenzon, "Uchenie o lichnosti," in idem, *Istoricheskie zapiski* (Moscow: Kushnerev, 1910), 25.

Kireevskii's personal life. At the time of his marriage to Natal'ia Arbeneva in 1834, he described himself as "incapable of belief."[19]

The circumstances of Kireevskii's "conversion" from casual to serious observance are recounted in a story reported by the philosopher's close friend, Aleksandr Koshelev (1806–1883), based on what Natal'ia told him after her husband's death.[20] This account is a set-piece of Russian intellectual history. At the start of their married life, Kireevskii had not shared his wife's religious convictions but agreed to respect them. For her part, Koshelev notes her recalling, she was willing, upon her husband's suggestion, to read Victor Cousin (1792–1867), and together they read Schelling. She remembers having responded in each case that the best of the philosophers' insights could already be found in the writings of the Church Fathers. She also recalls having introduced her spouse to her spiritual adviser, the monk Filaret (Novospasskii) (1758–1842), whom she credited with having, on the eve of his own death, finally overcome Kireevskii's lingering resistance and doubts.

In dating Kireevskii's spiritual turning point to 1842, Abbott Gleason notes, Natal'ia ignores the fact that her husband had already come to see Orthodoxy as the defining feature of Russian culture. His first important essay, "The Nineteenth Century," published in 1832 in the journal *Evropeets* (*The European*) under his own editorship, focused on the differences between Russian and European culture. It also offered an appreciation of what the European tradition had to offer and a critique of what Russia lacked. In the anxious aftermath of the Decembrist Uprising and the Polish revolt, the authorities censured Kireevskii for harboring allegedly subversive political intentions and ordered the journal suppressed.[21] Crushed by this defeat, Kireevskii retreated to private life. In 1834 he married. Coming increasingly to see East and West in terms of sharp oppositions, by 1838 he had formulated the ideas that characterized his later work. The occasion was a provocative position paper by Khomiakov, "On the Old and the New," which circulated in Moscow drawing rooms in 1838 and 1839. Kireevskii's informal "Answer to Khomiakov" (1838) articulated the distinctions between Western rationalism and Eastern faith; between the Western principle of "individual autonomy, meaning personal isolation," and the absence of "personal particularity" in Russian life. Here, too, he

---

[19] Kireevskii, Letter to A. I. Koshelev (6 July 1833 or 1834), in Gershenzon, *Polnoe sobranie*, 2:226.

[20] "Istoriia obrashcheniia Ivana Vasil'evicha," in Gershenzon, *Polnoe Sobranie*, 1:265–86. See also Abbott Gleason, *European and Muscovite: Ivan Kireevsky and the Origins of Slavophilism* (Cambridge, Mass.: Harvard University Press, 1972), 139–41; and editors' comments in James M. Edie, James P. Scanlan, and Mary-Barbara Zeldin, eds., *Russian Philosophy*, with George L. Kline, 3 vols. (Chicago: Quadrangle Books, 1965), 1:166.

[21] Gleason, *European and Muscovite*, 141, and chaps. 5–6.

recognized the Church Fathers as the font of Orthodox wisdom and praised the monasteries as "the spiritual heart of Russia," guardians of its "distinctive culture" (*samobytnoe prosveshchenie*).[22]

Writing the essay was clearly part of Kireevskii's intellectual transition; it may also have contributed to the shift in his personal sensibility. The widow's account is important not so much for its accuracy of detail, however, as for its function as myth. The incidents she describes, looking back over the span of her married years, dated to the early stages of a relationship that was later filled with conflict and misunderstanding. It was also a relationship that allowed her to serve as her husband's intellectual collaborator, by assisting with his publication projects. In recounting his conversion, she depicts herself not merely as a routinely pious female but as a person who read and formed opinions. She describes Kireevskii's transformation not as the fruit of solitary reflection or direct communion with God but partly as the result of her own efforts. At the very least, she views it as the effect of conversation and human contact—with her and the monk Filaret. Having felt neglected in life and deprived of access to her husband's private thoughts, she retroactively assigned herself a central role in the unfolding of his inner drama.

Alexander Herzen, who had little sympathy for Slavophile ideas, interpreted Kireevskii's turn to religion not as a constructive step toward inner harmony but as a compensation for frustrated ambition. After the suppression of *The European* in 1832, Kireevskii again tried to publish his work but without success, and he finally stopped writing. Until 1845 he divided his time between Moscow and Dolbino, his country estate in Kaluga Province, suffering greatly from the imposed silence. He needed the discipline of deadlines to focus his thoughts and energies; he yearned to reach what he called the "so-called educated public that still believed in Western systems." He complained of isolation and boredom. He wanted "to stop living in the countryside, which I am unable to love, despite many years of trying, and [return to] Moscow, which, despite equally long effort, I cannot distinguish from water, air, and light."[23] "Ivan Kireevskii's prematurely aged face," Herzen writes in *My Past and Thoughts,* "bore the deep marks of suffering and struggle, already succeeded by the mournful calm of the sea swell engulfing the sunken ship. His life was a failure." He had left Moscow, "harboring a deep grief and the unrequited thirst for public activity. A man as hard and pure as steel had been eaten away by

---

[22] "O starom i novom," in A. S. Khomiakov, *Sochineniia v dvukh tomakh,* Vol. 1, *Raboty po istoriosofii,* ed. V. A. Koshelev (Moscow: Medium, 1994), 456–70; 578n.; I. V. Kireevskii, "V otvet A. S. Khomiakovu," in Gershenzon, *Polnoe sobranie,* 1:109–22, 125.

[23] Letter to V. A. Zhukovskii, Moscow, 28 January 1845, in Gershenzon, *Polnoe sobranie,* 2:236 (all quotes).

the corrosion of this terrible time. Ten years later he returned to Moscow from his seclusion an Orthodox mystic."[24]

From Herzen's secular, pro-Western perspective, this outcome was a symptom of intellectual defeat, but, in Kireevskii's view, it was a step toward the integration of his emotional and intellectual worlds. By making religion a more active part of his personal life, he also found someone to talk to and something to do. After the death in 1842 of his wife's spiritual counselor, Filaret (Novospaskii), Kireevskii formed a close relationship with the monk Makarii (Ivanov) of the Optina Hermitage, not far from their estate. Makarii collaborated with the couple in producing Russian translations of the writings of the Church Fathers, and he also became their spiritual counselor. Though Kireevskii chafed at the boredom of rural existence and resented his exclusion from the public exchange of ideas, he found a way to put into practice the philosophical principles he associated with the virtuous life.

The ideal personality, in his opinion, was one in which the different faculties had achieved a state of balance, but in which the movements of the heart (the seat of spiritual sensibility) took precedence over those of the logical mind. "The Eastern thinkers, in their effort to attain the complete truth, sought to achieve an inner wholeness of the intellect—that concentration of intellectual powers which brings all the separate faculties of the mind together in a supreme and living unity. The Western philosophers, on the other hand, assumed that the complete truth could be discerned by separate faculties of the mind, acting independently and in isolation." Comparing Europe and Russia, he noticed "there an inner anxiety coupled with an intellectual conviction of virtue, here a profound peace and tranquility of the inner self, coupled with constant self-mistrust and an incessant striving for moral improvement; in a word, there an inner division of the spirit,...of thought ...; while in Russia...a predominant reaching out for wholeness of being, both external and internal, social and individual, intellectual and mundane, man-made and moral."[25]

Schelling's great contribution, in Kireevskii's eyes, was to have recognized the inadequacy of rational cognition as the path to truth and to have adopted the goal of reconciling reason and revelation. Kireevskii thus saw his own philosophical project as an approach to the same problems posed in Western thought. But Western thinkers were limited not only by the culture's inordinate dependence on rationality but also by the character of the religions to which they could turn. Finding both Catholicism and Protestantism lacking, Schelling "has only one alternative," Kireevskii writes: "to seek out and obtain with his own powers from the confused Christian

---

[24] A. I. Gertsen, *Byloe i dumy* (Moscow: Detskaia literatura, 1974), 458.
[25] Kireevskii, "O kharaktere," 1:201, 218; idem, "On the Nature," 193, 205 (translation modified).

tradition whatever corresponds to his inner notion of Christian truth. A lamentable task—creating a faith for oneself!" For the Orthodox philosopher, things were simpler. "Traces [of Orthodox Christian philosophy] have been preserved in the writings of the Holy Fathers of the Orthodox Church like living sparks ready to flare up at the first contact with believing thought and again to light the beacon for reason in search of truth." It was useless and impossible to return to the tradition in its original form, "but the truths expressed in the philosophical writings of the Holy Fathers could serve the renewal of philosophy as a life-bearing germ and a bright guiding light."[26]

The Orthodox philosopher is able to achieve the desired synthesis precisely because he does not use pure reason as his tool. He achieves his intellectual goal by living out the synthesis he posits as the philosophical ideal. The project of philosophy is inseparable from the philosopher's personal project: his inner sensibility is his instrument. "Every Orthodox person," Kireevskii writes, "is conscious in the depths of his soul that Divine truth cannot be embraced by consideration of ordinary reason and that it demands a higher spiritual view, a view acquired not through external erudition but through the inner wholeness of existence.... For him there is no thought separated from the memory of the inner wholeness of the mind, of that focal point of self-consciousness which is the true locus of supreme truth."[27]

This "craving for synthesis," as Father Vasilii Zenkovskii (1881–1962) reminds us, though it contrasted with the European penchant for drawing analytic distinctions, reflected the influence of German Romantic philosophy, as did Kireevskii's "doctrine of the 'inner focus of the soul.'" In demanding that "the intellectual life of the Orthodox world free itself from the distorting influences of foreign thought," Kireevskii spoke not as an outsider, Zenkovskii notes, but with the authority of someone who "knew the West's 'distorting influences,' not from the accounts of others, not from outside—but from within." Yet, despite Kireevskii's knowledge of Western culture, Zenkovskii is convinced, the philosopher's "whole personality and spiritual world were shot through with the rays of religious consciousness. His was a genuine and profound religious experience, and in giving it meaning he drew very close to the immense spiritual wealth that was opened to him in the Optina Cloister."[28]

---

[26] I. V. Kireevskii, "O neobkhodimosti i vozmozhnosti novykh nachal dlia filosofii," in Gershenzon, *Polnoe sobranie*, 1:262, 253–54; in English: "On the Necessity and Possibility of New Principles in Philosophy" (1856), in Edie et al., *Russian Philosophy*, 1:211, 203 (quotes, respectively; translation modified).

[27] Kireevskii, "O neobkhodimosti," 1:251–52; idem, "On the Necessity," 200–201 (translation modified).

[28] V. V. Zen'kovskii, *Istoriia russkoi filosofii*, 2 vols. (Paris: YMCA, 1948), 1:218, 221 (quoting Kireevskii, followed by his own comments), 220; V. V. Zenkovsky, *A History of*

Indeed, the opportunity to live out his ideal was an exercise in living philosophy—the very concept that Kireevskii strove to articulate in his philosophical work. As Zenkovskii puts it, Kireevskii followed the Church Fathers in believing that "the principle of wholeness—which conceals in itself the root of individuality and the condition of its specific quality—is hidden from us. We must seek it within ourselves in order to draw sustenance from it."[29] Kireevskii valued the writings of the Church Fathers not because they articulated particular ideas but because they provided a model of this achievement. In Kireevskii's words: "The truths they expressed were acquired directly as a result of inner experience and are presented not in the form of logical conclusions, such as our own minds might draw, but in that of an eyewitness's account of a land he has visited himself."[30]

Another such visitor was the Optina monk Makarii, in whom Kireevskii found a personal guide to the inner self. Scholars differ on how to understand his role. Abbott Gleason considers Kireevskii's relationship to the monk an "almost unhealthy spiritual-psychological dependence."[31] He describes the philosopher's last years as gloomy, his piety as Calvinist in its severity. He sees Kireevskii's attraction to monastic culture and patristics as a rejection of the contemporary world and secular values. Eberhard Müller, by contrast, understands Kireevskii's interest in patristics not as an effort to evade the dilemmas of the present but as a way to resolve them. Through his contacts with Makarii, Müller believes, Kireevskii discovered a form of experience, both personal and cultural, out of which he felt useful wisdom might grow.[32] Vladimir Kotel'nikov, writing in 1989, ignores the influence of Optina on the philosopher's development, but in an article published four years later (on the other side of perestroika) he describes the type of religious experience cultivated by the Optina monks as an important element in the evolution of Kireevskii's thought.[33]

The Optina Hermitage, Kireevskii said, was the hearth on which the "living sparks" of the old wisdom were to "flare up" and illuminate the contemporary spiritual horizon.[34] Established in the late fourteenth century, the monastery was at the point of extinction by the early eighteenth. Reconstructed on the initiative of local gentry, with the endorsement of

---

Russian Philosophy, trans. George L. Kline, 2 vols. (London: Routledge and Kegan Paul, 1953), 1:210, 213–14 (translation modified).

[29] Zen'kovskii, *Istoriia russkoi filosofii,* 1:223; Zenkovskii, *History of Russian Philosophy,* 1:215.

[30] Quoted without source, in Gershenzon, "Uchenie o lichnosti," 30.

[31] Gleason, *European and Muscovite,* 242.

[32] Eberhard Müller, *Russischer Intellekt in europäischer Krise. Ivan V. Kireevskii 1806–1856.* Beiträge zur Geschichte Osteuropas, bd. 5 (Cologne: Böhlau, 1966), 397–413.

[33] V. A. Kotel'nikov, "Optina pustyn' i russkaia literatura," *Russkaia literatura,* no. 1 (1989): 61–86; no. 3 (1989): 3–31.

[34] Kireevskii, "O neobkhodimosti," 1:253; idem, "On the Necessity," 203.

Metropolitan of Moscow Platon (Levshin),[35] by the early nineteenth century it had become the center of a form of spiritual guidance known as starchestvo. Drawing on the hesychast tradition of inner concentration, which had come to Russia in the fourteenth century, monastic counselors, called *startsy*, or elders, dedicated themselves to the comfort and illumination of laypeople as well as fellow monks.

An elder, as Dostoevskii later explained in *The Brothers Karamazov,* when introducing the character of Father Zosima, relinquishes worldly power and self-satisfaction in order to lead others away from willfulness and self-indulgence. The demands of the ego, as endorsed by social convention, are doomed to frustration. In a seemingly paradoxical way, only their defeat can lead to self-realization. In Dostoevskii's words:

> An elder is one who takes your soul, your will into his soul and into his will. Having chosen an elder, you renounce your will and give it to him under total obedience and with total self-renunciation. A man who dooms himself to this trial, this terrible school of life, does so voluntarily, in the hope that after the long trial he will achieve self-conquest, self-mastery to such a degree that he will, finally, through a whole life's obedience, attain to perfect freedom—that is, freedom from himself—and avoid the lot of those who live their whole lives without finding themselves in themselves.[36]

Dostoevskii describes Father Zosima as coming from a family of noble rank, having served in the military as a young man, scoffed at his brother's piety, and frequented the drawing rooms of polite society. In the wake of a spiritual crisis, he renounces the world. In providing the elder with a life story, Dostoevskii is adapting a current genre. The details of Makarii's background, for example, were recorded in 1861, soon after the monk's death, by Archimandrite Leonid (Kavelin) (1822–1891), who had served at Optina since 1852.[37] In renouncing their social position, both the real-life Makarii and the fictional Zosima represent an alternative to the solution that Kireevskii found for his own personal dilemma: how to overcome the legacy of modern skepticism and live a life of holiness in the contemporary world.

---

[35] Robert L. Nichols, "The Orthodox Elders (*Startsy*) of Imperial Russia," *Modern Greek Studies Yearbook* 1 (1985): 8; also Kotel'nikov, "Optina pustyn' i russkaia literatura," *Russkaia literatura,* no. 1 (1989): 62.

[36] Fyodor Dostoevsky, *The Brothers Karamazov,* trans. Richard Pevear and Larissa Volokhonsky (New York: Vintage, 1991), 27–28.

[37] *Skazanie o zhizni i podvigakh blazhennye pamiati Startsa Optinoi Pustyni Ieroskhimonakha Makariia* (Moscow: V. Got'e, 1861); rpt. as Arkhimandrit Leonid Kavelin, *Optinskii starets Makarii: Zhizneopisanie i zapisi* (Platina, Calif.: Saint Herman of Alaska Brotherhood, 1975). See also Sergei Lizunov and Elena Pomel'tsova, eds., *Zhizneopisanie optinskogo startsa ieroskhimonakha Makariia* (Moscow: Otchii dom, 1997).

Like Kireevskii (and Zosima), Makarii was of noble stock. Born Mikhail Ivanov, he did not, like the youthful Zosima, cut a dashing figure or, like Kireevskii, impress the intellectual lights of his day. Cross-eyed and stuttering, shy and bookish, he spent his early years in his native Orel Province reading the lives of monks and saints, as others would later read about him, and playing the violin. After attending parish schools and working as an accountant, he rejected the chance to marry and in 1810, at the age of twenty-two, entered a local monastery, prompted, so his biographer suggests, by his reading. In the monastery Makarii made the acquaintance of Leonid (Nagolkin) (1768–1841), whom he followed to Optina in 1834, serving as his assistant until the elder's death.

Observing the principles articulated by his teacher, Paisii Velichkovskii, the founder of eighteenth-century starchestvo, Leonid defined the spiritual practices that came to characterize Optina in its heyday. The type of asceticism (podvizhnichestvo) he promoted did not involve strict bodily discipline and mortification; in fact, it downplayed dramatic gestures. Developing themes elaborated by Nil Sorskii (1433–1508) in the fifteenth century, Leonid emphasized self-examination, self-knowledge, and spiritual self-improvement, techniques aimed at developing the spiritual personality (dukhovnaia lichnost'). The elder's role was to guide the believer in the mechanism of inner self-ordering (vnutrenee ustroenie). The goal was to free oneself from the compulsions of desire and worldly entanglement. Self-liberation was achieved when willfulness (svoevolie) was replaced by humility (smirenie). As Kotel'nikov explains it, "Smirenie is the deep awareness of a person's own imperfection in relation to the moral-religious ideal. From this awareness comes the ascetic imperative of intensive work on oneself, on one's inner purification and arrangement."[38]

Self-awareness was achieved through the process of confession, but ordinary monasteries did not encourage believers to confess more than once a year, enough to maintain their good standing with the Church. The Optina elders, by contrast, demanded that their pupils confess the deepest secrets of their souls as the key to mastering their desires and emotions. The experience, as one described it, could be shattering: "The elder himself told me about everything I had forgotten, only partially expressed, or never understood. My entire life and soul were as open to him as an open book. He knew everything better than I did myself."[39]

The Optina style of spiritual discipline thus encouraged personal development, but it did not suggest that monks or laypersons should practice this discipline in isolation. The "subjective effort" was not a solitary

---

[38] Kotel'nikov, "Optina pustyn' i russkaia literatura," Russkaia literatura, no. 1 (1989): 68 (asketicheskii imperativ napriazhenneishego truda nad soboiu, nad vnutrennim ochishcheniem i ustroeniem).

[39] Quoted in ibid., 72.

process but a communicative one. Likewise, to fight the passions one ought not retreat from the world but should bring one's powers of resistance to bear on the struggles of everyday life. Charity was a prized value and activity. The elders held audiences with lay visitors as well as fellow monastics. They also received many letters asking for blessings and advice, and much of their time was devoted to responding. Indeed, Makarii's first years at Optina were spent helping Leonid cope with his correspondence. He himself spent a good portion of his two decades as head of the hermitage in replying to letters. Assistants answered simple requests or expressions of gratitude; Makarii wrote the more complicated and personal replies.

Upon his death, the correspondence was published as a guide to spiritual enlightenment for the general public. The editors eliminate the identity of the recipients from whom they retrieved the letters, but the collection demonstrates the way Makarii combined personal attention with general precepts. In the case, for example, of forty-one letters addressed to a single man between 1840 and 1851, the monk focuses on the correspondent's spiritual uncertainties. The supplicant says he does not experience the proper emotion when he prays; he complains of depression and worries about his career. Makarii warns him that he cannot think his way to virtue but must renounce the feelings of pride associated with achievement. He must relinquish his intellect in favor of his heart, and he must have patience. Spiritual discipline is a process of learning. He should read the writings of the Church Fathers and strive for humility; understanding takes time. Better to be imperfect than conceited. Playing cards with his colleagues is no sin. The inner life is what matters.[40]

For the letter writers, the correspondence was therapeutic. Seeking help with specific problems, they received advice about how to change their conduct and redirect their emotions in more constructive (virtuous) ways. Some of the advice consisted of quotations from the writings of the Church Fathers, which the monks considered the source of their own wisdom. In addition to their pastoral activities, the elders continued to translate and edit the texts that Velichkovskii had brought back from Athos and trained his first students to study. Not many laypeople had the means, however, to purchase manuscript copies. In 1846, during one of Makarii's visits to the Dolbino estate, Kireevskii complained that Orthodox believers had few literary sources to consult for spiritual guidance and proposed that he and Makarii prepare the Optina manuscripts for publication. By 1860 the pair had supervised the preparation and publication of sixteen books, most in Slavonic but some in Russian, set in civil script, with annotations.[41]

---

[40] Kozel'skaia Vvedenskaia Optina, ed., *Sobranie pisem blazhennyia pamiati optinskogo startsa ieroskhimonakha Makariia* (Moscow: V. Got'e, 1862); cf. Macarius, Starets of Optino, *Russian Letters of Direction, 1834–1860*, trans. and ed. Iulia de Beausobre (Westminster, U.K.: Dacre Press, 1944), 1–78.

[41] *Skazanie o zhizni i podvigakh*, 174–75.

Kireevskii's relationship to Father Makarii thus had a professional as well as personal dimension. Much of the practical side of publication—the correction of proofs, the arrangements with printers, the distribution of copies—was handled by Natal'ia. In her correspondence with Makarii, she kept him informed of these matters, as well as appealing for advice on family and private life. Kireevskii, on his side, wrote Makarii with technical questions about editing and translation, with updates on his state of mind, and occasional pleas for guidance. Thus husband and wife each had a direct personal relationship with the monk, who also served as a link between them.

The Family Triangle

Kireevskii wanted to publish the teachings of the Church Fathers, because he was dissatisfied with what Orthodoxy had to offer in the way of intellectual stimulation. Educated Russians, he complained, turned to Catholic or Protestant theologians to find the answers to complex questions not addressed in Orthodox books. He urged Makarii not to avoid publishing difficult texts, because "publishing only what is generally accessible is also harmful. Many [Russians] for this reason do not read our religious books, but choose foreign ones, because ours only repeat the obvious truths."[42] Just as the routine observance of the Church calendar could not satisfy the spiritual needs of serious believers, so Orthodox sermons, Kireevskii complained, were dry and formulaic. Though he criticized Catholicism, and Protestantism as its logical outcome, for their reliance on abstract reason and their focus on the isolated individual, Kireevskii nevertheless admired Protestant sermons for their personal stamp. "The German pastor," he wrote, "delivers wonderful sermons. The Russian priest, no matter what his heart may tell him or how life may cause him to cry out in want or pain, cannot express his feelings in prayers burning with vital emotion direct from the soul. He can only follow the prayer book, which he learns in advance."[43] Measured against the Christian culture of the West, Orthodoxy thus seemed intellectually deficient, its impact limited by the repetition of ritualistic forms. Kireevskii's purpose was to revitalize the intellectual resources of the Church and discover a more meaningful way for individual believers to practice.

By entering into dialogue with the faithful and offering them a personal resource connected to specifically Orthodox beliefs, the Optina elders were competing with other sources of information and guidance. Educated

[42] Prot. Sergii Chetverikov, *Optina pustyn': Istoricheskii ocherk i lichnye vospominaniia* (Paris: YMCA, 1926), 133–34.

[43] Entry, 12 August 1853, in Eberhard Müller, "Das Tagebuch Ivan Vasil'evič Kireevskijs, 1852–1854," *Jahrbücher für Geschichte Osteuropas* 14, no. 2 (1966): 176.

Russians, looking for psychological direction, might turn to the wordy and eclectic handbook by Aleksandr Galich (1783–1848), who offered a summary of the latest in European philosophy and science pertaining to the constitution and improvement of "the self" (samost').[44] Readers might also turn to the classic manual of spiritual self-discipline, Pratique de la perfection chrétienne (1609), by the Spanish Jesuit Alfonso Rodríguez (1526–1616), available in many translations.[45] Kireevskii cites the French version as an example of the difference between the Roman and Eastern churches,[46] but the habits of modesty, silence, humility, "conformity to the will of God," and "examination of conscience" promoted by Rodríguez were common Christian ideals. Indeed, the art of Christian perfection was precisely Kireevskii's focus in the wake of his conversion.

His relationship to Makarii was central to this endeavor. Kireevskii sometimes visited Optina; Makarii sometimes spent time at the Kireevskii estate. When separated, the two corresponded. From June 1852 to May 1854 Kireevskii also kept a personal journal, in which he recorded his daily activities and reflected on his moods and cares. He does not say whether Makarii suggested the exercise, but he uses the diary as a way to fortify his willpower and deepen his self-knowledge. Not as playful or energetic as the letters he wrote to friends in the same years,[47] the journal is self-reflective but also reveals a full intellectual and social life. Kireevskii often visited his mother and the poet Zhukovskii's widow. Brief notes indicate evenings and conversations with a list of figures, including Chaadaev, Khomiakov, Shevyrev, Iuri Samarin (1819–1876), and Koshelev. He mentions reading the Protestant theologians Alexandre Vinet (1797–1847) and August Neander (1789–1850). He spent time with Karl Söderholm (d. 1878), the son of a Lutheran pastor residing in Moscow, who, under the influence of the Optina monks, converted to Orthodoxy and entered a monastery. The subject of a biography by Konstantin Leont'ev, Söderholm embodied the triumph of Orthodox over Western piety that Kireevskii hoped for on a grander scale.[48] He also represented the model of piety chosen by Makarii, that of withdrawal from the world.

[44] A. I. Galich, Kartina cheloveka, opyt nastavitel'nogo chteniia o predmetakh samopoznaniia dlia vsekh obrazovannykh soslovii (St. Petersburg: Tip. Imp. Akademii nauk, 1834).

[45] See Alphonsus Rodriguez, S. J., Practice of Perfection and Christian Virtues, trans. Joseph Rickaby, S. J., 2 vols. (London: Manresa Press, 1929).

[46] Entry, 3 June 1852, in Müller, "Das Tagebuch," 170.

[47] For example, letter to Koshelev, spring 1851, in Gershenzon, Polnoe Sobranie, 2:253–55.

[48] K. Leont'ev, Otets Kliment Zedergol'm, Ieromonakh Optinoi Pustyni (Moscow, 1882; rpt. Paris: YMCA, 1978); Leonard J. Stanton, "Zedergol'm's Life of Elder Leonid of Optina as a Source of Dostoevsky's The Brothers Karamazov," Russian Review 49, no. 4 (1990): 443–55. See Kireevskii's comments on the Crimean War, 7 March 1854, in Müller, "Das Tagebuch," 185.

This was not an option for Kireevskii. He remained entangled in everyday life, trying to infuse its mundane details with new awareness. It is not clear that he succeeded. The journal entries sometimes sound forced and formulaic. "As the entire mass expresses the same idea—about the salvation of the world through the mystery of the Incarnation of the Son of God, so the vespers are permeated with the idea of the Holy Trinity and Its secret relationship to the creation and to human understanding."[49] The diary's main purpose, however, was not to repeat the obvious (in the spirit of the Orthodox books that Kireevskii dismissed) but to make the practice of belief pertinent to his own situation. On the one hand, he recorded the times he attended mass and when he took confession, as well as the times he stayed home because of illness or inclement weather. On the other, he noted the little details of daily life: stomachaches, toothaches, games of chess, evenings spent in other people's drawing rooms, the conduct of his lawsuit over property in Tambov Province. "Unpleasant incident with Vasia [his son] about the buttons." "Toothache, *Revue des Deux Mondes,* ... Samarin and chess until 3 a.m., Serezha has a toothache."[50]

He no doubt enjoyed the games of chess. He certainly enjoyed the company of his friends, the evenings at Madame Zhukovskaia's or his mother's. But the diary does not convey the sense of pleasure. It instead fixes on what is lacking. On 16 August 1853 he notes that "except [for mass] today was empty and disappeared without leaving the slightest trace on my heart or mind." Describing a day spent in government offices on legal business, Kireevskii calls it "boring and empty." He worries that "an empty person is someone who has let most of his life slip away, or has yawned it away, or squandered it away, or smoked it away." Against this monotony and inattention, moments of spiritual intensity stand out: "After communion," he writes on 4 August 1853, "I felt that same sort of extraordinary readiness to seek the will of God." The point was to focus on the vivid moments of awareness, to refuse the comforting sameness of habit. "Today," he writes on 18 August 1853, "I again experienced the visible sign of the Lord's grace. The Lord's Mercy protects us, despite our sins and unworthiness."[51]

Kireevskii seems to have contrasted the Christian ideal toward which he was striving with two contrary impulses he felt within himself: a sense of intellectual or moral superiority, on the one side, and feelings of passivity and unworthiness, on the other. The self-examination involved in keeping the journal could easily be seen as a form of selfishness (self-preoccupation),

---

[49] Entry, 11 August 1853, in Müller, "Das Tagebuch," 176. Compare Herzen's ironic reaction to similarly pious effusions: Gertsen, *Byloe i dumy,* 459.

[50] Entries, 29 July 1853, 28 August 1853, in Müller, "Das Tagebuch," 174, 179.

[51] Entries, 16 August 1853, 7 September 1853, 4 August 1853, 18 August 1853, in ibid., 177, 180, 175, 177.

but he hoped it could teach him humility. He did not want to remain "half-Christian, half-egotist." If his task as intellectual and writer was to preach the virtues of Orthodoxy to the Russian public, then he must beware his own moral pretensions. In a sermon directed at himself, he remarks: "Before teaching your neighbor how to behave, correct yourself in the very depths of your heart, or, more precisely, ask the Almighty for self-correction and try with all your might to receive it. Then you will feel that a person's well-being lies beyond the pull of the passions and your soul will warm itself with the thought of this higher well-being and your words will have a real effect on the heart of your neighbor, empathetically arousing in him the love for what is inexpressible but can be understood by a person's entire being."[52]

The issue here was partly the relationship between intellect and "the heart." It was not enough to speak the truth, one must experience it oneself. It must be reflected not only in ideas or behavior but in a sense of inner peace, a kind of inner wisdom. The appearance of virtue, Kireevskii reminds himself, can be a form of vanity: "Ignoring one's own defects and acting the part of another's savior, you only flatter your own pride and self-regard. You concern yourself with him not because you love him but because you admire your own qualities. But these, in fact, constitute your inner blindness." Any vestige of egotism is an obstacle on the road to the Heavenly Kingdom: "Only from the moment when the heart turns decisively and unreservedly toward Christ, excising any self-serving aspirations and inspiring steadfastness of will to the point of martyrdom, does the dawn of another day begin to work in the soul."[53]

Kireevskii had translated his personal sense of passivity and his hyper-intellectualism, which he experienced as a kind of spiritual numbness, into philosophical terms. He did not deny the power of science to solve practical problems,[54] but knowing how to live required a different kind of knowledge. In a letter to Khomiakov written in 1840, he explained the distinction between the object and functioning of abstract reason and the higher awareness that only a certain kind of faith could supply:

Logical consciousness translates deeds into words, life into a formula. . . . Living by this kind of reason, we follow the blueprint but do not occupy the house. Having drawn the plan, we think we have built the building. But when it comes to the actual construction, we are strong enough only to lift a pencil but not a stone. In our day, therefore, only the uneducated, or spiritually educated, possess any willpower. But since, in our day, like it or not, the thinking

---

52 Entries, 20 March 1854, 29 August 1853, in ibid., 186, 179 (quotes, respectively).
53 Entries, 29 August 1853, 20 March 1854, in ibid., 180, 186.
54 Chiding an ailing friend for treating himself with homoeopathy instead of finding a good physician: see letter to N. M. Iazykov, 4 June 1836, in Gershenzon, *Polnoe Sobranie*, 1:65–66.

person must submit his cognitive process [*poznanie*] to the yoke of logic, at least he should realize this isn't the highest level of knowledge. There is a higher one, that of hyper-logical knowledge, which isn't mere candlelight, but all of life. And at that level the will grows in tandem with knowledge.[55]

Translating these philosophical concerns back into personal ones, Kireevskii concentrated on the state of his soul, not in order to evade but to confront the demands of living.

These demands challenged his capacities. Suffering from feelings of depression, he sought in self-scrutiny a way to escape the confines of self-involvement. This self-involvement was in some sense forced upon him by his exclusion from an active role in public life. Deprived of the stimulation of public debate, he was left with private conversations, personal correspondence, and family problems. The problems he blamed in large measure on himself. "I must always remember that the Almighty Lord Himself constantly surrounds me with the events of my life, and what seems empty and difficult and nasty suits the condition to which I have reduced my soul." To improve his soul and therefore his life, it does not suffice to change his outward behavior. He must learn to discipline the deepest impulses of his inner consciousness. "I must resolutely, unshakably, indestructibly, set diamond-hard boundaries not only to my deeds but to the most inconspicuous of my desires, fearing like fire or dishonor the least conspicuous cunning of the most fleeting dreams. O Lord! Give me the strength and constancy of desire to be true in all the twists and turns of my mind and heart!"[56]

Kireevskii had an almost mystical attitude toward dreams, which he considered "an expression of the soul's inner feelings," and he paid close attention to what they had to say. "They are nonsense," he said, "but nonsense that goes straight to the heart."[57] He was not very good, however, at introspection. He neglects the diary for long spells;[58] he often finds nothing worth recording; and many entries consist of a few words or names. Occasionally he preaches against the modern type of selfishness, to which he contrasts the Christian ideal of true love. It is not far-fetched to understand his indignation as directed against the vestiges of worldly thinking and "egotism" that he must have encountered in "the most inconspicuous" recesses of his own mind. Of an acquaintance, Kireevskii writes that he "insisted there are neither devils nor angels and that everything the Gospels say about souls is allegorical." Once "a religious fanatic," the man

---

[55] Letter to A. S. Khomiakov, 15 July 1840, in ibid., 1:67.

[56] Entry, 3 October 1853, in Müller, "Das Tagebuch," 184.

[57] Quoted from Kireevskii's letter to his sister, written in 1830, in Gershenzon, "Uchenie o lichnosti," 19–20.

[58] Entries, 7 and 18 March 1854, in Müller, "Das Tagebuch," 185.

"came to his senses and established his own religion by rejecting some things in Church teachings, keeping others, and renaming some. In short, he takes from the Gospels only one great truth, the injunction to love God and one's neighbor."

> Almost the entire *educated* world thinks in this way, counting itself smarter than the rest and viewing the faithful as complete idiots. However, not believing in the Living and Almighty God, but only in themselves and their own intellect, and understanding Godliness only as an abstraction derived from their own thoughts, they think they can love God! Thinking that the goal of life is their own well-being and seeing in their neighbors only the necessary means to attain this goal, they think they love them! How surprised they would be to recognize the enormous difference between the true love of God and of one's neighbor and the self-regard they mistake for love![59]

The focus on the self, even in the context of spiritual introspection, raised the danger of selfishness in the negative sense, and Kireevskii seemed especially sensitive to this distinction. What he describes is the reverse of the Weberian model, in which pious habits give way to a secular understanding of the self. Here, by contrast, the attempt to recapture the feelings of interdependence and self-abnegation associated with the religious way of life succumbs to the deeply ingrained habits of the secular personality.

> When a person immersed only in the impulses of self-love and knowing nothing but self-seeking pleasures suddenly by some miracle experiences, if only for an instant, selfless love and the particular nature of the supreme pleasure it provides, then in this instant of course he feels all the superiority of this unfamiliar condition over his habitually sensual, self-serving limitations. However, when the radiant instant passes, when the lightning that penetrates the darkness of his life disappears, then his memory of it soon fades. The thought of returning to this special condition now seems unpleasant. Realizing he would have to break all the threads of his habitual passions, he begins to regard the highest good with fear, as something hostile that threatens to destroy his habitual well-being.[60]

Love was not, in fact, an easy subject in Kireevskii's own life. He worries that he has not been a good father to his children:

> Sometimes I vividly imagine them to be grown up and unhappy, suffering because I cared for them poorly. Then I weep and my heart sets out on the true

---

[59] Entry, 28 July 1853, in ibid., 174 (*sebialiubie*).
[60] Entry, 29 July 1853, in ibid.

road, ready to go through torments and suffer deprivation for the sake of my love. But in real life I don't know how to behave. And one thing distracts me from another and life passes in inaction. Lord! Enlighten my mind, save me, forgive me, and put me on the correct path and strengthen me in it![61]

As a young man he had shown greater confidence in his capacity for affection. His proposal of marriage to Natal'ia Arbeneva in 1829 was refused on the grounds that they were too closely related.[62] After five years of separation, he returned from the tour of Europe that included his visit with Hegel and renewed his suit. This time it was accepted. Writing to his stepfather, he gloried in his happiness: "I am now like a blind man who suddenly sees the light and still doesn't know how to distinguish one object from another, but sees only that everything is bright and clear." As late as 1851, he mentions Natal'ia in a tone of playful intimacy. Replying to a letter from his dear friend Koshelev, he explains that he is writing, "despite my obvious success every day in loafing around [*prilezhanie*]," commenting that "my wife claims I pinched this word from her, but I consider it my own property, because, although it's her invention, it is dedicated exclusively to my own person."[63]

Perhaps his feelings soured, or, more likely, they were simply mixed. The diary mentions Natal'ia only briefly: "Got up late because I was caring for N. P. [Natal'ia Petrovna] until 3 a.m." "This evening I sat with my wife." "Wife's name-day."[64] The fleeting notes do not, however, indicate a happiness taken for granted. In the letters belonging to the early period of the diary, Kireevskii complains to Makarii of vague family troubles: "In my last letter to you I wrote about certain empty anxieties caused by our empty thoughts. As is usually the case, after writing to you this unease diminished, thank God, at least on the surface." A diary entry of 4 June 1852 mentions: "Conversation about domestic disorder."[65] A year later nothing seemed to have changed, and he blames himself for the problems: "The disarray in my outer life—household, domestic order, paperwork, children's upbringing—all that results from the disorder of my inner forces. The outer is only the imprint, the mirror of the inner. If God would cure me of my inner weakness, blindness, deformity, and poverty, then perhaps

---

[61] Entry, 3 October 1853, in ibid., 184.

[62] N. A. Elagin, "Materialy dlia biografii I. V. Kireevskogo" (22 March 1861), in Gershenzon, *Polnoe Sobranie*, 1:14. Also Gershenzon, "Uchenie o lichnosti," 13.

[63] Letter to A. A. Elagin, March 1834; letter to A. I. Koshelev, spring 1851, in Gershenzon, *Polnoe Sobranie*, 2:228, 253–55.

[64] Entries, 4 September 1853, 22 August 1853, 26 August 1853, in Müller, "Das Tagebuch," 180, 178–79.

[65] Letter to Makarii from 1852, in Chetverikov, *Optina*, 115; entry, 4 June 1852, in Müller, "Das Tagebuch," 170.

my external life would acquire a healthy wholeness."[66] Two years later, in 1855, he complains in a letter to Makarii:

> I beg you, Father, pray to Merciful God for our family to have peace, concord, love, and well-being. Thank God, we have no misfortunes or calamities, but there are spiderwebs that throw an imperceptible gloom on the insignificant nuances of the heart's movement, out of which gradually are woven entire fabrics that prevent us from seeing straight and distance us from each other. It would seem that a mere puff of the holy breath would dispel all that, as if it had never been. But this nothing has real effects.[67]

Kireevskii had resolved in 1853 to exert "diamond-hard" control not only over his conduct but even over his dreams and desires. The effort was unsuccessful. He could not dispel the webs of misunderstanding and bad feeling that entangled him and his wife. Prevented "from seeing straight," he asked Makarii to pray for his relief. But Kireevskii did not always welcome the monk's interference. When it came to the struggle with tobacco, he was less compliant. Victimized by habit and powerless to achieve the detachment and serenity he claimed to want, Kireevskii was unable to submit entirely to the elder's direction.

He described the conflict as follows. In 1852 Kireevskii had been obliged by illness to stop smoking. This was a habit he had indulged, as he put it, in his every waking moment since the age of thirteen. The "empty man" who "smoked away his life" (1853) was a self-portrait. Responding to the concern expressed by Makarii and the other startsy, Kireevskii decided to renounce his habit and for two years did not touch the pipe. But by 1854 he could no longer stand the strain and tried smoking in moderation. Makarii, however, withheld his blessing. This refusal put Kireevskii in "a very difficult situation," he complained. "On the one hand, I feel the need to return in moderation to the old, immoderate habit, too deeply ingrained in me and too abruptly broken off. On the other hand, I know that even the most useful thing done without your blessing can only do me harm." For all his pious talk, Kireevskii does not simply accept Makarii's decision. "Please recall, dear Father," he writes, "that when I first decided to stop smoking, *I clearly and definitely avoided any promise or vow* to stop smoking forever. I even decided not to accept your blessing, when you wanted me to promise to give up the pipe forever. In this respect I therefore cannot consider myself obligated in any way."[68] This does not sound like a man who wants the heart to dominate the mind; rather, Kireevskii appears to be rallying the power of argument to justify his submission to

---

[66] Entry, 15 August 1853, in Müller, "Das Tagebuch," 177.
[67] Letter of 1855, in Chetverikov, *Optina*, 136–37.
[68] Letter of 1854, in ibid., 126 (emphasis in original; letter dated by place in sequence).

impulses he wishes to dominate but cannot defeat. His self-knowledge is not the path to self-mastery or self-discipline but the explanation for why he cannot escape a basic form of self-involvement. He strikes a note more realistic than meek.

In seeking Makarii's approval, Kireevskii provides a vivid description of his dependency. During the thirty-three years of constant smoking, he claims not to have noticed any harm to his health. Only on the rare occasions when forced to do without the pipe did he suffer—not only physically but also mentally. His memory would weaken, his thoughts wander. After the illness, however, he responded to the urging of Makarii and the Metropolitan, who worried about the danger of excess, but he decided it would be easier to stop altogether than just to cut back. Now he realizes he had been mistaken. "My habit was so strong that it had become second nature." The mental weakness he had occasionally noticed before now constantly plagued him: he cannot compose his thoughts or write. He searches for words, loses the thread of conversation. "But while my intellectual activity has diminished, my passions have grown more insistent." He hopes that the two years of abstinence, fortified by the power of Makarii's prayers, will now give him the strength to observe moderation. "I did not want to undertake anything important without your blessing," he writes, "and therefore asked for your grace and now sincerely beg for your holy blessing, but not for your permission, for I do not consider myself bound by it in this affair." God himself would make the final judgment.[69]

Kireevskii had trouble with himself, his wife, his children. His wife had trouble with him. The spiderwebs affected her, too, and she, too, turned to Makarii. In September 1846 she sent him the proofs of a text in preparation, adding: "My heart is heavy, some grief is gnawing away at me." She asks him to bless her efforts, and those of her husband and the whole family, to keep to the path of goodness. In December proofs again, and the comment: "My soul is suffering, my heart is troubled and in pain about everything and about all of us."[70] In another letter, describing her involvement in the details of publication, she concludes:

Yes, I am suffering terribly and for good reason—nothing acute but for the loving heart sometimes hard to bear. Forgive my lack of courage, Father dear! I beg you with loving tears to pray to the Lord to sustain him [Kireevskii] in his conjugal love and faithfulness, and give your blessing to the upbringing of our children. Teach me, make me understand, and forgive me for bothering you, but I consider you closer than my own father.[71]

[69] Letter of 1854, in ibid., 128.
[70] Letters of 20 September 1846, 13 December 1846, in ibid., 144–45.
[71] Letter of mid-December, in ibid., 145–46.

In January 1847 she asks him to pray for Kireevskii's health and reports that she is "very, very sad."[72] That same month:

> I'm worthless, my heart aches constantly: anxiety makes me sad. Sometimes prayer helps, but sometimes I don't have the strength for prayer. Sometimes in the present I see the past and unknown or hidden events and my thoughts are distracted by this. My spiritual suffering increases, my mental and physical forces diminish. So you see, Father, my worthless sinfulness. I confess to you, who can provide the cure for my spiritual weakness.[73]

Even before Kireevskii had fallen ill and given up his pipe, during a time he described as one of mental equilibrium, he constituted her heaviest burden. "I suffer terribly," she writes Makarii in January 1847, "from private coldness and inattentiveness, and it's very hard to bear. I beg sincerely for your holy prayers, to strengthen peace, love, and concord."[74] Two weeks later she describes in greater detail "the grief I feel in my heart, or really, in my soul":

> I'm often, very often depressed, indeed that's how I'm feeling right now. Our relations are somehow unstable: sometimes everything seems fine, but that's clearly forced. Sometimes, like now, there's a sudden coldness, inattention, and worse, something unpleasant, which has no place in love. He's even inattentive to illness, moreover causing a lot of it himself. When I was in danger, he was very concerned, but now, if he thinks I'm the one who needs something or that the least little thing is what's needed to calm me down, like going to bed before 2 a.m., then nothing will get him to do it, and he rewards me with serious unpleasantness. My heart aches from sadness, what should I do? Should I become colder toward him, or...[sic] I really don't know. Coldness can be mistaken for caprice, which will only push him further away. It would be easier if I loved him less.... If I remind him of [our troubles] in ever so affectionate and friendly a way, he remains silent, but if I mention [them] in ordinary conversation, he gets angry, answers sharply, and then there's unpleasantness again. I honestly don't know what to do, it's so unbearably hard. I put all my hopes in your holy prayers, Father! They are strong enough to change those stubborn habits so harmful to the family and the servants. I beg you, don't forsake me. Pray to the Lord to help our souls, and bring peace and concord.[75]

---

[72] Letter of 3 January 1847, in ibid., 148–49.
[73] Letter of mid-January 1847, in ibid., 149–50 (*stradaniia dushevnye, nemoshch' dushevnaia*).
[74] Letter of 13 January 1847, in ibid., 151.
[75] Letter of 24 January 1847, in ibid., 152–53. For a translation of part of this passage and commentary on Kireevskii's character and relationship with his wife, see Gleason, *European and Muscovite*, 270–71.

Writing to Father Makarii may have provided solace for the unhappy pair, but their unhappiness seems to have survived. The wife portrays herself as the patient, loving partner, ill-treated by an insensitive spouse. She asks what to do and berates herself as "worthless," but she never wonders how she might change her own character for the better. Kireevskii has a different objective in his diary and letters. But despite his efforts at self-control and self-reflection, he remains an egotist, in the very sense he himself deplored: impatient with those around him; preoccupied with work at the expense of personal ties; eager—in theory—to love but fearful he was unloving. Despite his devotion to self-improvement, he failed to penetrate deeply into his own heart. The self-portrait in the diary shows little insight into his conflicted emotions.

In contrast to Weber's ideal-type capitalists or Foucault's psychiatric patients, whose practices of self-scrutiny reflect the substitution of rational for spiritual goals, Kireevskii's diary demonstrates the reverse. The educated gentleman's self-regard and intellectual ambition were supposed to retreat before an infusion of warmth, a new kind of understanding and means of human connection. His efforts to achieve this objective left him suffering the weight of depression—an isolated, inward-looking man. It seems in this case that the Western-style upbringing that prepared young men for active careers, even if they declined to pursue them,[76] triumphed over the strategies of self-definition offered by the Orthodox faith. Even when Kireevskii had modified the techniques of piety to conform to his own desires, he was unable to leave the old self behind. Perhaps it was the custom-tailoring of his relationship to Makarii that defeated its ultimate purpose. In any case, Kireevskii confessed not long before he died that his efforts had only intensified "that inner dividedness which it is the primary object of spiritual thinking to destroy."[77]

Perhaps, as Herzen believed, Kireevskii was simply burdened with a mournful temperament, unlike the bold and contentious Khomiakov, who loved a good fight, or the indomitable Konstantin Aksakov.[78] Kireevskii himself admitted that he was not cut out for happiness: "The dominant feeling in the daily life of our family is a certain intensely anxious expectation of misfortune. Happiness is not compatible with such a feeling."[79] But happiness was not the purpose of spiritual self-discipline. No living mortal could attain the ideal of the harmonious personality; it was the arduous process of striving that constituted the virtuous life.

---

[76] For an analysis of this kind of upbringing, see N. N. Mazur, "K rannei biografii A. S. Khomiakova (1810–1820)," in *Lotmanskii sbornik*, ed. E. V. Permiakov, 2 vols. (Moscow: ITS-Garant, 1994–1997), 2:195–223.

[77] Quoted without source in Gershenzon, "Uchenie o lichnosti," 25.

[78] Gertsen, *Byloe i dumy*, 456–57, 461.

[79] Quoted in Gershenzon, "Uchenie o lichnosti," 21.

It is, of course, the tension between traditional and innovative elements, between abstract thought and emotional longing, that gives Kireevskii's work and life their modern flavor. This tension has also given rise to divergent interpretations of his thinking. Mikhail Gershenzon (1869–1925), who published an edition of Kireevskii's essays and letters in 1911, believes the philosopher's basic insights are not specific to Christianity. In seeing the emotions as the moving force of personality, Gershenzon asserts, Kireevskii anticipated the modern psychology of "subconscious psychic states," which recognizes the power of "sublimated" instinctual forces.[80] Agreeing with Gershenzon on the importance of Schelling and Russian literary Romanticism in the development of Kireevskii's ideas, Father Zenkovskii denies, however, that "feeling" is at the core of Kireevskii's concept of personality, which he understands as a reflection of a deeply Christian, and specifically Orthodox, anthropology.[81]

As for Kireevskii's own person, the "autobiography" constituted by his correspondence and journal leaves the impression of someone who found his passivity a burden but could not loosen its grip. Eager for the light of love to enter and warm his heart, Kireevskii spent much of his life resisting. The techniques designed to wear away the outlines of his worldly persona only etched them more sharply into his mind. Like everyone else in his aristocratic circle, his character evolved in the context of a network of personal and intellectual ties. Even the process of conversion and his experiment in the Christian art of self-perfection bound him to others. In this sense, he did not experience the "individual isolation" he deplored in secular Western versions of the self.[82] But nor did he achieve the "perfect freedom," which Dostoevskii describes as "freedom from oneself."[83] His dual role, as mediator between Western thinking and Eastern wisdom, on the one hand, and practitioner of an Orthodox sensibility, on the other, demanded that some tensions remain unresolved. His philosophical position was reflected in the structures of his inner consciousness and the contours of his personal life.

---

[80] Gershenzon, "Uchenie o lichnosti," 39–40.
[81] Zen'kovskii, *Istoriia russkoi filosofii,* 1:222, 224; Zenkovskii, *History of Russian Philosophy,* 1:215–16.
[82] Kireevskii, "V otvet," 1:113.
[83] Dostoevsky, *Brothers Karamazov,* 27–28.

CHAPTER SIX

Between Art and Icon

Aleksandr Ivanov's Russian Christ

Discovering the Past

Kireevskii wished to retrain himself. He tried to replace his worldly habits with those of a pious man, and he tried to provide this pious self with an Orthodox, rather than more generally Christian, inspiration. Despite his sense of frustration, he nevertheless succeeded. On the level of ideology, the Slavophile legacy imprinted itself on Russian political and cultural history, well beyond the conservative or church-oriented sphere. In personal terms, his failure to achieve private virtue injured the pride he determined to master. Yet pride itself was the problem. In falling short, he fulfilled the Christian injunction to strive continually toward a spiritual goal impossible to attain.

The case of Aleksandr Ivanov, nineteenth-century Russia's most celebrated (and debated) religious painter, illustrates, in another domain, the difficulty in creating a native religious identity. Here, it was not the artist himself who struggled with the project of self-transformation but the friends and interpreters who wished to enlist him in the task of shaping Russia's spiritual profile. The medium was not the retrieval of a textual canon or the lost practices of piety; it was the crafting of a visual language, in dialogue with Western conventions but emerging allegedly from a distinctively Eastern source.

* * *

The ghost of Ivanov is remarkably persistent. To begin with a digression, consider *Leto v Badene* (*Summer in Baden Baden*), the lyrical reflection on Dostoevskii and Russian literature written for the drawer by

Leonid Tsypkin (1926–1982) in the 1970s.[1] Tsypkin follows the writer and his second wife on their way to Germany. Leaving St. Petersburg in the spring of 1867, the couple pass first through Vilna, where they remark on the swarms of disagreeable Jews. Arriving in Dresden, they head for the art gallery where they go straight to the *Sistine Madonna*. Tsypkin himself recalls seeing Raphael's masterpiece, which the Soviets had transported to Moscow during the war, displayed in the Pushkin Museum.[2] "A photograph of this picture," Tsypkin continues, "was given to Dostoyevsky for his birthday many years after his visit to Dresden and shortly before his death, by someone supposing that this was his favourite picture."[3] The photograph had become "the family reliquary," his widow recalled.[4]

The *Sistine Madonna* is a leitmotif in Tsypkin's story. Tsypkin imagines the couple returning repeatedly to the Dresden gallery, where on one occasion the writer makes a spectacle of himself by climbing onto a chair. "Above the heads of the crowd, the painting could be seen to particular advantage, the Madonna floating in the clouds with the child in her arms, the apostle looking piously up at her from below, and the angels above."[5] The Russian realist painter Ivan Kramskoi (1837–1887) also visited the *Sistine Madonna*, which he, too, greatly admired. He nevertheless objected to the secondary figures, whose role as spectators seemed to mimic that of the actual viewers.[6]

Tsypkin evokes this same mirroring when describing his experience in a different museum, trying to catch a glimpse of a large canvas that had attracted an eager throng. "The crowd was besieging this painting which took up half the wall," he writes, "so that it was not so much a picture as a whole sheet of canvas, almost like the *Appearance of Christ to the People*."[7] Tsypkin knows that his Russian readers will easily visualize the painting by Aleksandr Ivanov that hangs in the Tretiakov Gallery in Moscow. They

[1] Leonid Tsypkin, *Summer in Baden-Baden: A Novel*, trans. Roger and Angela Keys, intro. Susan Sontag (New York: New Directions, 2001). The manuscript was smuggled out of the Soviet Union and first published in 1982 in Russian in New York, not long before Tsypkin's death in Moscow. A practicing physician of Jewish background, he had attempted unsuccessfully to emigrate. Now in Russian: *"Leto v Badene" i drugie sochineniia* (Moscow: Novoe literaturnoe obozrenie, 2005).

[2] The painting was eventually returned to Dresden, where it still resides. See Konstantin Akinsha and Grigorii Kozlov, with Sylvia Hochfield, *Beautiful Loot: The Soviet Plunder of Europe's Art Treasures* (New York: Random House, 1995).

[3] Tsypkin, *Summer*, 4.

[4] A. G. Dostoevskaia, *Vospominaniia*, ed. S. V. Belov and V. A. Tunimanov (Moscow: Khudozhestvennaia literatura, 1971), 356.

[5] Tsypkin, *Summer*, 11.

[6] Reflections on 1869 visit, in I. N. Kramskoi, *Ob iskusstve*, ed. T. M. Kovalenskaia (Moscow: Izd-vo Akademii khudozhestv SSSR, 1960), 102.

[7] Tsypkin, *Summer*, 32.

will recall the structure of its composition and realize that this structure is echoed by the experience of the people surrounding Tsypkin.

Based on the *Gospel According to St. John,* Ivanov's painting shows John the Baptist (or John the Precursor), who calls himself "the voice of one crying in the wilderness" as he fulfills his God-sent mission to prepare for the coming of Christ. Positioned just left of center, he directs the attention of the groups clustered in the foreground to the figure of Jesus, positioned high and to the right, diminished in size against the far horizon. Interrupted in their various activities, the figures turn their eyes upward, in the same way that the painting itself causes visitors to stretch their necks toward the image from which they expect some revelation. Contemporaries noticed this doubling. Recalling the reaction evoked at the painting's first showing in Rome in 1857, the art critic Pavel Kovalevskii (1823–1907) later wrote: "It seemed as though the ecstasy of those being baptized in the Jordan communicated itself to the viewers. Holding their breaths, they joined the figures in the painting as they observed the Messiah draw near."[8]

As in other versions of this scene, Ivanov's canvas depicts not merely the historical moment of Christ's appearance on earth but the moment in which the light shown by God in the Darkness is manifest in the person of His Son and becomes visible to men. John has been sent "to bear witness of the Light, that all *men* through him might believe. He was not that Light, but *was sent* to bear witness of that Light.... [A]s many as received him, to them gave he power to become the sons of God, *even* to them that believe on his name" (John 1:7–12).

Ivanov's subject is therefore the impending transformation of humankind. It has both anthropological and narrative dimensions. The Pharisees on the right turn away; the figures on the left follow John's upward gesture. Some tremble, some show signs of joy; others are naked and vulnerable, and still others are clothed in the garments of social station; youth is paired with old age; the slave crouches in bondage; soldiers represent the worldly power helpless before the "grace and truth" of Christ. The subject can also be said, however, to constitute the event of seeing itself, which depends on reception of the Light. In this sense the theme touches also on the function of art.

In *The Invisible Masterpiece,* Hans Belting singles out Raphael's *Sistine Madonna* as the icon not only of Christian art but of art itself in the modern era. Transferred to the Dresden museum in 1853 from its

---

[8] Pavel Kovalevskii, "Vstrechi na zhiznennom puti: Aleksandr Andreevich Ivanov," in D. V. Grigorovich, *Literaturnye vospominaniia, s prilozheniem polnogo teksta vospominanii P. M. Kovalevskogo,* ed. V. L. Komarovich (Leningrad: "Academia," 1928), 364. Also: A. Novitskii, ed., *Istoriia russkogo iskusstva s drevnieishikh vremen,* 2 vols. (Moscow: Lind, 1903), 2:260–62.

original setting in a church, the Madonna is no longer venerated as the incarnation of divinity. She represents instead the miracle of artistic creation, which becomes itself an object of adoration. "Raphael had painted a vision as if experienced by the viewer," Belting writes, and spectators indeed gazed for hours in rapt fascination. The effect was a synthesis of secular and sacred emotion. "The painting itself showed a useful ambiguity," Belting notes, "for it depicted religious subject-matter and did so with a beauty that might well rekindle its beholders' feelings for religion.... Revelation, a religious concept, now came to signify revelation through art."[9]

Raphael's *Madonna* thus represented the transition from literal to symbolic icon. It is not by accident, then, that Tsypkin connects his account of Dostoevskii's fascination with this work to the effect of another secularized icon. Ivanov's *Iavlenie Khrista narodu* (*Appearance of Christ to the People*), first displayed in Russia in 1858, was the Russian *Sistine Madonna*.[10] Raphael's masterpiece was, in fact, a model and inspiration for Ivanov, who kept a copy in his studio in Rome,[11] as he grappled with the problem of how to express, in terms accessible to the modern viewer, the impact of a revelation that many no longer believed in but that still had the power to move them. The *Appearance of Christ to the People*, which resulted from these efforts, became the center of a prolonged discussion about the relationship between religion and art, and simultaneously about Russia's relationship to European culture.

The repositioning of the *Sistine Madonna* in a shrine to art (the museum) at the onset of the modern age (the Age of Enlightenment) defined its new cult status. "Paradoxically," writes Belting, "it was only after it had become a museum piece that it became the focus of a cult, which it should have been as an altarpiece."[12] The painting now functioned as a bridge between two forms of wonderment and also as a junction between two historically distinct modes of representation. Art, in Belting's terms, is "a new function that fundamentally transformed the old image. We are so deeply influenced by the 'era of art,'" he remarks, "that we find it hard to imagine

[9] Hans Belting, *The Invisible Masterpiece*, trans. Helen Atkins (Chicago: University of Chicago Press, 2001), 50, 58–59 (quote).

[10] For this direct comparison, see A. S. Khomiakov, "Kartina Ivanova (pis'mo k redaktoru *Russkoi besedy*, bk. 3 [1858])," in *Polnoe sobranie sochinenii A. S. Khomiakova*, 8 vols. (Moscow: Universitetskaia tipografiia, 1900), 3:365. Ivanov himself referred to the painting as *Appearance of the Messiah* (*Iavlenie Messii*); when exhibited in 1858 it acquired the title *Appearance of Christ to the People* (*Iavlenie Khrista narodu*). See I. A. Vinogradov, ed., *Aleksandr Ivanov v pis'makh, dokumentakh, vospominaniiakh* (Moscow: XXI vek-Soglasie, 2001), 709.

[11] M. V. Alpatov, *Aleksandr Andreevich Ivanov: Zhizn' i tvorchestvo*, 2 vols. (Moscow: Iskusstvo, 1956), 1:380, 2:25.

[12] Belting, *Invisible Masterpiece*, 67.

the 'era of images.'"[13] The "we" he invokes is, however, Western. From that vantage point, Russia appears as the land of the icon. Yet Russians began to see the icon as a symbol of native tradition only once the era of art had transformed holy images into objects of aesthetic contemplation.

In the wake of the Napoleonic Wars, when Europeans experienced a new interest in national identity, Russians also reappraised their cultural heritage. Restorers began to salvage holy images discarded by priests who had no sense of the icons' aesthetic value; scholars analyzed style and historical pedigrees; families took a new look at the objects hanging above the icon lamps; private collectors laid the basis for future museums.[14] To Russians, the image held the key to their cultural authenticity. Belting describes Eastern Europe, including Russia, as using "the icon as a means of self-assertion against the established culture of the rest of Europe by placing the icon outside the realm of historical thought."[15] When Slavophile-inclined philosophers turned their attention to the theology of Eastern Orthodox icons, they insisted on their character as unmediated conduits of the divine: these painted boards were not representations but incarnations, thus inherently different from any visual object a museum might purvey.[16]

Russia's self-definition as a culture "before art"—and in some sense beyond historical time—is thus both a response to and a product of secularization. The original image (icon), in its unself-conscious form, exists only in the context of an unself-consciously religious culture. In this sense, "art" is always "modern." Modernism, as a stylistic movement, then revolts against art's own tradition, embracing the immediacy and naïveté of the icon age. Thinking to escape the aesthetic tyranny of "art," modernists do so in the terms that art provides—as an aesthetic statement. Russia's experience of the "age of art" can thus be considered a vexed romance with the image. It seems less surprising, therefore, that the nineteenth-century artist who came closest himself to achieving iconic status and whose work came closest to being considered "an icon in art's clothing," and thus a successful translation of Russia's visual tradition into art-historical terms, should have been Aleksandr Ivanov. Famous for his monumental depiction of Jesus Christ, Ivanov became the emblem of modern Russia's cultural dilemma.

---

[13] Hans Belting, *Likeness and Presence: A History of the Image before the Era of Art*, trans. Edmund Jephcott (Chicago: University of Chicago Press, 1994), 9.

[14] Shirley A. Glade, "A Heritage Discovered Anew: Russia's Reevaluation of Pre-Petrine Icons in the Late Tsarist and Early Soviet Periods," *Canadian-American Slavic Studies* 26, no. 1–3 (1992): 145–95. On the belatedness of this discovery, see Evgenii Trubetskoi, "Umozrenie v kraskakh: Vopros o smysle zhizni v drevnerusskoi religioznoi zhivopisi" (Moscow, 1916), rpt. in *Filosofiia russkogo religioznogo iskusstva XVI–XX vv.: Antologiia*, ed. N. K. Gavriushin (Moscow: Progress-Kul'tura, 1993), 201.

[15] Belting, *Likeness*, 17.

[16] Trubetskoi, "Umozrenie v kraskakh."

Ivanov was the exact contemporary of the leading lights of the first Slavophile generation: Aleksei Khomiakov and Ivan Kireevskii. He shared their central preoccupations: the place of tradition in an era of change and the status of universal principles in the face of cultural difference. The *Appearance of Christ to the People* was interpreted as a response to these questions. It was first exhibited in Russia, upon the artist's return from twenty-eight years spent living and working in Rome. The picture and Ivanov's sudden death of cholera (the disease that also took the lives of Khomiakov and Kireevskii) sparked a flurry of comment in the press.

The issues raised by the controversial work were not, however, uniquely Russian. Ivanov's story reflects the well-known paradox of the age. Critics and writers across Europe discussed the connection between art, religion, and national self-definition. The language of art—style, technique, genre, theme—everywhere carried a political burden. Like Romantic nationalists elsewhere, Russian nativists rejected the abstract principles of the Enlightenment. In celebrating the distinctive features of their own tradition, they nevertheless displayed a broadly European style of thinking. Those who aimed to resurrect religion acknowledged the fact of interruption. Those who identified their patrimony with the Christian mission made culturally transcendent claims. Ivanov's long years in Rome brought him into contact with the European artists who gathered there.[17] In that environment he developed a visual vocabulary that his compatriots understood as both universal and culturally specific (Russian and European, Eastern and Western, sacred and secular), and they construed these qualities in political terms.

The political interpretation of Ivanov and his work began in his lifetime and intensified after his death. He was championed as a great artist on both sides of the aisle: by Khomiakov and the Slavophile-oriented Nikolai Gogol (1809–1852); by the "Westernizer" Alexander Herzen, the radical Nikolai Chernyshevskii, the anti-establishment culture critic Vladimir Stasov (1824–1906), and the realist painter Ivan Kramskoi.[18] Confirmation of the artist's reputation reached the general public through the illustrated magazine *Niva* (*The Cornfield*), which featured a thumbnail biography

---

[17] On Rome in this period, see Belting, *Invisible Masterpiece*, 33.

[18] N. V. Gogol, "Istoricheskii zhivopisets Ivanov" (1846), in *Vybrannye mesta iz perepiski s druz'iami* (1847; rpt. Moscow: Patriot, 1993); N. G. Chernyshevskii, "Zametka po povodu predydushchei stat'i," *Sovremennik*, no. 11 (1858): 175–80; rpt. in N. G. Chernyshevskii, *Polnoe sobranie sochinenii*, 16 vols. (Moscow: Khudozhestvennaia literatura, 1950), 5:335–40; Khomiakov, "Kartina Ivanova," 346–65; A. I. Gertsen, *Byloe i dumy* (1852–68) (Moscow: Detskaia literatura, 1974), pt. 7; V. V. Stasov, "O znachenii Ivanova v russkom iskusstve," *Vestnik Evropy* (January 1880), rpt. in idem, *Izbrannye sochineniia*, 3 vols. (Moscow: Iskusstvo, 1952), 2:38–89; I. N. Kramskoi, "Khudozhnik A. A. Ivanov i ego znachenie dlia russkogo iskusstva," *Istoricheskii vestnik* 5 (1881): 806–20; and I. N. Kramskoi, "Izobrazheniia iz sviashchennoi istorii, ostavlennykh eskizov Aleksandra Ivanova," *Khudozhestvennyi zhurnal* (January 1881), rpt. in idem, *Pis'ma, stat'i*, ed. S. N. Gol'dshtein, 2 vols. (Moscow: Iskusstvo, 1966), 2:354–55.

of Ivanov in 1880 and an appreciation of his life and work in 1908, the fiftieth anniversary of his death. He was also the subject of a volume in the popular series, "Lives of Remarkable People."[19]

Twentieth-century critics continued to debate the character and purposes of Ivanov's art. Fin-de-siècle Silver Age commentators used Ivanov as an occasion to dispute the relationship of art and religion.[20] Despite his religious focus, the painter was regarded, even in Soviet times, as a major figure in the cultural pantheon. The status of his work as a key moment in the evolution of Russian painting has never seriously been questioned. For the bicentenary of his birth in 2006, the Russian Museum in St. Petersburg organized an exhibition designed to confirm his status as a great master.[21]

Despite the patriotic consensus uniting Slavophiles and Westernizers, Silver Age decadents and Soviet academics, Marxist ideologues and post-Soviet neo-Slavophiles, they have chosen different approaches to the tensions in Ivanov's biography and his work. In one version of the story, the artist-as-saint leaves home (earthly Russia) for the heavenly city (Rome), where he dispenses with attributes of social station and becomes a hermit dedicated to art. On canvas, he manages to capture a moment of spiritual transformation frozen in time. Like the icon painters of old, he creates a symbolically pregnant image and leads a spiritually coherent life. In the competing version, an Ivanov of changing convictions deals not in eternal truths but in human stories. His character is not fixed in youth but experiences doubt and spiritual crisis. The canvas and sketches produced by this Ivanov focus on narrative—movement and change in human existence. Still another version combines features of these two: an intellectually coherent Ivanov struggles to express a consistently secular and rational approach to the world. Without question, no single portrait goes unchallenged. In that sense, the case of Ivanov as an interpretive dilemma is a modern story.

---

[19] "Aleksandr Andreevich Ivanov: Ocherk," *Niva*, no. 12 (1880): 242–44; "A. A. Ivanov," *Niva*, no. 37 (1908): 638–40; A. I. Tsomakion, *A. A. Ivanov: Ego zhizn' i khudozhestvennaia deiatel'nost'* (St. Petersburg: Tip. Kontragenstva zhel. dorog, 1894). See also the extensive treatment in N. P. Sobko, ed., *Slovar' russkikh khudozhnikov...s drevnieishikh vremen do nashikh dnei (XI–XIX vv.)*, 3 vols. (St. Petersburg: M. M. Stasiulevich, 1893), 1: cols. 5–297.

[20] Aleksandr Benua [Benois], *Istoriia zhivopisi v XIX veke: Russkaia zhivopis'* (St. Petersburg: Znanie, 1901); D. Filosofov, "Ivanov i Vasnetsov v otsenke Aleksandra Benua," *Mir iskusstva*, no. 10 (1901): 217–33; Vasilii Rozanov, "Aleks. Andr. Ivanov i kartina ego 'Iavlenie Khrista narodu'" (1906), in Gavriushin, *Filosofiia russkogo religioznogo iskusstva*, 145–50; text rpt. from V. V. Rozanov, *Sredi khudozhnikov* (St. Petersburg: A. S. Suvorin, 1914). See also N. Mashkovtsev, "Tvorcheskii put' Aleksandra Ivanova," *Apollon*, no. 6–7 (1916): 1–39; M. M. Allenov, *Aleksandr Andreevich Ivanov* (Moscow: Izobrazitel'noe iskusstvo, 1980), 73.

[21] See cover of *Illiustrirovannyi slovar' russkogo iskusstva*, ed. D. V. Sarab'ianov et al. (Moscow: Belyi gorod, 2001); Grigorii Goldovskii, "Aleksandr Andreevich Ivanov: Iubileinye razmyshleniia," in *Russkii muzei: Aleksandr Ivanov* (St. Petersburg: Palace Editions, 2006), 5–27. Thanks to Dr. Aleksei Kurbanovskii for sending me the catalogue.

Ivanov in Life and Letters: The Slavophile View

Ivanov was the son of the academic painter Andrei Ivanov (1776–1848). In 1830, at the age of twenty-four, already recognized for canvases executed in the approved classical style, the young man received a modest stipend from the St. Petersburg Society for the Encouragement of the Arts, an independent association supported largely by private donations, which allowed him to leave St. Petersburg for Rome.[22] There, among other European painters, he met the German Nazarenes, Johann Friedrich Overbeck (1789–1869) and Peter von Cornelius (1783–1867). He also attended gatherings in the villa of Zinaida Volkonskaia (1791–1862), a writer and art patron from a prominent family who had studied with Ivanov's father in St. Petersburg. In 1830 she, too, settled in Rome, where she converted to Catholicism and ended her days as a lay Franciscan. Her guests included Nikolai Gogol, whom Ivanov first encountered in 1838.[23]

By the mid-1840s, having labored at his great, still unfinished task for fifteen years, Ivanov was desperate for money.[24] In December 1845 Nicholas I visited the painter's studio, but his situation did not change. Wishing to help his friend, Gogol wrote to Count Matvei Viel'gorskii (1794–1866), a prominent musician and music patron. Published in *Vybrannye mesta iz perepiski s druz'iami* (*Selected Correspondence with Friends*) (1847), the letter first aroused interest in Ivanov and his work among the Russian public.[25] It also established one of the standard versions of the painter's story: the artist as saint.

A profile in self-abnegation, the portrait showed Ivanov living only for his art, indifferent to professional rewards or personal comforts. A true ascetic, "devoting himself to his task, like a monk to the monastery," Gogol wrote, Ivanov had abandoned "the idea of ever taking a wife and starting a family or household, leading instead a truly monastic existence, . . . ceaselessly praying." In itself, the subject of the great painting imparted an intensely spiritual dimension to the creative process, Gogol stressed. As John the Baptist heralds the approach of Christ, the moment of impending recognition is reflected in the consciousness of the figures grouped at

---

[22] See P. N. Stolpianskii, *Staryi Peterburg i Obshchestvo pooshchreniia khudozhestv* (Leningrad: Komitet populiarizatsii khudozhestvennykh izdanii, 1928).

[23] Nadejda Gorodetzky, "Princess Zinaida Volkonsky," in *Oxford Slavonic Papers*, ed. S. Konovalov, Vol. 5 (1954): 93–106; Stasov, "O znachenii Ivanova," 72; Allenov, *Aleksandr Andreevich Ivanov* (1980), 40.

[24] Anticipating a visit from a representative of the Academy, Ivanov organized a daguerreotype of the group of Russian artists then working in Rome. He sent prints to his father in St. Petersburg, hoping they would attract financial support. See E. N. Guseva, "O dagerrotipe 'A. A. Ivanov v gruppe russkikh khudozhnikov v Rime,'" *Pamiatniki kul'tury: Novye otkrytiia. Ezhegodnik 1995* (Moscow: Nauka, 1996): 253–68.

[25] On the letter's impact and for an example of an interpretation of Ivanov that follows Gogol's lead, see Kovalevskii, "Vstrechi na zhiznennom puti," 356.

the forefront of the picture. They are shown at the point when realization dawns and they await their own transformation. To convey this dynamic moment, Gogol explained, realism was not sufficient. The artist must experience a corresponding transformation: "As long as the artist himself has not experienced a true conversion to Christ, he cannot depict it on canvas. Ivanov has prayed to God to send him such a complete conversion. He has shed silent tears, begging Him for the power to carry out His holy idea." Warmed by "the fire of grace," Ivanov was sure to avoid "the cold callousness from which many of the best and most good-hearted people suffer these days." Ivanov, Gogol proclaimed, possessed the inner spiritual conviction lacking in "today's secular artists."[26]

Gogol's interest in Ivanov's piety reflected the writer's own quest for spiritual meaning.[27] In the Slavophile circles to which Gogol belonged, others shared this mood. Ivan Kireevskii, as we have seen, had also moved from casual observance of Orthodox ritual to intense personal commitment in the same years. Even in Europe, where the Enlightenment had done the most damage, religion was recovering its strength. Writing for *Sovremennik (The Contemporary)* in 1846, the amateur art critic Fedor Chizhov, who was close to Gogol and Kireevskii, praised Overbeck as "the greatest talent of our time."[28] The German was not, Chizhov insisted, a throwback to outmoded conventions; he was an artisan toiling in "the common workshop called modernity." Painters in general, Chizhov was pleased to report, were now "turning to the soul as the source of art and to religion as the highest inspiration."[29]

Just as Russians, in the wake of the Napoleonic Wars, began to understand Orthodox icons as the native language of pictorial expression, so, too, did Germans move back in time, beyond the onset of the confessionally divisive Reformation, to an allegedly native cultural source. Friedrich Schlegel praised the heritage of medieval northern art as specifically German, rejecting the classical standard so admired by Johann Joachim Winckelmann (1717–1768) and defended by Goethe (1749–1832), who

---

[26] Gogol, "Istoricheskii zhivopisets Ivanov," 138, 145, 146 (quote), 140–42 (quote).

[27] Mikhail Allenov believes that Gogol was drawing a portrait of himself which he projected onto Ivanov (Allenov, *Aleksandr Ivanov* [Moscow: Trilistnik, 1997], 13).

[28] F. V. Chizhov, "Overbek," *Sovremennik* 43 (1846): 17–68 (quote, 22). Chizhov's own biography demonstrates the attempt to mediate between traditional and modern demands. His interest in art and Slavophile ideas occupied his middle years, but he was trained in mathematics and engineering. Among his publications were a history of the steam engine and a book on silk farming, which he practiced commercially. He achieved stunning entrepreneurial success and amassed considerable wealth later in life in connection with railroads, steamship transport, and banking. See *Entsiklopedicheskii slovar'* (St. Petersburg: Brokgaus-Efron, 1903), 38:821–22; Inna Simonova, *Fedor Chizhov* (Moscow: Molodaia gvardiia, 2002); Thomas C. Owen, *Dilemmas of Russian Capitalism: Fedor Chizhov and Corporate Enterprise in the Railroad Age* (Cambridge, Mass.: Harvard University Press, 2005).

[29] Chizhov, "Overbek," 20, 30–31.

disliked the new patriotic religious art.[30] It was this neo-Christian Romantic spirit that infused Overbeck and the other Nazarenes with whom Ivanov consorted in Rome. Overbeck's 1824 painting of Christ's arrival in Jerusalem, which was widely diffused as a lithograph, directly inspired the composition of Ivanov's canvas.[31]

The Nazarenes adopted a religious model of the artist's calling. They converted to Catholicism, called themselves a brotherhood, and lived in monastic austerity. They derived their ideas about the spiritual character of art and the dedicated artist not, however, from medieval sources but from the writings of Wilhelm Heinrich Wackenroder (1773–1798), and especially from his essay, *Herzensergiessungen eines kunstliebenden Klosterbruders* (*Heart-Felt Confessions of an Art-loving Monk*) (1796), which Ivanov himself was able to read in Russian translation.[32] In the case of Raphael's *Sistine Madonna,* Wackenroder and Johann Gottfried Herder (1744–1803) established the legend that the work's celestial power was the product of the artist's personal vision. As Belting comments, "a *topos* from the miracle legends associated with medieval cult images has been put to the service of the new cult of art."[33] Gogol and Chizhov saw Ivanov, like the Germans, as engaged in the re-sacralization of the artist and of art itself.

Indeed, this period witnessed the production of "secular devotional pictures" not only in Germany but also in France, in connection with Protestant and Catholic revivals.[34] The inner tranquility and spiritual intensity promoted by Wackenroder bore some resemblance, moreover, to the Orthodox spiritual tradition admired by Kireevskii and the Optina fathers. In France, the major influence was exerted by the aesthetic theories of Victor Cousin, encapsulated in his published lectures of 1815–1821, *Du vrai, du beau, du bien.* Kireevskii had read Cousin, along with Friedrich Schelling,

---

[30] See Keith Andrews, *The Nazarenes: A Brotherhood of German Painters in Rome* (Oxford: Clarendon, 1964); Mitchell Benjamin Frank, *German Romantic Painting Redefined: Nazarene Tradition and the Narratives of Romanticism* (Burlington, Vt.; Hants, England: Ashgate, 2001); Hans Belting, *The Germans and Their Art: A Troublesome Relationship,* trans. Scott Kleager (New Haven, Conn.: Yale University Press, 1998), 19–21; and Lionel Gossman, "Unwilling Moderns: The Nazarene Painters of the Nineteenth Century," *Nineteenth-Century Art Worldwide: A Journal of Nineteenth-Century Visual Culture* 2, no. 3 (fall 2003). Available at http://www.19thc-artworldwide.org/autumn_03/articles/goss.shtml. Also idem, "Beyond Modern: The Art of the Nazarenes," *Common Knowledge* 14, no. 1 (2008): 45–104.

[31] D. V. Sarab'ianov, *Russkaia zhivopis' XIX veka sredi evropeiskikh shkol* (Moscow: Sovetskii khudozhnik, 1980), 99 (*Einzug Jesu in Jerusalem*).

[32] See Wilhelm Heinrich Wackenroder, *Confessions and Fantasies,* trans. and ed. Mary Hurst Schubert (University Park: Pennsylvania State University Press, 1971). See also Allenov, *Aleksandr Andreevich Ivanov* (1980), 15.

[33] Belting, *Invisible Masterpiece,* 55.

[34] Cordula A. Grewe, "The Invention of the Secular Devotional Picture," *Word and Image* 16, no. 1 (January–March 2000): 48–49.

on the eve of his conversion to serious Orthodox devotion. "God is revealed to us," Cousin affirmed, "through the idea of the true, the idea
of the good, and the idea of the beautiful.... True beauty is ideal beauty
and ideal beauty is a reflection of the infinite. Thus art is essentially moral
and religious."[35] In the 1830s, therefore, as the dominance of classicism
waned, some French painters turned to the pre-Raphaelite masters for stylistic inspiration. What the French admired in their work was its "aesthetic
and ascetic spirituality." Artists, like monks (and sometimes, as monks),
were both inspired and devout. Like the Nazarenes, French artists assembled in Rome and formed their own, neo-medieval brotherhood, on the
same model.[36]

Acknowledging the European context of Ivanov's aesthetic quest, his
contemporaries nevertheless tried to define what was particularly Russian
about him. For Slavophiles, the answer was simple. Europeans, Chizhov
argued, labored under a cultural disadvantage. Cold and rationalistic,
Protestantism was damaging to the plastic expressivity of art. Overbeck's
work therefore tended to the illustrative and schematic.[37] In yearning for
the warmth of unreflective faith, secularized Westerners turned to medieval religion, but this, in Chizhov's view, merely demonstrated the "un-
natural religiosity of the West." Russians, by contrast, had never lost their
spiritual immediacy. While borrowing Western stylistic conventions, modern Russian artists benefited from direct contact with the sacred sources.
"On questions of form," Chizhov wrote, "we submit to the Europeans,
but on matters of the spirit, we insist on revealing our soul in its own
image [obraz]."[38]

Khomiakov, like Chizhov, viewed Ivanov as the embodiment of the specifically Russian Slavophile vision: "He was a sacred artist because of his humble attitude toward religious art, which constituted his entire life."[39] Writing
in 1858, in the shadow of Ivanov's death, Khomiakov tried to distinguish
this ideal from the European Romantic version it closely resembled. The
first task of the re-sacralized artist, Khomiakov remarked, was to renounce
the goal of originality and self-expression essential to post-Renaissance art.
Invoking the self-effacing monk of Gogol's letter, Khomiakov praised Ivanov
for brilliantly succeeding at this task. The painter, he asserted, labored not

[35] Quoted in Bruno Foucart, Le Renouveau de la peinture religieuse en France (1800–
1860) (Paris: Arthéna, 1987), 18 (quote); also 16–17.

[36] Ibid., 9, 26–33; 45; 33 (quote).

[37] Chizhov, "Overbek," 38. Even the Germans thought of themselves as abstract and theoretical: Belting, Germans and Their Art, 6–8; Frank, German Romantic Painting, 3, 5–6.

[38] Chizhov, "Overbek," 60 (neestestvennaia religioznost' Zapada), 68.

[39] Khomiakov to A. I. Koshelev, quoted in E. I. Annenkova, "Problema sootnosheniia
iskusstva i religii v vospriiatii slavianofilov," in Slavianofil'stvo i sovremennost': Sbornik
statei, ed. B. F. Egorov, V. A. Kotel'nikov, and Iu. V. Stennik (St. Petersburg: RAN-Nauka,
1994), 67.

to leave his own personal mark but to serve a truth larger than himself. Italians must have regarded the Russian as "a strange, northern ascetic, who had retreated into his imagined creation, as into the desert, there to serve art with all his soul." The self-denial practiced in his personal life also became the guiding principle of his art. Ivanov believed, as Khomiakov puts it, "that the artist should not stand like a visible third party, between the subject and its expression, but should be a transparent medium, through which the image of the subject imprints itself on the canvas."[40]

To explain this process, Khomiakov, the inventor of a steam engine, used a figure of speech that reflected his own fascination with technology, as well as his yearning to connect the broken threads of tradition with the reality of modern times. He celebrated Ivanov's mastery of contemporary craft as well as his dedication to ancient principles. For Khomiakov, art in the age of mechanical reproduction had decidedly not lost its mysterious glow. "Ivanov," the philosopher wrote, "wanted the subject to transfer itself to the canvas by means of some sort of spiritual daguerreotype that causes the personality of the artist to disappear." On his canvases, Khomiakov observed, physical bodies became "transparent envelopes of thought." The great subject of Christ's appearance, a theme of universal human importance, demanded for its true expression "the complete exclusion of [the artist's] personality." This, Khomiakov believed, is what Ivanov had so magnificently achieved in wedding the spirituality of the old icons and the icon-painting craft to the techniques of modern art. "Never had a material image so transparently enfolded the secret of the Christian idea."[41]

In fact, however, Ivanov had not taken his models from the Russian icon tradition but from the Italian pre-Raphaelites. Fourteenth-century painters, such as Giotto (1266–1337), had similarly inspired the Nazarenes. Europeans, too, were responding to the inadequacies of modern-day individualism, which they associated with the stylistic hallmarks of Renaissance art. But in pursuing this same strategy, Khomiakov believed, Ivanov was not engaging in a double imitation—of contemporary artists, on the one side, and early European art, on the other. He enjoyed an advantage that the pre-Raphaelites lacked. In searching for the unspoiled simplicity of pre-secular art, Ivanov was able to reconnect with his own cultural tradition. In Khomiakov's words: "Ivanov did not fall into the same error as today's pre-Raphaelites. He did not imitate a simplicity foreign to himself. He was sincere, not theatrical, in his artistic simplicity. He was able to be simple because he was fortunate to belong not to the outmoded one-sidedness of Latin Christianity but to the fullness of the Church that cannot outlive its time."[42]

---

[40] Khomiakov, "Kartina Ivanova," 347, 360 (quote), 352 (quote).

[41] Ibid., 353, 360, 354, 361 (quotes, respectively).

[42] Ibid., 355.

The Byzantine icon tradition, which had left its mark on the Italian Old Masters, also provided the basis for Russian icon-painting. Therefore, in turning to the pre-Raphaelites, Ivanov was opting not for Europe but for Russia. "Our Ivanov, standing on firm soil, could achieve what was impossible for European artists. He was able to master the form, to study and transmit the secrets of the corporeal image, while remaining true to his own spiritual principles. He was a student of the icon-painters,...[but he] seems to have created something *new* in painting."[43] In short, Russian artists, because of their very distance from secular culture, were better placed than Europeans to resolve their common malaise. Unhappy with the present, all sought inspiration in the past, but, in returning, found different sources. The European pre-Renaissance led the Russians, via Byzantium, to the core of Orthodox tradition, which, in their case, invested the new sacred art with the power of cultural continuity. In that sense, from Khomiakov's perspective, Ivanov was able to mend the rupture in historical time.

Two forms of synthesis were at work in the philosopher's conception: first, the joining of modernity with the past; and, second, the triumph of personality in and through the collective spirit. Khomiakov claimed to identify both these postulates of Slavophile thinking in Ivanov's case. On the one hand, Ivanov's adaptation of the icon was not a mere reproduction but a more complex version of the original. On the other hand, by tapping the native heritage—language, way of life, habits of worship—the artist was "able to express in his soul the features that exceed the limits of the individual self. They become the private expression of the common Russian spirit [*vsenarodnyi Russkii dukh*], illuminated by the Orthodox Faith....His triumph is the collective triumph."[44]

Ivanov in Life and Letters: The Westernizer View

Ivanov's single-minded devotion to the great Christian theme and the austerity of his artistic calling matched him perfectly to the Slavophile ideal. Yet intellectuals of the Westernizer camp also celebrated his life and work. Alexander Herzen praised him as a martyr to tsarist oppression and to the smug cultural establishment. Indeed, Herzen's tone is hardly distinguishable from that of the Slavophiles. "Ivanov's life," he writes, "was an anachronism. Such sacred devotion to art, such religious dedication, combined with self-doubt, awe, and faith, we find only in stories about medieval hermits, who prayed with their brushes and for whom art was an act of moral heroism, a sacred rite, and a study."[45] Back in Russia,

---

[43] Ibid., 357.

[44] Ibid., 365, 358–59 (*ego torzhestvo est' torzhestvo obshchee*).

[45] Herzen quoted in Stasov, "O znachenii Ivanova," 79 (*nravstvennyi podvig zhizni, sviashchennodeistvie, nauka*).

Herzen observes, Ivanov "seemed like a stranger when he displayed his picture to the crowd of scheming art professionals, uncaring ignoramuses, and aesthetes in uniform.... Ill and tormented by poverty, Ivanov did not survive the crude contact with the imperial court—and died." The novelist Ivan Turgenev also complained that Russia had deprived Ivanov of a well-deserved welcome. Instead of accolades, he had been met by "an insulting newspaper article, various delays [in paying for the work], and calculated scorn."[46]

The radical thinker Nikolai Chernyshevskii was himself a cultural icon, exemplar of self-abnegation, and prophet of secular self-fashioning.[47] He, too, deplored the hostility with which Ivanov had been greeted by the academic establishment. Chernyshevskii's goal, however, was to rescue Ivanov not from criticism or neglect but from the praise of the wrong people: the Slavophiles. "Having outlived Gogol," Chernyshevskii wrote, "Ivanov had the time to see his error, correct it, and become a new man."[48] In St. Petersburg Chernyshevskii reported to have found the artist dissatisfied with his great painting, which he felt he had by now outgrown. Painters should not look to the past for inspiration, Chernyshevskii heard Ivanov say, but should reflect the achievements of the current age.

According to Chernyshevskii, *Das Leben Jesu* (*The Life of Jesus*), by David Friedrich Strauss (1808–1874), first published in German in 1835, which Ivanov read in 1851 in French translation, had changed the artist's attitude toward religion itself. By the 1850s he no longer aspired to imitate the Old Masters but had decided to apply the techniques introduced by Raphael to the expression of contemporary themes. Rejecting the German enthusiasm for the "pre-Raphaelite style" and the parallel Russian fascination with "Byzantine style" as "impermissible...steps in reverse," Ivanov had told Chernyshevskii that only when art confronted the problems of the present day could it "recover the significance it now lacks in public life."[49]

Thus each of Ivanov's commentators paints him in his own image. For Gogol, he was the monkish devotee of a holy craft. For Khomiakov he managed to reconcile modernity with the sacred tradition, integrating aesthetic enjoyment with the power of the divine. Raphael's *Sistine Madonna,* in the philosopher's opinion, was one of the few works to have managed this feat. In Khomiakov's words: "Seeing Ivanov's picture is not merely a supreme pleasure, but much more than that—it is a life event."[50] Chernyshevskii,

---

[46] Quotes, cited in commentary to Chernyshevskii, "Zametka," in *Polnoe sobranie sochinenii*, 5:931–32.

[47] Irina Paperno, *Chernyshevsky and the Age of Realism: A Study in the Semiotics of Behavior* (Stanford: Stanford University Press, 1988).

[48] Chernyshevskii, "Zametka," 340 (*sdelat'sia novym chelovekom*).

[49] Ivanov quoted in ibid., 338–39.

[50] Khomiakov, "Kartina Ivanova," 365 (*proisshestvie v zhizni*).

in claiming the painter for his own purposes, not surprisingly questioned Ivanov's dedication to religious truths. He saw him rather as a man of the present, concerned with social issues, eager to influence public opinion, convinced that art had the ability to "refashion life itself."[51] Perhaps it is here that the extremes meet. Khomiakov's insistence on the active power of the icon (its meaning as a "life event") and Chernyshevskii's desire for art to "transform life," though pointed in opposite directions (one toward God, the other toward society), converge on the notion of transfiguration. Chernyshevskii's Ivanov had ceased to believe in the literal Christ, but his alleged negative conversion, from faith to reason, echoed the Christian one: it had made him "a new man."

The most influential of these commentators was Vladimir Stasov. Like Chernyshevskii, the prominent culture critic wished to rescue the painter not only from his detractors but also from the Slavophiles' misguided acclaim. Khomiakov admired Ivanov's style as a reflection of the allegedly integrated character of the Orthodox faith, but this view, Stasov complained, derived less from the aesthetic qualities of Ivanov's work than from a general desire to celebrate the national spirit in art. So eager were the Slavophiles to identify a truly Russian national artist, the critic observed, that they uttered "everything patriotic and national that came into their heads." Under the influence of his Slavophile friends, Ivanov had claimed he wanted "to create in the icon style," but Stasov denied that there was anything "national" about the result. He nevertheless praised the artist for his sensitivity to the question of national culture (narodnost') and national types (*natsional'nyi istoricheskii tip*).[52]

What did Stasov mean by these terms? Like other neo-religious painters of the time, Ivanov modeled his figures on recognizable ethnic models. In order to re-create the historical setting for Christ's appearance, Ivanov visited Roman synagogues to observe the appearance, dress, and behavior of living Jews. He was therefore able to convey "the actual appearance of the Jewish type," as Stasov put it, claiming that Ivanov had even developed a degree of sympathy for the Jews, as the birth-nation of Jesus. His interest in the "nationality" of the Jews drew Ivanov's attention to Russian identity. "Soon," wrote Stasov, "he began to admire yet another nation [natsional'nost']—the Russian. His best thinking and greatest efforts at artistic development were dedicated to its study and, as far as he was able, to shaping a great future for it."[53]

Conceding that this interest had drawn Ivanov to the Slavophiles, Stasov took pains to dismantle Gogol's Slavophile-style portrait of the artist as

[51] Chernyshevskii, "Zametka," 339 (*preobrazovyvat' zhizn'*).

[52] Stasov, "O znachenii Ivanova," 60 (icon style); 47 ("*natsional'nosti,*" *kotoroi v etoi kartine imenno-to i ne bylo*), 61.

[53] Ibid., 62–63.

saint. The painter was certainly impoverished and dedicated to his work. But, the critic insisted, Ivanov was ascetic neither by temperament nor calling; he would have taken a wife had he been able to afford one. Indeed, he regretted being unable to combine marriage and work and admitted to sexual relations with prostitutes.[54] The record shows, in fact, that even before Gogol's death in 1852, Ivanov had begun to question some of his former ideas. In 1848 he wrote to Chizhov that history was "preparing humanity for a better life." Contemporaries, he said, were living in a "difficult transitional time." By 1855 he had begun to describe himself as also caught in a personal transition. "I seem to have abandoned the old habits of art," Stasov quoted him as saying, "but haven't yet laid the foundation for new ones. In this situation I have inadvertently become a transitional artist." In fact, Strauss's *Life of Jesus* seems to have shaken his earlier beliefs. In 1857 he traveled to Germany and England, meeting with Strauss, Guiseppe Mazzini (1805–1872), and Herzen, and a year later he wrote his brother that he was searching for a new path in art.[55]

Having derided Khomiakov's idealized vision of Ivanov, Stasov nevertheless sounded a similar note: "I consider Ivanov one of the greatest artists who has ever lived and at the same time one of the greatest and most original Russian figures." The Slavophile idiom seems inescapable. "I make bold to say," wrote Stasov, "that in all European painting there is no other Christ like Ivanov's Christ. None matches his majesty, simplicity, and deep sincerity. None matches the artistic perfection of Ivanov's historical types and the supreme originality of his images." But Stasov was not a Slavophile, and he was looking for something else to admire in Ivanov's work besides the ineffable Russian spirit. This something was realism. Ivanov, wrote Stasov, is a "deep and authentic realist." "We value him as a profound and accurate observer of real life, extraordinarily talented at conveying nature, people, human types and characters, expressions of the soul, and movements of the heart."[56]

Where the Slavophiles wished to see the imprint of a transcendent spirit, the radicals saw a response to questions of earthly human existence. However, in Stasov's opinion, it was not until the turning point of 1848 that Ivanov had been able to free himself from his classical academic training. At that time the painter resolved to devote himself to what Stasov quoted him as calling "the idea of a new art, suitable to modern concepts and

---

[54] Ibid., 64. On alleged celibacy, see "Mysli, prikhodiashchie pri chtenii Biblii (1846–47)," in Vinogradov, *Aleksandr Ivanov*, 659–60. On regrets, see Alpatov, *Aleksandr Andreevich Ivanov*, 2:97. Mention of his rejecting the possibility of marriage with his "beloved girl-friend" in order to go abroad and study art: Benua, *Istoriia zhivopisi*, 98.

[55] Stasov, "O znachenii Ivanova," 76–77 (*perekhodnyi khudozhnik*).

[56] Ibid., 79, 83, 81 (quotes, respectively).

needs." In this vein, Stasov described the post-1848 Ivanov as "a new man, a new artist," who had at last found his own distinctive voice.[57]

Stasov believed that the encounter with Strauss had been decisive, not in weakening Ivanov's faith but in changing his approach to the Bible. Toward the end of his life, the painter had produced a series of sketches on themes taken from the Old Testament. These sketches remained in the hands of his architect brother, Sergei (1822–1877), who willed them to the Prussian Archeological Society in Rome, of which he had been an active member. Following his instructions, the Society published the sketches in a series of albums, beginning in 1879.[58] The originals were later transferred to the Rumiantsev Museum, in Moscow, which already housed the great canvas. Access to the sketches and to a collection of Ivanov's correspondence, first published by the academic painter Mikhail Botkin (1839–1914) in 1880, dramatically transformed the artist's overall profile.[59]

The biblical sketches, in Stasov's view, constituted Ivanov's "main claim to immortality."[60] They reflected an intensified immersion in the biblical texts, which, ironically enough, given the Slavophile faith in Ivanov's deeply Orthodox spirit, Ivanov read in French translation.[61] But what kind of realism was this? Not, Stasov insisted, the realism of contemporary French art, guided by the empirical standards of natural science. Rather, the sketches represented a form of religiously inspired monumentalism. Eager to distinguish his interpretation from the pious enthusiasm of Ivanov's Slavophile admirers, Stasov invoked the authority of Alexander Herzen. But, on this subject, the Westernizer Herzen sounded very much like the Slavophile Khomiakov, who insisted on the distinctively Russian character of Ivanov's creation. As cited approvingly by Stasov, Herzen

[57] Ibid., 85–88.

[58] *Izobrazheniia iz Sviashchennoi istorii ostavlennykh eskizov Aleksandra Ivanova*, Vols. 1–14 (Berlin, 1879–1887): citation from "Ivanov, Aleksandr Andreevich," in *Khudozhniki narodov SSSR: Biobibliograficheskii slovar'*, ed. T. N. Gorina et al., 6 vols. (Moscow: Iskusstvo, 1983), Vol. 4, pt. 1, 387. The first of the albums were reviewed in January 1881 by Kramskoi, "Izobrazheniia." Thanks to Edward Kasinec for bibliographic assistance.

[59] Kramskoi, "Khudozhnik A. A. Ivanov," 806. Mikhail Botkin, ed., *Aleksandr Andreevich Ivanov: Ego zhizn' i perepiska, 1806–1858 gg.* (St. Petersburg: M. M. Stasiulevich, 1880). On the impact of both these sources, see also Kramskoi's letter to V. V. Stasov, 8 January 1880, in I. N. Kramskoi, *Pis'ma*, 2 vols. (Leningrad: Gosudarstvennoe izdatel'stvo izobrazitel'nykh iskusstv, 1937), 2:194. Cf. V. M. Zummer, "Svobodomyslie khudozhnika Aleksandra Ivanova: K 150-letiiu so dnia rozhdeniia," *Voprosy istorii religii i ateizma: Sbornik statei*, Vol. 4 (Moscow: Akademiia nauk SSSR, 1956), 180; see also Goldovskii, "Aleksandr Andreevich Ivanov," 24.

[60] Stasov, "O znachenii Ivanova," 87.

[61] Mashkovtsev, "Tvorcheskii put' Aleksandra Ivanova," 17. More ironic still, the translation was the work of Samuel Cahen (1796–1861), a French Jew who translated both Testaments and composed guides to religious thought for his French-speaking co-religionists. See Filosofov, "Ivanov i Vasnetsov," 223.

praised Ivanov for expressing "the unspoiled, intact Russian nature that we comprehend through our feelings, which we sense with our hearts, and for the sake of which...we so love Russia and have such passionate hopes for her future."[62]

Stasov's own ideological-aesthetic program embraced realism as the expression of a distinctively Russian cultural identity. Difficult to explain, however, was how the conventions of a European-wide movement applied to a narrative of universal significance, such as the appearance of Christ, could serve these particular goals. The solution for Stasov was to stress Ivanov's alleged sensitivity to narodnost'—his feel for the spirit of the nation, whether embodied in so-called national types or in concrete social details.

The nineteenth-century Russian painters who best embodied Stasov's ideal of socially conscious realism were the group called the *Peredvizhniki* (Itinerants). Breaking with the Imperial Academy in 1863, under the leadership of Kramskoi, they rejected official sponsorship and the aesthetic conventions of officially sponsored art. Their independent association was dedicated to bringing realist painting to the attention of the public in the form of traveling exhibitions.[63] Twenty years Ivanov's junior, Kramskoi completed his own interpretation of the Messiah, *Khristos v pustyne* (*Christ in the Desert*), in 1872. In contrast to Ivanov's composition, Kramskoi's Savior has moved to the foreground. Entirely alone, he sits hunched on a barren rock, lost in thought. No crowd, no greenery, no historical context—just a young man draped in a dark mantle. The picture thus compels a direct confrontation between viewer and figure, in which the viewer's gaze is not returned. Gone are the intrusive spectators, which troubled Kramskoi in the *Sistine Madonna* because they distanced the subject from the actual viewers and emphasized the devotional character of the work. Later Kramskoi supplied a humanistic interpretation of his painting, minimizing the Christian element, emphasizing the symbolic.[64]

Kramskoi considered Ivanov "an authentic and great artist." Influenced by the newly published correspondence, which exposed the painter's prolonged struggle for recognition, Kramskoi described Ivanov's ideas about art as well ahead of his time and portrayed his failure as a tragedy of Shakespearean proportions.[65] "Ivanov's significance is growing and...will continue to grow," Kramskoi predicted, but the public's initial coldness was not a mystery: "The 'character' of his work, the level of artistic

[62] Stasov, "O znachenii Ivanova," 89.

[63] Elizabeth Valkenier, *Russian Realist Art: The State and Society: The Peredvizhniki and Their Tradition* (New York: Columbia University Press, 1989).

[64] See letter to V. M. Garshin, 16 February 1878, in Kramskoi, *Ob iskusstve*, 191–94.

[65] Kramskoi, letter to P. M. Tret'iakov, 29 December 1879, in Kramskoi, *Pis'ma*, 2:188 (*istinnyi i velikii khudozhnik*); letter to V. V. Stasov, 8 January 1880, in ibid., 2:193–94.

development, and the artistic tastes that prevailed among the public at the time of the picture's appearance were so far apart that a misunderstanding was unavoidable."[66]

Kramskoi's description of the obstacle to understanding presented by Ivanov's work echoes the impediment to understanding depicted within the canvas itself: the painting "appears," as Christ "appeared"—also to "the people." In the case of the Messiah, some saw but others were blind. Regarding the painting, only a handful grasped its power, but most were unable to see it at all. Perhaps they needed a prophet (the critic?) to show them what was before their eyes. Unintentionally, therefore, Kramskoi understood the painting as functioning in the manner of a holy icon, though now in the service of art: manifesting in its mere presence (appearance) the spiritual quality inherent in the aesthetic as well as the religious domain.

And, indeed, Kramskoi used the occasion of Ivanov's misunderstood work to explicate how art in general acquires meaning. What does it mean to *see* art, which in itself is about seeing? How does taste change? For an artist to alter the way people see, to make them feel that they grasp what is before them, he must, of course, have talent. But the work itself must grab viewers' attention by its vitality and seeming ease. If its visual qualities do not please, if it demands too much explanation, then viewers will object that "they don't understand." "Long before it was shown," Kramskoi commented, "Ivanov's painting aroused great expectations, but when it appeared, most people said—'I don't understand.' And the majority was right, since this is in fact a painting that one must above all *understand.*"[67]

Kramskoi and the Peredvizhniki represented a movement for change in the conditions and conventions of artistic production. Taking their work directly to the broad public, they aspired to reflect the life this public knew without realizing what it was they knew because they did not see it. In view of the nature of this project, therefore, perhaps it is not surprising that Kramskoi's Christ confronts the viewer directly, without the intervention of the deputized viewers that Ivanov inserts within the narrative frame. In Kramskoi's architecture, "the story" is exported to the real world in which the painting itself exercises its power.

Kramskoi's explanation of Ivanov's difficulty in finding a language for his time reflects a rebel's understanding of what it means to forge a new path. It is hard, he said, for a work to engage the viewer's sympathy if its conventions are out of harmony with the current mood. Only rarely do great works appear at historical moments when that mood itself is in turmoil, when the old seems out of date, the new not yet developed. During

---

[66] Kramskoi, "Khudozhnik A. A. Ivanov," 807.
[67] Ibid., 808.

"moments of crystallization," Kramskoi explained, "when talents can build on a foundation of creativity already at hand, no one disputes them, they are generally accepted.... In such fortunate historical moments the artist works rapidly, with ardor and talent.... Such moments produce artistic work of the highest content and form. Ivanov did not draw such a lottery ticket."[68]

Ivanov's innovation, Kramskoi claimed, was to base his canvases on extensive studies from life. Each figure was carefully individuated, in terms of body type, anatomy, and temperament. He also pioneered in the use of natural lighting, the "*plein air*" style later developed by the French. He subordinated the "beauty of the line" to the logic of the composition. Beauty would emerge as a consequence of the expressive structure of the whole. "No artist has done more for Russian art than Ivanov," Kramskoi concluded. "Define the ideals of the art of today and you will see that Ivanov already understood them fifty years ago, defined himself in their terms, and attempted to realize them."[69]

Ivanov's true contribution was to open the way, but he could not fully apply his own innovations. "Ivanov was a realist of the most rigorous and honest kind," Kramskoi wrote, but his work remained cerebral. Each study of each head contributed to the final portrait on the canvas, but that final portrait—though at a higher level of perfection—had lost the energy and spontaneity of the drafts. The tragedy lay in Ivanov's own awareness of his failure. By 1848 he had stopped work on the great canvas, having begun to doubt its value. With the painting behind him, he approached new tasks such as the biblical sketches that occupied his last years.[70]

Leonardo da Vinci (1452–1519), to whom Kramskoi did not hesitate to compare Ivanov, was recognized as a great artist because his aesthetic impulses were at one with his time; his talent could draw on a national tradition. Ivanov, by contrast, had to free himself from the constraints imposed on his talents by the artificial academic style. The biblical sketches represented both the breakthrough and its necessary lack of completeness. "These compositions went so far in seizing the future that even today, more than twenty years after his death, not a single European artist can interpret the Gospels as seriously, directly, realistically, and respectfully as he did." But the promise was unfulfilled. Ivanov remained a lonely and tragic figure—Christ in the Desert, waiting for the viewer outside the frame truly to grasp his purpose. "By the time Ivanov forced himself to return to Russia," Kramskoi commented, "both he and Russia had become something new." Ivanov presented the great work which he himself had

---

[68] Ibid., 811.

[69] Ibid., 815. For the same emphasis on observation from nature and the value of the preparatory studies, see Novitskii, *Istoriia russkogo iskusstva*.

[70] Kramskoi, "Khudozhnik A. A. Ivanov," 814–15.

already surpassed but which nevertheless, in Kramskoi's view, constituted "an enormous intellectual [*ideinyi*] turning point in art." Ivanov recognized his own value, but no one was there to plead his case. In response to the crude reception that greeted him on his return, "his childishly pure nature did not hold out."[71]

Discovering the Future

In contrast to both the democrats' socially oriented realism and the Slavophiles' traditionalist nostalgia, the Silver Age defined itself as a time of aesthetic modernism and eccentric spiritual tastes. Writers and artists, in various ways, rejected the conventions of realistic representation, whether academic or civic-minded. They searched instead for meaning in symbolic forms or in purely formal relations. Both artists and art critics in this period showed a renewed interest in the Orthodox icon. The icon, in Belting's sense, took them back beyond the individualist, now also bourgeois, post-Renaissance modes of representation to a flattened idiom rooted both in a native cultural tradition and in abstract principles of design. Devoted, again in Belting's terms, to the mission of art in the modern sense, they understood the aesthetic dimension as a medium of spiritual exploration.

Given their conception of art as a spiritual enterprise, the Silver Age critics who embraced Ivanov were inclined to see him as an artist with a religious, not a social or political, mission. They nevertheless disagreed on how successful he had been in shaping a visual language that was both inspiring and identifiably Russian. Consider, for example, the views expounded by Alexandre Benois (1870–1960) in his history of nineteenth-century Russian painting. A painter in his own right and an original member of the World of Art association founded by Sergei Diaghilev (1872–1929), Benois, like Kramskoi, deplored the impact of Ivanov's academic training and hailed the biblical sketches as the painter's greatest moment. Like Gogol, he considered Ivanov a saintly figure, possessing a "childlike, angelic, sensitive soul, the soul of a true prophet, thirsting for truth and undaunted by martyrdom." This inner strength, according to Benois, gave Ivanov the "intellectual courage" to resist both the Academy and his own academically trained father, the kind of courage Benois considered "an unmistakable mark of divinity and...his lifelong salvation." For this commentator, however, the opposite of academic classicism was not realism, as it was for Stasov and Kramskoi, but spiritual intuition. "Ivanov's nature," Benois asserted, "was too impassioned and inspired for him to exchange

[71] Ibid., 817–19.

his deeply mystical outlook for the shallow positivism evident in Proudhon or Courbet's art."[72]

In Rome, surrounded on all sides by the classical style, Ivanov managed to make his way to the anti-classical Nazarenes. His encounter with "those holy artists," as Benois called them, was "the beginning of his salvation." Regretting that Overbeck had been led astray by "Catholic fanaticism," Benois praised him nevertheless as "the first in modern times to reveal in art a comprehension and spiritual recognition of Christian ideals." Describing the German as a "good-hearted, honest, and saintly, but limited" man, "whose theories were mystical but whose practice was dry and cerebral,"[73] Benois blamed Overbeck's influence for Ivanov's failure to realize his own aesthetic and spiritual calling. Convinced that art must derive from inspiration, Ivanov nevertheless approached his great canvas as Overbeck would have done, as an intellectual problem needing a technical solution. In contrast to the lively creativity of the original sketches, the final work was "heavy and tormented."[74]

Benois believed that "the mission of Russian art, as a reflection of Russian spiritual life, [was] to express in images the Russian relationship to the Mystery."[75] This was the goal Ivanov hoped to achieve in his great work—"to express not only his personal understanding of Christ, but the understanding of the Russian people." Unlike Khomiakov, however, who viewed the canvas as the triumph of the common spirit, Benois believed Ivanov had failed to achieve either national or spiritual authenticity in the monumental canvas. An unsuccessful attempt to merge classical models with the "archaic" Byzantine style, it "did not convey the holy message Ivanov intended....By nature a prophet, sage, martyr, and saint," Benois concluded, "Ivanov destroyed his youth in its creation."[76]

Only toward the end had the painter begun to craft a visual language that broke with his academic past. The year 1848 was crucial, in Benois's account, not, as in Stasov's view, because of the impact of revolution or the influence of Strauss but owing to the death of Ivanov Senior. A small inheritance gave Aleksandr the financial independence to devote himself to the task that Benois considered his true calling—the cycle of biblical

---

[72] Benua, *Istoriia zhivopisi,* 96, 97, 111. Pierre-Joseph Proudon (1809–1865) was a socialist philosopher; Gustave Courbet (1819–1877) was a realist painter, who produced, among other works, a portrait of Proudon (1865).

[73] Ibid., 99 (*obnaruzhil ponimanie i voodushevlennoe priznanie khristianskikh idealov v iskusstve*), 102. For another criticism of Ivanov's over-intellectualized, abstract approach to the subject as manifest in the canvas, see A. Andreeva, "Eskizy A. A. Ivanova iz bibleiskoi istorii," *Mir iskusstva,* no. 10 (1901): 234, 245.

[74] Benua, *Istoriia zhivopisi,* 106 (*muchitel'noe, tiagostnoe*); 107 (*vialoe i skuchnoe*). Other critics also preferred the studies over the completed canvas: see Novitskii, *Istoriia russkogo iskusstva,* 2:271.

[75] Benua, *Istoriia zhivopisi,* 127; quoted in Filosofov, "Ivanov i Vasnetsov," 218.

[76] Benua, *Istoriia zhivopisi,* 100, 107.

sketches.[77] Ivanov "was mistaken," Benois maintained, "in thinking that Strauss's book had shaken his faith. The German scholar's scientific study of Christ did succeed in shaking his external, scholastic faith and even destroyed it... but in place of his former, timid religiosity Ivanov experienced the birth of a different faith. This was a philosophically informed and truly Christian faith—free, daring, and infinitely more vital than the former one, which was that of his father." Ivanov, in Benois's opinion, had at last discovered a truly universal visual and spiritual style.[78]

Other commentators equally sympathetic to the exalted view of art and of Russian spiritual identity, as championed by the Slavophiles and lately by Benois, were even harsher on Ivanov's failings. Dmitrii Filosofov (1872–1940) was an active member of the St. Petersburg Religious-Philosophical Society, the gathering of lay philosophers engaged in revitalizing Orthodox intellectual life, and also a contributor to the journal *Mir iskusstva* (*World of Art*). There he engaged in polemic with Benois on the subject of Ivanov. Despite his devout habits, Filosofov declared, the artist had lost touch with the Orthodox spirit. His work did not express the Russian "national-religious ideal."[79] On the contrary: "Ivanov did not study, understand, or love Russia.... In fact, there is nothing *Russian* in Ivanov's work. By 'Russian' I do not mean Russian 'themes,' but the completely unthinking, spontaneous element of nationality that all great artists possess."[80]

Rome, Filosofov complained, had not liberated Ivanov but instead had deflected him from the source of true inspiration. "Ivanov's enthusiasm for the Italian school, the influence of the Catholic Overbeck, his association with the Catholic-accented Gogol—all this erased the national features from Ivanov's work and cast a Western-Catholic shadow." His vision, however grand, could not be claimed for the Russian heritage. "To represent Ivanov as an inspired embodiment of purely Russian national religious ideals, some kind of homegrown nineteenth-century Russian philosophy, as Benois does, is incorrect and unfounded."[81]

Where Benois explained Ivanov's inconsistencies as a product of a mystical yet independent turn of mind, Filosofov saw "the stubbornness of an honest but limited man," who agreed with Gogol, on the one side, and with Herzen and Chernyshevskii, on the other, and then became "slavishly dependent" on the ideas of Strauss. Unstable in his thinking, Ivanov was

---

[77] Ibid., 108–9. Agreeing on the power of the sketches to express the mystical dimension of Ivanov's belief, in a visually realistic idiom: Andreeva, "Eskizy," 240–42.

[78] Benua, *Istoriia zhivopisi*, 109–10.

[79] Filosofov, "Ivanov i Vasnetsov," 219 (*voploshchenie natsional'no-religioznogo ideala*). Filosofov attributes this opinion to Benois, but Benois is actually paraphrasing the views of the painter Viktor Vasnetsov (1848–1926). For his general views, see D. V. Filosofov, *Neugasimaia lampada: Stati po tserkovnym i religioznym voprosam* (Moscow: I. D. Sytin, 1912).

[80] Filosofov, "Ivanov i Vasnetsov," 225–26.

[81] Ibid., 225, 227.

equally incoherent in his tastes, falling at one point under the sway of the early Italians and the Byzantine style, later rejecting the Byzantine model and preferring Raphael to the early masters. In short, Filosofov concluded, "no precise conclusions can be drawn" from Ivanov's diverse opinions, which, moreover, "contain nothing to stimulate the creative rebirth of national religious painting."[82]

Ivanov's career indeed unfolded in a sequence of disparate stages—the academic training, the magisterial canvas, the biblical sketches. It also presented a mixture of styles—the conventional compositions of his early years; the probing studies for the large canvas; the tightly controlled choreography and smooth finish of the canvas itself, reflecting the influence of the mock-medieval Nazarenes; and, finally, the translucent fluidity of the biblical scenes. On an intellectual level, Ivanov also lacked coherence: moving from the Slavophile-inclined Gogol and the Catholic-inspired Germans to the humanistic skepticism of Strauss and the secular social consciousness of Herzen and Chernyshevskii.

Yet, if Ivanov's confusion defeated attempts to assess his overall achievement, it made him an enduring subject of controversy. The biblical sketches, like the great canvas, also provoked a range of opinion. Some critics found them "fragmentary and incomplete";[83] others praised their freshness. The art historian Nikolai Mashkovtsev (1887–1962), writing in 1916, denied that Ivanov had ever been a "proper realist." Likening him to Paul Cézanne (1839–1906), also better at ideas and studies than finished products, Mashkovtsev considered the biblical sketches an inspired stylistic jumble.[84]

Incoherence, by contrast, did not trouble the religious philosopher and culture commentator Vasilii Rozanov, who disliked neatly organized systems of thought and prized self-contradiction. His discontent focused instead on the work as a medium of religious expression. When, in 1906, the centenary of Ivanov's birth, Rozanov contemplated the artist's contribution to Russian culture, he found the vision fundamentally deficient. The great canvas, Rozanov complained, failed to transcend its moment but was fatally limited by the intellectual perspective of its day. Like Benois, whose history of Russian painting he undoubtedly had read, and in contrast to Stasov, Rozanov judged Ivanov's attempt at realism a failure. Elements of moribund academic classicism marred the final effect, he complained, creating an awkwardly composite style. In subject matter, too, Ivanov's success was only partial. Wanting to express the "simple, the natural, the *vital* and *real*," the painter had intended to depict "the true faith, his own

---

[82] Ibid., 221, 224, 226.
[83] Andreeva, "Eskizy," 235 (*otryvochnost' i nezakonchennost'*).
[84] Mashkovtsev, "Tvorcheskii put' Aleksandra Ivanova," 2, 28–30.

and the people's, but he captured it not in its living dimension, as in prayer, but in the abstract and general."[85]

Taking Ivanov's pious intentions for granted, Rozanov claimed that the striving for realism had led him astray. "Instead of interpreting 'Christianity' as a 'spiritual fact' or 'spiritual turning-point,' a page in *my own spiritual story*,' Ivanov decided to depict 'the historical meaning of Christianity,' 'its role in history.'" Not only did "the artist pick the wrong theme," Rozanov protested, but he was unable to convey the spiritual dimension of the scene he had chosen. Unlike Khomiakov, who described the picture as vibrating with sacred, and specifically Eastern Orthodox, emotion, Rozanov saw nothing either Russian or even Christian about it. Its failure was rooted, he maintained, in its stylistic choices. "The essence of the *Appearance of Christ to the People* is *not an ethnographic fact* but a spiritual one. Ivanov, however, has all too clearly drawn an ethnography." On the one hand, the painting was too specific—depicting the physical appearance of the landscape and the human figures; on the other, it was not specific enough. In selecting "a theme of extremely general meaning, half-historical, half-philosophical," Rozanov asserted, Ivanov had expressed "nothing of our own; everything was imported or borrowed."[86]

Rozanov's response raised basic questions. What kind of plastic or pictorial representation could penetrate the surface to convey the emotion and meaning of belief? How could painting ever move us in the spiritual dimension? How could it avoid abstraction and express the experience of faith for individual believers and historically specific cultures? But Rozanov did not, in this connection, recommend the traditional icon as a way to embody the sacred that produces, rather than describes, the spiritual moment. Among art professionals, by contrast, the ancient icon had become the focus of attention.

Icon into Art

In discovering the icon as a work of art, nineteenth-century specialists claimed to identify an authentically Russian medium rooted deep in the past. Yet the charm of the newly appreciated images inhered not only in their pre-illusionist simplicity, two-dimensionality, and material immediacy but also in their retrospective incompleteness. Damage had turned them into the outlines of realized works the viewer would never see. Just as Ivanov's studies and biblical sketches seemed expressive in their unfinished state, whereas the completed *Appearance of Christ to the People* seemed conventional and resolved, so the old icons had the allure of lost

---

[85] Rozanov, "Aleks. Andr. Ivanov," 146.
[86] Ibid., 147–49.

or unachieved wholeness. Appreciated for their formal qualities and their unplanned imperfections (the damage of time), they had become modern.

Indeed, for art journals of the period modernism and the icon went hand in hand. The intersection of past and future is illustrated by the two exhibitions organized in 1913, the year of the Romanov tercentenary, both devoted to Russian Orthodox icons, one sponsored by the Moscow Imperial Archeological Institute, the other by the leading avant-garde couple Mikhail Larionov (1881–1964) and Natal'ia Goncharova (1881–1962), in their neo-primitive phase.[87] The icon's temporal conjuncture prompted the Ukrainian painter Aleksei Grishchenko (1883–1977) to reflect more generally on the relationship between ancient and modern conventions. In his view, the conflict between art and image had found its resolution not in nineteenth-century realism but in the simplicity of modernist forms. Cézanne, for example, had "bridged the chasm between the old art of painting and the new." Drawing on traditional models of the artistic vocation, Cézanne's work had a moral, as well as aesthetic, dimension, in Grishchenko's view. "The deep and simple spirit of Cézanne's painting, his remarkable hermit's life, filled with diligent labor and creative exaltation: all this has been the lodestar for artists pursuing the task of pure painting."[88]

In Grishchenko's rendition, Europe and Russia were no longer at odds. European modernists, such as Henri Matisse (1869–1954), admired Old Russian art (the icons), at the intersection of the Italian and Greek traditions.[89] "Twentieth-century Paris," Grishchenko commented, "in an odd way has something in common with barbaric Muscovy." For the same reason Russian modernist painting was deeply national, because it derived its principles from the art of Russia's past, that is, the Byzantine tradition. Though Grishchenko derided the programmatic work of the realist Peredvizhniki, Ivanov earned his admiration: "Aleksandr Ivanov emerges as an exceptional personality in the history of [Russian] painting. His convictions and profound attitude toward art raised him high above the level of his contemporaries, not only in Russia but in Europe as well." If Ivanov's true painterly eye saved him from the banality of social-minded realism, it did not, however, protect him from influences of a different kind. "Alas," Grishchenko wrote, "his timid spirit soon succumbed to the lamentations of the inept Nazarenes, who then dominated Rome, as well

[87] *Vystavka drevne-russkogo iskusstva.* Imperatorskii moskovskii arkheologicheskii institut imeni Imperatora Nikolaia II (Moscow: Delovoi Dvor', 1913); *Vystavka ikonopisnykh podlinnikov i lubkov,* organized by M. F. Larionov; foreword by M. F. Larionov and N. S. Goncharova (Moscow: Bol'shaia Dmitrovka, Khudozhestvennyi salon, 1913).

[88] Aleksandr Grishchenko, *O sviazakh russkoi zhivopisi s Vizantiei i zapadom XIII–XX v.: Mysli zhivopistsa* (Moscow: Levenson [izd. A. Grishchenko], 1913), 7 (*udivitel'naia zhizn' otshel'nika*).

[89] On Matisse in Russia, see Elizabeth Kridl Valkenier, *Valentin Serov: Portraits of Russia's Silver Age* (Evanston, Ill.: Northwestern University Press, 2001).

as to the Christian mysticism of Gogol and the materialism of Strauss and Herzen. This ruined his remarkable Russian gift for painting." Even now, Grishchenko complained, few Russians had followed Cézanne's example in trying "to span the abyss of false realism and retrospective individualism, to connect with the best elements of the native artistic past."[90]

Not everyone found these arguments convincing. The icon's dual perspective might evoke the fractured planes of modernist compositions, but, some objected, these had nothing to do with the juxtapositions found in icons, which derived from an entirely different worldview and served different expressive aims.[91] Nikolai Punin (1888–1953) expressed this opinion. For many years the companion of the celebrated poet Anna Akhmatova (1889–1966), Punin was associated with the futurist avant-garde. After the Bolshevik Revolution he soon ran into trouble. First arrested in 1921, he worked at the Russian Museum and lectured on art history during the 1930s but stopped publishing. Arrested again on several occasions, for the last time in 1949, he died in a labor camp shortly after Stalin's death.

Punin began his professional career in 1913, when he joined the Department of Christian Antiquities at the Russian Museum and published his first article in the avant-garde journal *Apollon* (*Apollo*). It concerned the relationship between contemporary art and the icon tradition.[92] Punin shared Grishchenko's distaste for the didactic realism of the Peredvizhniki, but he denied that modernist abstraction had anything in common with the tradition of icon art. The icon, he insisted, reflected the artist's direct contact with the natural world, as well as his direct access to spiritual meaning, qualities that modern art, with its individualist focus and formal preoccupations, had lost. Art on the one side, icon on the other.

Denouncing the current trends in European art as empty formalism, devoid of spiritual meaning, Punin blamed the Renaissance for "the erosion of human spiritual creativity." Linking realism, impressionism, and "art-for-art's sake," he regretted that technique had become the sole purpose and meaning of art. It is ironic that Punin should have been targeted during the postwar Soviet campaign against "formalism" and "bowing to the West." The anti-formalism he expressed in 1913 was quite different from the Stalinist accusation. In contrast to what he considered the pale, lifeless palette of the "plein air" style, Punin celebrated the vibrant, "mystically"

---

[90] Grishchenko, *O sviazakh*, 26 (*Muskovy*), 54, 60, 89.

[91] Comments à propos Grishchenko, in "Bibliografiia: Vystavka drevne-russkogo iskusstva," *Svetil'nik*, no. 3 (May 1913): 34.

[92] N. Punin, "Puti sovremennogo iskusstva i russkaia ikonopis'," *Apollon*, no. 10 (1913): 44–50. On Punin, see the preface to N. Punin, *Mir svetel liubov'iu: Dnevniki, pis'ma*, ed. L. A. Zykov (Moscow: Artist-Rezhisser-Teatr, 2000), 7–16; and V. N. Petrov, "N. N. Punin i ego iskusstvovedcheskie raboty," in *Russkoe i sovetskoe iskusstvo: Izbrannye trudy o russkom i sovetskom izobrazitel'nom iskusstve*, ed. I. N. Punina (Moscow: Sovetskii khudozhnik, 1976), 7–32.

infused colors of the ancient icons. He found the much-touted Cézanne "strange and disappointing"—"a victim, indeed a martyr, of barbaric realism." Despite the artist's talent and love for paint, which Punin admitted Cézanne approached with "religious devotion," the work was lifeless. What is important in art, Punin said, is "not how to see, but the purpose for which you are seeing."[93]

The icon was not the inspiration for modern art, in Punin's view, but its antidote. "Icon art [is] something of a *revelation*, showing a way out of the deadly stagnation of European realism toward the broad, eternal seas, toward the kind of free art vital to the human personality worthy of art at all." For Russians, he wrote, icons "are not so much works of art as they are living organisms, vessels of some special spiritual values, enveloped in a form as beautiful as it is expressive." Whereas icon painters shared with the rest of society a language of symbolic meaning, modern painters were enclosed within themselves and fixated on formal relationships. Art was thus faced with the choice between formalism, on the one hand, and self-resurrection through "the resurrection of forgotten traditions," on the other.[94]

These traditions were in fact being rediscovered. The Society for the Study of Ancient Russian Icon Painting sponsored a series of lavishly illustrated volumes, which appeared in 1914 under the title *Russkaia ikona* (*The Russian Icon*). Punin was among the editors. In the first issue, the painter Nikolai Roerikh (1874–1947) noted that until recently interest in icons was considered a "curiosity," a sign of arrested aesthetic development. Only now were they understood as art.[95] Another contributor complained that the first modern scholars to study the old icons had treated them not as creative works of art but as relics of an inflexible craft. Careful attention to style and proper restoration, however, had revealed the icon painter's individual touch, the aesthetic variety, rather than formulaic rigidity, of the genre.[96]

Punin, by contrast, did not try to justify the icons in terms of art. On the contrary, he insisted on the separation of image and aesthetics.

[93] N. Punin, "Puti sovremennogo iskusstva: Po povodu 'Stranits khudozhestvennoi kritiki' Sergeia Makovskogo," *Apollon*, no. 9 (1913): 56–57, 59–60.

[94] Punin, "Puti sovremennogo iskusstva i russkaia ikonopis'," 45–48, 50. The editor of a recent volume of Punin's writings remarks on the irony that Punin was later stigmatized as a formalist, whereas, in fact, he defended realism for what he considered its objectivity, accessibility, and connection to shared values. He disapproved of art that was individualistic, Romantic, and archaic: Punin, *Mir svetel liubov'iu,* 15.

[95] Nikolai Rerikh, "Pis'mo khudozhnika," *Russkaia ikona: Sbornik,* 3 vols. (St. Petersburg: T-vo R. Golike i A. Bilborg, 1914), 1:14.

[96] N. M. Shchekotov, "Ikonopis' kak iskusstvo (po povodu sobranii ikon I. S. Ostroukhova i S. P. Riabushinskogo)," *Russkaia ikona,* 2:115–42.

Fig. 2. Aleksandr Ivanov, *Iavlenie Khrista narodu* [Appearance of Christ to the People] (1837–1857). Oil on canvas. 540 x 750 cm. [18.7 x 24.6 ft.] © State Tretiakov Gallery, Moscow. The final version of the canvas.

Fig. 3. Aleksandr Ivanov, *Arkhangel Gavriil porazhaet Zakhariiu nemotoi* [Archangel Gabriel Striking Zachariah with Muteness]. Watercolor, whitening, pencil on paper, 26.2 x 39.9 [or 39.3] cm. © State Tretiakov Gallery, Moscow. From Ivanov's cycle of biblical sketches executed in the 1840s and 1850s.

There is no longer any doubt that the icon is a form of painting and constitutes an artistic unity. But raising the icon to the level of ordinary aesthetic values, however elevated that level may be, deprives it of its true meaning and to a great extent negates its value. The icon, one must not forget, is more than an example of style, a plethora of rich coloration. Its specific content is a particle of eternity, the incarnation of a life and spiritual rhythm different from the life and rhythm that until now have nourished our artistic senses. Ancient Russian icon painting cannot teach us to draw or paint better or in different ways. But it can teach us to think differently, to see the artistic design differently and approach its fulfillment in new ways. We can affirm that before speaking of art, one must speak of life. In any case, for us it is important to see the icon not so much as a historical or even aesthetic phenomenon, but as the deepest spiritual foundation without which the icon would not have achieved such powerful painterly and artistic qualities and would never have acquired the importance we assign it today.[97]

If the icons owed their spiritual intensity to the Byzantine legacy, he conceded, it was not until the fifteenth century that painters learned to free themselves from its formal constraints and convey the direct power of religious experience. Only then, in his view, did the icons become Russian, "express[ing] with particular and surprising intensity the distinguishing features of national identity."[98] Yet this identity was not entirely separate from the sources that fed European art. At its peak, the icon tradition reflected not only the impact of Byzantine Orthodoxy but also that of Hellenic Greece. "The Russian icon owes its harmony to Greece," Punin wrote, "the same Greece to which the best of European art is also indebted."[99]

Art and Icon among the Godless

With the Bolshevik Revolution, the legacy of scientific positivism and figurative realism triumphed over the philosophical idealism and spiritual improvisations of the Silver Age (now branded "decadent"), as well as the dogma and rituals of organized religion. But as before 1917, when the autocracy sponsored the Academy of Arts and endorsed the classical style, and when Nicholas I personally visited Ivanov's studio in Rome, political authority again intruded on issues of style and official sponsorship. For all its hostility to religion, the Soviet art establishment also embraced

---

[97] N. Punin, "Zametki ob ikonakh iz sobraniia N. P. Likhacheva," *Russkaia ikona*, 1:22–24.

[98] Punin, "Zametki ob ikonakh," 34.

[99] N. Punin, "Ellinizm i vostok v ikonopisi: Po povodu sobraniia ikon N. S. Ostroukhova i S. P. Riabushinskogo," *Russkaia ikona*, 3:191.

Ivanov as a native son. Following the lead of Stasov and Kramskoi, as well as Herzen and Chenyshevskii, the new experts interpreted his work as "progressive," in the secular Soviet sense.

Over the years successive editions of *Bol'shaia sovetskaia entsiklopediia* (*The Great Soviet Encyclopedia*) stressed the elements linking Ivanov to the outlook of the so-called democratic intelligentsia. Changes in ideological temperature are apparent, however, in the way each portrait deals with the breaks and contradictions in the artist's life and career. The entry in the 1933 edition, composed by the art historian Aleksei Fedorov-Davydov (1900–1969), characterizes Ivanov's early, classical style as an expression of aristocratic class perspective but credits him with evolving, "though not without contradictions, uncertainties, and vacillations," toward "the radical, rationalist orientation of the urban petty bourgeois." By the end, Fedorov-Davydov maintains, the painter had adopted "a new positivist attitude toward religion, seeing art as an instrument of the people's moral education, a way of resolving social contradictions." He was not, however, an essentially spiritual artist. The "decadent critics" of the turn of the century were wrong to praise the biblical sketches "as the 'mystical' culmination of Ivanov's work." Despite the shortcomings of the great canvas, Fedorov-Davydov considers it Ivanov's principal contribution. In short, Ivanov's thematic preoccupations do not prevent him from emerging as an exponent of rational positivism whose religious feelings are not at the center of his art.[100]

The *Encyclopedia*'s 1952 profile finds a different solution to the dilemma of Ivanov's political and social ambiguity, insisting even more emphatically that Ivanov's story is not only coherent but profoundly secular. Instead of condemning his background as aristocratic, the essay maintains that he had been "raised in an atmosphere of lively interest in the progressive ideas of his time." He is said to have harbored subversive attitudes even during his student years and to have sustained a concern for social questions while in Rome, despite his "religious illusions." The great canvas is praised as a depiction of the people's struggle for liberation. While acknowledging Ivanov's friendship with Gogol, whose honorable patriotism he is said to have shared, the essay rejects the image propagated by the Slavophiles and by "decadent" critics, who hailed Ivanov as "a God-seeking artist,

---

[100] Aleksei Fedorov-Davydov, "Ivanov, Aleksandr Andreevich," *Bol'shaia sovetskaia entsiklopediia* (Moscow: Sovetskaia entsiklopediia, 1933), 27:333–35 (*vydaiushchiisia russkii zhivopisets*). In the 1920s Fedorov-Davydov adhered to the sociological school of Soviet art history: John E. Bowlt, "Some Thoughts on the Condition of Soviet Art History," *The Art Bulletin* 71, no. 4 (December 1989): 546 (calling him a "vulgar Marxist"). In contrast to Fedorov-Davydov, see the passing comment by Adam Efros (1888–1956), who compares *Appearance* ("the failure of a genius") to the studies and sketches ("the inventions of a genius"), which he considers better suited to the 1910s than the 1840s: Abram Efros, ed., *Sil'vestr Shchedrin: Pis'ma iz Italii* (Moscow-Leningrad: Academia, 1932), 14. In the 1920s Efros was involved in the Moscow Yiddish Theater. On Efros, see Bowlt, "Some Thoughts," 545.

trying to resurrect the icon craft." Instead, the essay endorses his work as a model for late-nineteenth-century realism and a precursor of future Soviet art.[101]

The basic elements of this account survive into the 1972 edition, though by then the tone has cooled. The entry by the distinguished scholar Dmitrii Sarab'ianov (b. 1923) describes Ivanov as a member of "the progressive Russian intelligentsia" concerned with "injustice and oppression," whose painting, in a realistic mode, depicted "the spiritual turning point in the life of oppressed humanity, the beginning of its liberation and moral regeneration." Sarab'ianov characterizes the biblical sketches as a combination of "classical monumentalism" and "realistic methods," uniting the past and future of art. He praises the great canvas for its social message and social observation, but notes "the contradictory impression" produced by the mixture of academic and realistic styles.[102]

These, then, were the parameters governing the limits of what could be written on the subject. That Punin should have continued to think about Ivanov is not surprising, given the critic's earlier interest in icon art and the spiritual roots of artistic creativity. In 1947 he embarked on a study of the painter, which he intended as his doctoral dissertation. The work was interrupted two years later by the arrest that led to his death in 1953. The completed sections of the draft were published only in 1976 and 1990.[103]

Following the contours of the official version, Punin stressed Ivanov's ideological coherence. Noting that Ivanov père was familiar with the ideas of Winckelmann, associated in Europe with admiration for classical democracy, Punin assumed that the elder Ivanov held enlightened views on social questions. The ideas the son adopted after contact with Herzen and Chernyshevskii must therefore have been grounded in attitudes implanted by his father. "Aleksandr Ivanov," Punin wrote, "gives evidence of a coherent personality, which developed in a logical manner, though not without wavering along the way." "It seems evident," Punin added, "that Ivanov's ideas on social and political issues followed the same logical progression as his artistic views."[104]

---

[101] "Ivanov, Aleksandr Andreevich" [unsigned], Bol'shaia sovetskaia entsiklopediia, 2nd ed. (Moscow: Gosudarstvennoe nauchnoe izdatel'stvo, 1952), 17:272–74 (genial'nyi russkii khudozhnik).

[102] Dmitrii Sarab'ianov, "Ivanov, Aleksandr Andreevich," Bol'shaia sovetskaia entsiklopediia, 3rd ed. (Moscow: Sovetskaia entsiklopediia, 1972), 10:8–9 (russkii zhivopisets). Sarab'ianov remains a highly respected scholar: Bowlt, "Some Thoughts," 548.

[103] N. N. Punin, "Aleksandr Ivanov" (1947), in Russkoe i sovetskoe iskusstvo, 56–80; N. N. Punin, "'Bibleiskie eskizy' Aleksandra Ivanova," in Problemy izobrazitel'nogo iskusstva XIX stoletiia, Vol. 4, ed. N. N. Kalitina (Leningrad: Leningradskii gosudarstvennyi universitet, 1990), 4–36. On publication history, see M. Iu. Evsev'ev and I. N. Punina, "K 100-letiiu so dnia rozhdeniia N. N. Punina (1888–1953)," in ibid., 3–4.

[104] Punin, "Aleksandr Ivanov" (1947), 60–61 (natura tsel'naia). Reference to "wavering" echoes the phrasing of the 1933 Encyclopedia entry.

Indeed, Punin's point is to demonstrate the continuity between Ivanov's early academic training and his later style. To support this contention Punin marshaled arguments somewhat at odds with the standard Soviet accounts while at the same time affirming basic Soviet values. The Academy, he asserted, had preserved the conventions of classical Greek painting, with its underlying "mythopoetic principle." This classical legacy, which had left its mark on Russian art of the fourteenth and fifteenth centuries and persisted into the nineteenth, was, according to Punin, fundamentally supra-individual and moral in character. Its impact on Russian painting of the eighteenth and nineteenth centuries was evident in "the allegorical expression of the social-ethical norms of a patriarchal-religious worldview.... Russian art, like Greek art, in their most significant phases, never aimed merely to express aesthetic values. In positive terms, they were always the bearers of a civic-minded social ideology."[105]

Just as he described the legacy of classical Greece in terms compatible with the ideology of Socialist Realism, Punin praised Old Russian art not as a conduit for the divine but for its materialism, objectivity, social-mindedness, and artisanal craftsmanship—a catalogue of Soviet-era virtues. The icon, Punin insisted,

> has nothing mystical about it.... [T]he emphasis on art as a kind of miracle is completely absent in the Russian icon, at least in the examples that can be considered the most national [*natsional'nyi*] or native [*narodnyi*] expressions.... There is something severely practical, some common sense, a remarkable sobriety in the icon-painter's thinking, which endows the world of his images with that visually tangible objectivity, concreteness, and materiality that became the legacy of Russian icon art.[106]

Punin, earlier in his career, had insisted that the icon was an aesthetic achievement, but not in the modern sense, when art had lost something essential to the creative experience. Now he links the qualities of religiously motivated art with the antireligious attitudes of Soviet ideology. Old Russian art was "calm, objective and concrete, constructive and practical," not "specifically aesthetic." The materiality of the image was a function of the material itself: "Precisely this organic link with the board gives the icon a compositional objectivity rare in pictures that are understood as illusionist reproductions of a piece of reality." These were the qualities that also distinguished Ivanov's *Appearance of Christ to the People,* which, wrote Punin, "was not a picture in the nineteenth-century sense."[107]

---

[105] Punin, "Aleksandr Ivanov" (1947), 64, 65 (*ideino-soderzhatel'nyi i sotsial'no-obshchestvennyi*).

[106] Ibid., 66–67.

[107] Ibid., 67, 68, 69 (quotes).

The features of Old Russian art that Punin called "an expression of the national character" (*natsional'nyi kharakter*) or "native tradition" (*narodnaia traditsiia*) had, in his view, survived the subsequent imposition of European art. These features were: "the attempt...to give art the greatest possible objectivity, to make it...materially tangible, retain its connection to the principles of craftsmanship, and thus prevent it from entering the sphere of purely aesthetic values." Art that adhered to this tradition was "oriented toward collective reception" and offered "the supra-individual image of its age." Ivanov's work, as part of the Russian school, shared this legacy. His paintings presented objective facts in a manner that was "adequate to reality but that goes beyond 'individual cases' to express reality's ideal being." This is what connected the Russian school to the "native" Russian tradition.[108]

It was precisely these "native" influences, Punin maintained, that Ivanov sensed and reflected. Like all creative geniuses, he was able "intuitively to penetrate the past," without necessarily having known it directly. "The artistic traditions that lie at the heart of Ivanov's creative evolution as hidden tendencies," the critic noted, "were barely acknowledged by the artist himself." Drawing on the mythopoetic element in the "Russian folk tradition" that expressed the worldview of the common people, Ivanov aspired "to reconstruct the Christian myth, to resurrect it for a new life in the circumstances of his own historical moment." The "great artist's myth-making impulse" was a "progressive principle" linking him to the tradition of Old Russian art, and through it with the legacy of ancient Greece.[109]

Punin thus echoed the official description of Ivanov as "democratic" and quintessentially Russian. He explained these qualities, however, as rooted in the aesthetic conventions of sacred art, which, at the same time, he seemed to deprive of its spiritual dimension. His treatment of the biblical sketches emphasized this point. Rejecting the Silver Age view of these fluid and translucent images as an expression of Ivanov's alleged mystical tendencies, Punin proclaimed him a realist. He contended, perhaps in a gesture toward the "anti-cosmopolitan" spirit of the postwar Stalinist day, that the sketches owed little to the influence of European art but demonstrated, instead, the same artisanal-type realism at work in the Orthodox icon. Despite his twenty years in Rome, Punin insisted, Ivanov's vision was strong enough to resist the weight of the West. His work remained an expression of the "purely Russian spirit."[110]

The fundamental concept of the sketches was certainly religious, but it was a religion enlightened by the insights of Strauss's rational approach. Strauss, Punin agreed, was of crucial importance in shaping Ivanov's later

---

[108] Ibid., 69, 70, 71, 72 (quotes).
[109] Ibid., 73–74, 78, 80.
[110] Punin, "'Bibleiskie eskizy'," 4–36.

years and inspiring the biblical cycle. Yet, as an expression of his Lutheran heritage, Strauss's outlook was abstract and rational. Ivanov's "humanism," by contrast, was distinctly "national." Here, however, Punin struggled with the clash of categories. Praising Ivanov's attempt to replace "the illusions of religious belief" with faith in living people, Punin conceded that Ivanov's nonconformist bent was not (pace Chernyshevskii) directed at the political or social world of his day but remained within the conceptual universe of religion.[111] It was, after all, the ancient icon style, emerging at a subconscious cultural level, in its "mythopoetic," highly concrete but also synthetic and "collective" mode, that rendered the painter "national," "progressive," and modern.

Punin built his portrait of Ivanov by engaging the chain of art-critical interpretations that had preceded him and continued around him. The resulting profile allowed him to integrate ideas he had been nursing since the start of his career with the orthodoxies of postwar Stalinism. His views did not, of course, enter the discussion of Ivanov until years later. In the 1950s others wrestled with the challenge of making Ivanov acceptable. Ivanov emerged then as a practitioner of realism, the sketches not as expressions of the Christian truth but as historical narratives, presenting the biblical stories as legends or myths. His debt to the Slavophiles is minimized, the impact of rational Bible criticism enhanced.[112] As in Punin's (unavailable) account, 1848 looms as a turning point, but no one argues for the importance of the Orthodox icon tradition. The most extreme version predictably credits Strauss and the revolutionary events of 1848 with curing Ivanov of his early religious faith and his naive attachment to Slavophile ideas. He emerges as a critic of "the myth of religion," in the spirit of the Museum of the History of Religion and Atheism in Leningrad, whose director, Vladimir Bonch-Bruevich (1873–1955), praises the "artist-enlightener" for his proto-Soviet "materialist" worldview.[113]

The most extensive treatment of Ivanov in these years was provided by Mikhail Alpatov (1903–1983), professor at Moscow University and the Academy of Art, in a two-volume study that appeared in 1956, the 150th anniversary of Ivanov's birth.[114] Alpatov hewed, of course, to the

[111] Ibid., 18–19, 21.

[112] N. Dmitrieva, "Bibleiskie eskizy Aleksandra Ivanova (K 150-letiiu so dnia rozhdeniia khudozhnika)," *Iskusstvo*, no. 5 (1956): 50–60. She claims (54) that Ivanov's rendition of the Bible tales reflected the views of Ludwig Feuerbach (1804–1872), as expressed in *Das Wesen des Christentums (The Essence of Christianity)* (1841). Offering no evidence that Ivanov had read the book, she notes that Feuerbach's ideas were widely accepted at the time. See also B. Bernshtein, "A. Ivanov i slavianofil'stvo," *Iskusstvo*, no. 3 (1959): 58–66.

[113] Zummer, "Svobodomyslie" 159–81 ("myth of religion," 172). Zummer was an art historian whose earliest publications on Ivanov appeared in 1915. Punin cites him frequently.

[114] Alpatov, *Aleksandr Andreevich Ivanov*. On Alpatov's early career: Bowlt, "Some Thoughts," 547. Toward the end of his life, Alpatov admitted that he was dissatisfied with this work. In the atmosphere of the time, he recalls, he had pulled his punches: M. V. Alpatov,

basic Soviet line: although Ivanov "still thought in the traditional categories of Christian morality," he was "an active fighter for progressive ideals." Among the first Russian artists to embrace the democratic ideas of
popular liberation, he placed the suffering and struggles of the "people"
at the center of his canvas, emphasizing the "social questions" so prominent in the 1830s and 1840s. Having promised his sponsors an interpretation of Scripture, Ivanov delivered "a historical depiction of the life of the
people."[115] Admiring Raphael as a model of technical perfection, he believed in the social purposes of art and was among the pioneers of socially
conscious realism, the precursor to Soviet realist art.[116] The iconic quality
of Raphael's *Madonna*—a moment seized outside of time, and therefore
eternal—was replaced by a narrative of life on earth.

In the 1920s Alpatov had published studies of the ancient icons. He now
interpreted the biblical sketches as a stage in Ivanov's progressive emancipation from religious views. Like the *Appearance of Christ to the People*,
the scholar contended, they were historical, not mystical. Influenced by
Strauss and the defining year of 1848, Ivanov depicted the idea of Christ
as a human myth. The biblical sketches, Alpatov wrote, "had the ability
to liberate human awareness."[117] In the postwar spirit of Soviet nationalism, Alpatov claimed Ivanov both as a native son and a world-class genius.
"The Russian national character left a deep mark on Ivanov's art. It has
simplicity and immediacy; it is natural without being precious or forced."
For this very reason his work attained the status of "a classic of world
art," great precisely because it was also an expression of "the national
characteristics of [the artist's] native people."[118]

How do all these versions of Ivanov add up? Except for the contrarian
Rozanov, all commentators—whether Romantic, realist, "decadent," or
Party-line—agree that Ivanov was not only a great Russian painter but was
a great painter *tout court*. His stylistic inconsistency and the contrasting
phases of his work allow critics to focus on the aspect they find most congenial. In the Soviet portrait, he is modern and democratic, and surmounts
the debilitating influence of the Slavophiles' mystical worldview. Punin, in
1947, attempts to link these same positive features to the icon style, by associating the aestheticism of high art with bourgeois individualism and the

---

*Vospominaniia: Tvorcheskaia sud'ba, semeinaia khronika, gody ucheniia, goroda i strany,
liudi iskusstva*, ed. I. E. Danilova (Moscow: Iskusstvo, 1994), 133.

[115] Alpatov, *Aleksandr Andreevich Ivanov*, 1:378, 8, 206 (quotes, respectively).

[116] Ibid., 1:9. Writing in 1947, during the anti-Western campaign, Punin claimed that although Ivanov confessed to admiring Raphael, he in fact resisted the Italian influence: Punin,
"'Bibleiskie eskizy'," 29.

[117] Alpatov, *Aleksandr Andreevich Ivanov*, 2:154, 145, 161, 185 (quote).

[118] Ibid., 2:280–82. On the "anti-cosmopolitanism" of the postwar Stalin years, see, for
example, Ethan Pollock, *Stalin and the Soviet Science Wars* (Princeton: Princeton University
Press, 2006).

production of religious images with the era of craftsmanship and socially rooted forms. He does not, however, celebrate the spiritual dimension of this religiously motivated art, as he had before 1917. At the end of the 1970s Sarab'ianov focuses on Ivanov's debt to European Romanticism, to which, via the Nazarenes (as well as the Slavophiles), the painter owed his belated interest in the national roots of Russian art and, in particular, the ancient icons. In making this point, Sarab'ianov cites the recently published text of Punin's 1947 essay, which, after a silence of thirty years, finally entered the scholarly conversation.[119]

Soviet-era critics continued, however, to praise Ivanov for his rationality, realism, and social conscience. Today's leading Ivanov expert is Mikhail Allenov (b. 1942), who composed his doctoral dissertation in the early 1970s, achieving what Punin had been forced brutally to abandon thirty years before.[120] The world historical event conveyed in the great canvas, Allenov predictably asserts, is constituted not so much by the appearance of Christ as by the shift in human consciousness it occasioned.[121] "Christian mysticism provided the terminological arsenal for the artist's thought but did not define his worldview.... The orientation toward the future, the striving to change Russia's current condition transformed the religious mythologem of 'paradise lost' into the condemnation and rejection of the contemporary conditions of social life."[122] The focus is not the discovery of a revealed God but humanity's path toward self-discovery. "Ivanov's painting," Allenov concludes, "depicts the departure from myth into history, from the past into the present."[123]

Approaching Ivanov from the secular Soviet position, Allenov nevertheless respects the tensions in the painter's outlook. He shows how the realism of the great canvas and the stylistic eclecticism of the biblical sketches allowed Ivanov to integrate his religious sensibility with the increasingly rational approach to religion he encountered in contemporary European thought. Both phases of his work, in different ways, also allowed him to combine elements of classicism with the conventions of pre-Renaissance art—whether the plastic immediacy of Old Russian icons, the storytelling composition of Orthodox frescos, or the simplified forms of Egyptian painting.

---

[119] D. V. Sarab'ianov, *Russkaia zhivopis' XIX veka sredi evropeiskikh shkol* (Moscow: Sovetskii khudozhnik, 1980), 104–6.

[120] M. M. Allenov, "Kartina A. Ivanova 'Iavlenie Khrista narodu' ('Iavlenie Messii'): Ideino-khudozhestvennaia problematika," 2 vols., Diss. for Candidate's Degree in Art History, Moscow State University, Department of History, Section on the History of Russian and Soviet Art, 1975. Typescript courtesy of the author.

[121] Allenov, *Aleksandr Andreevich Ivanov* (1980), 121–26, 132.

[122] Ibid., 143.

[123] Ibid., 174.

In his post-Soviet reflections on the painter, Allenov continues to invoke the ideological context for Ivanov's work, but he focuses more centrally on the way the various components of Ivanov's thinking and religious belief—unstable and ambiguous as they may have been—found visual expression. Not surprisingly, given the history of the subject, he begins by contrasting the "icon" with the "picture."

> The picture, or pictorial form of representation [*kartinnaia forma izobrazitel'nosti*], as distinct from the icon form of representation, appeared in the world in order to show everything that exists on earth in horizontal dimension, on the horizon of human sight, according to the norms of what is naturally possible for the experience of sight. However, a miracle is miraculous precisely because it occurs outside these norms. Therefore, the reaction of people encountering God as Christ should also include an element of the supernatural and paradoxical, pointing to the exceptional, or, which is the same thing, extra-normal character of the occurrence. But in this exceptionality its universal humanity is lost. For the essence of what is human is by definition what is common to all people—the norm, the rule, but not the exception.[124]

A picture such as Ivanov's *Appearance of Christ to the People* is precisely not religious, Allenov still insists, but historical. It tells a story and conveys meaning according to the rules of human perception. Viewers or critics do not need to believe in order to get the message, but they need to know how to see. Indeed, says Allenov, Ivanov's picture centers on the very process of seeing. As viewers, we are confronted by the same problem facing the figures depicted in the painted scene: we must not merely look but must also see. The scene depicts a moment of transition in the life of humanity: the witnesses to Christ's coming are themselves transformed by their new awareness. But the painter has also figured himself into the picture: the person of the pilgrim, nestled under the upraised arm of John the Baptist, represents the artist, indeed the process of art itself. This figure, says Allenov, is a "mental mirror" (*umstvennoe zertsalo*), an observing organ. His activity is the quiet "activity of contemplation" (*deiatel'nost' sozertsaniia*), which enables him to see and make visible to others what they might not have seen on their own. This figure, Allenov asserts, is "a kind of representational hieroglyph, whose sign is the all-seeing eye, gazing not down from the heavens but up from earth. The artist is nothing more or less than the earthly organ, the tool of the divine 'all-seeing eye.'"[125]

---

[124] Allenov, *Aleksandr Ivanov* (1997), 4. This volume was nominated for the Minor Booker in 1999. Allenov is also the author of the entry on Ivanov in *Illiustrirovannyi slovar' russkogo iskusstva*, 171–72.

[125] Allenov, *Aleksandr Ivanov* (1997), 4, 8, 19, 20, 22.

Allenov's formulation thus returns us to Hans Belting's distinction: art is not the icon. Art is a form of human communication, not a mediation between human and divine. Yet art also acquires some of the attributes of religion. Here the artist appears in the role of "all-seeing eye." From Allenov's secular perspective, Ivanov speaks the language of this world, enabling us to see what we otherwise could not see, but the object of our attention is the human condition. The painter certainly believed in Christ, but he dedicated his life to art, not God. With this reading, we return both to the opening scene of the *Gospel According to St. John* and to the Romantic concept of art as the instrument of modern transcendence.

The historical character of Ivanov's art—its central interest in narrative, not revelation—is the key to its modern and secular status. This insistence brings Allenov, even in 1997, back to the canonical Soviet version of Ivanov as the man of the (progressive) political moment. In returning to Russia in 1858, when the era of the Great Reforms was just under way, Allenov contends, Ivanov was able to connect the theme of his great canvas—the theme of epoch-making transformation—with the events of his time. He was therefore also able to bridge the representational gap between the unmoving image of spiritual truth and the narrative structure of modern thinking. In displaying his work, Ivanov "allowed everything symbolic in the picture to be experienced as historical, individualized portraiture, and everything historical that was occurring in contemporary Russia to be seen in the symbolic perspective that illuminated that same picture."[126] Nurtured in the Soviet art establishment, and having survived the decades of Thaw, Perestroika, and post-Communism, Allenov is no stranger to shifting historical contexts. In relation to Ivanov, he divests the social-contextual elements of Soviet-era art commentary of its ideological heavy-handedness, but the structure of the argument remains.

No less persistent is the Slavophile model. In 2000 the city of Moscow, together with the Russian Culture Foundation established by film-maker Nikita Mikhalkov (b. 1945), sponsored an exhibition on the theme of "Image and Transfiguration in Art," which received the formal blessing of Aleksei Rediger, Patriarch of Moscow and All Russia (1929–2008). The selections, all Russian works, were designed to illustrate the idea that "Orthodoxy is Russia's historical destiny." In this context, Ivanov is praised for having finally freed himself from the Catholic-influenced academic style and returned in the biblical sketches to the techniques of ancient Russian frescos.[127] Also, in 2000, on the occasion of the second millennium, the Russian Federation issued a series of commemorative stamps featuring

---

[126] Ibid., 99.

[127] O. A. Gostev, ed., *Obraz i preobrazhenie v iskusstve* (Moscow: Ministerstvo kul'tury Rossiiskoi federatsii, Rossiiskii fond kul'tury; Izd. "Atel'e URS," 2000), 9 (quote), 13.

nineteenth-century paintings, including Kramskoi's *Christ in the Desert* and Ivanov's *Appearance.*

A more emphatic version of the neo-Slavophile view can be found in the commentary to a collection of Ivanov's correspondence and other documents, published in 2001 by the Gogol scholar Igor' Vinogradov (b. 1958). Focusing on reflections recorded by Ivanov in 1846–1847, Vinogradov emphasizes the artist's monarchist feelings and his faith in Russia's spiritual mission.[128] He welcomes Ivanov's conviction that, in the artist's words, "Russia can be expected to legislate for all humanity, thus bringing about the universal Kingdom of Heaven for the entire planet earth." The artist's role is to elevate the monarch's moral standing, educating him in the wisdom of the Bible and showing him "the secret of Russia's future...a goal both glorious and blessed."[129]

Vinogradov nevertheless thinks that the great canvas failed precisely in its religious mission. Stasov had praised Ivanov for his care in depicting historically and ethnically accurate figures, commending his interest in the representation of the Jews. Ivanov himself was proud of the attention with which he had observed and re-created the Jewish faces. Vinogradov, however, echoes the complaints of commentators who believed that the work's realism detracted from its message. He cites a witticism attributed to the poet Fedor Tiutchev (1803–1873): "These are not apostles and believers, but simply the Rothschild family." Vinogradov agrees: "This naturalistic [*naturalistichnost'*] and even 'portrait-like' [*portretnost'*] quality of *The Appearance of the Messiah,* damaging to the iconographic tradition, was noticed both before and after Tiutchev by many contemporaries."[130] Ivanov's mistake was to abandon the icon in favor of art. His realism led him to introduce the foreign element (the Jews) into the native, Christian story (where historically the Jews of course belonged).

His other mistake was to think he had suffered a spiritual crisis. "Seduced" by reading Strauss, Ivanov rejected his deepest personal convictions, Vinogradov assures us, and was thus "in this respect...beneath the level of his own work."[131] A deeply religious man to the day of his death, Ivanov created images that functioned as an antidote to the antireligious feeling of the time, even though they suffered from the influence of "secular and non-Orthodox knowledge," and particularly from the impact of Roman Catholicism, as experienced in Rome.[132] Concluding with a rhetorical

---

[128] Ivanov, "Mysli, prikhodiashchie pri chtenii Biblii (1846–1847)," in Vinogradov, *Aleksandr Ivanov,* 646–69.

[129] Vinogradov, *Aleksandr Ivanov,* 654 (quotes); also 657.

[130] Ibid., 19.

[131] Ibid., 22 (quote; also citing views in Botkin, *Aleksandr Andreevich Ivanov*); 23 (citing Tsomakion, *A. A. Ivanov*).

[132] "Leonid Uspenskii is right to observe that 'the transfer of the Roman Catholic image [*obraz*] onto Orthodox soil...[sic] contributed to the general weakening of church influence

flourish, Vinogradov applauds Ivanov's reference to Russia as the Savior nation, citing the artist's appeal to his countrymen to "labor for the Glory of God" and thus also the glory of Russia.[133]

Most recently, the catalogue of an exhibition organized in 2006 by the Russian Museum in St. Petersburg to mark the bicentenary of Ivanov's birth counts Ivanov among "the Titans" of Western art, a creative genius whose "universal human mission transcended historical circumstances." Like many before him, the editor finds the great canvas noble in its aspirations but lacking "the decidedly innovative pathos of his later revolutionary quests and epoch-making achievements."[134] It is the biblical sketches that will endure "among the ranks of the greatest creations of world art." Citing Allenov's view, in the secular Soviet tradition, that the sketches depict "not the Passion of Christ but the human Passion," the editor nevertheless finds traces of the divine in this late work, which reaches beyond the human senses to "grasp the ungraspable."[135] The sketches, he affirms, embodied Ivanov's concept of the missionary purpose of the artist and of art, which is "the spiritual transformation of the world."[136] Although that mission is universal—the Christian truth is the same for all humankind—it is Russia, as Ivanov believed, that shoulders the special, God-given mission to "usher in the golden age."[137]

Rounding out 150 years of interpretation, this latest addition to the corpus of Ivanov criticism agrees that he must continue to represent the triumph of universal values (aesthetic and spiritual), while at the same time reflecting the distinctive character of Russian culture. In post-Soviet Russia, when Orthodoxy has resumed its pre-1917 role as partner to the imperial state, Ivanov's religious focus suits him once again to nationalist appropriation. Yet across the years it has always been difficult to define what, in fact, was "Russian" (or even Orthodox) about his work, whether the carefully manicured canvas or the loosely expressive sketches. In general terms, the Slavophiles hoped to make Orthodoxy Russia's defining feature, but the traditional status of this Orthodoxy itself needed revision. The question of what constituted Russian national identity (in the face not only of ruptures with the past but also of the culturally composite character of the

---

on Orthodox consciousness [*rastserkovlenie pravoslavnogo soznaniia*]'" (ibid., 23–24). Ouspensky (1902–1987) spent his mature years in Paris, involved in the study of Orthodox theology and the practice of icon painting. Leonid Ouspensky, *Theology of the Icon* (Crestwood, N.Y.: St. Vladimir's Seminary Press, 1978); Leonid Ouspensky and Vladimir Lossky, *The Meaning of Icons*, trans. G. E. H. Palmer and E. Kadloubovsky (Crestwood, N.Y.: St. Vladimir's Seminary Press, 1982).

[133] Vinogradov, *Aleksandr Ivanov*, 24 (citing Ivanov).

[134] Goldovskii, "Aleksandr Andreevich Ivanov," 5, 7.

[135] Ibid., 22 (including direct cite of Allenov).

[136] Ibid., 21 (Goldovskii's words).

[137] Ibid., 13 (citing Ivanov).

empire) was not amenable to easy solutions. The celebration of the ancient icon coincided in 1913, as we have seen, with the centenary of Romanov rule. A year later the empire was at war and searching for a useable ideology of popular mobilization. The question of religion intruded here as well, with directly political consequences.

CHAPTER SEVEN

The Old Slavophile Steed

Failed Nationalism and the Philosophers' Jewish Problem

As suggested by Tiutchev's snide remark about the Rothschild family, noted in the previous chapter, the question of the Jews created difficulties for those espousing a Christian approach to Russian cultural identity. The "people" to whom Ivanov's Christ was appearing were, after all, mostly Jews, and the painter expended his talent for realistic depiction on making them look the part. Those who turned toward Him at this historical moment, as on the massive canvas, were about to forsake their past. Those who turned away continued through the centuries to repeat their gesture in daily life a hundred times over. Crowded into the annexed Polish lands, the stubborn descendants of the biblical Jews were not merely different, in the sense that Muslims, or even Protestants and Catholics, were different. Joined to Christianity at the root, they represented a conscious rejection of the original authority on which the monarchy claimed to rest. In the context of the broader challenge that nineteenth-century nationalism posed for Romanov rule, the Jewish Question therefore occupied a special place. The dilemma was exacerbated in 1914, when the western territories, including historic Poland, became the site of military conflict and when Russian intellectuals faced the task of shaping a patriotic identity suited to a mass-mobilization war.[1]

* * *

The spirit of nationalism that emerged in Europe in the wake of the French Revolution posed a challenge to dynastic states that embraced a

---

[1] Hubertus F. Jahn, *Patriotic Culture in Russia during World War I* (Ithaca: Cornell University Press, 1995).

diversity of peoples. Nicholas I faced this challenge dramatically in 1830–1831, when the wave of European revolutions inspired a rebellion in the Russian-ruled Kingdom of Poland. In its wake, the tsar adopted the formula "Orthodoxy, Autocracy, Nationality" as an antidote to the nationalist appeal. The third term, narodnost', was vague enough to invite a broad range of interpretation on the question, hotly debated in the decades to come, of what in a positive sense constituted the Russian identity.[2] In the religious domain, the slogan also targeted a potential threat, in this case reaffirming the historic ties between the Orthodox Church and the imperial state. Roman Catholicism had enjoyed a certain fashion in the court of Alexander I, which seemed all the more deplorable after the recent treachery of the Catholic Poles.[3]

The autocracy thus defined its power in terms specific to the Russian core. But the empire by definition was wider and less uniform than its core. By the late nineteenth century the population, measured by religious affiliation, was 70 percent Eastern Orthodox and Uniate, 11 percent Muslim, 4 percent Jewish (10 percent in the western provinces to which the Jews were largely restricted), 9 percent Catholic (most in the Kingdom of Poland), and 3 percent Lutheran (most in the Baltic region). The regime endorsed the basic structures of hierarchy and obedience within the minority confessions, as a means of enforcing administrative control. However, when the lines of division coincided with geographically vulnerable areas and political insubordination (anticipated or actual) coincided with religious allegiance, the authorities quickly moved from tolerance to repression.[4] The threat was particularly acute along the western borders. The Poles lost the last vestiges of autonomy they still enjoyed after 1831 when they revolted again in 1863.[5]

---

[2] On the evolution of the concept of narodnost', from its interpretation by the original Slavophiles to its aggressively chauvinistic use by right-wing groups at the turn of the century, see K. K. Arsen'ev, "Na temy dnia: Natsionalizm i liberalizm," *Vestnik Evropy* (January 1915): 365.

[3] Elena Gretchanaja, "Marginalität als Mechanismus der Selbsterkenntnis: Autobiographische Texte russischer Katholikinnen des frühen 19. Jahrhunderts," in *Autobiographical Practices in Russia—Autobiographische Praktiken in Russland*, ed. Jochen Hellbeck and Klaus Heller (Göttingen: Vandenhoeck & Ruprecht, 2004), 49–76; Andrei Zorin, "Ideologiia 'Pravoslaviia-Samoderzhaviia-Narodnosti': Opyt rekonstruktsii," *Novoe literaturnoe obozrenie*, no. 26 (1997). The desire to separate Aleksandr Ivanov, as an Orthodox icon, from the Catholic influence of Rome is part of this reaction.

[4] On the official link between religious and political allegiance, see M. A. Reisner, "Veroterpimost' i natsional'nyi printsip po deistvuiushchemu pravu," in idem, *Godusarstvo i veruiushchaia lichnost': Sbornik statei* (St. Petersburg: Obshchestvennaia pol'za, 1905), 156–61. See also Robert P. Geraci and Michael Khodarkovsky, eds., *Of Religion and Empire: Missions, Conversion, and Tolerance in Tsarist Russia* (Ithaca: Cornell University Press, 2001).

[5] The Kingdom of Poland, established by the Congress of Vienna in 1815, lost its separate status after 1863. For recent scholarship, see Theodore R. Weeks, *Nation and State in Late Imperial Russia: Nationalism and Russification on the Western Frontier, 1863–1914*

This second rebellion occurred in the midst of the Great Reforms, which reorganized patterns of authority in the countryside and loosened the reins on public life. In this transitional moment, nationalism was not the only ideology to challenge the imperial regime, which also confronted the menace of a home-grown revolutionary movement. Inspired by European theories of popular sovereignty and social justice, the radicals succeeded, in 1881, in assassinating the tsar-liberator Alexander II. The anti-Jewish pogroms that followed were inspired, no less than the revolutionaries themselves, but now from the political right, by modern models of political mobilization. The mob attacks on peaceful Jewish communities reflected both archaic prejudices and current tensions troubling to the urban and rural masses. They were instigated, however, by groups within the educated elite that embraced the new-style anti-Semitic ideology then emerging in Russia.

The intrusion of ideological anti-Semitism into the public arena was a pan-European development. The term itself was invented in 1879 by Wilhelm Marr (1818–1904), signaling a shift in the political context in which traditional anti-Jewish feeling now functioned.[6] By this time Russia had made its own contribution to the new tone, with the publication in 1869 of the virulent *Kniga Kagala* (*Book of the Kahal*) by Jakob Brafman (1825–1879), who initiated the myth of the world Jewish conspiracy. Novelists and journalists writing for a broad readership spread the idea that the Jews were hostile to the empire and its interests.[7]

Such views provided a language with which an agitated public could respond to moments of political crisis or tension. The Jewish Question did not become a matter of public controversy, however, until the aftermath of the Russo-Turkish War of 1877–1878. During the conflict Jewish journalists (some writing for the not yet anti-Semitic daily *Novoe vremia* [*Modern Times*]) were among the war's strongest supporters. However, after military setbacks and diplomatic defeat, Jewish suppliers were accused of profiteering and the Jews in general were reproached with lack of patriotic

---

(DeKalb: Northern Illinois University Press, 1996); Alexei Miller, *The Ukrainian Question: The Russian Empire and Nationalism in the Nineteenth Century* (Budapest: Central European University Press, 2003); idem, *The Romanov Empire and Nationalism: Essays in the Methodology of Historical Research*, trans. Serguei Dobrynin (Budapest: Central European University Press, 2008); Robert D. Crews, *For Prophet and Tsar: Islam and Empire in Russia and Central Asia* (Cambridge, Mass.: Harvard University Press, 2006).

[6] Shulamit Volkov, *Germans, Jews, and Antisemites: Trials in Emancipation* (Cambridge: Cambridge University Press, 2006), 82–84.

[7] In the 1880s these ideas were widely disseminated in Russia by the popular writings of Vsevolod Krestovskii (1840–1895). Iokhanan Petrovskii-Shtern, *Evrei v russkoi armii: 1827–1914* (Moscow: Novoe literaturnoe obozrenie, 2003), 300–302. Also, Gabriella Safran, "Ethnography, Judaism, and the Art of Nikolai Leskov," *Russian Review* 59 (April 2000): 236–37.

feeling.[8] When the issue of minority rights was raised at the Congress of Berlin in 1878, Foreign Minister Aleksandr Gorchakov (1798–1883) declared: "In Serbia, Romania, as in Russia, the Jews represent a danger: they don't resemble the Jews of Paris, London, Berlin and Vienna, and therefore the equalization of their rights would have harmful consequences for these countries."[9]

The tsar's assassination strengthened the association of the Jews with Russia's misfortunes. Although only one of the perpetrators was Jewish, conservative journalists attributed the deed to Jewish machinations and justified the ensuing pogroms as a legitimate expression of the people's desire for revenge. Prominent among those who propagated these views was Ivan Aksakov (1823–1886), the younger brother of Konstantin Aksakov, one of the original Slavophile thinkers.[10] Ivan Aksakov's fulminations created, by implication, a line of continuity between the original Slavophile ideas and the more politically and socially oriented antipathy toward the Jews that emerged after 1881.

The distinction between the later period and the pre-Reform years was the use of physical violence. The post-1881 pogroms were followed in 1903 by similar riots in Kishinev. Pogroms accompanied the mobilization for the Russo-Japanese War in 1904 and punctuated the 1905 Revolution (peaking after the October Manifesto and continuing into 1906).[11] The Kiev journalist Vasilii Shul'gin (1878–1976), an avowed anti-Semite, deplored the violence but also deplored the Jews. After the October Manifesto, he later recalled, the Jews rejoiced. "This bald insult to the feelings of Russian patriots...provoked the Jewish pogrom."[12] The tone of public discussion also

---

[8] See Petrovskii-Shtern, *Evrei v russkoi armii*, 299; see also John Doyle Klier, *Imperial Russia's Jewish Question 1855–1881* (Cambridge: Cambridge University Press, 1995), 392–94. On connections between Slavophilism, pan-Slavism, and anti-Semitism linked to the supply question, see, too, N. R. Ovsianyi, *Russkoe upravlenie v Bolgarii v 1877–78–79 gg.* Izdanie Voenno-Istoricheskoi Komissii Glavnogo Shtaba (St. Petersburg: T-vo Zhudozhestvennoi Pechati, 1906), 35. For anti-Semitism in Europe, related to the war, see Sir Tollemache Sinclair (1824–1912), *A Defence of Russia and the Christians of Turkey* (London: Chapman and Hall, 1877). Hannah Arendt cites this work as an example of the way anti-Jewish themes were involved with the Eastern Crisis in Britain: "Antisemitism" (1938–39), in Hannah Arendt, *The Jewish Writings*, ed. Jerome Kohn and Ron H. Feldman (New York: Schocken, 2007), 60.
[9] Cited in Klier, *Imperial Russia's Jewish Question*, 395.
[10] I. S. Aksakov, "Iudaizm kak vsemirnoe iavlenie," *Rus'* (13 June 1881); "Evreiskaia agitatsiia v Anglii," *Rus'* (23 January 1882); "Normal'no li polozhenie Evreev na nashem Zapade i Iuge, i ikh otnoshenie k mestnomu naseleniiu?," *Rus'* (24 April 1882), rpt. in *Polnoe sobranie sochinenii I. S. Aksakova*, vol. 3, *Pol'skii vopros i Zapadno-Russkoe delo. Evreiskii vopros* (Moscow: M. G. Volchaninov, 1886), 725–34, 757–71.
[11] John D. Klier and Shlomo Lambroza, eds., *Pogroms: Anti-Jewish Violence in Modern Russian History* (Cambridge: Cambridge University Press, 1992).
[12] V. V. Shul'gin, "1917–1919" (1970), ed. R. G. Krasiukov; commentary B. I. Kolonitskii, in *Litsa: Biograficheskii al'manakh*, Vol. 5 (Moscow-St. Petersburg: Feniks-Atheneum, 1994), 147. Jewish commentators blamed the government: see, e.g., I. V. Gessen, M. B. Ratner, and

sharpened. In the Duma, positions on the Jewish Question (equal rights, access to education, and abolition of the Pale) reflected broader party divisions. Right-wing deputies spewed anti-Semitic venom, angering their liberal opponents, who denounced the discriminatory laws still in force.[13] The imperial authorities at the highest levels did not, however, endorse mob violence.[14] In trials following the major pogroms, perpetrators were charged under criminal statutes that penalized "violence against persons, also theft of, or damage to property on the basis of economic relationships or religious, tribal, or status hatred."[15] Hostility toward the Jews was disseminated nonetheless, not only by conservative ideologues but also by various branches of the imperial bureaucracy. The army high command began distributing anti-Semitic tracts to the ranks in the 1890s.[16] In 1911, when the Ministry of Justice brought charges of ritual blood slaughter against Mendel Beilis, the cream of the professional intelligentsia mobilized in his defense. The trial resulted in Beilis's unexpected acquittal in 1913 by a jury of ordinary Russians. The courtroom drama, widely covered in the press, nevertheless placed the vision of Jews as the perpetrators of anti-Christian violence squarely in the public eye and provided this vision with official sanction.[17]

L. Ia. Shternberg, eds., *Nakanune probuzhdeniia: Sbornik statei po evreiskomu voprosu* (St. Petersburg: Pravo, 1906).

[13] On the span of rhetoric on the Jewish question, compare the remarks of Markov 2 with those of Vasilii Maklakov: *Gosudarstvennaia Duma: Stenograficheskie otchety*. Tretii sozyv. 1911 g. Sessiia chetvertaia. Chast' II. Zasedaniia 39–73 (s 17 ianvaria po 5 marta 1911 g.) (St. Petersburg: Gosudarstvennaia tipografiia, 1911), zasedanie 54 (9 February 1911), cols. 1543–1614.

[14] For an analysis of tsarist policy and the denial of high-level official responsibility for the pogroms, see Hans Rogger's classic work *Jewish Policies and Right-Wing Politics in Imperial Russia* (Berkeley: University of California Press, 1986).

[15] Statutes 269, 1490, and 1606. *Delo o pogrome v g. Tomske v 1905 g. (Ochet o sudebnom zasedanii Tomskogo okruzhnogo suda)* (Tomsk: tip. Sibirskogo T-va Pechatnogo Dela, 1909), 4. N. S. Tagantsev, ed., *Ulozhenie o nakazaniiakh ugolovnykh i ispravitel'nykh 1885 goda*, 11th ed. (St. Petersburg: Gosudarstvennaia tipografiia, 1901), 266–67. Records of other trials include *Delo o pogrome v Orshe 21–24 oktiabria 1905 goda: Obvinitel'nyi akt i sudebnoe sledstvie* (St. Petersburg: tip. Busselia, 1908); *Delo o pogrome v Belostoke 1–3 iiunia 1906 g.: Obvinitel'nyi akt, sudebnoe sledstvie, rechi poverennykh* (St. Petersburg: tip. Busselia, 1909); *Delo o pogrome v Belostoke 1–3 iiunia 1906 g.: Obvinitel'nyi akt, sudebnoe sledstvie, rechi poverennykh*, 2nd ed. (St. Petersburg: "Trud," 1909). For a list of pogroms following 17 October, see "Prilozhenie: Khronika oktiabr'skikh dnei. III: Posle Manifesta," *Pravo*, no. 48–49 (4 December 1905): cols. 135–206.

[16] Semen Gol'din, "Russkoe komandovanie i evrei vo vremia pervoi mirovoi voiny: Prichiny formirovaniia negativnogo stereotipa," in *Mirovoi krizis 1914–1920 godov i sud'ba vostochnoevropeiskogo evreistva*, ed. O. V. Budnitskii et al. (Moscow: ROSSPEN, 2005), 29–46. Objections raised in the Duma by Maksim Vinaver (1862–1926): Sessiia I, zasedanie 33 (26 VI 1906 g.), in *Gosudarstvennaia Duma: Stenograficheskie otchety 1906 god. Sessiia pervaia. Tom II* (St. Petersburg: Gosudarstvennaia tipografiia, 1906), 1735.

[17] V. Maklakov, "Spasitel'noe predosterezhenie: Smysl dela Beilisa," *Russkaia mysl'*, no. 11 (1913): 135–43; G. M. Reznik et al., eds., *Delo Mendelia Beilisa: Materialy Chrezvychainoi*

The Jews were an easy target. They were at once vulnerable (in their impoverished small-town masses) and powerful (as international bankers and entrepreneurs, perhaps also as members of the russophone professional elite and the political parties, from liberal to radical, so distasteful to die-hard supporters of autocratic rule). Having entered the empire in large numbers as a result of the eighteenth-century Polish partitions, the Jews were associated, in their historic origins and continuing (enforced) residential patterns, with the treacherous Poles. Inhabitants of many nations, they owed their loyalty to none. They represented, on the one hand, the challenge of modernity—urban, commercial, and adaptable—and, on the other, the ancient and enduring affront to the Christian tradition.[18] Having crucified Christ to begin with, they had denied his sovereignty ever since. They were inimical to Orthodoxy, Autocracy, and Narodnost'.

In short, even before 1914 the notion of the Jew as "the inner enemy" was firmly lodged in the spectrum of Duma rhetoric, the practice of mass politics, and the ideology of empire.[19] The Jewish Question was powerful because it resonated at so many levels—economic, geopolitical, religious, ideological, and philosophical. The original Slavophiles had engaged the question of Judaism from a theological but not a social or political perspective.[20] Their legacy nevertheless established a discourse of Russian cultural identity anchored in an antisecular worldview. Consider, for example, the position of the philosopher Vladimir Solov'ev, whose ideas inspired the Orthodox revival among lay intellectuals at the turn of the century. Publicly condemning Ivan Aksakov's diatribes, Solov'ev argued not on civic or political grounds but from an explicitly Christian standpoint.[21]

His Christian orientation did not make Solov'ev a political conservative. As in the time of the Slavophiles and Westerners, antiestablishment

---

sledstvennoi komissii Vremennogo pravitel'stva o sudebnom protsesse 1913 g. po obvineniu v ritual'nom ubiistve (St. Petersburg: Dmitrii Bulanin, 1999); Rogger, Jewish Policies, 40–55.

[18] On Jewish integration and the association of Jews with modernity, see, respectively, Benjamin Nathans, Beyond the Pale: The Jewish Encounter with Late Imperial Russia (Berkeley: University of California Press, 2002); and Yuri Slezkine, The Jewish Century (Princeton: Princeton University Press, 2004).

[19] William English Walling, Russia's Message: The True World Import of the Revolution (New York: Doubleday, 1908), chap. 5 (Creating the "Internal Enemy").

[20] On the multilayered nature of Russian anti-Semitism, see Klier, Imperial Russia's Jewish Question, 389–90; 387 (original Slavophiles). For Khomiakov's view of the Jews, whom he characterizes in terms of their social and cultural features, in particular, their focus on money and material life and their propensity for abstraction, see "O vozmozhnosti Russkoi khudozhestvennoi shkoly," Moskovskii sbornik (1847), rpt. in Polnoe sobranie sochinenii Alekseia Stepanovicha Khomiakova, 3rd rev. ed., 8 vols. (Moscow: Universitetskaia tipografiia, 1900), 1:88–90.

[21] V. S. Solov'ev, "Evreistvo i khristianskii vopros," Pravoslavnoe obozrenie (August 1884): 755–72; (September 1884): 76–114; rpt. in Taina Izrailia: "Evreiskii vopros" v russkoi religioznoi mysli kontsa XIX–pervoi poloviny XX vv., ed. V. F. Boikov (St. Petersburg: Sofiia, 1993), 31–80.

intellectuals occupied a range of philosophical positions. Some preferred secular liberalism (the hallmark of the Kadet Party), others scientific positivism or materialist socialism (associated with Social Democracy). Some shared the fin-de-siècle European fascination with the irrational and spiritual dimensions of human existence.[22] Inspired as well by the native examples of Fedor Dostoevskii and Vladimir Solov'ev, the neo-idealists reclaimed the philosophical legacy that liberals and post-1848 socialists had spurned.[23] The Religious-Philosophical Society, established in St. Petersburg in 1901 and in Moscow in 1905, provided Orthodox-identified thinkers with a forum in which they embarked on the intellectual equivalent of discovering the ancient icon as a work of art—shaping a modern Christian idiom tied to the legacy of the historic Russian church, but enlivened by dialogue with modern thinking.[24]

In the aftermath of 1905, when revolutionary violence had been matched by the violence of government repression, a group of thinkers already associated with the turn toward philosophical idealism articulated a position critical of the secular left but distinct from the conservatism in official circles. The essay collection titled *Vekhi* (*Landmarks*), published in 1909 to considerable controversy, reasserted the importance of religious values.[25] Managing the practical implications of these ideas was not always easy, however, since the political context kept changing. The case of Vasilii Rozanov illustrates the difficulty they faced.

Known for his fascination with both the Sexual and the Jewish Questions, Rozanov was a principled antirationalist, in the Dostoevskian mold, refusing to acknowledge the demands of logical consistency. Though writing for publications violently hostile to the Jews, Rozanov claimed to admire the Jewish people. Deploring the violence of pogroms, he expressed himself occasionally in ways that lent themselves to the opposite

[22] On the antirational turn, see Fedor Stepun, *Byvshee i nesbyvsheesia* (New York: Chekhov, 1956; rpt. St. Petersburg: Aleteiia; Moscow: Izd. Progress-Litera, 1994), 217.

[23] George F. Putnam, *Russian Alternatives to Marxism: Christian Socialism and Idealistic Liberalism in Twentieth-Century Russia* (Knoxville: University of Tennessee Press, 1977); Randall A. Poole, ed., *Problems of Idealism: Essays in Russian Social Philosophy*, trans. idem (New Haven, Conn.: Yale University Press, 2003).

[24] Jutta Scherrer, *Die Petersburger Religiös-Philosophischen Vereinigungen: Die Entwicklung des religiösen Selbstverständnisses ihrer Intelligencija-Mitglieder (1901–1917)*. Forschungen zur Osteuropäischen Geschichte, Bd. 19 (Wiesbaden: Otto Harrassowitz, 1973); A. V. Sobolev, "K istorii religiozno-filosofskogo obshchestva pamiati Vladimira Solov'eva," *Istoriko-filosofskii ezhegodnik '92* (Moscow: Nauka, 1994), 102–14; Kristiane Burchardi, *Die Moskauer "Religiös-Philosophische Vladimir-Solov'ev-Gesellschaft" (1905–1918)* (Wiesbaden: Harrassowitz Verlag, 1998). On the origins, see Zinaida Gippius, *Vospominaniia* (Moscow: Zakharov, 2001), 120–21, 124.

[25] N. A. Berdiaev, S. N. Bulgakov, M. O. Gershenzon, A. S. Izgoev, B. A. Kistiakovskii, P. B. Struve, S. L. Frank, *Vekhi: Sbornik statei o russkoi intelligentsii* (Moscow: Kushnerev, 1909). See Jeffrey Brooks, "*Vekhi* and the *Vekhi* Dispute," *Survey* 19, no. 1 (winter 1973): 21–50; V. V. Sapov, ed., *Vekhi: Pro et contra: Antologiia* (St. Petersburg: Russkii khristianskii gumanitarnyi institut, 1998).

interpretation. His fellows in the Religious-Philosophical Society valued his independence of mind, unfettered imagination, and gift for the literary language. Most disliked his anti-Semitic views, but they accepted him, as the politically moderate Petr Struve (1870–1944) put it, on the grounds that he was not "morally accountable."[26] Tolerance for his idiosyncrasies came to an end, however, in late 1913, when Dmitrii Merezhkovskii (1865–1941), a guiding spirit of the "new religious consciousness" and founding member of the Society, called for his expulsion.[27] Public opinion at that point was consumed by the drama unfolding in the Kiev courtroom. While liberals rushed to Beilis's defense, Rozanov published a series of pamphlets endorsing the blood libel legend.[28] Some Society members objected to Merezhkovskii's motion as a form of intellectual censorship or the unwanted intrusion of political opinion into the philosophical sanctum; the majority prevailed, however, and Rozanov was excluded.[29]

Still, not everyone considered the opinions themselves entirely outrageous. Describing Rozanov's prose as "nightmarishly frivolous," Sergei Bulgakov (1871–1944), a contributor to *Vekhi*, nevertheless found much of value in his presentation of the "tragedy" of the Jewish religion.[30]

---

[26] Struve, cited in Evgeniia Ivanova, "Ob iskliuchenii V. V. Rozanova iz Religiozno-Filosofskogo obshchestva: Doklad Soveta i preniia po voprosu ob otnoshenii obshchestva k deiatel'nosti V. V. Rozanova," *Nash sovremennik*, no. 10 (1990): 114. Struve was a former Marxist, active in the Liberation Movement after 1901; Kadet Party deputy in the second State Duma, 1907; and contributor to *Vekhi*. He joined the White forces in the civil war and spent his remaining years in Paris. For his political views in this period, see P. B. Struve, *Patriotica: Politika, kul'tura, religiia, sotsializm: Sbornik statei za piat' let (1905–1910 gg.)* (St. Petersburg: Izd. D. E. Zhukovskogo, 1911). More generally, see Richard Pipes, *Struve: Liberal on the Right, 1908–1944* (Cambridge, Mass.: Harvard University Press, 1980). For background on Rozanov: Laura Engelstein, *Keys to Happiness: Sex and the Search for Modernity in Fin-de-Siècle Russia* (Ithaca: Cornell University Press, 1992), chap. 8.

[27] The prolific Symbolist novelist and literary critic Merezhkovskii was an outspoken opponent of Bolshevik rule; after 1917, he spent his final decades in Paris. See "Religiozno-filosofskie idei V. V. Rozanova i D. S. Merezhkovskogo," in *Istoriia russkoi filosofii*, ed. M. A. Maslin et al. (Moscow: Respublika, 2001), 393–404; and *D. S. Merezhkovskii: Pro et contra: Lichnost'i tvorchestvo Dmitriia Merezhkovskogo v otsenke sovremennikov: Antologiia*, ed. D. K. Burlaka et al. (St. Petersburg: Russkii khristianskii gumanitarnii institut, 2001).

[28] *Oboniatel'noe i osiazatel'noe otnoshenie evreev k krovi*, reprinting articles from 1911–1913; *Angel Iegovy u evreev (Istoki Izrailia)*; *Evropa i evrei; V sosedstve Sodoma (Istoki Izrailia)*—all published by A. S. Suvorin in St. Petersburg, 1914. See A. N. Nikoliukin, "K voprosu o mifologeme natsional'nogo v tvorchestve V. V. Rozanova," in V. V. Rozanov, *Sakharna*, ed. A. N. Nikoliukin (Moscow: Respublika, 1998), 417. *Oboniatel'noe i osiazatel'noe* rpt., ibid., 276–413.

[29] For the minutes of the debate, see Ivanova, "Ob iskliuchenii," 111–21. Ivanova herself believes that a Masonic plot was behind the initiative to exclude Rozanov, whom she absolves of all moral blame. As an example of how styles of thinking persist, her view sounds like a thinly veiled accusation that the Jews themselves (the expected formula is the *zhido-masonskii zagovor* [Yid-Masonic Conspiracy]) were, in fact, responsible for the injury to an irreproachable Orthodox thinker, whose life, she asserts, was ruined by the event.

[30] S. N. Bulgakov to A. S. Glinka (15 January 1914), in *Vzyskuiushchie grada: Khronika chastnoi zhizni russkikh religioznykh filosofov v pis'makh i dnevnikakh*, ed. V. I. Keidan (Moscow: "Iazyki russkoi kul'tury," 1997), 568; cited in Evgenii Gollerbakh, *K nezrimomu*

Unrepentant, either in relation to his feelings about the Jews or in response to the action taken against him, Rozanov did not moderate his views. In June 1914 he warned Merezhkovskii, his principal critic, not to publish in left-wing "Yid" newspapers such as *Rech'* (*Speech*) and *Russkoe slovo* (*The Russian Word*), suggesting he publish in *Novoe vremia* instead. "The Yids," Rozanov explained, "will first f—k you..., then drag you through the mud. They're always like that...They are fundamentally traitors."[31]

The Beilis case demonstrated the damaging consequences of ideas that in other circumstances might be confined to private conversations or particular social circles. Rozanov's familiar diatribes were considered now in a new light. With the outbreak of hostilities in summer 1914, intellectuals became ever more conscious of their responsibility in shaping public opinion. The same critically minded artists and writers who had applauded the heroes of 1905 joined more conservative thinkers, such as those in the *Vekhi* group, in responding to the patriotic call. Outside the political parties, the creative intelligentsia, from boulevard to avant-garde, contributed generously to the illustrated albums, essay collections, charitable soirées, and mass-market journalism devoted to civic mobilization. Publications that had decried the government crackdown after 1905 now endorsed the struggle against German aggression.

Searching for patriotic shorthand, artists and writers drew on the iconography of Orthodoxy, bulwark of the imperial enterprise. The Christian imagery they once employed to sanctify the martyrs of Bloody Sunday and the regime's punitive brigades now served to glorify the call to war. In the Russo-Turkish War of 1877–1878, General Mikhail Skobelev (1843–1882), mounted on his white steed, had invented himself as a latter-day St. George, patron saint of old Muscovy.[32] Images of St. George, emblem of empire and of victory over the infidel, appeared everywhere in 1914. Skobelev's name was attached to the imperial war-charity association, the so-called Skobelev Committee. The modernist artist Natal'ia Goncharova, who had run afoul of the censor for her controversial early work, now produced *lubok*-style

gradu: Religiozno-filosofskaia gruppa "Put'" (*1910–1919*) *v poiskakh novoi russkoi iden-tichnosti*, ed. M. A. Kolerov (St. Petersburg: Aleteiia, 2000), 52. The son of a priest, Bulgakov was drawn to legal Marxism, then returned to religion via Tolstoi; participated in the revival of idealism in 1902–1903; was a Christian Socialist Duma deputy in 1906; was ordained in 1918 as an Orthodox priest; was expelled from the Soviet Union, together with 160 other intellectuals, in 1922; and spent his final years in Paris. On Bulgakov, see "'Religioznyi materializm' S. N. Bulgakova," in Maslin et al., *Istoriia russkoi filosofii*, 417–26; Putnam, *Russian Alternatives to Marxism;* Catherine Evtuhov, *The Cross and the Sickle: Sergei Bulgakov and the Fate of Russian Religious Philosophy* (Ithaca: Cornell University Press, 1997).

[31] Letter from V. V. Rozanov to D. S. Merezhkovskii (15 June 1914), in Keidan, *Vzysku-iushchie grada,* 580.

[32] See Hans Rogger, "The Skobelev Phenomenon: The Hero and His Worship," in *Oxford Slavonic Papers,* ed. Robert Auty, J. L. I. Fennell, and I. P. Foote, n.s., vol. 9 (Oxford: Clarendon, 1976), 46–78.

Fig. 4. Natal'ia Goncharova, "Sviatoi Georgii Pobedonosets [St. George the Victor]," in *Misticheskie obrazy voiny: 14 litografii* [Mystical Images of War: 14 Lithographs] (Moscow: V.N. Kashin, 1914). 32.4 x 24.8 cm. Print Collection, Miriam and Ira D. Wallach Division of Art, Prints and Photographs, The New York Public Library, Astor, Lenox and Tilden Foundations.

Fig. 5. Georgii Pashkov (b. 1886), Cover: *Klich: Sbornik na pomoshch' zhertvam voiny* [The Call: A Collection to Benefit War Victims] (Moscow: A. A. Levenson, 1915). Courtesy Sterling Memorial Library, Yale University. Pashkov was known for his postcards, posters, and commercial art.

block prints in the neo-icon mode, endorsing the sacred cause of a defensive war, which is how the public understood this conflict.[33]

"The Times are Going Slavophile"

That the challenge of war, a mere seven years after the ebb of revolution, should have raised concerns about the empire's internal cohesion is not surprising. Suspicion fell on those domestic populations—the Poles and the Jews—close to the vulnerable western periphery and already suspect by virtue of their religious and cultural self-containment. Not only did these two mutually distrusting peoples intermingle on the Russian side of the border; both also inhabited contiguous areas under German and Austrian rule—East Prussia to the north, Galicia to the south: remnants of the original partitions. To these familiar objects of distrust were now added domestic groups of German origin: the Baltic nobility, the inhabitants of agricultural colonies dating from the eighteenth century, and Protestant-inspired Christian sects such as the Baptists.

The need to fortify the empire against internal discord and betrayal acted, at least at first, as a unifying force in its own right. Convened in an extraordinary session on 26 July/8 August 1914, the Duma deputies from the Baltic and Polish regions, including Naftal Fridman (1863–1921) from Kovno Province, speaking on behalf of the Jews, rose to assert the loyalty of their respective peoples.[34] From the pinnacle of power, Commander-in-Chief Grand Duke Nikolai Nikolaevich (1856–1929) issued two appeals. The first promised the reconsolidated Polish people "autonomy under the Russian scepter" at the victorious conclusion of the war. The second urged the "Russian people" (*russkii narod*) to respect their non-Russian domestic neighbors.[35] Similar sentiments were expressed, from the far

---

[33] Natal'ia Goncharova, *Misticheskie obrazy voiny: 14 litografii* (Moscow: V. N. Kashin, 1914). See Jane Ashton Sharp, *Russian Modernism between East and West: Natal'ia Goncharova and the Moscow Avant-Garde* (Cambridge: Cambridge University Press, 2006). More generally, see Aaron Joseph Cohen, *Imagining the Unimaginable: World War, Modern Art, and the Politics of Public Culture in Russia, 1914–1917* (Lincoln: University of Nebraska Press, 2008).

[34] *Stenograficheskii otchet: Gosudarstvennaia Duma.* Chetvertyi sozyv. Sessiia II. Chast' V. Zasedanie Gosudarstvennoi Dumy, sozvannoi na osnovanii Vysochaishego Ukaza Pravitel'stvuiushchemu Senatu ot 20 Iiulia 1914 g. Subbota, 26 Iiulia 1914 g. (Petrograd: Gosudarstvennaia tipografiia, 1914), cols. 20–28.

[35] "Poliaki!" *Niva*, no. 33 (16 August 1914), 641. Text of the appeals: General-Ad"iutant Nikolai, "Vozzvanie Verkhovnogo Glavnokomanduiushchego—Poliaki!" (1/14 August 1914); General-Ad"iutant Nikolai, "Vozzvanie Verkhovnogo Glavnokomanduiushchego—Russkomu narodu!" (5/18 August 1914), *Voennyi sbornik*, no. 12 (December 1914): 205–8. See Aleksander Achmatowicz, *Polityka Rosji w kwestii polskiej w pierwszym roku Wielkiej Wojny 1914–1915* (Warsaw: Wydawnictwo Neriton, Instytut Historii PAN, 2003); see also

reaches of the sophisticated literary elite, by the poet Osip Mandel'shtam (1891–1938). A ditty published in *Niva,* the mass-circulation illustrated magazine, echoed the official line, urging Poles to rally to the Russian imperial banner.[36]

The tendency to demonize the opposing forces—from the German perspective, the Asiatic Cossack hordes; from the Russian standpoint, the Teutonic barbarians—served all combatant nations as a rallying point. The role of atrocity claims on the western front is well known; lurid rhetoric and imagery on this theme characterized Russian propaganda as well.[37] In the context of inflamed passions, responsible public figures attempted to maintain a semblance of intellectual decorum, while also endorsing the patriotic cause. Participants in the Religious-Philosophical Society were among those who rose to the civic occasion. The Moscow branch organized a reading on the subject of the war, held in the Polytechnic Museum on 6 October 1914, and it drew a large crowd.[38] Those who missed the event could study the lectures in the thick journal *Russkaia mysl' (Russian Thought)*. The lectures were also discussed in the general and Orthodox press, and in special wartime publications.[39]

The speakers, as expected, distinguished the spiritual roots of Russian cultural identity from the Western tradition (as exemplified by German culture), but they were obliged to confront the empire's embrace of the

---

Jeffrey Mankoff, "Russia and the Polish Question, 1907–1917: Nationality and Diplomacy" (Ph.D. diss., Yale University, 2006).

[36] Poliaki! Ia ne vizhu smysla / V bezumnom podvige strelkov! / Il' voron zakliuet orlov? / Il' potechet obratno Visla? / Ili snega ne budet bol'she / Zimoiu pokryvat' kovyl'? / Ili o Gabsburgov kostyl' /Pristalo opirat'sia Pol'she? / I ty, slavianskaia kometa, /V svoem bluzhdan'e vekovom / Rassypalas' chuzhim ognem, / Soobshchnitsa chuzhogo sveta! (Poles! I do not see the point / In the marksmen's mad feat / Does the raven peck the eagles? / Does the Vistula run backward? / Will the snow no longer / Cover the feather-grass in winter? / Does leaning on the Hapsburg crutch / Befit Poland? / And you, Slavonic comet / In your eternal wandering / Have been scattered by another's fire / Transmitting another's light!). O. Mandel'shtam, "Poliaki!" *Niva,* no. 43 (25 October 1914): 833. The raven appeared on the crest of Austrian Galicia; the two-headed eagle was the Romanov symbol; the marksmen (*Strzelcy*) were a Polish military formation.

[37] On the western front, see John Horne and Alan Kramer, *German Atrocities, 1914: A History of Denial* (New Haven, Conn.: Yale University Press, 2001); Isabel V. Hull, *Absolute Destruction: Military Culture and the Practices of War in Imperial Germany* (Ithaca: Cornell University Press, 2005); Jeff Lipkes, *Rehearsals: The German Army in Belgium, August 1914* (Leuven: Leuven University Press, 2007). For Russia, Laura Engelstein, "'A Belgium of Our Own': The Sack of Russian Kalisz, August 1914," *Kritika* 10, no. 3 (2009).

[38] On the 6 October event: V. F. Ern to E. D. Ern (6 October 1914), V. F. Ern to E. D. Ern (7 October 1914), in Keidan, *Vzyskuiushchie grada,* 600–601. Also: Ben Hellman, "Kogda vremia slavianofil'stvovalo: Russkie filosofy i pervaia mirovaia voina," in *Problemy istorii russkoi literatury nachala XX veka,* ed. L. Biukling and P. Pesonen (Helsinki: Helsinki University Press, 1989), 211–39.

[39] For example, "V chem ideologicheskaia i psikhologicheskaia sila slavianofil'stva?" *Biulleteni literatury i zhizni,* ed. V. Krandievskii, no. 6 (November—[pt.] II, 1915–16), 281. On the impact of these discussions, see Stepun, *Byvshee i nesbyvsheesia,* 297.

Catholic Poles and its alliance with Protestant England and Catholic France. They also addressed the problem of the Jews, obstinate co-claimants to the Judeo-Christian legacy, from which Russia's own, nonsecular identity, as they saw it, derived.[40] No more successfully than the original Slavophiles could their philosophical heirs resolve the tension between Christian universalism and cultural particularity, but under the pressure of wartime patriotism, they returned to the dilemma with a heightened concern.

The October session presented two contrasting views of the war, reflecting different degrees of identification with the Slavophile position. On the more emphatic side, Sergei Bulgakov credited "the holy war and the humble self-sacrifice of the great Russian armed forces for this [current] spiritual rebirth."[41] Echoing sentiments widely expressed at the time, he contrasted Russia's spiritual power to the efficient but soulless German military machine.[42] In a similar vein, the Symbolist poet and philosopher Viacheslav Ivanov (1866–1949) described the Germans as true barbarians. Armed by modern ideas of racial superiority, they represented the "face of the dark demon"—blasphemy and atheism. Russia, by contrast, was fighting in the name of Christ for a universal sacred cause.[43]

The *enfant terrible* of the occasion was Vladimir Ern (1882–1917). Ern, who had studied philosophy at Moscow University, was of mixed parentage, his father Lutheran, his mother Eastern Orthodox. Perhaps in a moment of Oedipal passion, he described his paper as a "land mine" designed to shatter the foundations of German culture. Its title—"From Kant to Krupp"—became a wartime catch-phrase,[44] as did the title of his 1915 essay collection, *Vremia slavianofil'stvuet* (*The Times Are Going Slavophile*).[45] Ern's underlying premise, that national cultures were

---

[40] For the "Jewish Question" in the context of the Orthodox religious revival, see essays by the major figures, rpt. in Boikov, *Taina Izrailia*.

[41] S. Bulgakov, "Russkie dumy," *Russkaia mysl'*, no. 12 (1914): 121. In wider circulation format: Prof. S. N. Bulgakov, "Tri imperii," in *Velikaia voina v obrazakh i kartinakh*, ed. Iv. Lazarevskii, Vol. 10 (Moscow: D. Ia. Makovskii, 1916), 50–56.

[42] Bulgakov, "Tri imperii," 56. Cf. Leonid Andreev, "Krestonostsy," *Otechestvo: Illiustrirovannaia letopis'*, no. 6 (14 December 1914): 85; "Poucheniia nastoiashchei voiny," *Voennyi sbornik* 57, no. 9 (September 1914): 3. On similar attitudes in Britain and Germany during World War I, see Alan Kramer, *Dynamic of Destruction: Culture and Mass Killing in the First World War* (Oxford: Oxford University Press, 2007), 77.

[43] Viacheslav Ivanov, "Vselenskoe delo," *Russkaia mysl'*, no. 12 (1914): 97–107 (quotes, 97, 101, 103). Ivanov left for Italy in 1924.

[44] V. F. Ern to E. D. Ern (28 September 1914), in Keidan, *Vzyskuiushchie grada*, 599; S. Askol'dov ("*krylatye slova*"), cited ibid., 602. For Ern's biography and the reaction to his wartime posture, see D. K. Burlaka et al., eds., *V. F. Ern: Pro et contra: Lichnost' i tvorchestvo Vladimira Erna v otsenke russkikh myslitelei i issledovatelei: Antologiia* (St. Petersburg: Russkaia khristianskaia gumanitarnaia akademiia, 2006). More generally: "V. F. Ern: Bor'ba za Logos," in Maslin et al., *Istoriia russkoi filosofii*, 491–97.

[45] V. F. Ern, *Vremia slavianofil'stvuet: Voina, Germaniia, Evropa i Rossiia* (Moscow: I. D. Sytin, 1915). Series: Voina i kul'tura. For another venue for his ideas, see V. F. Ern, "Vozvrat

defined by their religious traditions, was nothing new, but his incendiary language set off sparks. "As war descends, suddenly, from under the soft skin of German culture, rapacious, bloodthirsty claws emerge," he wrote, in the idiom of the boulevard press, citing a string of well-known atrocity cases. "The visage of 'the people of philosophers' is distorted by bestial cruelty." It was wrong, he insisted, to see the recent outrages as a betrayal of German culture. Krupp, no less than Kant, represented the German spirit.[46] German brutality on the battlefield, in fact, derived from Kant's attempt to replace the mystery of the heavens with "bare sensual experience." It was "Orthodox Russia's liberationist mission" to rescue German culture from its own dark side.[47]

Ern later published this lecture in a collection of essays titled *Mech i krest* (*The Sword and the Cross*). Merging philosophy and rabble-rousing, he played the atrocity card yet again. "Alas, we cannot say that the hands holding this sword are pure. The blood of old men and women, the murder of children, the ashes and dust of the holy sites of culture cannot be washed away even by the death, however 'glorious' a death, of the sons of the *Faterland* [*sic*]." The Germans spring to war, "like a beast that pounces on its prey." Violence, however, is all on one side. "For Russia the sword is an instrument. The cross, in its holiness, is higher than the sword. Russia is powerful not through sheer physical might, but through the truth and only the truth.... Against the brutal German sword (not by accident become brutal), Russia battles with a sword *illuminated* by the faith in a higher truth."[48]

In the Slavophile tradition, Ern insisted not only on the Christian but also the specifically Eastern Orthodox character of Russian national identity. He could therefore not deny that Russian-Polish conflicts also involved a confrontation between faiths. Both nations defined themselves in religious terms; both claimed a messianic destiny. The solution, however, must be religious, not legal or political. "We do not need frosty toleration!" he declaimed. "It would constitute a terrible mutual insult if Russians and Poles, in the name of the nihilistic principle of misunderstood liberalism, began to 'tolerate' what each other holds sacred, just as enlightened states tolerate the existence on their territories of shamanism or other forms of

na Balkany," in Lazarevskii, *Velikaia voina v obrazakh i kartinakh*, Vol. 12 (1916), 147–50. On the Slavophile approach to nationalism: N. Ustrialov, "Natsional'naia problema u per-vykh slavianofilov," *Russkaia mysl'*, no. 10 (1916): pt. 2, 1–22. For the major entries in the wartime debate, see M. A. Kolerov, ed., *Natsionalizm: Polemika 1909–1917: Sbornik statei* (Moscow: Dom intellektual'noi knigi, 2000), 143–230.

[46] V. F. Ern, "Ot Kanta k Kruppu" (lecture in Moscow Religious-Philosophical Society, 6 October 1914), rpt. in V. F. Ern, *Mech i krest: Stat'i o sovremennykh sobytiiakh* (Moscow: I. D. Sytin, 1915), 308–9. Originally in *Russkaia mysl'*, no. 12 (December 1914): 116–24.

[47] V. F. Ern, "Sushchnost' nemetskogo fenomenalizma," in idem, *Mech i krest*, 327–28.

[48] V. F. Ern, "Introduction," in *Mech i krest*, 297–98.

Fig. 6. Ivan Bilibin (1876–1942), "Strazhi [The Guards]," *Lukomor'e: Ezhenedel'nyi illius-trirovannyi literaturno-khudozhestvennyi i satiricheskii zhurnal*, no. 12 (Petrograd: Suvorin, 1915): Paskhal'nyi numer [The Shore: A Weekly Literary-Artistic and Satirical Illustrated Magazine, Easter Number]. Courtesy Helsinki University Slavonic Library. Known for book illustration, commercial art, set and costume design, in his signature "neo-Russian" style, Bilibin contributed to satirical journalism after 1905, worked with Sergei Diaghilev in Paris, and died in Leningrad.

ancient, long-outmoded errors." Yet the two branches of the Christian faith must unite to defend the primacy of faith itself, threatened by the secularizing momentum of Germanic Protestantism.[49]

Those on the other side of the debate agreed that Russia could be defined in terms of a distinctive spiritual principle. They were uncomfortable, however, with the use of this idea for crudely political aims. Nikolai Berdiaev, who had rejected the Marxist convictions of his youth in favor of an existential approach to Christian philosophy, accused both Ern and Ivanov of "jingo patriotism, boasting, readiness to grovel before the police, denial of the facts—all in colossal proportions."[50] Semen Frank (1877–1950), who had converted to Orthodoxy from Judaism in 1912, objected to the demonization of German culture.[51] Prince Evgenii Trubetskoi (1863–1920), one of the Society's founders and a leader in the Kadet Party, had concluded even before the war that Russia's political purpose could no longer be identified with a Christian calling. The idea of the "Russian Christ" was insulting not only to non-Christians, he declared, but to non-Orthodox Christians as well. The notion ill suited the realities of the multiconfessional state.[52] The only solution, he said,

---

[49] V. F. Ern, "Ostrië russko-pol'skikh otnoshenii," *Novoe zveno*, no. 3 (17 January 1915): 14–17; rpt. in idem, *Mech i krest*, 333–37. For positions on Poland by other philosophers, see Larisa Leshchenko, *Pol'skii vopros v russkoi filosofsko-religioznoi mysli na rubezhe XIX–XX vekov* (Wroclaw: Wydawnictwo Universytetu Wrocławskiego, 2006).

[50] Cited in Aleksandr Vadimov, *Zhizn' Berdiaeva: Rossiia* (Oakland, Calif.: Berkeley Slavic Specialties, 1993), 159. Expelled from the Soviet Union in 1922 together with 160 other intellectuals, Berdiaev settled in Paris; he is known for *The Russian Idea* (1946). See "Ekzistentsial'no-personalisticheskaia filosofiia N. A. Berdiaeva," in Maslin et al., *Istoriia russkoi filosofii*, 435–47; A. A. Ermichev, ed., *N. A. Berdiaev: Pro et contra: Antologiia* (St. Petersburg: Russkii khristianskii gumanitarnyi institut, 1994).

[51] S. L. Frank, "O poiskakh smysla voiny," *Russkaia mysl'*, no. 12 (December 1914); similarly, Ivan Il'in (1882–1954): I. A. Il'in, *Dukhovnyi smysl voiny* (Moscow: I. D. Sytin, 1915). Objections were also raised by Evg. Adamov, in *Kievskaia mysl'* (October 1914); N. Efros, "Kant i Krupp," *Rech'* (October 1914); P. Ryss, "Ot Vladimira Solov'eva k Vladimiru Ernu," *Den'* (27 November 1914); M. Rubinshtein, "Vinovat li Kant?" *Russkie vedomosti*, no. 33 (1915). Ern's reply: "Sushchnost'," 319. For the full debate, see Burlaka et al., *Ern: Pro et contra*, 442–518, and commentary. Of Prussian parentage, the Orthodox philosopher Fedor Stepun (1884–1965) also appreciated the need to separate the wartime distortions of German culture from its deep (in his mind) religious roots: F. A. Stepun [N. Lugin], *Iz pisem praporshchika-artillerista* (Tomsk: Izd-vo "Vodolei," 2000), 129–37. This is a reprint of the full 1918 edition, which restored the censor's cuts in the first publication: *Severnye zapiski*, no. 7–9 (1916). On Stepun's philosophy: V. K. Kantor, "F. A. Stepun: Russkii filosof v epokhu bezumiia Razuma," in F. A. Stepun, *Sochineniia*, ed. V. K. Kantor (Moscow: ROSSPEN, 2000), 3–33. Frank and Stepun were both expelled from the Soviet Union in 1922.

[52] E. N. Trubetskoi, "Staryi i novyi natsional'nyi messianizm," *Russkaia mysl'*, no. 3 (1912), rpt. in idem, *Smysl zhizni*, ed. A. P. Poliakov and P. P. Apryshko (Moscow: Respublika, 1994), 341. From an old aristocratic family, Trubetskoi studied law and philosophy at Moscow University; taught in Iaroslavl, Kiev, and Moscow; was a member of the State Council (1916–1917) and Council of the Orthodox Church (1917–1918); after 1917 joined

was to abandon the Slavophile postulates, to dismount from "the old Slavophile steed."[53]

The war challenged Trubetskoi to shape his antisecular, but nonconfessional, vision of Russia's destiny to the demands of national mobilization. Russia, he now asserted, would succeed in being national, namely, motivated and integrated, only when it embarked on a liberationist mission; to be truly Christian, however, this mission had to be universal. Russia would only become national when it transcended nationalism. "Russia will be healed," Trubetskoi declared, a week after hostilities began, "only when it forgets itself and serves the cause of *universal human* culture." Echoing the contrast implied in the Nicholaevan triad between the "national'nost'" that threatened the empire and the "narodnost'" that sustained it, Trubetskoi insisted that Russia must raise the "national/native cause [*narodnoe delo*] above the level of national egotism [*natsional'nyi egoizm*]." Selfless nationalism had the advantage also of accommodating Russia's desire to liberate the other Slavic nations: restore Polish unity, establish a greater Serbia, and free the Slavs under Austrian rule. Poland, in particular, was "Russia's bastion against Germanism."[54] For Trubetskoi, whose diplomat brother Grigorii (1873–1930) helped draft the Grand Duke's appeal to the Poles, imperial ambitions were a moral substitute for the divisive and self-centered character of nationhood.[55]

Indeed, nationalist ideology suited neither the complexity of Russia's internal composition nor its geopolitical ambitions. It was associated rather with the bold self-assertion of the recently unified German state. Trubetskoi believed that Russia must therefore find an alternative inspiration, which he defined as "the Christian resolution of the national question."[56]

the Whites; and died in Novorossiisk on the Black Sea, as the White Army prepared to leave. See "E. N. Trubetskoi: Obosnovanie smysla zhizni," in Maslin et al., *Istoriia russkoi filosofii*, 483–91; Randall A. Poole, "Religion, War, and Revolution: E. N. Trubetskoi's Liberal Construction of Russian National Identity, 1912–20," *Kritika* 7, no. 2 (2006): 195–240. Trubetskoi and Sergei Bulgakov had experienced the 1905 Revolution in Kiev, where both took a stand against the intensified anti-Semitism and anti-Jewish violence: see Faith Hillis, "Between Empire and Nation: Urban Politics and Community in Kiev, 1863–1907" (Ph.D. diss., Yale University, 2009).

[53] Trubetskoi, "Staryi i novyi natsional'nyi messianizm," in idem, *Smysl zhizni* (1994), 346 (*kon' starogo slavianofil'stva*).

[54] E. N. Trubetskoi, "Smysl voiny," *Russkie vedomosti* (8 August 1914); rpt. in idem, *Smysl zhizni* (1994), 352–53 (emphasis in original). As a separate publication: idem, *Smysl voiny* (Moscow: Put', 1914) (5,000 copies); rpt. (Moscow: I. D. Sytin, 1915).

[55] Poole, "Religion, War, and Revolution," 210–11, citing Gollerbakh, *K nezrimomu gradu*, 249–50. Gollerbakh traces the publication history of this lecture, which made its way through the secular and Orthodox press.

[56] Kn. Evgenii Trubetskoi, "Voina i mirovaia zadacha Rossii," *Russkaia mysl'*, no. 12 (December 1914): 88–96; idem, *Voina i mirovaia zadacha Rossii*, 2nd ed. (Moscow: I. D. Sytin, 1915), 11. See also idem, "Patriotizm protiv natsionalizma," in Lazarevskii, *Velikaia voina v obrazakh i kartinakh*, Vol. 4 (1915), 197–98.

Unlike Ern, who blamed the entirety of German culture for the disaster of German nationalism, Trubetskoi feared the nationalist spirit as a universal temptation—"the inner monster, the terrible and evil beast that hides in every nation." Russian victory, he insisted, must serve a "higher cultural principle"—"the spiritual unity of peoples."[57] Such Christian universalism would solve the dilemma of Russia's national identity in an age of increasingly narrow nationalist claims. Poland must belong to Russia, because Russia was an empire, but the Poles could only be imperial Russians (*rossiiskie*) if Russia were not defined in Orthodox terms.

Trubetskoi's ideas evoked a range of responses but did not appeal, of course, to conservatives. Dmitrii Khomiakov (1841–1918), the elder son of the Slavophile philosopher, belonged to the militantly right-wing Union of the Russian People. In February 1915 he wrote to a friend: "All the same, your Prince E. Trubetskoi is an idiot. He just doesn't understand what he's talking about, though he speaks sincerely."[58] Liberal readers appreciated what they considered Trubetskoi's enlightened views on the nationality question, but some challenged his rosy vision of Russia's wartime mission. What about the Jewish Question—inequality, pogroms, Polish anti-Semitism? Was it not hypocritical to denounce Germany, in view of Russia's brutal conduct in Galicia?[59]

The philosophers' ideas thus circulated widely and resonated with the major themes of wartime propaganda. Consider, for example, a pamphlet of civic instruction, *Velikaia voina: Chto dolzhen znat' o nei kazhdyi russkii?* (*What Every Russian Should Know about the Great War*), which hailed the conflict as a chance for Russians to unite behind the imperial banner. Echoing the pervasive mood of spiritual exaltation, the brochure described the country's new-found pride not in political terms but in the language of Christian renewal that was supposed to distinguish Russia from the secular European states. The "dawn" of Russia's national existence would "illuminate the banner of the Cross—the symbol of suffering and the resurrection of nations."[60]

The conflict between Russian and German culture was another theme not confined to the world of Orthodox philosophers. Contributors to a volume of civic-minded reflection on the war represented the cosmopolitan face of the Russian intelligentsia. Here a Polish scholar with professional ties in both Russia and Germany urged Slavs of all nations to rally against

[57] Trubetskoi, *Voina i mirovaia zadacha Rossii,* 15–16, 22.

[58] D. Khomiakov, Moscow, 3 February 1915, to Ego Prev. K. N. Paskhalov, Tula Province: GARF, f. 102, op. 265, d. 1012, l. 281.

[59] E. Levontin, Riazan, 22 October 1914, to Prince E. N. Trubetskoi, Moscow: GARF, f. 102, op. 265, d. 1002, ll. 2202–22020b. Also, letter to Trubetskoi criticizing his approach to Germany, 9 December 1914: GARF, f. 102, op. 265, d. 1001, l. 2023.

[60] *Velikaia voina: Chto dolzhen znat' o nei kazhdyi russkii?* (Petrograd: Tekhnicheskoe izdatel'stvo inzhenera N. G. Kuznetsova, 1914), 51 (*voskresenie narodov*).

German militarism.[61] Here also a philosopher of Jewish background viewed what he called "the tragedy of the German spirit" as an outgrowth of Germany's religious heritage. The path from Luther to Nietzsche, he believed, led away from religion toward the celebration of "the bare life instincts [and] the urge to conquer."[62]

Russian intellectuals were not alone, of course, in blaming the deep structures of German culture for the nation's current belligerence. Émile Durkheim (1858–1917), whose work was known in Russia, argued that a pervasive "*mentalité*" explained a number of Germany's characteristic features: the cult of power, the over-valuation of state authority, and the desire to dominate other nations. These traits generated a style of warfare that Durkheim described as "systematically inhumane," reflecting a deep-seated "social pathology."[63] Durkheim himself did not point to religion as a determining feature of German culture, but this view, so prevalent in Russia, could be found in Europe as well. A religious conception of the national mission was articulated by certain clergymen on the German side.[64] The story that launched the legend of the "Angels of Mons," first published by Arthur Machen (1863–1947) in September 1914, played on the contrast between cold German rationality and the simple faith of the British foot soldier.[65] The ideas expounded in the confines of the Religious-Philosophical Society thus converged with styles of thinking that traversed Europe.

[61] F. Zelinskii, "Slavianskoe vozrozhdenie," *V tylu: Literaturno-khudozhestvennyi al'manakh* (Petrograd: M. V. Popov, 1915), 80–86. Classicist Faddei Zelinskii (1859–1944), aka Tadeusz Zieliński, who wrote in German as well as Russian and often published in Germany, belonged to the faculties of both St. Petersburg and Warsaw universities.

[62] David Koigen, "Tragediia germanizma," in *V tylu*, 180–214. See idem, *Ideen zur Philosophie der Kultur: Der Kulturakt* (Munich: G. Müller, 1910); idem, *Die Kultur der Demokratie, vom Geiste des volkstümlichen Humanismus und vom Geiste der Zeit* (Jena: Diederichs, 1912). Koigen (1879–1933), born in Volhynia, studied in Europe before moving to St. Petersburg in 1913, where he became an editorial writer for the Kadet newspaper *Den'*. In 1921 he fled Kiev, where he had been professor of philosophy and sociology, for Berlin.

[63] Émile Durkheim, *"L'Allemagne au-dessus de tout," la mentalité allemande et la guerre* (Paris: A. Colin, 1915). Another of Durkheim's pamphlets was available in Russian translation: Émile Durkheim and Ernest Denis, *Qui a voulu la guerre? Les origines de la guerre d'après les documents diplomatiques* (Paris: A. Colin, 1915): Komitet frantsuzskikh uchenykh: Bergson, Butru [Émile Boutroux], Diurkgeim, Sen'ebos [Charles Seignobos] et al.: *Issledovaniia i dokumenty otnosiashchiesia k voine*: E. Diurkheim and E. Deni, *Kto khotel voiny?* (Petrograd: Izd. "Biblioteki Velikoi voiny," 1915).

[64] Some Protestant and Catholic German clergymen envisioned the war as a holy mission; a number of French Catholic intellectuals declared Protestantism the root of German evil: Kramer, *Dynamic of Destruction*, 176–78. See also Doris L. Bergen, "Christianity and Germanness: Mutually Reinforcing, Reciprocally Undermining?" in *Religion und Nation, Nation und Religion: Beiträge zu einer unbewältigten Geschichte*, ed. Michael Geyer and Hartmut Lehmann (Göttingen: Wallstein, 2004), 76–98.

[65] Arthur Machen, *The Angels of Mons: The Bowmen, and Other Legends of the War* (London: Simpkin, Marshall, Hamilton, Kent, 1915); see Barbara Korte, ed., *The Penguin Book of First World War Stories* (London: Penguin, 2007), 373.

The philosophers were also aware, from press reports and their contact with the excited public, of the atmosphere at home. None more so than the recently disciplined Rozanov, who always aimed to capture the prevailing mood on whatever subject caught his attention. His wartime writing is a good guide, therefore, to the tone of bellicose exaltation that greeted the outbreak of hostilities on 19 July 1914—1 August, in Europe. Hailing the conflict as an Easter of the Slavic nations, he called the war a redemptive bloodletting—a "great racial and cultural struggle" between "two worlds"—the Slavic and Teutonic. "Forgotten but now justified," the Slavophiles were right, he proclaimed, to have valued the native Russian tradition over the empty abstractions of European culture. "The dawn of the new war is not only a tribal struggle with the Germanic world but the cultural rebirth of Russia on primordial [*iskonnye*] Russian principles."[66]

Like the other Slavophile-oriented thinkers, Rozanov viewed the difference between these two civilizations as expressions of their religious traditions. He went further than most of them, however, in his embrace of instinct and emotion, and hence, in the context of war, of disorder and violence. When a mob destroyed the German Embassy in Petrograd on 22 July/4 August 1914, Rozanov excused the attack as misguided but forgivable, even touching.[67] "Illusions are as sacred as facts," he remarked. "The dear people of Petersburg spent a splendid night of illusions—and God bless them."[68] The outbursts of the Russian folk were joyful and instinctive; the depredations of the Germans calculated and inhuman. Their brutality stemmed from the fact that they "are essentially trained in civic virtues, but not in morality or religion."[69] Europeans, in their rational positivism, had lost the spirit of Christ, but Russian soldiers were "Christ-loving" in their simplicity.[70]

---

[66] V. V. Rozanov, *Voina 1914 goda i russkoe vozrozhdenie* (Petrograd: A. S. Suvorin, 1915), 2–3, 6, 31–32, 40, 47, 69 (pieces first published in *Novoe vremia*). See discussion in Ben Hellman, *Poets of Hope and Despair: The Russian Symbolists in War and Revolution (1914–1918)* (Helsinki: Institute for Russian and East European Studies, 1995).

[67] Rozanov, *Voina 1914 goda*, 9. For condemnation, see I. I. Tolstoi, *Dnevnik, 1906–1916*, ed. L. I. Tolstaia (St. Petersburg: Evropeiskii dom, 1997), 526. Official protest: *Memorandum Concerning the Treatment of German Consuls in Russia and the Destruction of the German Embassy in St. Petersburg*. Published by the Imperial German Foreign Office (Berlin: Carl Heymanns, 1915).

[68] Rozanov, *Voina 1914 goda*, 16.

[69] Rozanov, *Voina 1914 goda*, 51, 81. Atrocities as expression of cold calculation, not thirst for blood or desire to inflict suffering: idem, "Latinskaia i germanskaia kul'tury: K zasedaniiu v Sorbonne, posviashchennomu latinskoi kul'ture," *Novoe vremia*, no. 13973 (4/17 February 1915), 6.

[70] V. V. Rozanov, *V chady voiny* (Petrograd-Moscow: "Rubikon," 1915), 55, 21. His wartime journalism is collected in: *Na fundamente proshlogo: Stat'i i ocherki 1913–1915 gg.*, ed. A. N. Nikoliukin (Moscow: Respublika, 2007); idem, *V chadu voiny: Stat'i i ocherki 1916–1918 gg.*, ed. A. N. Nikoliukin (Moscow: Respublika, 2008).

The German declaration of war gave Russia the opportunity to depict itself as the victim of unwarranted aggression. The spectacular violence committed by German troops and the belligerence of German propaganda reinforced the contrast with what Russians thought of as their own, merely defensive posture. Thus, for all their differences, Rozanov and Trubetskoi could both condemn the spirit of nationalism as inherently un-Russian. "We fight against '*Deutschland über alles,*'" Rozanov proclaimed, "but will never replace it with '*Russland über alles.*' Our hearts are inclined by God to find this simply *repulsive*. Repulsive, unnecessary, and inimical. We *always* want to live among the nations [*narody*], as *one among them,* with no thought of leadership, hegemony, or superiority."[71]

Reacting to Rozanov's endorsement of spontaneous mob violence, which he excused as an outpouring of exuberant indignation, some of his Orthodox-minded colleagues were not surprised to find him "descend[ing] into the mud." They recognized this posture as the signature of his art: "the tiger's bloodthirstiness is as innocent as Rozanov's dirt," one wrote, dismissing the wartime essays as frivolous journalism. Their recycled clichés smacked of jingoism but failed to capture the spiritual essence of the war—"the mystical, mysterious meaning of the current *horrors.*"[72] Such criticism was framed, however, in terms of shared assumptions. The contrast between Russia's profound spiritual essence and the shallow, "petty bourgeois" or "bourgeois" positivism of German culture was a standard feature of current Orthodox thought.[73]

Church-sponsored Orthodox publications reflected the same set of themes that preoccupied the neo-Orthodox philosophers in the Religious-Philosophical Society. When endorsing the war, they defined it primarily in religious and cultural, not political or national, terms. Contributors applied the Slavophile scheme of opposing civilizations—Western rationalism arraigned against the spiritual virtues of the East. They vilified the Germans as materialist, militarist, egotistical, and fundamentally antireligious. Some writers targeted European culture as a whole; others distinguished the Latin nations, including, of course, Russia's ally France, which allegedly had preserved the best of the Roman legacy, from the Teutonic barbarians, who devoted their energy to conquering the Slavic peoples in the East. The war was a punishment for the sins imported from Western culture, but the conflict was a purifying flame.[74] The philosopher

---

[71] Ibid., 59.

[72] Ivan Chernokhlebov, "V. V. Rozanov i voina," *Golos zhizni*, no. 16 (15 April 1915): 8–11.

[73] For example: Sergei Bulgakov, *Voina i russkoe samosoznanie (publichnaia lektsiia)* (Moscow: I. D. Sytin, 1915), 45.

[74] "Bor'ba za khristianskie idealy," *Tserkovno-obshchestvennyi vestnik*, no. 38–39 (25 September 1914): 1–3; Vasilii Teplov, "Religioznyi smysl nastoiashchei voiny," ibid., no. 48 (4 December 1914): 1–5; sv. M. Stepanov, "Rol' dukhovenstva v gosudarstve vo vremia voiny,"

Vasilii Zenkovskii (1881–1962), writing in the Kiev-based *Khristianskaia mysl' (Christian Thought)*, urged Russians to recognize the power of their own Orthodox tradition, which would "lead Europe *out from under the nightmarish power of Germanism.*"[75] At home, the Tolstoyans and the so-called rationalist sects, the Anabaptists, Shtundists, and Evangelicals, were branded as "instruments of pan-Germanism."[76]

Like their secular colleagues, Orthodox writers denounced German "atrocities" as violations of the Geneva and Hague Conventions, which they praised Russia for upholding. Biblical images reinforced the message. Invoking the familiar litany of German crimes and desecrations, one writer denounced the destruction of the Rheims Cathedral as an act of "Satanic sadism." A missionary journal featured Germany as the anti-Christ. Exploring the "religious meaning of the war," Orthodox writers concluded, not surprisingly, that Russians had a sacred obligation to fight it. Christianity was a religion of peace, but until the Christian ideals of love and brotherhood had penetrated each human heart, the self-sacrifice demanded by military service must be considered a "feat of Christian love."[77] Exhortations to obey the secular powers are a continuous motif.[78] Even the Baptists supported the war effort and pledged their loyalty to the cause.[79]

The Question of the Jews

Construing Russian cultural identity in religious terms, the intellectual exponents of Orthodox revival were obliged to confront the question of the

---

Strannik (February 1915): 172–96; E. P. Belousov, "Germanskaia ideia i russkii ideal: Po povodu russko-germanskoi voiny 1914–15 gg.," *Missionerskoe obozrenie*, no. 1 (January 1916): 28–39; no. 2 (February 1916): 183–91 (citing Religious-Philosophical Society texts in *Russkaia mysl'*; also speeches from the 17 January 1915 Duma session); sv. N. N. Pisarev, "K voprosu o prichinakh i zadachakh sovremennoi voiny," *Pravoslavnyi sobesednik* (September 1914): 266–67; 293 (citing Khomiakov); "Pravoslavie i voina: K voprosu o sovmestimosti voiny s khristianstvom" [unsigned], *Russkii palomnik*, no. 36 (7 September 1914): 570–71.

75 V. V. Zen'kovskii, "Rossiia i Pravoslavie," *Khristianskaia mysl'* (January 1916): 101–18; (February 1916): 102–19; (April 1916): 85–102 (emphasis in original).

76 sv. Vasilii Markov, "Khristianskie idealy i voina," *Strannik* (January 1915): 43–57; I. Aivazov, "Baptizm—orudie pangermanizma," *Golos tserkvi*, no. 7–8 (July–August 1915): 114–39. Even Old Believer publications joined in these attacks, possibly to demonstrate their own good standing: V. Senatov, "Nachalo nemetskogo zasil'ia," *Slovo tserkvi*, no. 7 (15 February 1915): 153–54; *Slovo tserkvi*, no. 25 (21 June 1915): 587.

77 "Pravoslavie i voina: K voprosu o sovmestimosti voiny s khristianstvom"; Iosif Barkov, "Dukh antikhristov: Po povodu nastoiashchei voiny," *Golos tserkvi*, no. 1 (January 1916): 57–69; no. 2 (February 1916): 55–63; "Bor'ba za khristianskie idealy"; Teplov, "Religioznyi smysl"; S. A. S., "Khristianskii smysl sovremennoi voiny," *Strannik* (February 1915): 163–71; Markov, "Khristianskie idealy i voina."

78 Antonii Arkhiepiskop Khar'kovskii, "Khristianskaia vera i voina," *Russkii inok*, no. 21 (November 1916): 872–77.

79 On Baptists and the war: Heather J. Coleman, *Russian Baptists and Spiritual Revolution, 1905–1929* (Bloomington: Indiana University Press, 2005), 115–22.

Jews and Judaism, in relation to Christianity as a whole and to Russian culture in particular. The wartime context, which magnified the power of religious-cultural stereotypes, altered the terms of discussion. Concentrated by law in the area that bore the brunt of German aggression, where they mingled with the unreliable Poles, always resentful of Russian domination, the Jews spoke a dialect of German and maintained communal and commercial contacts across the border. With the ground prepared by the preceding decades of official sponsorship and right-wing agitation, patriotic anti-Semitism flourished.

Although incitement to ethnic animosity was against the law, the censor turned a blind eye to such provocations. The nationalist press did not mince words: "The Yids have treason in their blood. You cannot trust a single Yid, even those who volunteer to fight, not to betray the army to the enemy." Expelling "this harmful, treacherous nation would multiply the power of our fighting forces."[80] The brutality with which the army high command treated the Jewish population in the western provinces, well publicized at the time, made a mockery of official appeals to domestic solidarity in the face of the German threat.[81]

Not everyone in the Orthodox fold embraced these extreme views. Some Church publications espoused a crude anti-Semitism, others denounced it; still others found a middle way. A Petrograd theological journal that counted Sergei Bulgakov among its authors defined itself in opposition to the anti-Semitic Right. In 1914 its editors attacked the Union of the Russian People for its vulgar hostility toward the Jews.[82] At the other extreme, the organ of Orthodox Church missionaries denounced the Jews as the greatest enemies of the Christian faith. Not only did they insinuate themselves into the Orthodox fold in the guise of crafty sects, but they translated their Talmudist obsessions into the atheist creed of socialism. Promoting socialism as a means to further the religious and national interests of the

---

[80] From Fedor Sologub's clipping file: *Russkoe znamia* (18 December 1914), *Groza* (6 July 1915), *Zemlia* (17 February 1915): IRLI, f. 289, op. 6, ed. khr. 33, ll. 185–860b.

[81] For a description of the Jews' situation, the impact of policy, and the debate among Kadets on how to respond, see M. M. Vinaver, "Doklad po evreiskomu voprosu Tsentral'nogo Komiteta partii" (7 June 1915), in *S''ezdy i konferentsii konstitutsionno-demokraticheskoi partii 1905–1920 gg.*, 3 vols., Vol. 3, bk. 1: 1915–1917 gg., ed. O. V. Volobuev et al. (Moscow: ROSSPEN, 2000), 52–94. See also Yohanan Petrovsky-Shtern, "The 'Jewish Policy' of the Late Imperial War Ministry: The Impact of the Russian Right," *Kritika* 3, no. 2 (2002): 217–54; R. Sh. Ganelin, "Gosudarstvennaia duma i antisemitskie tsirkuliary 1915–1916 gg.," *Vestnik Evreiskogo universiteta v Moskve*, no. 3(10) (1995): 4–37; idem, "Evreiskii vopros vo vnutrennei politike Rossii v 1915 godu," ibid., no. 1(14) (1997): 41–65; Peter Gatrell, *A Whole Empire Walking: Refugees in Russia during World War I* (Bloomington: Indiana University Press, 1999). A well-informed summary of what was happening, what was known about it, and how the Russian public was responding: *The Jews in the Eastern War Zone* (New York: American Jewish Committee, 1916).

[82] "Ot redaktsii," *Tserkovno-obshchestvennyi vestnik*, no. 1 (1 July 1912): 1–3; "Starye i novye tsennosti," ibid., no. 41 (13 October 1914): 1–2.

tribe, so the missionaries warned, the Jews became agents of pan-German domination.[83]

Atheism, however, was not the only danger the Jews posed: their piety was also a menace. Another contributor to the missionary journal, who fancied himself "enlightened," reproached the Jews for clinging stubbornly to their traditional beliefs. Resisting the Christian message, they refused to join with Holy Russia in the struggle to "cleanse humanity of the beast"—in this case, the Germans. It was the patriotic duty of enlightened Jews to accept Christ and join with the rest of humankind, he admonished. "Otherwise, the Jewish people, blind and deaf at the moment of the world's greatest catastrophe, will vanish from the historical arena, like helpless, hopelessly sterile dust. They will be the pitiful laughing stock of all the nations."[84]

Thus, in the moment of wartime crisis, a single style of thinking could support divergent political views. The case of Nikolai Berdiaev is instructive in this regard. An outspoken opponent of political anti-Semitism, whether on the part of government officials or reactionary ideologues, he nevertheless shared some of their assumptions. In 1912, while the Beilis trial was still in progress, he published an essay outlining an approach to the Jews compatible with a politically liberal, but Christian perspective. Here he denounced in no uncertain terms the nationalist type of anti-Semitism, as exemplified by the Union of the Russian People and *Novoe vremia*. Relying on the press and the street, such "vulgar anti-Semitism" promoted hatred of the Jews as an incitement to political action. It was "a sickness," Berdiaev claimed, that was in fact "alien" to Russia. It was not only modern but also "bourgeois"—a term he employed "not as a social category. A bourgeois person does not believe in the other world and is thus overly occupied with the affairs of this one....Nationalism is deeply bourgeois, not in the social, but in the spiritual sense of the word."[85]

While rejecting racial and political anti-Semitism, as "incompatible with the Christian faith," Berdiaev nevertheless expressed antipathy toward the Jews on theological grounds: "religious anti-Semitism is obligatory for all Christians."[86] "To a certain extent," as he put it a few years later, "by overcoming the Jewish spirit, Christianity is in religious terms unavoidably anti-Semitic....Christianity must free itself from Semitic religious materialism and from the vestiges of the Old Testament attitude

[83] "Pravoslavnaia missiia i evreistvo," *Golos tserkvi*, no. 3 (March 1916): 119–22; I. Iankov, "Sotsializm na sluzhbe pangermanizma," *Tserkovnyi vestnik*, no. 43–35 (6–13 November 1916): 804–7.

[84] Sergei Brodskii, "Evreiskii vopros," *Golos tserkvi*, no. 9–10 (September–October 1915): 120–30; quote 122.

[85] Nikolai Berdiaev, "Natsionalizm i antisemitizm pered sudom khristianskogo soznaniia," *Russkaia mysl'*, no. 2 (February 1912), 132, 129, 127 (quotes, respectively).

[86] Ibid., 134, 138.

toward God." Among these vestiges, he believed, was precisely the kind of hatred and violence directed by self-professed Christians at their Jewish neighbors. "The Christian attitude toward the Jews is the great shame of the Christian world." It was a great shame precisely in religious terms, because the persecution of the Jews was itself un-Christian: "Christians who crucify the Jews for having crucified Christ, themselves continue to crucify Christ."[87]

Even if Christians treated Jews with forbearance, in the Christian spirit, the underlying challenge would still remain. "After the crucifixion of Christ," Berdiaev explained, "the Jews became the bearers of the anti-Christian spirit, the eternal negation of the redemptive power of the sacrifice on Golgotha." Persisting in their tribal separatism, they opted out of the Christian story. Only they, therefore, had the power to solve the Jewish problem: by abandoning their isolation. "The history of the Jews is providential," Berdiaev wrote. "No human force can exterminate the Jews." So long as they continued to exist, "anti-Semitism will never entirely be overcome. The fate of the Jewish people is absolutely tragic."[88]

There is no doubt that Berdiaev rejected the belligerent politics of the mobilized Right, but in describing the Jews' mundane existence, he nevertheless did not avoid the stereotypes favored by political anti-Semites. "The Jews are more powerful than all others and invincible," he wrote. "Enormous material wealth is concentrated in their hands. They have an exceptional grasp on life and also spiritual endurance and energy, overcoming all persecutions and repression. But nevertheless the Jews are exceptionally unfortunate.... The Jew, who bears the idea of anti-Christian chiliasm, of the earthly kingdom and its blessings, does not know and will never know, happiness and joy. He will wander forever."[89]

In Berdiaev's view, therefore, the victims of anti-Semitic aggression, deplorable in its own right, represented an underlying menace that such tactics were powerless to combat. Indeed, violence and persecution only enhanced the Jews' moral stature. "Of course, pogroms will certainly cease. They are the vestige of primitive barbarism. The political limitation on Jewish rights will end. The vulgar forms of anti-Semitism in daily life will disappear. But the Jewish Question will remain even more tragic and profound. In the West, where there are no pogroms and where the Jews have equal rights, anti-Semitism is stronger even than in Russia."[90]

---

[87] N. A. Berdiaev, "Religioznaia sud'ba evreistva," *Khristianskaia mysl'* (April 1916): 123–24. In this vein, see also Solov'ev, "Evreistvo i khristianskii vopros"; Lev Karsavin, "Rossiia i evrei," *Versty*, no. 3 (Paris, 1928), rpt. in L. P. Karsavin, *Malye sochineniia*, ed. S. L. Karsavina et al. (St. Petersburg: Aletiia, 1994), 447–69.

[88] Berdiaev, "Natsionalizm i antisemitizm," 136, 133 (*istrebit'*), 137 (quotes, respectively).

[89] Ibid., 137.

[90] Ibid.

At this point, the paradoxical character of Berdiaev's position separates him from the secular liberals who shared his conclusions but not the logic from which they derived. "One can even say," Berdiaev observed, "that the horror of the pogroms and the injustice of legal discrimination put the Jews in Russia in a morally privileged situation in the eyes of the majority of the Russian intelligentsia, preventing them from speaking honestly about the Jewish Question. The everyday anti-Semitism of our primitive nationalists and the political anti-Semitism of the government do not weaken, but intensify, the moral and cultural power of the Jews in Russia. Such anti-Semitism paralyzes the will of the Russian people, who are morally reluctant to fight against groups who are persecuted and oppressed."[91]

The right-wing Kadet Vasilii Maklakov (1869–1957), one of Beilis's legal defenders, had observed that sensible anti-Semites, such as Vasilii Shul'gin, who boasted of his convictions, had nevertheless repudiated the government position. They realized that the charges against Beilis and the conduct of the trial reduced their own beliefs to the absurd. The fanatics had discredited a worthy cause.[92] Berdiaev's tortured reasoning, published when the outcome of the trial was still in doubt, suggests a similar attempt to rescue the valid premises from distortion. Unlike Shul'gin, however, he did not consider himself an anti-Semite. Indeed, he wrote: "The anti-Semitism of our 'rightists' arouses a feeling of disgust and loathing." Yet his theological anti-Semitism led him sometimes to sound just like them: "I deeply believe that the liberation of Russian culture and the Russian intelligentsia from the anti-Christian Jewish idea, from the distinctive Jewish morality, will at the same time liberate them from anti-Semitism and nationalism."[93]

Berdiaev thus approached the Jewish Question from two angles—the practical and the theological. The first led him to condemn the right-wing use of anti-Semitism to promote un-Christian behavior (including physical violence); the second led him to condemn the Jews for rejecting the Christian spirit. Not all Orthodox thinkers drew the same conclusions from their devotion to Christian values, but, confronted by the challenge of the war, they had difficulty fashioning a coherent position on the subject. Consistent with his earlier pronouncements, Evgenii Trubetskoi rejected the identification of Russia and Russian culture with the Christian idea. "Every nation should be holy and great in our eyes," he wrote his beloved friend,

[91] Ibid.

[92] Maklakov, "Spasitel'noe predosterezhenie," 139, 141. For boasting, see V. V. Shul'gin, "*Chto nam v nikh ne nravitsia...*": *Ob antisemitizme v Rossii* (Paris: Russia minor, 1929; rpt. St. Petersburg: Natsional'no-respublikanskaia partiia Rossii: Izd-vo "Khors," 1992), 7. Vladimir Meshcherskii (1839–1914) also repudiated the government's position: M. N. Luk'ianov, "'Rossiia—dlia russkikh' ili 'Rossiia—dlia russkikh poddanykh'? Konservatory i natsional'nyi vopros nakanune pervoi mirovoi voiny," *Otechestvennaia istoriia*, no. 2 (2006): 42.

[93] Berdiaev, "Natsionalizm i antisemitizm," 140–41.

the philanthropist Margarita Morozova (née Mamontova, 1873–1958), in March 1915. The very idea of "Holy Russia," as propagated by Berdiaev, and lately by Struve, Trubetskoi complained, was incompatible with this universal view. This idea, he mordantly observed, might comfort such "Russian Germans" as Struve and Ern, uncertain of their own identity. True Russians like Morozova and himself had no need for national self-assertion, still less in religious guise.[94]

Despite her devotion to the prince and his philosophical enterprise, Morozova persisted in her defense of Holy Russia. Regarding the Jews, she expressed distaste for "the complete horror of their religious life."[95] Trubetskoi considered anti-Semitism an imitation of the worst of German-style nationalism, but his disagreement with Morozova did not create a barrier between them. Even among the liberal intelligentsia, a range of feeling on the Jewish Question was taken for granted. For those in this camp who rejected a strictly secular outlook, the issue was bound to present contradictions.

The type of anti-nationalism promoted by Trubetskoi also animated the thinking of Dmitrii Merezhkovskii.[96] Merezhkovskii, too, continued to assert the religious essence of Russian culture while rejecting the political abuse of this idea, as he had in pressing for Rozanov's exclusion from the Religious-Philosophical Society two years earlier. Denouncing "the sham, irreligious assertion of individuality" underlying the nationalist militarism of Protestant Germany, he celebrated Russia as a "holy nation."[97] Russian-style Christianity could function as a powerful mobilizing force, uniting the intelligentsia and the people in the business of war. Ultimately, however, in Merezhkovskii's view, a Christian position on war was incompatible not only with nationalism but with war itself. The pacifist implications of his argument, suppressed by the censor in 1915, appeared only in the 1917 edition of his wartime essays.[98]

---

[94] E. N. Trubetskoi to M. K. Morozova (19 March 1915) and (24 March 1915), in Keidan, *Vzyskuiushchie grada*, 628, 633–34. On Morozova's role in the Religious-Philosophical Society and *Put'*, see ibid., 65–66. Also Michael A. Meerson, *"Put'* against *Logos:* The Critique of Kant and Neo-Kantianism by Russian Religious Philosophers in the Beginning of the Twentieth Century," *Studies in East European Thought* 47, no. 3–4 (1995): 225–43. For Trubetskoi's critique of Struve, see E. N. Trubetskoi, "Razvenchanie natsionalizma: Otkrytoe pis'mo P. B. Struve," *Russkaia mysl'*, no. 4 (1916): 79–87.

[95] E. N. Trubetskoi to M. K. Morozova (31 August 1914), in Keidan, *Vzyskuiushchie grada,* 590 (*ves' uzhas ikh religioznoi zhizni*). See also E. N. Trubetskoi to M. K. Morozova (? August 1914), in ibid., 586.

[96] See D. S. Merezhkovskii, "O religioznoi lzhi natsionalizma," *Golos zhizni,* no. 4 (1914): 2–4, rpt. in Burlaka et al., *Ern: Pro et contra,* 450–57; 928–29nn.

[97] D. Merezhkovskii, "Voina i religiia," in *V tylu,* 87–89 (sham individuality); Merezhkovskii, in *Kniga Korolia Al'berta: Posviashchaetsia Bel'giiskomu Koroliu i ego narodu predstaviteliami narodov i gosudarstv vsego mira* (Moscow: "Ideia," 1915), 16 (holy nation).

[98] D. S. Merezhkovskii, "Voina i religiia," *Nevoennyi dnevnik: 1914–1916* (Petrograd: Ogni, 1917), 175–79.

Like Berdiaev, Merezhkovskii addressed the question of the Jews from the perspective both of Christian philosophy and current Russian politics. His 1915 essay, "The Jewish Question as a Russian Question," appeared in the all-purpose patriotic vehicle, *V tylu* (*On the Home Front*), but also, more pointedly, in *Shchit* (*The Shield*), a volume intended explicitly to counteract the right-wing use of anti-Semitism as a mobilizing strategy and defuse the hostility toward Jews intensified by wartime policies and propaganda.[99] Adopting the familiar neo-Slavophile assumptions (Germans are materialist egotists, Russians are selfless communitarians), Merezhkovskii insisted that Russian patriotism should distinguish itself from German-style nationalism by making toleration its guiding principle. Like Trubetskoi, he therefore detached the religious conception of Russian culture from the anti-Semitic attitudes with which it was often allied. At the same time Merezhkovskii rejected the basic principle of nationalism, including Jewish nationalism, as a form of ethnic exclusivity that detracted from the collective enterprise.

In trying to address the Jewish Question in the context of the war, no group was entirely consistent. The neo-Orthodox philosophers, as well as the Church-oriented publications, and even the members of the Progressive Bloc in the Duma, demonstrated a range of attitudes and emotions.[100] Indeed, no social group at the time was immune to anti-Jewish sentiment, but norms and expectations varied. Virulent anti-Semites were the exception among the literary, artistic, and academic intelligentsia.[101] Hence the eventual censure of Rozanov's views. Unabashed anti-Semitism was, by contrast, the rule in official and court circles. The liberal mayor of Petrograd, Count Ivan Tolstoi (1858–1916), was anomalous in his privileged milieu.[102] In visiting the city's Choral Synagogue in November 1914, where

[99] D. Merezhkovskii, "Evreiski vopros, kak russkii," in *V tylu*, 109–11; rpt. in *Shchit: Literaturnyi sbornik*, ed. Leonid Andreev, Maksim Gor'kii, and Fedor Sologub, 3rd rev. ed. (Moscow: Mamontov, 1916), 163–65; and in Merezhkovskii, *Nevoennyi dnevnik*, 135–38.

[100] Ganelin, "Gosudarstvennaia duma"; idem, "Evreiskii vopros." Also: O. V. Budnitskii, *Rossiiskie evrei mezhdu krasnymi i belymi (1917–1920)* (Moscow: ROSSPEN, 2005), 345. On the tension between liberal ideals of equal rights and the integrative demands of nationalist ideology, see Arsen'ev, "Na temy dnia."

[101] For some of these exceptions, see Mikhail Prishvin (1873–1954), *Dnevniki: 1914, 1916, 1917* (Moscow: Moskovskii rabochii, 1991), 120; Sergei Nebol'sin, "Iskazhennyi i zapreshchennyi Aleksandr Blok," *Nash sovremennik*, no. 8 (1991): 183. Both cited in Viktor Kel'ner, "The Jewish Question and Russian Social Life during World War I," *Russian Studies in History* 43:1 (summer 2004): 15 [trans. of "Evreiskii vopros i russkaia obshchestvennaia zhizn' v gody pervoi mirovoi voiny," *Vestnik Evreiskogo universiteta v Moskve* no. 1 (14) (1997): 66–93]. Prishvin also made sarcastic remarks about Jews in connection with Rozanov's expulsion from the Religious-Philosophical Society; see Ivanova, "Ob iskliuchenii," 108. On the violently anti-Semitic sentiments of Pavel Florenskii, see chapter 4.

[102] Tolstoi, who had been minister of education in Witte's government from late 1905 until the spring of 1906, was known for his defense of Jewish rights. See Count I. I. Tolstoi, "Antisemitizm v Rossii," in I. I. Tolstoi and Iulii Gessen, *Fakty i mysli: Evreiskii vopros v*

he and his children occupied an honorary place next to the families of the Barons Gintsburg, he made a dramatic public statement. In May 1915 he noted in disgust and disbelief that the police had searched the same Choral Synagogue for a cordless telephone supposedly in use by Jewish spies. Skeptical that the efforts of the group associated with *Shchit* would do any good, he nevertheless lent his name to their endeavor.[103]

Arguments for the Defense: The *Shchit* Project

Shchit was conceived as an expression of moral and civic consciousness on the part of the non-Jewish intelligentsia, not merely for the benefit of the Jews, but on behalf of the Russian cultural nation.[104] It was the brainchild of three writers whose work attracted a diverse readership and whose political views were not defined by any single ideology. Leonid Andreev (1871–1919) wrote realist fiction on topical themes, some of them sensationalistic; his wartime publications were energetically patriotic.[105] Maksim

Rossii (St. Petersburg: Obshchestvennaia pol'za, 1907), 139–220. On his career and accomplishments (including as a specialist in Old Russian coins), see: D. N. Shilov, *Gosudarstvennye deiateli Rossiiskoi imperii, 1802–1917: Biobibliograficheskii spravochnik* (St. Petersburg: Dmitrii Bulanin, 2001), 663–66; B. V. Anan'ich, *I. I. Tolstoi i peterburgskoe obshchestvo nakanune revoliutsii* (St. Petersburg: Liki Rossii, 2007). For Tolstoi's comments on the virulent anti-Semitism of various highly placed aristocratic figures, see Tolstoi, *Dnevnik*, 642, 591. Another exception was Prince Sergei Urusov (1862–1937). See his intervention in *Gosudarstvennaia Duma: Stenograficheskie otchety 1906 god*. Sessiia pervaia. Tom II. Zasedaniia 19–38 (s 1 iiunia po 4 iiulia) (St. Petersburg: Gosudarstvennaia tipografiia, 1906), zasedanie 23 (8 July 1906 g.), 1125–41. S. D. Urusov, *Zapiski gubernatora: Kishinev, 1903–1904* (Berlin: J. Ladyschnikow, 1907).

[103] Tolstoi, *Dnevnik*, 573, 634, 622, 630. See B. V. Anan'ich and L. I. Tolstaia, "I. I. Tolstoi i 'Kruzhok ravnopraviia i bratstva,'" in *Osvoboditel'noe dvizhenie v Rossii*, no. 15 (Saratov: Saratovskii universitet, 1992), 155–56. On the Gintsburg family, see Gershon David Hundert, ed., *The YIVO Encyclopedia of Jews in Eastern Europe*, 2 vols. (New Haven: Yale University Press, 2008), 1:601–3.

[104] Andreev had at first contacted Jewish writer and editor Solomon Pozner; Zinovi Grzhebin (1877–1929) was approached as a possible publisher. Grzhebin, an artist and editor associated with the World of Art, who was involved in the production of satirical journals during the 1905 Revolution, now edited the patriotic literary journal *Otechestvo: Illiustrirovannaia letopis'*, devoted to the war. Details on origins of essay volume: memo by F. Sologub, IRLI, f. 289, op. 6, ed. khr. 33, l. 249.

[105] Leonid Andreev, *V sei groznyi chas: Stat'i* (Petrograd: Knigoizdatel'stvo "Prometei" N. N. Mikhailova, 1914); a paean to Belgium, *Belgiitsam* (Moscow: Knigoizdatel'stvo "Obshchee delo," 1914/1915); the insipid drama, *Korol', zakon i svoboda*, in English: *The Sorrows of Belgium: A Play in Six Scenes*, trans. Herman Bernstein (New York: Macmillan, 1915); and the didactic account of an indifferent citizen finally rising to the civic occasion: "Igo voiny (Priznanie malen'kogo cheloveka o velikikh dniakh)," *Metel': Literaturnye al'manakhi izdatel'stva "Shipovnik,"* bk. 25 (Petrograd, 1916), 143–233; translated into English and French in 1917. See Ben Hellman, "Leonid Andreev v nachale pervoi mirovoi voiny: Put' ot 'Krasnogo smekha' k p'ese 'Korol', zakon i svoboda,'" in *Literaturnyi protsess: Vnutrennie zakony i vneshnie vozdeistviia*, ed. P. S. Reifman. Trudy po russkoi i slavianskoi filologii.

Gor'kii (pseud. of Aleksei Peshkov, 1868–1936), the plebeian playwright and novelist, combined Bolshevik sympathies with a quest for spiritual meaning. In these years he was known for his portrayals of lower-class life and his autobiographical writings. The initial idea for the project came, in fact, from the third partner, Fedor Sologub (1863–1927), an idiosyncratic Symbolist poet and writer, whose wife, Anastasiia Chebotarevskaia (1876–1921), also cooperated in the enterprise. Essentially apolitical, he wrote patriotic verses during the war.[106]

Some Jews welcomed the gesture; others found it condescending.[107] The participants themselves had difficulty drawing the line, under circumstances exacerbated by the war, between benign and dangerous opinions. When the editors invited Berdiaev to contribute, he offered them the essay on good and bad anti-Semitism that he had published during the Beilis trial.[108] Gor'kii and the writer and editor Solomon Pozner (1876–1946) now found those ideas offensive. Berdiaev, indignant, expressed his anger to Sologub:

> I consider it completely objectionable for the Jew Pozner to censor a Russian writer who has been requested to express an independent opinion on the Jewish Question and to demand from that Russian writer a particular philo-Semitic ideology. I wish to serve truth and justice, not Jews specifically. My article mounts a fervent practical defense of Jewry and is replete with indignation against anti-Semitism in its racial, political, and day-to-day manifestations. Though I am not a philo-Semite in my religious consciousness and cultural ideals, it would seem especially valuable when someone who is not philo-Semitic defends Jewry in practical ways and takes a stand against anti-Semitism. The exclusion of my article would be justified had I preached practical anti-Semitism in politics, morality, and everyday life. But what I was preaching was exactly the opposite.[109]

Literaturovedenie. Studia Russica Helsingiensia et Tartuensia, II (Tartu: Tartuskii universitet, 1990), 81–101.

[106] Fedor Sologub, *Voina: Stikhi* (Petrograd: Izd. zhurnal "Otechestvo," 1915); A. Chebotarevskaia, ed., *Voina v russkoi poezii: Stikhotvoreniia vybrany,* intro. F. Sologub (Petrograd: M. N. Popov, 1915); numerous contributions to Grzhebin's *Otechestvo.*

[107] "K russkoi intelligentsii" (Petrograd, December 1914): IRLI, f. 289, op. 6, ed. khr. 33, ll. 55–57. Israel Isidor El'iashev (Baal-Makhshoves) (1873–1924), in *Evreiskaia mysl'* (1916), cited in Kel'ner, "Jewish Question," 35–36. An American translation served as a vehicle for interventionist propaganda: Maxim Gorky, Leonid Andreyev, and Fyodor Sologub, eds., *The Shield,* foreword by William English Walling; trans. A. Yarmolinsky (New York: Knopf, 1917). Russian-Jewish émigré Avrahm Yarmolinsky (1890–1975) headed the New York Public Library Slavonic Division, 1917–1955. A socialist trade unionist and civil rights activist, Walling (1877–1936) attributed Russian anti-Semitism to German influence and hailed the February revolution as a defeat for the German-backed tsarist regime. On his 1906 visit to Russia: Walling, *Russia's Message.*

[108] Berdiaev, "Natsionalizm i antisemitizm," 125–41.

[109] Berdiaev quote, cited from IRLI, in Kel'ner, "Jewish Question," 32.

Berdiaev published the essay instead in an Orthodox theological journal.[110]
As in the case of Rozanov's exclusion from the Religious-Philosophical Society, the political context altered the impact of ideas which earlier had fallen within a range of morally acceptable opinion. Anti-Jewish sentiments attached to wartime propaganda and promoted by official policy now justified massive violence against the Jews and deeply affected public opinion.[111] In an effort to counteract the right-wing campaign, the organizers of *Shchit* also sponsored public lectures by an array of non-Jewish speakers, who emphasized the Jews' positive role in Russian economic and cultural life, stressing the damage inflicted by ethnic and religious hatred on the patriotic cause.[112]

Mirroring the expanse of Russia's civic-minded public life, the contributors to *Shchit* included a former cabinet minister, future ministers of the Provisional Government, populists and radicals, Realists and Symbolists, professionals and artists, philosophers, economists, journalists, and literary critics. A number were active contributors to patriotic journalism.[113] The cover featured a charcoal sketch by the impressionist painter Leonid Pasternak (1862–1945), known at the time for his war-charity posters.[114] The sketch depicts a sorrowful Jewish workman at the bedside of a young woman with a bandaged brow, the implied victim of an anti-Semitic attack. The theme of empathy is extended in the several literary sketches offering admirably patriotic Jewish characters in the counter-stereotype mode.[115] Mobilizing typical anti-German arguments, here in defense of

[110] Berdiaev, "Religioznaia sud'ba evreistva." See n. 87.

[111] See numerous examples in the private correspondence intercepted by the censor: GARF, f. 102, op. 265.

[112] Speakers included the Polish specialist on classical Greek religion Faddei Zelinskii, historian Paul Miliukov, economist Mikhail Bernatskii (b. 1876), Ukrainian writer Maksym Slavinskyi (1868–1945), literary critic Georgi Chulkov (1879–1939), Orthodox Church historian Anton Kartashev, Andreev, and Sologub. Program and summaries: "Russkie ob evreiakh; Programma publichnoi besedy" (n.d.): IRLI, f. 289, op. 6, ed. khr. 33, ll. 50–51. The editors also published a questionnaire in various newspapers, surveying attitudes toward the Jews. Gor'kii presented the results in December 1915 in a public lecture, which was itself then published, completing the pedagogical circuit: M. Gor'kii, "Po povodu odnoi ankety," *Letopis'*, no. 1 (January 1916): 189–220.

[113] For background, see Kel'ner, "Jewish Question." Contributors overlapping with *V tylu*: Andreev, Sologub, Teffi (1876–1952), Valerii Briusov (1873–1924), Gippius, Sergei Gusev-Orenburgskii (1867–1963), Bekhterev, and Tatiana Shchepkina-Kupernik (1874–1952); overlapping with *Velikaia voina v obrazakh i kartinakh* (1914–1917): Count Aleksei Tolstoi (1882–1945), Prince Pavel Dolgorukov (1866–1927), Maksim Kovalevskii (1851–1916), and Sergei Bulgakov. Memo by F. Sologub, IRLI, f. 289, op. 6, ed. khr. 33, l. 249.

[114] Pasternak was a nonobservant Jew, whose poet son Boris (1890–1960) converted to Orthodoxy. Ronald Hingley, *Pasternak: A Biography* (New York: Knopf, 1983), 14. Pasternak père left for Berlin in 1921, fled to England in 1938, and died in Oxford.

[115] Mikhail Artsybashev (1878–1927), "Evrei: Rasskaz," in Andreev, Gor'kii, and Sologub, *Shchit*, 15–24; Sergei Gusev-Orenburgskii (former Orthodox priest, turned writer, later known for his factual account of the 1919 anti-Jewish pogroms), "Evreichik," in ibid.,

Fig. 7. Leonid Pasternak, Title page. *Shchit: Literaturnyi sbornik* [The Shield: A Literary Collection], ed. Leonid Andreev, Maksim Gor'kii, and Fedor Sologub, 3rd rev. ed. Russian Society for the Study of Jewish Life (Moscow: Mamontov, 1916). Courtesy Sterling Memorial Library, Yale University.

the Jews, one essayist insisted that "contemporary anti-Semitic ideology" was itself "a product of the German culture industry." The old hatreds, he wrote, were emerging "in a scientific, or rather, pseudo-scientific guise," propelled by the "militant Germanism" of the unified nation.[116]

The overall orientation of the volume was secular—in defense of equal rights and civic virtues. But the appeal to Orthodoxy was a centerpiece of patriotic as well as anti-Semitic discourse. The subject could not be ignored. Merezhkovskii's wife, the poet and essayist Zinaida Gippius (1869–1945), reminded her readers that Christ himself was a Jew. The eminent psychiatrist Vladimir Bekhterev, writing as an amateur poet, recounted the case of a rabbi attached to the French army, who, in the spirit of Jesus, had given his life for a wounded Christian soldier.[117] The insistence on resolving the Jewish Question from a progressive, but nevertheless nonsecular, perspective is reflected in the comments of Anton Kartashev (1875–1960). A historian of the Russian Orthodox Church associated with the Religious-Philosophical Society, Kartashev hailed Vladimir Solov'ev as a "great Christian philo-Semite," who admirably derived his principles of toleration not from "imported intelligentsia liberalism" but as a consequence of the Church's own beliefs. Viacheslav Ivanov also proposed what he considered a Christian solution to the problem: "If we were truly with Christ," he proclaimed, the Jews would finally acknowledge Him as the Messiah.[118]

The combination of toleration and religious conviction was not always easy to achieve. Sergei Bulgakov took a different approach. At first he had been reluctant to contribute to the volume. As he wrote to an acquaintance in December 1914, he was out of sympathy with the overall tenor of the project.

The Jewish Question grows ever more painful, thanks to the complexity of feelings about it. I am certain that of all the questions, not excluding that of

---

70–75; and Aleksei Tolstoi, "Anna Ziserman: Ocherk," in ibid., 226–34. For examples of the philo-Semitic counter-myth genre: Iakov Okunev (1882–1932), "Smert' soldata Branfmana," in *Evrei na voine: Dvukhnedel'nyi illiustrirovannyi zhurnal,* ed. D. Kumanov, no. 11 (Moscow: Moskovskoe izdatel'stvo, 1915): 9–10 (the journal was dedicated to celebrating Jewish military courage); Iakov Okunev, *Na peredovykh pozitsiiakh: Boevye vpechatleniia* (Petrograd: M. V. Popov, 1915). Also: Vadim Belov, *Evrei i poliaki na voine: Vpechatleniia ofitsera uchastnika* (Petrograd: Izd. "Biblioteki Velikoi voiny," 1915).

[116] Fedor Kokoshkin (1871–1918), "Korni antisemitizma," in Andreev, Gor'kii, and Sologub, *Shchit,* 120–30.

[117] Tikhoberezhskii, "Smert' ravvina: Iz sobytii na zapadnom teatre voiny," in ibid., 225. The well-known story concerned Abraham Bloch (1859–1914), a rabbi from Lyons, who was killed by shrapnel while ministering to a dying Christian soldier on the battlefield. Bekhterev, who enjoyed an international reputation, remained in the Soviet Union after 1917 (see chapter 1).

[118] A. Kartashev, "Izbrannye i pomilovannye," in ibid., 113 (*nanosnyi intelligentskii liberalizm*); Viacheslav Ivanov, "K ideologii evreiskogo voprosa," in ibid., 97–99.

the war, the Jewish Question is the most difficult, and in various respects, fatal and decisive for Russia. In Petrograd they are planning a collection on the Jewish Question. I declined to participate because . . . it is impossible and also not at all timely to tackle the essence of the matter (and that's the only way to write about it). However the Jewish publishers think otherwise. Considering my antinomian attitude to the Jews—extreme philo-Israelite and extreme anti-*Zhidovstvo*—it is extremely difficult to enter into this frame.[119]

By antinomian, Bulgakov had in mind the reproach directed at the Jews for failing to accept the "law of grace." Rejecting Christ as the son of God, they clung for moral guidance to the laws expounded in the Old Testament. In valuing the precepts of earthly conduct over the power of the Holy Spirit, they set themselves on the path that easily led to the loss of sacred meaning altogether, the path toward secular modernity. Distinguishing "Israel" from "Zhidovstvo" (derived from the disparaging Russian term *Zhid*), Bulgakov objected to the tendency of Jews to become a culturally, not religiously, defined community—the people of Yiddish, of trade, of the *mestechko*. These cultural Jews were distinct from Christians in the mundane sense, but they had lost their spiritual calling.

Where Berdiaev objected to Jewish exclusivity as a form of nationalism at odds with the universal Christian spirit, which the Jews stubbornly refused to accept, Bulgakov, by contrast, urged the Jews to strengthen their sense of themselves as a nation. This nation, however, was not to constitute an enclave within the empire but an independent state of its own. When he ultimately agreed to contribute to *Shchit*, he wrote on the subject of Zion.[120] The Jews, he advised, should reject the Diaspora; they were justified in wanting more than equal rights and the abolition of the Pale of

---

[119] S. Bulgakov, Moscow, 23 December 1914, to Dr V. K. Khoroshko, Brest-Litovsk: GARF, f. 102, op. 265, d. 1002, l. 2120. Vasilii Khoroshko (1881–1949) was a neurologist and a member of the Moscow Psychological Society, to which Bulgakov also belonged; both left Moscow University in 1911. The text of this note exists in two versions: the one in GARF (23 December 1914), transcribed by the imperial perlustration department; another (22 December 1914), published in *Novyi mir* in 1989 based on a handwritten archival manuscript. The term "philo-Israelite" appears in the censor's version as "filo-izraelizm" but appears in *Novyi mir* as "filoiudaizm." Bulgakov may have changed his mind between what appears to be a draft and the version actually mailed. But in conjunction, the variants underscore what he intended by the contrast with "Zhidovstvo." Manuscript version: "Pis'mo B. K. Khoroshko," Moscow, 22 December 1914 [autograph in the Manuscript Division of the Russian State Library], cited in S. N. Bulgakov, "Moia rodina: Stat'i, ocherki, pis'ma," ed. I. B. Rodnianskaia, *Novyi mir*, no. 10 (1989): 241. The same version is also cited in Kel'ner, "Jewish Question," 23; also in Gollerbakh, *K nezrimomu gradu*, 49.

[120] Sergei Bulgakov, "Sion," in Andreev, Gor'kii, and Sologub, *Shchit*, 43–46. On the similarity of this position to that of the Allies in Paris in 1919, refusing to grant Jews "national rights" as minorities within political states but supporting the creation of a Jewish state in Palestine: Mark Levene, "Nationalism and Its Alternatives in the International Arena: The Jewish Question at Paris 1919," *Journal of Contemporary History* 28, no. 3 (1993): 519.

Settlement. What they needed was a political state (excluding, of course, the Christian holy places) as a national home for Israel, where they would achieve rebirth as a people (*vozrozhdenie svoego naroda*). Zionism, he wrote, had emerged not only in response to prejudice and persecution but also for fear of assimilation and secularization. Jews were forgetting what it meant to be Jewish. The only way to retain the idea of Jewishness, in his view, was either to suffer continual persecution or bring the Diaspora to an end. The Jews must assert their national character (*utverzhdenie svoego natsional'nogo lika*), Bulgakov believed, by establishing a "national center" (*natsional'nyi tsentr*) in the land of Palestine given to them by God.[121]

The inclusion of writers with a Christian orientation by the organizers of *Shchit* was important, first, because they represented a significant current within the progressive fold; and, second, because the Jewish Question itself was never entirely secular. Nevertheless, the focus of the enterprise remained primarily political. Both the radical Gor'kii and the moderate Andreev worried about the impact of anti-Semitism on the Russian political nation—on its chances in the war and its prospects for the future. Anti-Semitism was not itself peculiar to Russia, they knew. It was anti-Jewish violence, Andreev insisted in the volume's opening essay, that set Russia apart.

> Yes, we are still barbarians. The Poles do not trust us. We fill Europe with fear....But we no longer want to appear this way....The Jews' tragic love for Russia corresponds to our own love *for Europe*, which is just as loyal, inextricable, and tragic. Indeed, we ourselves are the *Jews of Europe*. Our border is our own Pale of Settlement, our unique Russian Ghetto....Here is the equality in which we all may take bitter solace. This is the penalty with which life justly repays the Russians for the suffering of the Jews....The end to Jewish suffering is the beginning of Russian self-respect, without which Russia *cannot exist*.[122]

Employing the terms of abuse lavished on German "atrocities" in wartime propaganda, Gor'kii condemned the "hatred of Jews [as] a bestial, zoological phenomenon."[123] Identifying the "uncultured mob [that] transcends social categories" as "the principal bearer of zoological impulses such as Judeophobia," Gor'kii described how anti-Semitic rhetoric and propaganda had distorted public consciousness. "In recent years, rather many people have learned to believe that...the non-Russians among them are the enemy, and most of all the Jews. Such people are convinced that all Jews are restless people, strikers and rebels. They learn," in the case of

---

[121] Bulgakov, "Sion," in Andreev, Gor'kii, and Sologub, *Shchit,* 43–45.
[122] Andreev, "Pervaia stupen'," in ibid., 7–8.
[123] M. Gor'kii, "***," in ibid., 59.

Beilis, "that the Jews like to drink the blood of furtive boys. These days," during the war, "we are told the Jews of Poland are spies and traitors."[124]

Pavel Miliukov (1859–1943), the historian and Kadet Duma deputy, was central to the liberal roster.[125] His contribution to *Shchit* demonstrated that nationalism remained a dilemma for patriotic liberals in wartime. Advocating the rule of law as the best foundation for the multiethnic Russian state, he defended the integrity of empire. In the present chauvinistic atmosphere, therefore, he advised the Jews to avoid the mistake of forming a separate national movement, since they depended for their own welfare on the liberation of Russia as a whole.[126] A similar admonition might also have been aimed at the Poles, but the Polish question was largely neglected in an enterprise designed to repair, rather than deepen, ethnic and religious cleavage. In accord with its anti-nationalist outlook, the volume included a contribution from the Polish linguist Jan Niecisław Baudouin de Courtenay (1845–1929), who had publicly opposed the anti-Jewish boycott inaugurated by the National Democrats in 1912.[127]

The Polish case, in fact, revolved around the Poles' repeated efforts to extricate themselves from the empire and reestablish their own nationally defined state. The Jewish case was less straightforward, since the Jews had never had a national state and did not consider themselves a nation in the political sense. Imperial anti-nationalism could not satisfy the Poles; Christian universalism could not accommodate the Jews, who refused to see it as universal. Polish nationalists also had trouble accepting the Jews, for different reasons. The editors of *Shchit* promoted a civic vision in which individuals

---

[124] Ibid., 64–65. Part of this passage is in Gorky, Andreyev, and Sologub, *The Shield*, 15.

[125] P. Miliukov, "Evreiskii vopros v Rossii," in *Shchit*, 166–74; translated in Gorky, Andreyev, and Sologub, *The Shield*, 53–73. See Melissa Kirschke Stockdale, *Paul Miliukov and the Quest for a Liberal Russia, 1880–1918* (Ithaca: Cornell University Press, 1996); and the most recent edition of his memoirs: P. N. Miliukov, *Vospominaniia*, ed. M. G. Vandalkovskaia, 2 vols. (Moscow: "Sovremennik," 1990); condensed: Paul Miliukov, *Political Memoirs, 1905–1917*, ed. Arthur P. Mendel; trans. Carl Goldberg (Ann Arbor: University of Michigan Press, 1967).

[126] Arguing for the abolition of the Pale in 1911, Vasilii Maklakov denounced Jewish nationhood not only as injurious to the empire but also to the Jews. He also noted the paradox that official policy was largely responsible for creating this inner Jewish nation: "This policy has managed to unite the Jews into a separate nation [*natsiia*]. It has turned the Jewish Question in Russia from a social or confessional question to a national one. It has united the Jews as objects of government injustice, has forced the Jews to hate Russian authorities, and then uses this hatred, incited by itself, as justification for its anti-Semitism." *Gosudarstvennaia Duma: Stenograficheskie otchety*. Tretii sozyv. 1911 g. Sessiia chetvertaia. Chast' II. Zasedaniia 39–73 (s 17 ianvaria po 5 marta 1911 g.) (St. Petersburg: Gosudarstvennaia tipografiia, 1911), zasedanie 54 (9 February 1911), col. 1549.

[127] De Courtenay, "Svoeobraznaia 'krugovaia poruka,'" in Andreev, Gor'kii, and Sologub, *Shchit*, 143–46. See Theodore R. Weeks, *From Assimilation to Antisemitism: The "Jewish Question" in Poland, 1850–1914* (DeKalb: Northern Illinois University Press, 2006), 167. Also: Edward Stankiewicz, ed., *A Baudouin de Courtenay Anthology: The Beginnings of Structural Linguistics*, trans. and intro. idem (Bloomington: Indiana University Press, 1972).

and groups enjoyed equal rights in a neutral, secular framework, but the question of what kind of "Russia" this would be remained inconclusive.

Conclusions

In the context of the war, the Jewish Question took on added meaning. Since the mid-nineteenth century the Jews had been viewed by imperial Russian cultural nationalists (an irresolvable contradiction in terms) as the quintessential "inner enemy." In terms of geographical location they inhabited the porous western borders, intimately connected to the unreliable Poles, linked by trade and kinship to co-religionists in nations hostile to Russian imperial ambitions. Caught in a perpetual double-bind, some persisted in their religious and customary self-isolation, whereas others, more ominously, managed to penetrate the bastions of the native elite—in the universities and professions. In economic terms, they represented at once the worst of backwardness—crowded into their dusty provincial towns, trading in alcohol and lending money—and simultaneously the most intimidating forms of modern life—the factories, banks, and stock exchange. Before and during the war they were the objects of Polish nationalist anti-Semitism, itself a destabilizing force from the perspective of the center.[128] They were the targets of anti-Semitism on the part of imperial officials and of organized violence at the hands of the armed forces and enthusiastic "mobs," acting with or without official backing.

Berdiaev was right. The test for enlightened Russians was not whether you liked the Jews. Instead, the test was whether, not liking them, you defended their right to exist on equal terms with their Christian neighbors in the civic sphere. Violence against peaceful communities was, of course, abhorrent; even ideologues who justified the pogroms did so by claiming that the Jews were the aggressors—preying on Christian children, exploiting the peasantry, murdering the tsar, conspiring with the enemy, plotting

---

[128] For some recent scholarship on this large question, see Frank Golczewski, *Polnisch-Jüdische Beziehungen 1881–1922: Eine Studie zur Geschichte des Antisemitismus in Osteuropa* (Wiesbaden: Franz Steiner Verlag, 1981); Pawel Korzec, "Polish-Jewish Relations during World War I," in *Hostages of Modernization: Studies on Modern Antisemitism 1870–1933/39: Austria—Hungary—Poland—Russia*, ed. Herbert A. Strauss (Berlin: Walter de Gruyter, 1993), 1022–37; Brian A. Porter, *When Nationalism Began to Hate: Imagining Modern Politics in Nineteenth-Century Poland* (New York: Oxford University Press, 2000); Robert Blobaum, ed., *Antisemitism and Its Opponents in Modern Poland* (Ithaca: Cornell University Press, 2005); Konrad Zieliński, *Stosunki polsko-żydowskie na ziemiach Królestwa Polskiego w czasie pierwszej wojny światowej* (Lublin: Wydawnictwo Uniwersytetu Marii Curie-Skłodowskiej, 2005); Weeks, *From Assimilation to Antisemitism.* For contemporary treatments: Grigorii Landau, *Pol'sko-evreiskie otnosheniia: Stat'i i zametki* (Petrograd: Trud, 1915); *K evreiskomu voprosu v Pol'she: Sbornik statei,* intro. N. N. Polianskii (Moscow: "Moskovskoe pechatnoe pr-vo," 1915).

world domination. But allowing them to coexist or refraining from murdering and despoiling them was not the same as admitting them to the cultural fellowship of Orthodox Russia.

Just as Bulgakov styled himself a Christian socialist, Berdiaev might be called a Christian liberal. Recognition of religious diversity from a Christian perspective was not, however, in the words of Vladimir Ern, the same as "frosty toleration"; nor was it the "imported intelligentsia liberalism" repudiated by Anton Kartashev. Christian liberalism did not presuppose a neutral public sphere in which religious faith becomes a matter of personal conviction and no one form of observance or vision of the divine claims pride of place. Solov'ev, Berdiaev, Bulgakov, Ern—all maintained a theological perspective in which the ultimate goal was the triumph of Christian truth. Like the secular liberals, they were universalists—but in spiritual, not political, terms. Positing, on the one hand, the absolute value of Christian revelation, identifying, on the other, the root of Russian cultural integrity in Eastern Orthodoxy, they found the Jews to be a problem they could not solve. For that reason Trubetskoi, who favored an imperial rather than confessional definition of the Russian mission, challenged the Slavophile conflation of culture and faith.

Rozanov, by contrast, was a particularist. He was also blissfully free of the need for coherence. Unlike Berdiaev or Bulgakov, he appreciated the Jews in both their everyday and Old Testament dimensions. He had no interest in civil rights or civilized behavior. He was inspired by the irrational, the corporeal, the instinctual, and the virtuous—the latter only as a movement of the heart, not a matter of principle. Therefore, Rozanov (who abjured politics) was, politically speaking, a conservative. For him there was no contradiction in valuing the Old Testament and writing for the anti-Semitic gutter press.

Neither Rozanov nor the Christian liberals could be neutral about the Jews. It was a highly charged preoccupation they shared, despite Berdiaev's demurral, with the unabashed political anti-Semites. Not all self-described anti-Semites, for their part, endorsed mistreatment of the Jews—some for pragmatic reasons and based on the same logic that caused them to fear and dislike them. Minister of Finance Petr Bark (1869–1937), for one, criticized the ruthless policies implemented by the army high command during World War I, but not on moral grounds. The empire, he argued, could ill afford to antagonize the international banking networks controlled by the Rothschild clan. Their willingness to extend credit to the tsarist regime depended on how the Jews in Russia were treated.[129] Supporting the position

---

[129] Ganelin, "Evreiskii vopros," 50–51. See Bark's retrospective explanation of the need to placate international Jewish networks: Bark (unpublished) Memoirs—English typescript (n.d.), 41–42: Bakhmeteff Archive, Columbia University.

of the Progressive Bloc in the Duma, the Bessarabian aristocrat Aleksandr Krupenskii (1861–1939) took the same tack. Describing himself as "a congenital anti-Semite," he had "come to the conclusion that it is now necessary for the good of the homeland to make concessions to the Jews. We need the support of the Allies. One cannot deny that the Jews are a great international power and that our hostile policy toward them weakens our credit abroad."[130]

Political liberals were similarly pragmatic. Vasilii Maklakov, who had defended Mendel Beilis during the notorious trial, later deplored the anti-Semitism of the White forces in the civil war as harmful to the anti-Bolshevik cause, just as he had denounced imperial policy as harmful to the empire.[131] But liberals were ambivalent: Maklakov and Trubetskoi declined to join the two hundred intellectuals and public figures who signed a petition in favor of Jewish rights, organized by Gor'kii and Sologub in 1915 and published in *Russkie vedomosti* (*The Russian Gazette*), the leading liberal newspaper.[132] The Progressive Bloc itself had difficulty shaping a unified position on the Jewish Question. Given the climate of the times, that is not surprising.

Nor did the Left entirely avoid the problem. The Social Democrats rejected anti-Semitism in no uncertain terms, as a vestige of pre-Enlightenment obscurantism, like religion itself, but they shared the anti-capitalist, anti-bourgeois animus of the populist anti-Semites. This rhetorical elision had ugly consequences after the Bolshevik victory. Social Democrats were also clear in their repudiation of national claims, including the Zionist version, that might impede the international thrust of socialist solidarity. In that sense, their position bore a structural relationship to the position assumed by imperial liberals, who, in their case, viewed nationalism as a threat to the integrity of empire. For Orthodox-identified Russian intellectuals who distanced themselves from both the reactionary Right and the secular Left, the philosophical question of the Jews translated awkwardly in political terms. From their perspective, the Jews, like the Russians, were a cultural nation defined by religion, in a world in which the

[130] Ganelin, "Evreiskii vopros," 56–57 (both quotes). Krupenskii: marshal of the nobility and zemstvo president, headed the Red Cross in Southern Russia, 1914–18, represented Bessarabia at the Paris Peace Conference.

[131] Maklakov, "Spasitel'noe predosterezhenie." Also: O. V. Budnitskii, ed., "Belye i evrei (Po materialam rossiiskogo posol'stva v Parizhe i lichnogo arkhiva V. A. Maklakova)," in *Evrei i russkaia revoliutsiia: Materialy i issledovaniia*, ed. O. V. Budnitskii (Moscow; Jerusalem: Izd-vo "Gesharim," 1999), 269–85.

[132] Miliukov and Anatoli Koni (1844–1927) also refused, claiming it was not timely. "Pis'mo v redaktsiiu," *Russkie vedomosti* (1 March 1915), 5. Cited in R. M. Khin-Gol'dovskaia, "Iz dnevnikov 1913–1917," intro. and ed. E. B. Korkina, notes by A. I. Dobkin, *Minuvshee: Istoricheskii al'manakh* 21 (Moscow-St. Petersburg: Atheneum-Feniks, 1997), 554 (commentary, 589); Budnitskii, *Rossiiskie evrei mezhdu krasnymi i belymi*, 345.

political nation was the framework for loyalty and the engine of war. The delicate balance the enlightened neo-Orthodox philosophers attempted to strike between civic tolerance and cultural identity was difficult to maintain. In the context of empire, neither Russians nor Jews could escape this dilemma.

Index

Page numbers in *italics* indicate illustrative material.

abortion law in Russia and Soviet Union, 29–30
Akhmatova, Anna, 177
Aksakov, Aleksandr, 117
Aksakov family, 113
Aksakov, Ivan, 195, 197
Aksakov, Konstantin, 6, 129–30, 149, 195
Aleksandrov, Petr, 61
Alekseev, Petr (archpriest), 105, 106, 118
Aleksei (Rediger), 188
Alexander I (tsar), 21, 36, 39–42, 46, 83–84, 107, 108, 111, 128, 129, 193
Alexander II (tsar), 22, 46, 47n35, 48, 58, 62, 66–69, 73, 80, 88, 107, 194
Alexander III (tsar), 22, 66
Allenov, Mikhail, 159n27, 186–88, 190
Alpatov, Mikhail, 184–85
Andreev, Leonid, 221, 223n112, 224, 227
Angels of Mons, 211
anti-Semitism, 11, 123–24,192–232; Beilis, Mendel, blood libel against, 97, 196, 199, 200, 216, 218, 222, 228, 231; Social Democrats and, 231; National Democrats and, 228; of Dostoevskii, 152; Ivanov's Jewish figures and, 189, 192; revolutionary movement and, 69, 72–73; *Shchit*, 220–29, 224; of Slavophiles, 195. *See also* Aksakov, Ivan; Brafman, Jacob; Florenskii, Pavel; Rozanov, Vasilii; Shul'gin, Vasilii; Union of the Russian People
Appearance of Christ to the People (Ivanov), 152–59, 162, 169, 175, 182, 185, 187, 189, 192
Arsenii (Matseevich), 105–6

art and religion, 10, 151–90; Nazarenes, 158, 160–62, 172, 174, 176, 186; Kramskoi and, 168–69; Romanticism, influence of, 160–61, 186, 188; *Sistine Madonna* (Raphael), 152–54, 160, 164, 168, 185; Slavophile view of, 158–63. *See also* icons; Ivanov, Aleksandr
Austrian Galicia, peasant uprising in (1846), 47
autocracy, Russian: anti-Semitism and, 195–96; 1905 Revolution affecting, 33–34; religion, involvement with, 2–3, 102–8, 128–29; rule of law, tsarist failure to produce, 21–22, 25. *See also* specific tsars by name, e.g. Nicholas I

Bakunin, Mikhail, 54–55, 68
Baptists, 121, 203, 214
Bardina, Sofiia, 61
Bark, Petr, 230
Baudouin de Courtenay, Jan Niecisław, 228
Bazarov, Evgenii, 50
Bazhenov, Nikolai, 32
Beccaria, Cesare, 38, 62
Beilis, Mendel, 97, 196, 199, 200, 216, 218, 222, 228, 231
Bekhterev, Vladimir, 28–29, 30n41, 223n113, 225
Belinskii, Vissarion, 50
Belting, Hans, 153–55, 160, 171, 188
Benois, Alexandre, 171–74
Berdiaev, Nikolai, 111, 115, 198n25, 208, 216–20, 222–23, 226, 229–30
Bernatskii, Mikhail, 223n112

Bezdna, 47–48, 69, 75
Bilibin, Ivan, 207
Black Repartition, 62
Blavatsky, Helena, 117
blood libel case against Mendel Beilis, 97,
    196, 199, 200, 216, 218, 222, 228, 231
Bloody Sunday (1905), 75
Bolshevik-Menshevik split (1903), 68
Bolshevik (October) Revolution (1917),
    26, 30, 35, 97–98
Bonch-Bruevich, Vladimir, 184
Botkin, Mikhail, 167, 189n131
bourgeoisie, 76–77, 216.
Brafman, Jacob, 194
Brothers Karamazov (Dostoevskii),
    110n49, 136, 140n48, 150n83
Bulgakov, Sergei, 199, 200n30, 205,
    209n52, 213n73, 215, 223n115,
    225–27, 230

Carlyle, Thomas, 100
castrating sect (Skoptsy), 121–22
Catherine the Great (tsar), 2, 4, 16, 32,
    36–39, 42, 83, 105–7, 109–11
Catholicism, 110, 111, 125–26, 128, 139,
    160, 172–74, 188, 189, 193
Cézanne, Paul, 174, 176–78
Chaadaev, Petr, 43, 84, 140
Charter of the Nobility (1785), 39
Chebotarevskaia, Anastasiia, 222
Chernyshevskii, Nikolai, 50–52, 99, 156,
    164–65, 173–74, 181, 184
Chicherin, Boris, 50, 117
Chizhov, Fedor, 128, 159–61, 166
Christ Faith (Khlysty), 122
Christ in the Desert (Kramskoi), 168,
    170, 189
Chulkov, Georgii, 223n112
civil death, 42, 51, 87
civil society, concept of, 9, 78–98; autoc-
    racy, politics, and the state, relationship
    to, 79–85; Great Reforms, 80, 82, 84,
    89; judicial system and, 85–88; Populists
    and, 86–88; in post-Soviet Russia, 80;
    religious toleration, 9, 89–98 (*See also*
    religious toleration); Russian Orthodox
    Church and, 89–91
Communism, 13, 45, 80, 101, 188. *See
    also* Marxism; socialism
Constantine (Grand Duke), 44, 48
Cornelius, Peter von, 158
corporal punishment in Russia, 38n14,
    39, 59
Cossack revolt (1773–1774) led by Pu-
    gachev, 34, 36–39, 42, 52, 54
Cousin, Victor, 131, 160–61
Crimean War, 34, 47, 48–49, 66
Criminal Code of 1845, 42–43, 91–93

da Vinci, Leonardo, 170
Dal', Vladimir, 117
Danilevskii, Nikolai, 116–17
Darwin, Charles, 100, 116–17, 119
death penalty in Russia, 37–38, 41–42, 43
Decembrist uprising (1825), 5, 34, 40–44,
    83–84, 128, 131
Diaghilev, Sergei, 171, 207
Dolgushin, Aleksandr, 52n48
Dostoevskii, Fedor, 46, 110n49, 116, 119,
    136, 150, 151–54, 198
Drentel'n, Aleksandr, 62
Dukhobortsy (Spirit-Wrestlers), 122–23
Duma, 82, 92, 95–97, 196, 197, 203, 220;
    Progressive Bloc, 220, 231
Durkheim, Émile, 211

Eastern Orthodox Church. *See* Russian
    Orthodox Church
Elagin, Aleksei, 130
Elagina, Avdot'ia, 130
eldership (startsy/starchestvo), 109, 110,
    113–14, 136–39
emancipation of serfs, 8, 46, 47–48, 80,
    107, 109; Bezdna, 47–48, 69, 75
Enlightenment ideals, 2, 3, 6, 7, 83,
    102–4, 111
Ern, Vladimir, 205–6, 208, 210, 219, 230
Evropeets (The European), 131, 132

Fathers and Sons (Turgenev), 6, 50n38
Fedorov-Davydov, Aleksei, 180
feminists and feminism, 30, 31, 87–88
Filaret (Drozdov), 108–9, 113, 115
Filaret (Novospasskii), 131–33
Filosofov, Dmitrii, 173–74
Florenskii, Pavel, 115–16, 220n101
Florovsky, Georges, 104, 108
Foucault, Michel, 13–20, 24, 30–32, 33,
    125–26, 149
France, WWI alliance with, 205, 213
Frank, Semen, 208
freedom of the press in Russia, 36, 83–84
Freemasons, 40, 83, 107, 199n29
French art, 161, 167, 170
French Revolution (1789), 1, 5, 8, 16, 33,
    44, 100, 107, 192
Fridman, Naftal, 203

Galich, Aleksandr, 141
Gapon, Georgii, 75, 120
Gavriil (Petrov), 105–7, 110
Gay, Peter, 100
Germany, 11, 14, 204–6, 209–10, 210–13,
    223–25. *See also* World War I
Gershenzon, Mikhail, 150
Gintsburg family, 221
Giotto, 162

Gippius, Zinaida, 225
Goethe, 159
Gogol, Nikolai, 52n44, 156, 158–61,
   164–66, 171, 173–74, 177, 180, 189
Golitsyn, Aleksandr, 107
Goncharova, Natal'ia, 176, 200–203, 201
Gorchakov, Aleksandr, 195
Gor'kii, Maksim, 221–22, 224,
   227–28, 231
Gospel According to St. John, 153, 188
Gramsci, Antonio, 79–80, 98
Great Reforms: civil society and, 80–82,
   84; Orthodox Church and, 89, 108, 118;
   emancipation of serfs, 8, 46, 47–48, 80,
   107, 109; intelligentsia, formation of, 4,
   7; Ivanov and, 188; Judicial Reforms of
   1864, 8, 21n21, 22, 47, 51n41, 52, 56,
   66, 85, 108; revolutionary movement
   and, 9, 47–48, 63–64
The Great Soviet Encyclopedia, 180–81
Gregory Palamas, 109–10n46
Grishchenko, Aleksei, 176, 177
Grzebin, Zinovi, 221n104

Hardy, Thomas, 100
Hegel, Georg Friedrich Wilhelm, 130
Herder, Johann Gottfried, 160
Herzen, Alexander: 4n6, 5–7, 20, 84; on
   Ivanov, 156, 163, 164, 166–68, 173,
   174, 177, 180, 181; on Kireevskii, 132–
   33, 141, 149; revolutionary movement
   and, 41, 43, 50, 53, 55
hesychasm, 109–10, 122, 136
Holy Synod, 92, 95, 96, 103, 104, 106,
   107, 108, 129
homosexuals, 1922 trial of, 27–29

icons: Ivanov and, 162–63, 181, 183,
   185–87; modern rediscovery as art and
   cultural legacy, 102, 155, 171, 175–79,
   188; pre-Raphaelite painters influenced
   by, 163; Punin on, 181–83; WWI propaganda drawing on, 200–203, 201–2, 207
individualism: Foucault's critique of, 14,
   125; Russian liberals and, 7, 31; radicals
   and, 23–24, 65; Slavophile understanding of, 6, 125, 126, 131, 150
Instruction of 1767, 36
intelligentsia: development of, 3, 4–7;
   professionals and bureaucrats, 25–27,
   64–65, 76–77, 81–82; revolutionary movement, as actors in, 35, 47,
   49–65, 67–76
Ishutin, Nikolai, 51n40, 54
Israel, state of, 226–27
Ivanov, Aleksandr (artist), 10, 151–90; *Appearance of Christ to the People*, 152–
   59, 162, 169, 175, 182, 185, 187, 189,

192; biblical sketches of, 167, 170–71,
   174–75, 180–81, 183–86, 188, 190;
   icons and, 162–63, 181, 183, 185–87;
   post-Soviet view of, 187–88; Slavophile
   view of, 158–63, 188–90; Soviet appreciation of, 156–57, 179–81, 183–86,
   188; Strauss's *Life of Jesus*, influence
   of, 163, 166–67, 172–74, 177, 183–85,
   189; Westernizer approach to, 163–71
Ivanov, Andrei (father of Aleksandr), 158,
   171, 172
Ivanov, Sergei (brother of Aleksandr), 167
Ivanov, Viacheslav (Symbolist poet and
   philosopher), 205, 208, 225

January Strikes (1905), 75–76
Japan, Russian war against (1904–1905),
   75–76, 195
Jesus Prayer, 109
Jews and The Jewish Question: Ivanov's
   figures of, 165; legal status of, 91, 96,
   97; percentage of imperial population,
   Jews as, 193; Judaism, 197, 215, 226;
   shtetl (*mestechko*), 226. *See also* anti-
   Semitism
John of Kronstadt, 120, 127
Joseph II (emperor), 106, 110
judicial system in Russia: Criminal Code of
   1845 and "crimes against the state," 42–
   43; Decembrists, trial and execution of,
   41–42, 44; reforms of 1864, 8, 21n21,
   22, 47, 51n41, 52, 56, 66, 85, 108; Populist trials (1860s–1881), 53–62, 86–88;
   Pugachev, trial and execution of, 37–38

Kadet Party, 198, 199n26, 208, 211n62,
   215n81, 218, 228. *See* Maklakov,
   Vasilii; Miliukov, Pavel; Nabokov, Dmi-
   trii; Trubetskoi, Evgenii
Karakozov, Dmitrii, 52n48, 54, 55
Kartashev, Anton, 223n112, 225, 230
Khlysty (Christ Faith), 122
Khomiakov, Aleksei, 10, 111–15, 125,
   129, 130–31, 140, 142, 149; Ivanov
   and, 154n10, 156, 161–67, 172, 175;
   on Jews, 197n20; photo of, 112
Khomiakov, Dmitrii, 210
Khoroshko, Vasilii, 226n119
Kireevskii, Ivan, 10, 111, 113–14, 126,
   129–51, 156, 159–60; Optina elder Fr.
   Makarii, association with, 113–14, 133,
   135–40, 145–49; Optina manuscripts,
   preparation and publication of, 138–40;
   religious conversion of, 131–33
Kireevskii, Natal'ia, 113, 126, 131, 139,
   145; Filaret (Novospasskii), association
   with, 113, 131
Kishinev, pogrom, 195

Kistiakovskii, Bogdan, 19, 22–24, 198n25
Koni, Anatolii, 59, 231n132
Koshelev, Aleksandr, 131, 140, 145
Kotel'nikov, Vladimir, 135, 137
Kovalevskii, Pavel, 153, 158n25
Koval'skii, Ivan, 60
Kramskoi, Ivan, 152, 156, 167n59, 168–71, 180, 189
Krestovskii, Vsevolod, 194n7
Krupenskii, Aleksandr, 231
Krylenko, Nikolai, 30
Kuhlman, Quirinus, 122

Land and Liberty, 53–54, 56, 62
Landmarks/Vekhi, and Vekhi group, 19n19, 22, 25, 198–200
Larionov, Mikhail, 176
Lavrov, Petr, 55, 68
law, rule of. See rule of law
Lenin, Vladimir, 24, 61, 68, 71, 73n109
Leonid (Kavelin), 136
Leonid (Nagolkin), 137–38
Leont'ev, Konstantin, 117, 140
liberals and liberalism: 7–9, 11–13, 20–22, 26, 29–32, 47, 49, 62, 77–79, 81, 97, 99, 117–18, 198–99, 206, 218, 225, 230–31; anti-Semitism and, 196, 199, 210, 218, 219, 229; civil society, concept of, 79, 81; religious toleration and (see religious toleration); revolutionary movement and, 9, 78
Liberation Movement, 95
The Life of Jesus (Strauss), 163, 166–67, 172–74, 177, 183–85, 189
Lomonosov, Mikhail, 106
Loris-Melikov, Mikhail, 66
Lossky, Vladimir, 110
Lotman, Iurii M., 40
Lutherans and Lutheranism in Russia, 117, 121, 140, 184, 193, 205

Machen, Arthur, 211
Makarii (Ivanov), 113–14, 133, 135–40, 145–49
Maklakov, Vasilii, 218, 228n126, 231
Mandel'shtam, Osip, 204
Manifesto of 17 October 1905, 77, 95
Marr, Wilhelm, 194
Martinist Freemasonry, 107
Marx, Karl, 33, 67, 68
Marxism, 6–7, 23, 26, 63, 67–68, 70, 127
Mashkovtsev, Nikolai, 174
Masons, 40, 83, 107, 199n29
Matisse, Henri, 176
Mazzini, Guiseppe, 166
Mendeleev, Dmitrii, 117
Mensheviks, 68

Merezhkovskii, Dmitrii, 199–200, 219–20, 225
Mezentsov, Nikolai, 60, 62
Mikhalkov, Nikita, 188
Miliukov, Pavel, 223n112, 228
modernism: icons as art in, 102, 155, 171, 175–79, 188; as stylistic movement, 155, 171
monarchy, 2–3, 14–17. See also autocracy, Russian
monks and monasticism in Russia, 105–10, 113, 130–33, 135–40, 146, 158
Mormonism, 93
Morozova, Margarita, 219
Muslims, 91, 95, 192, 193
Myshkin, Ippolit, 58

Nabokov, Dmitrii, 88
Napoleonic Wars, 1, 5, 34, 102, 107, 155, 159
Narodniki. See Populism
narodnost', 5, 165, 168, 193, 197, 209
nationalism, 3, 5, 10–11, 185, 192, 194, 209–10, 213, 216, 218–20, 226, 228, 231; Germany, nationalism of, 11, 209–10; Poland, 228; Romantic nationalism, 3, 6, 156. See also World War I
National Democrats, 228
Nazarenes, 158, 160–62, 172, 174, 176, 186
Nazism, 11, 14
Neander, August, 140
Nechaev, Sergei, 52n48, 54–55, 57, 59, 61
New Economic Policy, 28, 29
Newman, John Henry, 100, 114
Nicholas I (tsar), 5, 10, 11, 22, 28, 40, 46–48, 80, 84, 92, 107–9, 111, 128, 158, 179, 193
Nicholas II (tsar), 82, 108, 117
Nikolai Nikolaevich (Grand Duke), 203, 209
Nikon (patriarch), 120
Nilus, Sergei, 116
Niva (The Cornfield), 156
Novikov, Nikolai, 83, 107
Novoe vremia (Modern Times), 194, 200, 216

Ogarev, Nikolai, 50, 53
Old Believers, 90–91, 95, 105, 106, 120–22, 214n76
Onegin, Eugene, 50
Optina Hermitage, 110, 113–14, 122, 134–40, 160
Orthodoxy. See Russian Orthodox Church
Overbeck, Johann Friedrich, 158–61, 172, 173
Oxford Movement, 114, 119

Palmer, William, 114–15
Pashkov, Georgii, 202
Pasternak, Leonid, 223, 224
Paul I (tsar), 39, 40
peasants and peasant life: economic developments of late 19th century affecting, 63–64; emancipation of serfs, 8, 46, 47–48, 80, 107, 109; Bezdna, 47–48, 69, 75; religious traditions of, 119–23, 127; radicals and, 68–73; commune, 6, 23
Pelikan, Jaroslav, 114
penance (confession), 125, 127–28, 137
the People's Will/the People's Freedom, 62
Peredvizhniki, 168–69, 176, 177
perestroika, 135, 188
Perovskaia, Sofiia, 58, 61
Peter I the Great (tsar), 2, 3, 6, 36, 41n20, 83, 102–7, 109, 111, 117n75
Peter III (tsar), 36–37, 40
Petrashevskii, Mikhail, and Petrashevtsy, 43, 46, 52
Petrov, Anton, 48
Philokalia, 110
pietism, 107, 108, 110
Pinkerton, Robert, 104n17, 106n27
Platon (Levshin), 106–8, 110, 136
Pogodin, Mikhail, 129
pogroms, 69, 72–73, 75, 194–96, 198, 210, 217–18, 229. See also anti-Semitism
Poland: Jews of, 192, 197, 203, 215, 228, 229; Foucault and, 14; anti-Jewish boycott, 228; Uprising of 1830–31, 5, 34, 43–45, 193; Uprising of 1863, 34, 48–49, 193–94
Polizeistaat, 16, 18, 19, 24, 26, 28, 32, 89, 93, 94
Populism, 6–8, 23, 55–56, 59, 62, 64–65, 69; Marxism compared, 63, 67–68; trials of 1860s–1881, 53–63, 86–88; women's activism in, 87–88. See also Bakunin, Mikhail; Lavrov, Petr
post-Soviet Russia, ix, 80, 119, 157, 187–88, 190
Pozner, Solomon, 222
pre-Raphaelite painters, 161–64
press, freedom of, 36, 83–84
Progressive Bloc, 220, 231
proletariat, 65, 67, 68, 70, 76, 77. See also workers/working class
Protestantism/Protestants, 91, 95, 101, 103, 105, 106, 108, 110, 114, 115, 122, 125, 133, 139, 160, 161, 192, 203, 208
Protocols of the Elders of Zion, 116
Pugachev, Emelian, revolt lead by (1773–1774), 34, 36–39, 42, 52, 54
Punin, Nikolai, 177–79, 181–86

Pushkin, Alexander, 38n9, 52n48, 83–84
Putin, Vladimir, ix

Quakers, 122

Radishchev, Aleksandr, 39–40, 42, 83
Raphael (artist), 152–54, 160, 164, 168, 174, 185
Rasputin, 118
Rech' (Speech), 200
Rechtsstaat, 22, 24, 26, 89, 94–95. See also rule of law
Reisner, Mikhail, 93–95, 97–98
religion: See Baptists; Catholicism; Dukhobortsy; Jews; Khlysty; Muslims; Old Believers; Protestantism/Protestants; religious toleration; Russian Orthodox Church; Skoptsy
Religious-Philosophical Society, 118, 173, 198, 199, 204–11, 223
religious toleration, 9, 91–98, 206, 220, 225, 230; 17 April 1905 decree, 95–97
Revolution (1905), 33–35, 73–79, 82, 85; pogroms and, 195–96; Manifesto of 17 October 1905, 77, 95, 195
Revolution (1917): February ix, 31, 97; October (Bolshevik), 26, 30, 35, 97–98
revolutions of 1848 in Europe, 45–46, 172, 184
Rodríguez, Alfonso, 140
Roman Catholicism, 110, 111, 125–26, 128, 139, 160, 172–74, 188, 189, 193
Romanticism, 6, 7, 10, 14, 50, 107, 111, 128, 134, 150, 160–61, 186, 188; Romantic nationalism, 3, 156
Rozanov, Vasilii, 99, 115, 118, 174–75, 185, 198–200, 212–13, 219–20, 223, 230
rule of law, 8–9, 13–32; religious toleration and, 94–95. See also Rechtsstaat
Russian Orthodox Church, 89–91, 92, 95, 96, 97, 103, 107–9, 110–11, 118–19, 120–21, 123, 128, 130, 193, 215; Church Fathers, 110, 114, 131–35, 138–39; eldership, 109, 110, 113–14, 136–39; Holy Synod, 92, 95, 96, 103, 104, 106, 107, 108, 129; monks and monasticism, 105–10, 113, 130–33, 135–40, 146, 158; Peter and Catherine the Great's relationship to, 2–3, 103–7, 109, 111; hesychasm, 109–10, 122, 136
Russkoe slovo (Russian Word), 200
Russo-Japanese War (1904–1905), 75–76, 195
Russo-Turkish War (1877–1878), 66, 194–95
Ryleev, Kondratii, 41

Saint George, iconography of, 200–203, 201–2
Samarin, Iuri, 140
Sand, George, 50
Sarab'ianov, Dmitrii, 181, 186
Schelling, Friedrich, 130, 131, 133, 150, 160
Schlegel, Friedrich, 159
secularization thesis, 100–102, 123–24
self-castrating sect (Skoptsy), 121–22
serfs, emancipation of, 8, 46, 47–48, 80, 107, 109
Shchit, 220–29, 224
Shevyrev, Stepan, 129, 140
Shul'gin, Vasilii, 195, 218
Silver Age, 117, 157, 171, 179, 183
Sistine Madonna (Raphael), 152–54, 160, 164, 168
Skobelev, Mikhail, 200
Skoptsy, 121–23
Slavinskyi, Maksym, 223n112
Slavophilism: thought system, ix, 5–6, 8, 11, 23, 84, 90, 111, 113–15, 119, 121, 123, 125–27, 129, 151, 163, 190, 197; founding thinkers (*see* Aksakov, Konstantin; Khomiakov, Aleksei; Kireevskii, Ivan); minor thinkers (*see* Aksakov, Aleksandr; Aksakov, Ivan; Khomiakov, Dmitrii); Slavophil-influenced thinkers, 155–57, 173, 188, 205, 209, 212–13, 230
sobornost', 111, 114
Social Democrats, 63, 70, 73n109, 74, 198, 231. *See also* Lenin, Vladimir
socialism: anti-Semitism and, 215, 231; of Herzen, 6; of Populists and Marxists, 7, 23–24 (*see also* Marxism; Populism); revolutionary movement and, 3, 34, 43, 46, 55, 67, 70–71, 72, 74, 77
Socialist Revolutionary Party, 74
Söderholm, Karl, 140
Sofia (Princess), 122
Sologub, Fedor, 222, 224, 231
Solov'ev, Aleksandr, 62
Solov'ev, Vladimir, 118, 126, 197–98, 217n87, 225, 230
Solzhenitsyn, Alexander, 101–2, 119
Sorskii, Nil, 137
soviet (1905), 76
Soviet regime: ix, 26–29, 32, 80, 97–98
Soviet views on art, 156–57, 179–81, 183–86, 188. *See also* Allenov, Mikhail; Alpatov, Mikhail; Fedorov-Davydov, Aleksei; Punin, Nikolai; Sarab'ianov, Dmitrii
Sovremennik (The Contemporary), 159
Spasovich, Vladimir, 22n23, 60, 61–62
Spirit-Wrestlers (*Dukhobortsy*), 122–23
spiritualism and the occult, 117–18

Stalinism, ix, 11, 26–27, 29–30, 101, 177, 183–85
Stanley, Arthur Penrhyn, 109, 113
startsy/starchestvo (eldership), 109, 110, 113–14, 136–39
Stasov, Vladimir, 156, 165–68, 171, 172, 174, 180, 189
State and Revolution, 24
Stolypin, Petr, 95
Strauss, David Friedrich, 163, 166–67, 172–74, 177, 183–85, 189
Struve, Petr, 199, 219
Symbolists, 199n27, 205, 222, 223

Tagantsev, Nikolai, 58
terrorism, 53–63, 62–63, 65–66
Tertz, Abram [Andrei Siniavskii], 99
Thompson, E. P., 69, 72n107
Tiutchev, Fedor, 189, 192
Tkachev, Petr, 54, 68
Tolchenov, Ivan, 128
Tolstoi, Ivan, 212n67, 220–21
Tolstoi, Lev, 66, 126, 200n30
Trediakovskii, Vasilii, 106
Trepov, Fedor, 59
Trial of the 50 and Trial of the 193 (1877–1878), 57–58
Trotsky, Leon, 18n18
Trubetskoi, Evgenii, 155n14, 208–10, 213, 218–20, 230, 231
Trubetskoi, Grigorii, 209
Tsypkin, Leonid, 151–54
Turgenev, Ivan, 6, 50n38, 164
Turkey, Russian war against (1877–1878), 66, 194–95

Ukraine and Ukrainians, 1, 45, 121
Union of the Russian People, 210, 215, 216
Urusov, Sergei, 221n102

Vasnetsov, Viktor, 173n79
Vekhi/Landmarks, and *Vekhi* group, 19n19, 22, 25, 198–200
Velichkovskii, Paisii, 109–10, 137, 138
Viel'gorskii, Matvei, 158
Vinaver, Maksim, 196n16
Vinet, Alexandre, 140
Vinogradov, Igor', 189–90
Volkonskaia, Zinaida, 158
Voltaire, 106

Wackenroder, Wilhelm Heinrich, 160
Walling, William English, 222n107
Weber, Max, 3, 125–26, 144, 149
Westernizers: thought system, 5, 84; views of Ivanov, 163–71; thinkers (*see* Belinskii, Vissarion; Herzen, Alexander; Ogarev, Nikolai)

women in Russia: Populism and, 58–59, 61–62, 87–88; religion and, 120
What Is to Be Done? (Chernyshevskii), 50–51
Wilson, A. N., 100–102, 116
Winckelmann, Johann Joachim, 159
Wolin, Sheldon, 14
workers, working class, 25, 35–37, 56, 63–77, 120, 127. *See also* proletariat
World War I, 11, 26, 78–79, 123–24, 192, 200–232

Yarmolinsky, Avrahm, 222n107

Zasulich, Vera, 59, 61, 62
Zelinskii, Faddei, 223n112
zemstvos, 8–9, 46–47, 65–66, 73, 74, 76, 82, 84–85, 94–95
Zenkovskii, Vasilii, 134–35, 150, 214
Zheliabov, Aleksandr, 58
Zhukovskii, Vasilii, 130, 140
Zionism, 226–28